THE FOURTH ENEMY

JAMES CANE

THE FOURTH ENEMY

JOURNALISM AND POWER IN THE MAKING OF
PERONIST ARGENTINA, 1930–1955

THE PENNSYLVANIA STATE UNIVERSITY PRESS
UNIVERSITY PARK, PENNSYLVANIA

**Library of Congress
Cataloging-in-Publication Data**

Cane, James, 1968–
The fourth enemy : journalism and power in the making of Peronist Argentina, 1930–1955 / James Cane.
    p.   cm.
Summary: "An interdisciplinary study examining the newspaper industry in Argentina during the regime of Juan Domingo Perón. Traces how Perón managed to integrate almost the entire Argentine press into a state-dominated media empire"—Provided by publisher.
Includes bibliographical references and index.
ISBN 978-0-271-04876-5 (cloth : alk. paper)
ISBN 978-0-271-04877-2 (pbk. : alk. paper)
1. Government and the press—Argentina—History—20th century.
2. Press and politics—Argentina—History—20th century.
3. Censorship—Argentina—History—20th century.
4. Perón, Juan Domingo, 1895–1974.
5. Argentina—Politics and government—1943– .
I. Title.

PN4748.A7C36   2012
302.230982'0904—dc23
                    2011026168

Copyright © 2011 The Pennsylvania State University
All rights reserved
Printed in the United States of America
Published by The Pennsylvania State University Press,
University Park, PA 16802-1003

The Pennsylvania State University Press is a member of the Association of American University Presses.

It is the policy of The Pennsylvania State University Press to use acid-free paper. Publications on uncoated stock satisfy the minimum requirements of American National Standard for Information Sciences—Permanence of Paper for Printed Library Material, ANSI Z39.48–1992.

Contents

LIST OF ILLUSTRATIONS / *vii*
PREFACE AND ACKNOWLEDGMENTS / *ix*
LIST OF ABBREVIATIONS / *xv*

Introduction: From Fourth Estate to Fourth Enemy / 1

Part 1

1 The Fourth Estate / 25
2 Journalism and Power in the Impossible Republic / 58

Part 2

3 The Triumph of Silence / 91
4 Journalism as Labor Power / 116
5 Scenes from the Press Wars / 143

Part 3

6 The Die Is Cast / 177
7 The Fourth Enemy / 206
Conclusion: Journalism and Power in the New Argentina / 229

NOTES / 241
BIBLIOGRAPHY / 281
INDEX / 301

Illustrations

All images courtesy of Ministerio del Interior, Archivo General de la Nación.

1. Perón addresses public in the Teatro Colón opera house, March 8, 1947 / 2
2. The *La Prensa* offices, 1938 / 37
3. Statue to be placed atop *La Prensa* offices / 38
4. Printer at a Hoe printing press, November 1941 / 49
5. Printers at work in *La Prensa*, October 1924 / 50
6. News vendors prepare *El Mundo* for distribution, mid-1930s / 51
7. Octavio Palazzolo addresses the founding meeting of the Federación Argentina de Periodistas, Córdoba, 1938 / 85
8. Perón addresses the Fifth Congress of the Federación Argentina de Periodistas, Buenos Aires, October 20, 1944 / 135
9. Public gathering in front of the Casa Rosada, October 17, 1945 / 170
10. Perón signs the Estatuto del Periodista Profesional, December 24, 1946 / 185
11. Eva Perón meets representatives of the Sindicato de Vendedores de Diarios, Revistas y Afines, December 2, 1949 / 219
12. Eva Perón distributes funds from the Fundación Eva Perón to the staff of *La Prensa*, June 11, 1951 / 223
13. Eva Perón with the staff of *La Prensa*, May 23, 1951 / 223
14. Edificio ALAS, location of the offices of Editorial ALEA / 225

Preface and Acknowledgments

The research and writing of this book are bracketed by two events, one in Argentina, the other in Venezuela. While neither is directly related to the history of journalism in mid-twentieth-century Argentina, both bear upon my own approach to the topic in ways that deserve to be made explicit. This is more than an affirmation of the Crocean dictum that "all history is contemporary history"; it is also a confession of just how much the ghosts of the past haunt my understanding of the present.

At about the same time that I boarded a plane in San Francisco to return to Buenos Aires and begin my initial research on the Argentine press, hired gunmen stopped a small car on a highway near the resort town of Pinamar in the province of Buenos Aires and brutally assassinated its driver. For the next two years, monthly marches denouncing that January 1997 murder brought tens of thousands of Argentines into the already chaotic streets of Buenos Aires. Public outrage only increased as forensic teams performed first one and then another autopsy, while indications that the police of the province of Buenos Aires had destroyed crucial evidence at the crime scene drew public suspicion to the very organization in charge of the investigation.

At first, a simple black-and-white photograph of the victim found its way into every public corner of the city; within months, the eyes alone had become ubiquitous. The little-known José Luís Cabezas, handcuffed to the steering column of his car and shot twice before his assassins doused him with gasoline and set fire to his corpse, became a powerful and immediately recognizable symbol of both the disturbingly enduring legacy of state terrorism and the total impunity that powerful criminal interests seemed to enjoy in President Carlos Menem's Argentina.

Yet this still contentious case has an added element which, unlike the arguably even more serious crimes that jolted the country in those years, assured sustained media attention: Cabezas, a photojournalist, was clearly killed for exercising his profession. For the nation's media workers, this was more than the murder of a man obviously dearly loved by his family, friends, and coworkers. The assassination of a colleague "in the line of duty" was compounded by a level of symbolic violence against Cabezas clearly intended to silence not just him, but all Argentine journalists.

The killing, however, did just the opposite. Instead, it sparked heated public debates over the rights and obligations of journalists and newsworkers in Argentine society and the appropriate relationship between economic power, political power, and media power in a constitutional democracy. Moving beyond abstract affirmations, these controversies also challenged working journalists and media proprietors on the degree to which journalism and media practices conformed to these ideals.

These same broader media issues became explicitly contentious once again as I was engaged in shaping that initial research into the present text, though within a different public and on a grander scale. In May 2007, Venezuela's oldest and most watched television station, Radio Caracas Televisión (RCTV), went off the air. Long a forum for virulent criticism of president Hugo Chávez, the station had served as a basic point of reference for the Venezuelan opposition, and its owner, Marcel Granier, had become one of the country's more visible anti-Chávez public figures. To RCTV supporters, the station's inability to broadcast is yet more proof that the "Bolivarian Revolution" is little more than an anachronistic dictatorship set on violating the essential constitutional and human rights of opponents. Chávez silenced RCTV for no other reason, they claim, than his recognition of the threat that freedom of expression and public access to accurate information pose to his authoritarian ambitions.

Supporters of the Chávez government paint a different picture. They argue that the station did not go off the air by dictatorial fiat, but by the perfectly proper unwillingness of the country's constitutional authorities to rubber-stamp the renewal of a state-granted broadcast license whose expiration had been determined five decades earlier. For Venezuelan authorities, the crucial support that RCTV gave to conspirators in the April 2002 coup attempt, its repeated incitation to violence during the crisis, and the deliberate misinformation the station broadcast during the upheaval had long placed the station beyond the bounds of both proper journalism and democratic legality. Using the public's own airwaves, RCTV had betrayed the Venezuelan constitution and the same citizen right to accurate information that the station's supporters now hypocritically proclaimed as inviolable. Not renewing RCTV's privileged use of a public good—the nation's broadcast frequencies—beyond the terms established by a previous government was neither a violation of rights guaranteed to all Venezuelans nor an authoritarian assault on freedom of the press; it was a response to the station's violation of the public trust and a legally valid, legitimate defense of constitutional rule against those who would see its demise.

If the controversies surrounding the Cabezas assassination were often quite literally the background noise to my initial research, the RCTV case confirms that the kinds of conflicts that I examine in this book are more pervasive than they might at first appear. These disputes reveal just how ambiguous the ideological and juridical foundations of modern journalism truly are, and just how fluid and contested the relationships between public, state, and press remain. They betray the presence of long-running underlying differences of opinion among journalists, newspaper, and media corporation executives, politicians, and the general public over the precise nature of the media's role in modern society, and what its limits and attendant responsibilities—if any—should be.

In examining the conflict-ridden transformation of the commercial press with the rise of Peronism, I found myself immersed in debates on the nature of journalism and the press that were often strikingly similar to those of the 1990s. As a result, I necessarily engage many of these same larger questions of citizenship, representation, and democracy that swirled around me as I began my research, and I do so for a simple reason: the Menem years marked what many assumed were the death throes of a sweeping and surprisingly durable social and economic project established fifty years earlier. Just as the Argentine neoliberal turn of the 1990s coincided with broader global phenomena, the complex economic and ideological crises that gave rise to and found their "resolution" in the Peronist movement were far from exclusively local. It is my intention, then, that the present study form part of a broader scholarly debate on the transformation of journalism, media institutions, and civil society in the global crises of the 1930s, 1940s, and 1950s. Finally, as a historian of Argentina, I make no claims to any privileged understanding of contemporary Venezuela. I do hope, however, that my approach to the press conflicts of mid-twentieth-century Argentina might provide some signposts for navigating the Chávez-era media disputes (and others elsewhere that are sure to surface). If nothing else, this book sounds a cautionary note that such conflicts are likely more profound, more complex, and more ambiguous, but less unusual, than their participants either suspect or are willing to admit.

I could never have written this book without the support of what I found to be a surprising array of people. Readers should be as aware as I am of the degree to which whatever merit this book has rests with them, while all errors and shortcomings in this text are clearly my own.

First, to work with Tulio Halperín Donghi and receive his criticism and encouragement regarding this and other projects has proven absolutely invaluable. I am not sure that he fully realizes—or even cares to imagine—how many students of Latin American history here, in Argentina and elsewhere he has inspired through his insight, wit, common sense, and absolute candor. Still, my enormous debt to him is as much personal as it is professional, and I thank him for everything he has done for me over the years.

Also at UC–Berkeley, Professors Margaret Chowning, Julio Ramos, Linda Lewin, Martin Jay, and Alan Pred helped to shape my approach to the study of history. Margaret Chowning, especially, took interest in this project and continually offered detailed and insightful criticism while at the same time helping me secure the material means to help support my family in the Bay Area. Daniel Hallin of UC–San Diego also provided extremely useful critiques of early versions of several chapters. I am grateful to participants, commentators, and fellow panel members at multiple conferences for their input on papers related to this work, especially Michael Conniff, Joel Horowitz, Tom Klubock, Corinne Pernet, and Bryan McCann.

I owe a great debt to Sandy Thatcher of Penn State Press, who not only gave me excellent advice on the process of publication, but showed near-infinite patience as this text took final shape. I would also like to thank my copyeditor, John Morris, for so admirably taking on the daunting task of making my often tangled prose reader-friendly.

I have had the great fortune to be constantly surrounded by colleagues and friends who have taken an interest in this project and contributed to this text in ways that they might not recognize. Patrick Barr-Melej, Mark Healey, John Jenks, Vera Candiani, Max Friedman, Line Schjolden, Doug Shoemaker, John Brady, Alistair Hattingh, Myrna Santiago, and Paula de Vos, through conferences, dinners, hikes, coffee, and asados helped to shape this work from its earliest stages. Patrick, Max, and Mark in particular always proved more than willing to read multiple chapter drafts as well as answer early morning and late night e-mails on the most trivial matters with great clarity, insight, and patience. In the final stages of preparing the text, I also received invaluable advice from the sharp minds of Eduardo Elena, Oscar Chamosa, Chuck Walton, the anonymous readers at Penn State Press, Nicolás Quiroga, Liliana Da Orden, Jorge Nállim, and—again—Mark Healey. This book is much stronger for their advice; it would surely be stronger still if I had been capable of incorporating all of their suggestions.

It is always a pleasure to return to Buenos Aires, where I have repeatedly abused the hospitality of Bárbara Williams, Andrea Moleres, Pablo Blasberg, and, more recently, Marita Rossi. That Bárbara, Andrea, and Pablo have all emigrated is for me a personally painful reminder of just how much Argentina, and the world, have changed since I began this work. I am also grateful to the Carrasco Villegas family in Santiago de Chile, who provided a warm environment for my revision of large parts of this text.

In Argentina the support of the following groups and individuals proved crucial: the staff of the Archivo General de la Nación, especially Andrés Pak Linares; Norma González and Laura Morana of the Fundación Fulbright; the staffs of the Biblioteca Nacional and the Biblioteca del Congreso; Natalio Botana, Jorge B. Rivera, Oscar Terán, Elías Palti, Diego Armus, and Sylvia Saítta for their early encouragement; Enrique Israel, dedicated scholar, translator, political militant, and caretaker of the library of the Central Committee of the Argentine Communist Party; Luciano Kasio of the Archivo de Prensa (Presidencia de la Nación), not only for his tireless help in digging up dusty folders but for making me welcome in the Casa Rosada; the staff of *La Nación*, especially Pablo Blasberg; journalists and unionists Jorge Chinetti and Enrique Tortosa of the FAP/APBA and the UTPBA; and Sr. Rufino of the Círculo de la Prensa.

Funding for this work came through grants from the Mellon Foundation, the Fulbright Foundation, the Tinker Foundation, the Chancellor of the University of California, and the UC–Berkeley Department of History. Additionally, support has come from the University of Oklahoma's Vice President for Research, the College of Arts and Sciences, the School of International and Area Studies, and the Department of History. At OU I am particularly grateful to my colleagues Rob Griswold, Sandie Holguín, and Terry Rugeley for their invaluable professional advice, patience, and encouragement.

Finally, my wife, Claudia, has sacrificed more than either of us care to remember in the course of completing this project. She has constantly encouraged and supported me in my research, writing, and teaching of Latin American and Argentine history from our first days in San Francisco and Buenos Aires through the present. Along the way, we have had the good fortune of being accompanied by our beautiful daughter, Fiona Violeta, whose birth coincided with the first written words of this project. This book is as much theirs as mine. Now that it is finished, I can promise both Claudia and Fionita that the late-night typing will end—for a while.

Abbreviations

AGN	Archivo General de la Nación
AGN-AJ	Archivo General de la Nación—Archivo Justo
AdeP	Archivo de Prensa
ALN	Alianza Libertadora Nacionalista
AP	Associated Press
APBA	Asociación de Periodistas de Buenos Aires
ASNE	American Society of Newspaper Editors
CADEPSA	Compañía Argentina de Ediciones y Publicidad, Sociedad Anónima
CGT	Confederación General de Trabajo
FAP	Federación Argentina de Periodistas
FATI	Federación Argentina de Trabajadores de la Imprenta
FGB	Federación Gráfica Bonaerense
FORJA	Fuerza de Orientación Radical de la Juventud Argentina
GOU	Grupo de Oficiales Unidos
IAPA	Inter American Press Association
IAPI	Instituto Argentino de Promoción e Intercambio
PC	Partido Comunista
PE	Poder Ejecutivo
PL	Partido Laborista
PP	Partido Peronista
PS	Partido Socialista
PSI	Partido Socialista Independiente
SIP	Sociedad Interamericana de Prensa
STP	Secretaría de Trabajo y Previsión
SVDRA	Sindicato de Vendedores de Diarios, Revistas y Afines
UCR	Unión Cívica Radical
UD	Unión Democrática
UP	United Press

INTRODUCTION:
FROM FOURTH ESTATE TO FOURTH ENEMY

> The history of the Argentine people is the history of their liberties.
> The history of Argentine liberties is the history of the national press.
>
> —*La Prensa*, **November 11, 1943**

When Juan Domingo Perón announced his new government's economic agenda from the stage of the Teatro Colón, the working men and women sitting in the posh seats of the famed Buenos Aires opera house could not miss the symbolic importance of the act. Not only was the Argentine president directly addressing Argentine workers "as *compañero* to *compañero*," he was doing so from the cultural bastion of a national elite in clear retreat. Declaring his government "an extension of the working class in the Government House," Perón warned the audience that their newfound political power stood imperiled by a host of serious enemies. As he listed these enemies, the audience erupted in acclamation at mention of the fourth: the press. In the midst of the sweeping social transformation underway, at that March 1947 meeting the once powerful "fourth estate" of the old order formally became the besieged "fourth enemy" of the Peronist "New Argentina."[1]

If those involved in the events of that evening grasped the inversion of the social hierarchy implicit in the workers' symbolic occupation of the cultural sanctum of the oligarchy, they also understood that in decrying *la prensa*—the press in general—Perón was, in fact, railing against a specific newspaper: *La Prensa*, Latin America's most powerful commercial daily. Only the collective refusal of Argentine workers to buy or advertise in the paper, Perón insisted, could halt its repeated "lies" and continuous "betrayal" of the national interest.[2] Even as he spoke, government employees were already hard at work to drive home the severity of the threat posed by this "fourth enemy," as well as to remove any doubt as to precisely which member of the press stood as the greatest menace. When the crowd poured out of the Teatro Colón and into the streets, they found the walls of downtown Buenos Aires freshly plastered with

Fig. 1 Perón addresses public in the Teatro Colón opera house, March 8, 1947.

transcripts of the latest government radio commentary denouncing *La Prensa* as fundamentally anti-Argentine as well as ideologically, culturally, politically, and economically beholden to foreign interests.[3]

The boycott had little impact, despite Perón's personal appeal. Still, tensions between the owners of *La Prensa* and the Peronist movement grew to fever pitch, while Argentines became yet more polarized and the economic situation of the press as a whole rapidly deteriorated. Finally, nearly four years after the Teatro Colón meeting, Peronist news vendors mounted a total strike against the paper. When one newsworker died and fourteen were wounded in the ensuing violence, the minister of the interior intervened, formally declaring *La Prensa*'s closure.[4] Police and congressional investigations began as the paper's owner fled to Uruguay. In April 1951, the Argentine Congress invoked a constitutional provision that empowered the body to seize private property of public interest. Immediately, *La Prensa* and all of its productive infrastructure passed into the hands of the executive power, to be used "in the general interest and social perfection of the Argentine people."[5]

During the May Day celebrations two weeks later, Perón presented the union leaders who had organized the Teatro Colón gathering with the ultimate trophy: the newly expropriated *La Prensa*. A startlingly different newspaper soon hit the streets. Now property of the General Confederation of Labor (CGT)—the core of the Peronist movement—the new *La Prensa* had "ceased to be the capitalist instrument of a small group of proprietors to become the patriotic dominion of five million Argentine workers."[6] Just as the workers had occupied the space of elite culture on the night of March 7, 1947, they now ostensibly controlled what only months before had been the most powerful voice of that elite within the Argentine public sphere. From the Peronists' "fourth enemy," *La Prensa* had become, in the words of Perón himself, the "symbol of the New Press of the New Argentina."[7]

Peronism and the Transformation of the Argentine Press

The expropriation of the newspaper produced shock waves felt well beyond Argentina. Yet, as momentous as the Peronist seizure of *La Prensa* proved in itself, it also marked the culmination of an even more dramatic transformation of the entire Argentine newspaper industry. With the addition of the morning paper, Perón and his associates now controlled eight newspapers in the city of Buenos Aires alone, including what had been not just Argentina's, but Latin America's, five largest dailies at the time of Perón's election in February 1946.[8] Through a series of violent confrontations, backroom deals, economic pressures, and legal actions between 1946 and 1951, Juan Domingo Perón had managed to fashion the vast majority of one of the world's more extensive and developed newspaper industries into an enormous quasi-state media empire.

The present study traces this unparalleled transformation of the Argentine press from the crises of the 1930s to the height and dissolution of the region's archetypal populist experiment in the mid-1950s. This book is as much a history of the disputes that permeated the Argentine commercial press in the years 1930 to 1955 as it is a study of a key aspect of the growth and consolidation of Peronism as the focal point of Argentine political life. It is the story of the nation's major newspaper institutions, their proprietors, and the newsworkers who daily created the media in the midst of a series of often debilitating ideological, economic, and political crises. At the same time, it is an account of the conflict-ridden emergence of the Argentine military, Juan Domingo Perón, and the urban working class as the major protagonists of a social transformation more profound than even its architects imagined.

The press conflicts of these years have largely escaped careful scrutiny by scholars of modern Argentina, despite the wealth of literature on Argentine populism and the great significance that Peronists themselves placed on control of the press. Though passing reference to conflicts with *La Prensa* are frequent in histories of Peronism, modern Argentina, and Latin American journalism, scholars have tended to overlook the experiences of other major Argentine newspapers and have left the narrative put forth in the wake of Perón's overthrow in 1955 largely unchallenged.[9] In this view, the history of the press in the Peronist years has become little more than a manifestation of Juan Domingo Perón's authoritarian, unerring, relatively effortless, and perhaps inevitable subjugation of the whole range of institutions of Argentine civil society. In turn, those who have more directly engaged the question of populism and the Argentine media, as well as those scholars with a more nuanced understanding of Peronism's complexity, have either left the specific process by which Peronists came to control the commercial press underexplored or strayed little from that same interpretive framework.[10] For scholars of Peronism, then, the evolution of the movement's relationship with the press has tended to serve primarily as an illustrative anecdote that has little to do with the historical development of the Argentine press and everything to do with the widening sphere of Peronist power; scholars of the media—far fewer in number—have tended to view the Peronist transformation of the press essentially as an aberration imposed from without, a sudden authoritarian intromission into the otherwise progressive development of an internally coherent, autonomous press.[11]

Without doubt, the history of the Argentine press in the Peronist years is inseparable from the authoritarian tendencies of Perón, Eva Perón, and sectors of the Peronist movement. The military regime from which Perón emerged systematically silenced sectors of the press through strict censorship, the detention of journalists, and the withholding of government advertising. On several occasions, Peronist crowds violently attacked newspapers like *La Prensa*, *Crítica*, and *El Mundo*—most notably on the evening of October 17–18, 1945, the very night that gave birth to Peronism proper. Later, while eschewing overt censorship, the democratically elected Peronist government seized control of newsprint distribution and used bureaucratic measures to pressure the opposition press. State-run and sympathetic media mounted relentless propaganda campaigns to discredit opposing media. Even the decisive conflict between news vendors and the owners of *La Prensa* received open encouragement not just from broad sectors of the Peronist movement, but from President Perón and Eva Perón themselves. Finally, the practical consequences of the Peronist transformation of the press bore little resemblance to the rhetoric invoked for that transformation: it neither democratized the Argentine public sphere, nor did it create a newspaper industry that effectively served as a vehicle for the exercise of working-class citizenship. As Cristián Buchrucker has signaled, for all their differences, Perón's creation of a large propaganda apparatus stands as one of the more striking similarities between Peronism and the European fascisms.[12]

To ascribe the dramatic transformation of the Argentine press in the years 1946 to 1951 solely to Peronist authoritarianism, however, leaves several crucial questions unanswered and many of the specific moments of what was in fact a complex set of conflicts difficult to comprehend. Given the great power that Perón wielded and the enormous popular support he enjoyed, why did the process take so long? Why did Perón and his associates opt for the creation of a private media holding company, Editorial ALEA, to run much of the commercial press, rather than simply closing or nationalizing opposition papers? Why did many newsworkers endorse specific actions that set the stage for the transformation of the newspaper industry, and why did many journalists join the ranks of Peronism? If "the press" was under threat, what prevented commercial newspaper proprietors from forming a common front against first the military and then the Peronist governments? Why did Peronists put such intense and prolonged effort into articulating a coherent discourse of journalism and the press when, on the one hand, they had little hope of convincing the opposition of the validity of government press policies, and, on the other, Perón loyalists ostensibly needed no such persuasion? Finally, what does the nature of the multiple disputes surrounding the press—and even the fact of their existence—tell us about the ideological climate, the bases of press legitimacy, and the character of political conflict in mid-twentieth-century Argentina?

The approach to these questions that I adopt here owes much to the origins of this study and the particular path that this project took. Few books spring fully formed, like Minerva, from the foreheads of their authors; the present study is not one of these. This book began as an investigation of Argentine political ideology in the wake of the military coup of September 1930, the country's first unequivocal interruption of constitutional rule in the twentieth century. Like many other scholars, I turned to the press as both mirror and repository of a fairly broad segment of opinion and as a window into political, cultural, and social history.[13] Yet, as I examined the concrete manifestations of press discourses around particular themes, it quickly became clear that the proper role of journalism and the press was one of the more contentious issues of that decade. This was due, in no small measure, to the way that the conflict over the social role of journalism lent concrete expression to more fundamental issues regarding the distribution of power in Argentine society, the meanings of democracy, the shifting nature of citizenship, and the reworking of the boundaries between state and civil society and between public and private. Relatedly, actual control over the commercial press also became crucial in gaining influence in these and other political disputes, as newspapers grew in importance as vehicles of public mobilization with the severe crisis of the Argentine party system in the 1930s. Simply put, the press was more than a focal point of conflict for the duration of the decade; it was also a site at which a whole range of ideological, political, cultural, and class struggles intersected in tangible ways.

Nonetheless, the conflicts surrounding the press in the 1930s that first drew my attention had not only failed to reach even tentative resolution by the beginning of Perón's ascent in 1943, but they escalated with ever-increasing urgency with the Peronist transformation of Argentine society. Like many other historians of Argentina, I was pulled by the sheer gravity of the Peronist era—reluctantly at first, enthusiastically later—into its orbit. When I turned my attention to the press conflicts of the Perón years, however, I did so with the great advantage of having already seen the opening of multiple fissures in the Argentine newspaper industry over the course of the previous decades. In fact, it is the particular form of the Peronist engagement with these gestating conflicts that not only shaped the fate of the commercial press in the years 1946 to 1955, but constituted an important component of Peronism's rapid evolution into the nation's dominant political force.

In placing the battles surrounding the newspaper industry in Peronist Argentina within the greater trajectory of Argentine journalism history, then, I am responding less to a search for origins than to a recognition of what this approach reveals about the commercial press, Peronism, and mid-twentieth-century Argentina. The story of the transformation of the Argentine press between 1946 and 1955 emerges in its full complexity only when considered not merely as a consequence of the rise of Peronism or as an aspect of the Peronist experience, but also as a moment in the longer historical development of the Argentine press. Examining the Argentine press within the whirlwind of Peronism's emergence makes apparent the complexity of the newspaper industry's internal tensions, the intricacy of its interactions with other aspects of Argentine life, and the ambiguity of its ideological bases.[14] The conflicts of the Peronist era, in effect, reveal "the press" not as a static, unified, and monolithic entity, but as an internally divided array of institutions and a historically fluid set of less formal social relationships.

Similarly, these struggles belie any conception of Peronism as a singular movement responding to the preconceived designs of its founder and leader. A clearer understanding of the social history of Argentine journalism casts new light on the ways in which the heterogeneous ideological, political, social, and economic components of a frequently improvised and contentious political practice evolved in tense interaction not just with each other, but with the surprisingly resilient residual elements of liberal Argentina. To paraphrase *The Eighteenth Brumaire*, the protagonists of this story made their own history, but they did not make it as they pleased; they did so within the confines and opportunities inherited from deeply rooted historical circumstances. The story of journalism in this period illuminates the degree to which Perón and his followers built the "New Argentina"—and the Peronist movement itself—from the ideological and institutional debris of an old order that had begun to crumble from its own internal fissures more than a decade earlier, but whose definitive collapse remained stubbornly elusive.

Journalism and Power

In an initial impassioned plea and through his subsequent scholarship, David Paul Nord has long urged his more methodologically conservative colleagues to recognize that the "fundamental purpose of mass communication, and especially journalism, is the exercise of power."[15] Yet it is also clear that the discursive and textual practices of twentieth-century journalism can become socially meaningful only in relation to the productive infrastructure and distributive capacity of media institutions. As the media conflicts of mid-twentieth-century Argentina demonstrate, struggles for hegemony are over not only the mobilizing potential of ideas, but control of the material and institutional means necessary to forge the level of social consensus that hegemony entails. Underpinning this study of the specific conflicts surrounding journalism and the press in a decisive period of modern Argentine history are a more fundamental set of concerns and a more ambitious agenda: in the broadest sense, this book is an attempt to trace concretely the dialectical relationship between contests for the exercise of power and the institutions of civil society—that is, between struggles for hegemony and battles for control of the instruments through which hegemonic power is established, defended, contested, and perpetually reshaped.[16]

The importance of print media in Argentine daily life and their centrality for the fashioning of multiple forms of power also ensured that newspaper institutions would emerge as major battlegrounds—often literally—in the political, ideological, and cultural conflicts of the Peronist years. The Argentine capital in the mid–twentieth century was a world in which the media's permeation of everyday life was not only well underway, but increasingly rapid. Both urgent and ubiquitous, newspapers formed an integral part of the urban landscape, adorning the hands of pedestrians, job seekers, and subway and streetcar riders. At once symbols of the city's cosmopolitan character and catalysts for the nation's economic modernization, newspapers were also ephemeral. Discarded and disintegrating, dirty and crumpled on the city streets, by late afternoon the morning papers had already ceded their place to the evening dailies to assume a different role in the urban landscape as commonplace markers of the accelerating pace of modern life.

Though the growth of the press in the city of Buenos Aires overshadows that in the cities and towns of the Argentine interior, newspapers became an important part of daily life for Argentines across the nation. Between the mid-1880s and the 1930s the Argentine public ranked near the top in world per capita newspaper consumption.[17] As a result, the press played an increasingly important role in shaping both the mundane and extraordinary lived experience of what Beatriz Sarlo has aptly called Argentina's "peripheral modernity."[18] In the pages of popular dailies like *Crítica* and *Noticias Gráficas,* global culture, politics, and sports intersected with local concerns, while the divisions blurred between world and national events, public and private lives. Even the ritual of purchasing a newspaper, performed by few peoples anywhere more often than by Argentines, not only helped mark the rhythms of everyday life in the Argentine capital, it helped mold readers' collective and individual cultural, political, ethnic, gender, and class identities.[19]

More explicitly and insistently than most other commodities, newspapers served as an instrument for the creation of meaning and hierarchy regarding broad swaths of social, political, and cultural life. Indeed, the heterogeneity of newspaper content and the ubiquity of newspapers made the press a meaning-creating link between the minutiae of everyday life, the shifting events of city, nation, and world, and the abstract, universalizing expressions of the dominant ideology. This crucial role in the creation of meaning for such large sectors of the population makes the press an essential element of the shifting "structure of feeling" in modern Argentina; or, as James Carey has stated more emphatically, "journalism not only reveals the structure of feeling of previous eras, it *is* the structure of feeling of past eras, or at least significant portions of it."[20]

While Argentina did boast a vibrant partisan press in the first decades of the century, between 1880 and 1920 partisan proprietor-journalists largely gave way to politically and economically independent newspaper entrepreneurs tied not to specific political factions, but to the market. The size and diversity of the Argentine newspaper market facilitated an enormous degree of economic independence for the nation's press, with the owners of even medium-sized newspapers capable of maintaining themselves beholden primarily to the reading public and private advertisers rather than to state institutions and explicit forms of political power. Directors of the large commercial newspapers still regularly placed their papers' weight behind specific political figures, parties, and programs. Yet these endorsements were largely tactical alliances to be discarded at will, manifestations of the political convictions of autonomous newspaper proprietors, or commercial strategies directed at gaining the readership of a particular market segment. Thus, while media scholar Silvio Waisbord's assertion that "the [South American] press never attained independence from the state, and for the most part did not try to become separate" may hold true for much of the continent, the commercial press of Argentina—and, in particular, that of the Argentine capital—marks a clear and important exception.[21] Indeed, it is the progressive erosion of this autonomy and the corresponding formation of a more direct relationship between the power of the press and that of the state—an extremely contentious, two-decade process—that forms the basis for the multiple conflicts that I examine here.

The twentieth-century Argentine commercial press thus formed part of an array of institutions whose effectiveness as bulwark of the long-term vitality of the social and political order rested on its relative autonomy from state power proper. This distance from state power proper allowed for the fragmented presence of antisystemic political and cultural discourses within the popular press, giving voice to dissident intellectuals and articulating the interests of broad sectors of the Argentine public in more immediate ways than their formal political representatives. Often while at its most confrontational with regard to state power, the commercial press helped create the kind of pluralistic—even chaotic—public sphere that seemed to confirm rather than undermine the realization of liberalism's egalitarian promise of universal citizenship.[22] As an integral component of the broader Argentine social order, the press served as a crucial forum for the articulation of normative aspects of what remained powerful ideological precepts (for example, "democracy" in the abstract) as well as their practical implications (what "democracy" meant in concrete practice). On a daily basis and usually in the most mundane ways, the commercial press of mid-twentieth-century Argentina thus repeatedly served to generate consent around the dominant ideology as "common sense" and the larger social order as "natural," while at the same time giving voice to contestation in ways that generally tended to regenerate, rather than weaken, the legitimacy of the social order.[23] As a "fourth (e)state" (*cuarto estado*) beyond the state, Argentine newspapers formed "part of a process by which a world-view compatible with the existing structure of power in society is reproduced, a process which is decentralized, open to contradiction and conflict, but generally very effective."[24]

At the same time, the growing reading market that allowed for this relative autonomy from explicit forms of political power also fostered the emergence of newspapers as important economic entities by the 1920s, employing large numbers of journalists, graphic artists, and vendors, consuming productive inputs like newsprint and technologically advanced presses, and mediating between a broad range of producers and Argentine consumers. Just as journalism as a practice of power gains broad social significance through media institutions, media institutions themselves could not exist without newsworkers. To limit any understanding of the twentieth-century press to that of cultural institution, or to reduce newspapers to shapers of ideology and conduits for the exercise of power, is to overlook a fundamental aspect of the social reality of the modern media: the twentieth-century press is as much *industry* as it is *culture*. Not only do newspapers help produce social meaning, but people produce newspapers, through processes that involve tools, raw materials, and, from the 1880s onward, an increasingly elaborate division of labor.

Rather than simple instruments of power within the broad array of social contests, the institutions of the twentieth-century Argentine press constituted a *commercial newspaper industry*. As such, they were riddled not just with the tensions between the cultural/ideological and economic/productive practices of the modern press, but with the more profound struggles inherent in industrial relations of production. If, as Nord argues, the purpose of journalism "is the exercise of power," this power is not wielded by disembodied journalists through institutions above the social order, but by real people embedded in the real social conflicts of institutions themselves embedded in the broader social order. The tumultuous history of the press in Peronist Argentina is thus one of struggles not only for control of the instruments necessary for the socially meaningful exercise of journalism's ideological and cultural power, but within a set of institutions permeated by the more far-reaching social conflicts of modern Argentina.

Peronism and Journalism History

To examine at once the Argentine commercial press and Peronism, then, is to engage two "total" phenomena: the first, a set of fluid and internally fragmented cultural, political, and economic institutions that by the 1920s formed an integral part of the rhythms of urban life; the other, a movement inaugurating changes so dramatic as to reshape Argentina for the remainder of the century. As I show here, the Peronist relationship with the Argentine press was not a direct confrontation between two powerful historical agents, nor did it develop in linear fashion. Instead, it proceeded as an accumulation of multiple and often indirect disputes concerning the relative balance of power between newsworkers and newspaper proprietors, between individual newspaper owners, between public and press, and between state and press. It is in the course of a whole range of specific struggles like these, played out across the spectrum of Argentine society, that Peronism emerged and Peronists and non-Peronists alike forged their claims to hold the reins of power in the nation's political, cultural, and economic institutions. It is also the convergence of these many disputes and their contingent resolutions that constitutes the sweeping transformations of the Peronist era.

    The approach to journalism history that I adopt here is a pragmatic response to a surprisingly complex object of study. While historians have long relied upon newspapers as important sources for the study of the past, we have only begun to move beyond our tendency to accept them either as reflections of popular sentiment—while wrestling with the slippery question of audience reception—or as vehicles solely of elite opinion.[25] Too many media scholars, in turn, accept a historically static view of the press, anthropomorphizing "the press" as a coherent collective agent while reifying the ideological underpinnings of the newspaper industry—even though the specific, practical meanings of the latter are often the fiercely contested terrain of press-related conflicts. As a result, contemporary (often North American) norms frequently serve as a de facto transhistorical yardstick in media studies, bringing researchers to see ideologically charged notions like "freedom of the press" not as the contingent products of social contests, but as concrete and stable, existing or lacking in any given time and place, at once beyond history and capable of being born, dying, and even rising from the dead.[26]

The wide-ranging nature of the debates as well as the depth and complexity of the conflicts examined in this book caution against these approaches. In fact, these struggles bring to the fore the historically changing character of our own understanding of what, in fact, "the press" is. In his history of violence against the press in the United States, media scholar John Nerone offers a far more useful conception of what we study when we study the press. Nerone describes the press not as a static entity, but as a multifaceted "network of relationships," and sees violence directed against press institutions as part of episodic struggles over precisely what this network entails.[27] We can go further: disputes over the press are limited neither to moments of violent confrontation nor to periods of heated public debate. Instead, these mark points of inflection in the unceasing process of reproducing this network of relationships and readjusting the relative power held by the myriad parties involved.

Rather than fundamentally stable, then, the descriptive understanding and normative nature of the press—that is, what the press *is* and what the press *should be*, respectively—are contingent elements of a whole range of disputes in a network of relationships no more static than any other set of relationships in capitalist societies. Changes in the status of newspapers as commodities, the relative importance of commercial display and classified advertising, the complexity of newsroom relations of production, press jurisprudence, and the nature of the reading public all send ripples throughout the press's entire network of relationships. These relationships, in turn, are not above the social order. Instead, they form an integral part of more fundamental social norms and practices, embedding each newspaper institution in processes of historical change not as simple agent or object, but as an array of sites of contention.

The intricacy of the network of relationships that comprised the press and its interpenetration with the broader structures of power in Argentine society meant, quite simply, that the newspaper industry formed an integral part of the social and political order whose crises in the 1930s gave way to the unexpectedly profound transformations of the Peronist years. In its institutional character, the mid-twentieth-century commercial press was ambiguous and internally contradictory: at once political-cultural forum and commercial enterprise; indispensable medium of public opinion and source of private profit; channel of dissent and bolster of the social order. Similarly, with its thousands of newsworkers, high-tech capital goods, and extensive material inputs, the newspaper industry was an important element not just of the political and cultural spheres of Argentine society, but of the economic realm as well. Given its hybrid nature, the rapidly shifting distribution of power and accompanying political conflicts in Argentine society had inescapable consequences for the commercial press, and made it both weapon and prize.

Well before the emergence of Perón as a significant national figure, disputes surrounding the status of journalists' rights in the workplace and the social meaning of journalism practice had begun to expose the growing discrepancy between the ideological and juridical foundations of the press in nineteenth-century liberalism and the commercial practices of the twentieth-century newspaper industry. As a result, Perón-era conflicts for control of the press as an instrument of social power remained intimately linked to long-running struggles over the balance of class power within the newspaper industry. The attention I pay to working journalists in this study, then, stems less from a desire to restore newsworkers to the historiography of the press than from a recognition of the pivotal role that newsworkers played in the broader debates over the meaning of journalism, the clear impact of union militancy on the juridical standing of press institutions, and the importance of class cleavages within the newspaper industry for the reshaping of state-press relations in the 1930s and 1940s.[28] Similarly, I explore the links between changing relations of production in the newsroom, emerging notions of social citizenship, and the practical consequences of the profound economic and ideological crises that racked the country. In examining the transformation of the Argentine commercial press, I also point beyond the state-press conflicts of Peronist Argentina to the inherent volatility of relationships between state, market, public, and crucial institutions of civil society in the age of mass politics.

In engaging the press, Perón and the Peronists thus faced a powerful set of institutions permeated by the same set of profound crises that would give rise to Peronism. The increasingly strained relations between journalists and proprietors within an economically complex and capital-intensive newspaper industry, the consequences of the commercial press's legal and ideological dependence upon a faltering constitutional liberalism, and the growing legitimacy of state interventionism all shaped press development in the 1930s. Conflicts surrounding these processes did more than provide convenient excuses for authoritarian intromission in the Argentine press in the following decade. Though they certainly did that as well, more significantly, it was in no small measure the aggravation of these same crises in even more rapidly changing circumstances that determined at once the opportunities and limits—the realm of the possible—not just for Perón in his approach to the press, but for the shifting distribution of power between newsworkers, newspaper proprietors, the state, and the reading public in the Peronist years.

For this reason, the emphasis that I place on the evolution of state-press relations in both the 1930s and under the military regime of 1943 to 1946 responds to more than a desire to avoid condemning these years to the status of "prelude" to the Peronist heyday. Like other scholars, I consider the profound changes of the 1930s key to understanding not just the conditions that made Peronism possible, but also the social and political forces whose conflicts called the movement into existence.²⁹ The surprisingly sophisticated forms of media management developed by the Augustín P. Justo regime in the 1930s have remained virtually unexplored by scholars, despite their importance as crucial points of inflection in both the development of the Argentine press and the course of Argentine political history.³⁰ From 1943 to 1945, Perón and his military allies drew from these precedents when formulating their own media strategies; the nearly disastrous consequences of those strategies had important implications for the press following Perón's election to the presidency in 1946. Perón's heavy-handed press policies of the years 1947 to 1955, I argue, did not follow strictly from the demands of a scripted, preconceived totalitarian media project, nor were they merely a local adaptation of foreign media models. Instead, they responded as much to Perón's spectacular initial failures in engaging the press as to his unexpectedly resounding success in mobilizing public support in the crisis of October 1945—support that came, significantly, despite the unanimous opposition of "public opinion" as expressed in the pages of the nation's major newspapers.

Rather than unidirectional phenomena in which the press repeatedly stood as a simple target of Peronist action, the conflicts surrounding the newspaper industry that I examine here left not just the press transformed, but Peronism as well. Indeed, the public and private disputes for influence over—or outright control of—the Argentine press formed an integral part of the process through which Peronists forged the legitimacy of their project while simultaneously undermining that of their opponents. Long-running struggles over the institutional, political, and economic aspects of journalism practice played a crucial role in helping shape Peronism's passage from its roots in a military regime seeking civilian support in 1944 to a loose and contradictory reformist movement born of an abrupt democratic opening and unprecedented working-class mobilization in 1945 to 1947. These same disputes—and the seismic shift in the media landscape that they produced—also helped determine the Peronist government's consolidation by the early 1950s as an increasingly bureaucratic regime invoking formulaic and ritualized public acclamation.³¹

Thus, to view the "Peronization" of the Argentine press as an essentially linear process or as the preordained result of an unequivocal, fascist-inspired authoritarianism is to underestimate at once the gravity and consequences of Perón's miscalculations upon his entrance into national politics, the strength of the broader historical precedents and constraints within which Perón and the Peronists operated, and the shifting nature of Peronism over its first decade of existence. Similarly, to imagine "the press" as a coherent, passive, or helpless object of state intromission fails to account for the importance of deep, ongoing conflicts surrounding a socially powerful, institutionally diverse, internally fractured, and rapidly changing newspaper industry. The commonplace reduction of the Peronist transformation of the press to a manifestation of Perón and

Eva Perón's personal aspirations to power, finally, neglects what was both a crucial element in this particular process as well as a fundamental component in the broader unfolding of Argentine history in the second half of the twentieth century: the utopian appeal of Peronism as a force seemingly capable of resolving acute social contradictions, realizing long-neglected egalitarian promises of citizenship, and empowering Argentine workers in unprecedented—though ultimately ambiguous—ways.[32]

This book shares with other recent studies an emphasis on the articulation of a more heterogeneous "Peronist ideology" rooted not exclusively in the authoritarian Right but in the pragmatic incorporation of a broader array of political philosophy.[33] Looking at the articulation of that ideology in relation to the press, however, brings me to place even greater emphasis on the ambiguous persistence of fragmented liberal currents in Peronist discourse.[34] In its self-portrayal as at once revolutionary rupture with Argentina's liberal past and final realization of the unfulfilled emancipatory promises of that same past, Peronism came to occupy a vast ideological spectrum. This study helps to show that the movement's ability to manage the ambiguity of this stance owes much to an overarching set of contradictions in mid-twentieth-century Argentine political life. Well before the military coup of 1943, the nation's established liberal political forces had long proven themselves either unable or unwilling to bridge the gap between the promises of egalitarian political citizenship that they repeatedly invoked and the increasingly stark reality of political and social exclusion. That they had also become entangled in the degeneration of even the most basic of formal democratic practices in the course of the 1930s only served to make that abstract crisis of legitimacy all the more specific and real. By late 1945, those same contradictions had also engulfed the Argentine commercial press, making it a powerful set of institutions whose primary ideological vulnerability lay not in the liberal norms upon which it rested, but in the press's failure to embody those ideals convincingly in practice. As a result, Peronists found they could best challenge the legitimacy of the whole array of anti-Peronist newspapers less by directly confronting the liberal basis of journalism practice than by embracing and transforming it.

The course of these disputes reveals the incoherence and internal contradictions of "Peronist ideology" as flexibility and strength. I make no claim that Peronists convinced the unconvinced by repeatedly formulating their approach to the press in terms of the highest values of what Mariano Plotkin has called the liberal "unifying myth" of the opposition. The great energy that Peronists nonetheless put into justifying their press policies less as negation than as practical realization of liberal abstractions, however, suggests that many Peronist leaders believed that appeals to notions of "rights," "democracy," and "freedom"—regardless of the equivocal and instrumental manner in which

Peronists invoked them—constituted an important component if not of public support for the regime, then at least of public acquiescence to specific state actions. Similarly, by repeatedly proclaiming the construction of a truly open, democratic, and representative public sphere as the goal of government media policies, Perón and his allies could undermine the most salient element of opposition discourse. In this light, the objections of newspaper owners like *La Prensa*'s Alberto Gainza Paz not only ran counter to Peronist notions of "social justice" and "national sovereignty," but formed part of long-running attempts to subvert even the egalitarian political impulses of traditional liberalism itself. In turn, controversial state acts like the manipulation of newsprint distribution became set within the context of struggles for the creation of a "New Argentina" that would embody the whole range of utopian aspirations—liberal and illiberal alike—articulated by the Peronist movement.

The Limits of This Study

Readers will no doubt quickly become aware that this work, like most scholarship, leaves out more than it explicitly includes. First, my intention is not to determine whether Argentines in this period abided by a statically conceived "freedom of the press"—the ideological and juridical cornerstone of the modern media. I instead explore the ways in which the nature of the press as well as the ideological foundations upon which its legitimacy rests are not only historically contingent, but constitute key elements in broader social contests. This study serves as a caution that, when we are approaching the media, concretely historicizing competing discourses of "freedom," "class," "citizenship," "democracy," "rights," and even "the press" itself are of fundamental importance, especially when analyzing moments of rapid social and political change. I do not, however, deny qualitative distinctions in the functioning of the media under different political regimes; my use of such distinctions will become apparent throughout the course of this work.

Second, this is a study not of explicitly partisan periodicals, but of the commercial newspaper industry. This is not because the partisan press had become wholly irrelevant; in fact, the most widely read of these periodicals, the Argentine Socialist Party's *La Vanguardia*, had by 1945 achieved a circulation level equal to that of the largest newspapers of both Colombia and Chile.[35] Yet even *La Vanguardia* operated on a small scale compared to commercial dailies like *La Prensa, La Nación, El Mundo,* and *Crítica.* By the onset of the crises of the 1930s, explicitly partisan writing had become a subset of an increasingly broad array of journalism practices. More obviously, the so-called political press formed part of explicitly partisan conflicts that did not necessarily carry direct consequences for commercial newspapers; disputes involving the commercial press, on the other hand, tended to quickly encompass the press as a whole. Partisan media did play an important role in the period that I examine here, and formed part of the wave of press-related conflicts of the Peronist years. The more far-reaching struggles surrounding the press, however, played themselves out more dramatically and revealingly in the context of the major commercial newspapers.

Similarly, my focus does not extend beyond the federal territory of the city of Buenos Aires.[36] Not only did Buenos Aires hold what were without question Argentina's—and even Latin America's—largest newspapers, but the 1880 federalization of the city created a separate juridical universe for publishers in the new Federal Capital. Newspapers in the Argentine capital thus fell under the legal domain of a federal government whose Congress, unlike provincial legislatures, remained constitutionally prohibited from dictating "laws that restrict the freedom of the press, or establish federal jurisdiction over that freedom." As a result, legal measures affecting the Buenos Aires press also encompassed the provincial press; regulations of provincial newspapers, however, had no legal effect on the press of the capital. As with the partisan press, then, I have not incorporated a systematic discussion of provincial periodicals in this period, even as I hope that my own work opens avenues of exploration for both topics.[37]

Finally, the history of radio and other newer media falls beyond the scope of this book, even as I recognize the growing need for further research into this area. The Argentine Constitution of 1853 recognized not a general freedom of expression, but the more specific *libertad de imprenta*—perhaps most accurately translated as "freedom of the printing press"—leaving the constitutional guarantees for radio on much more ambiguous terrain.[38] In addition, prior to the Perón era many important radio stations operated as extensions of commercial newspaper organizations like *El Mundo* and *La Razón*. As a result, disputes around the Peronist appropriation of Latin America's largest private radio network took place in a legal gray area and remained to some degree subsumed in the more central debates surrounding the newspaper industry.[39] As with the partisan and provincial presses, the inclusion of these elements here would have proven unwieldy, while centering this study on commercial print journalism more accurately captures the contours of the multiple disputes surrounding the press in this period.

Journalism and Power in the Making of Peronist Argentina

The following chapters uncover the mid-twentieth-century contests to define the social role of the Argentine press both *as it should be* and *as it was in practice,* tracing the ways in which these disputes became instrumentalized in the struggle for hegemony within and over the Argentine newspaper industry. Drawing upon and advancing fundamental changes in conceptions of the social aspects of citizenship and the proper relationship between civil society and the state, Peronists adeptly inserted themselves into the institutional and ideological fissures that had begun to emerge within the newspaper industry in the 1930s. Their success in this struggle rested at once on the ability of Peronists to present the "resolution" of particular press-related conflicts as consonant with the creation of a socially just "New Argentina" as well as with the unrealized egalitarian promises of Argentine liberalism. This book is an examination of the competing claims to resolve the tensions between the twentieth-century commercial press and the ideals proclaimed by those nineteenth-century liberals who had established the ideological and juridical foundations of Argentine journalism practice. It is also the story, however, of how the volatile historical processes that had at once given birth to Peronism and undermined the legitimacy of the newspaper industry status quo ultimately militated against the realization of utopian media projects—Peronist and non-Peronist alike—in anything but an authoritarian simulacrum for the duration of the subsequent decade.

In addressing the multiple conflicts within and surrounding the Argentine newspaper industry, Peronists fashioned a discourse of the social role of journalism that posited the state not as a threat to the functioning of the press, but as a defender: of the "true press" from the corrupting influence of commerce; of public opinion from the distorting effects of powerful private interests; of newsworkers from newspaper proprietors; of smaller news organizations from more powerful ones; and of the newspaper industry as a whole from very real external economic shocks and internal production bottlenecks. Perón and his allies, with the balance of state power in their hands, portrayed their actions as falling within the bounds of this discourse, combining their arguments with a capacity for concrete action that outstripped, delegitimized, and divided the opposition. That the confiscation of *La Prensa* took place through formally legal channels and under conditions of constitutional normality reveals more than the extent to which Peronists had come to dominate Argentine political life. It also reveals the degree to which opponents of Perón failed to articulate convincing alternative visions of the social role of journalism and the press that recognized not just the profound changes inaugurated by Peronism, but the commercial transformation of the press itself in the twentieth century.

Four interrelated processes helped create these circumstances. First, the industrialization of newspaper production produced a press clearly different from that envisioned in classical liberalism, as newspaper institutions became increasingly capital-intensive, profit-oriented organizations. The potentially exclusionary implications of this process for the universal practice of public expression and the distorting power that commercial interests might exert on the means of social communication became important elements in criticism of the press as early as the 1910s. Allegations that the "marketplace of ideas" had degenerated into nothing more than a market in commodities and audiences only increased in the crises of the 1930s and 1940s, setting important precedents and providing useful fodder for subsequent Peronist critiques.[40]

Yet two other elements of this industrialization also played crucial roles in shaping the Peronist transformation of the commercial press: the increasingly clear and elaborate division of labor in the newspaper industry, and the growing importance of newspapers as economic entities. In the course of the 1930s, disputes within newspaper institutions between newsworkers and proprietors emerged into the open, while the worldwide newsprint crisis in the wake of World War II aggravated both those conflicts as well as the competition between newspapers. By the time of Perón's ascent, then, the industrialization of the Argentine press had produced a triple fissure: between conceptions of the press as a vehicle of general public expression and the private, capital-intensive and commercial nature of the newspaper industry; between labor and capital within the press; and between those newspaper institutions with access to increasingly scarce and expensive newsprint and those that approached bankruptcy.

Second, the economic crisis of the 1930s, together with the post–World War II restructuring of the world economy, brought a dramatic expansion of the legitimate realm of state activity, fundamentally shifting a view of the proper balance between public and private realms that had achieved broad consensus within the Argentine political class. In the course of the Depression, consensus grew within the Argentine political class for the expansion of state intervention throughout the economy as the primary corrective factor to the domestic impact of a world market in disarray and as a mediator between different sectors of capital.[41] The political crises of the 1930s and the multiple threats posed by the world war only boosted state coordination of the economy and lent weight to state intervention in information circulation (through censorship) and production (as wartime propaganda). Increasingly, traditional liberal claims that the state stood as the primary threat to the functioning of the press shared space with pragmatic appeals to the state's capacity to insulate sectors of the newspaper industry from the devastating effects of postwar economic restructuring. Many began to argue that the state, rather than being a categorical menace, could protect the press's proper mission from the far greater threats of irresponsible commercialism, monopoly formation, and financial ruin.

Third, the rise of the Argentine urban working class as a significant political force reshaped notions of the proper social role of the press and the ability to exercise the power of journalism in meaningful ways. The new style of politics that this rise inaugurated had at its core broader conceptions of the nature of citizenship and representation and, relatedly, emphasized the importance of the state as a mediator between collective and individual interests. As Daniel James has so convincingly argued, the basis of Perón's power lay in "his capacity to recast the whole issue of citizenship within a new social context."[42] In relation to the press, this renegotiation of the meanings of citizenship included assertions of the rights of Argentine workers to continuously articulate their aspirations, interests, and daily life through the means of social communication in ways that at once incorporated and transcended liberal notions of individual freedom of expression.[43]

Rather than negating traditional conceptions of the press as a vehicle for the citizen's constitutional right of expression and as an embodiment of public opinion, Peronists built upon them. Perón and his followers argued that the problem with the press lay less in the century-old liberal norms of journalism practice than in the refusal of newspaper owners to adhere to those norms in ways that recognized the increasing breadth of the Argentine polity. While proprietors unceasingly invoked the expression of public opinion in their newspapers as the cornerstone to press legitimacy, Peronists added a crucial caveat: the commercial press failed to embody that aspiration in practice, serving instead simply to "publicize the private opinion of newspaper owners." This failure points directly to a long-standing fissure between public and press that finally revealed itself with the sudden, unexpected political protagonism of a crucial section of that public. In explaining the unanimity of newspaper opposition to Perón in October 1945—just as popular support for the colonel became impossible to ignore—metalworker Ángel Perelman declared that "having neither means nor form of expressing ourselves, we [workers] did not constitute 'public opinion.'"[44] The gap between formal citizenship (full and equal membership in "the public") and the obviously unequal distribution of wealth and the exercise of power in Argentina would find its promised bridge, supporters of Perón argued, not just in the "social justice" policies of the Peronist state, but in the representation of working class interests in the pages of the daily press—provided that journalists faithfully fulfilled their true mission.

Finally, the growing political polarization of the 1930s became, in the following decade, what Tulio Halperín Donghi has evocatively called a *guerra civil larvada*—civil war in gestation, or veiled civil war.[45] Yet it was more than the depth of the cleavages that had opened within Argentine society that facilitated and even encouraged the instrumentalization of the more utopian elements of Peronist discourse in the struggles over the press: Peronists had also quickly come to control all three branches of a vastly more powerful Argentine state. It is within these conditions of unprecedented political dominance that Perón deftly managed to use long-running labor disputes within the newspaper industry, competition among different newspapers, the perception of an Argentine public sphere held captive by private interests, and the growing legitimacy of state economic interventionism to wholly refashion the Argentine media. This transformation culminated in the congressional expropriation of *La Prensa* in 1951.

Part 1 of this study examines the rise of the modern Argentine press from the period following the battle of Caseros (1852) through the multiple crises of 1930 to 1943. The rapid expansion of the Buenos Aires press transformed its nature: as capitalist relations of production came to dominate the newsroom, conflicts of interest emerged between a new class of professional journalists and the owners of newspapers, undermining notions of "the press" as an internally unified institution. Similarly, the increasingly capital-intensive nature of the newspaper industry began to belie the notion of press freedom as a universal right, while the growing economic weight of the newspaper industry threatened to undermine in important ways the nineteenth-century juridical and ideological foundations upon which the relationship between press, state, and public stood.

Chapter 1 examines the transition from the small partisan press of the nineteenth century to the massive commercial newspaper industry of twentieth-century Buenos Aires. Chapter 2 looks more closely at three particular aspects of the commercial press in the crises of political and economic liberalism in the 1930s: the resurgence of partisan journalism, though now in hybrid form; the increasingly complex state/press relations of that decade; and the unionization drive of Argentine journalists.

The press policies of the military regime (1943–46) that gave birth to the Peronist movement are the topic of part 2. Beyond rapidly expanding state authority in the realm of information production and dissemination, military reformers also fundamentally revised juridical definitions of the nature of the press, recognizing newspapers as commercial institutions and the newsroom as a site of class conflict. In addition, the sudden articulation by military officials of notions of citizenship centered on social rights implied a substantive change in conceptions of the proper relationships between the press, civil society, and the state. The dual fissure that had begun to emerge in the course of the 1930s now suddenly became impossible to ignore: the growing rift between working journalists and newspaper proprietors belied the coherence of the press as a unified collective subject; and the explosion of new social groups onto the political scene seriously undermined claims of newspapers as broadly representative institutions within the public sphere.

Chapter 3 examines initial regime attempts to bring the Argentine press into line with the dictates of military authoritarianism by means of increasingly bureaucratic—and ultimately counterproductive—forms of censorship. Chapter 4 uncovers the process behind the extension of collective bargaining rights to journalists and the multiple conflicts that this move engendered.

Chapter 5 analyzes the changing relations between the military regime, the press, and the public in the midst of the stark political polarization of 1945. Ironically, the circumstances surrounding the foundational moment for Peronism also revealed that the emulation of the methods of press cooptation that had served Augustín P. Justo so well for nearly a decade quickly ended in disaster for Perón, in no small measure due to the unexpected depth of the social transformation that the military had only tentatively unleashed. The vivid contradiction between the press's ideal role as the voice of "public opinion," expanding conceptions of citizenship, and the Buenos Aires commercial newspapers' overwhelming rejection of the clearly popular Juan Domingo Perón in his moment of crisis, I argue, forms the basis of the most violent episode of the mass mobilizations that gave formal birth to the Peronist movement on October 17, 1945: the sustained and deadly attack on the offices of the newspaper *Crítica*.

Part 3 explores the transformation of the Buenos Aires commercial press from the Perón's February 1946 electoral victory through the consolidation of the Peronist media apparatus in 1951. The failure of Perón's carefully cultivated ties to powerful newspaper owners like *Crítica*'s Raúl Damonte Taborda to provide him any support during his fall from grace in mid-1945 signaled to the newly elected president that alliances with figures possessing an autonomous capacity for political mobilization were simply too dangerous. The creation of a "New Argentina" called for a significantly more thorough reworking of the relationships between state, press, and public in ways that might address the growing political and cultural protagonism of Argentine workers; it also meant that the Peronist government would seek to avoid the tactical mistakes of the past and seek to build a media apparatus that might both generate consensus around the regime and make betrayal by newspaper owners impossible. Still, the creation of a properly Peronist communications conglomerate owes much to the particularly dire economic circumstances that most Argentine newspapers faced after the war. These conditions not only aggravated the existing fissures within the newspaper industry, but set the stage for the expropriation of Latin America's most powerful commercial daily by the Argentine Congress.

Chapter 6 traces the intricate process by which Perón replaced his set of alliances with powerful but unreliable newspaper owners in favor of hidden direct control of the majority of the Buenos Aires commercial press through the private holding company Editorial ALEA and the Undersecretariat of Information and the Press. Chapter 7 examines the complex legal, ideological, economic, and workplace conflicts that culminated in the Argentine Congress's expropriation of Latin America's most powerful commercial daily, *La Prensa*. I argue that the newspaper passed to Peronist hands not simply due to the authoritarian tendencies of Peronism, but also because Peronists managed to articulate relatively coherent solutions to the set of increasingly acute crises that had surrounded and permeated the Argentine newspaper industry since the 1930s. In doing so less by denying liberal claims of the press's proper role as a vehicle of expression open to all citizens than by asserting that *La Prensa* self-evidently and repeatedly failed to embody that lofty ideal in practice, they added a layer of ambiguity to opposition invocations of traditional liberal notions of "freedom of the press." Ironically, in consolidating a media apparatus that acted less as a forum of public expression—working-class or otherwise—than as a stage for the regime's public acclamation, the expropriation of *La Prensa* served to generate only an illusory unanimity and a silenced but increasingly desperate opposition.

In this study's conclusion, I briefly trace the history of the Argentine newspaper industry in the wake of the fall of Perón. It would become clear to a subsequent generation of Peronists that the movement's leader had proven unwilling and unable to move beyond a clearly authoritarian, sublimating "resolution" of the tensions within the Argentine press. Similarly, the bureaucratization of the newspaper industry had betrayed fundamental promises that the Peronist press might serve as a more open vehicle for citizen rights of collective and individual expression. For a more radical group of influential Peronist intellectuals, I argue, these failures called into question not only the possibility that any compromises with capitalist forms of media ownership might allow for a truly free and representative press, but also nothing less than the emancipatory potential of Peronism itself. Finally, I briefly place the Argentine press conflicts of the period 1930 to 1955 in their transnational context. Despite their uniqueness, these conflicts are not isolated phenomena; they form part of the perpetual, contentious negotiation of the relationship between state and civil society, the power of journalism and commercial media in the age of mass politics, and the nature of citizenship and democracy in capitalist societies.

1

THE FOURTH ESTATE

> Buenos Aires. Callao and Rivadavia: "Noticias Gráficas!" "Crítica!"
> And the whirlwind of the newsboy's cries —dark, dark—,
> that opens like a fan and invades the streets of the city:
> Like a lance.
> Like an arrow.
>
> **—José Portogalo, 1935**

> Nothing moves in a civilized nation if the printed press does not work. . . .
> The highest ideals, the most honorable aspirations for the common good
> have been sown, cultivated, and harvested through the columns of newspapers.
>
> **—*La Nación*, September 1, 1935**

Disconcertingly well-stocked periodical kiosks crowded the sidewalks of mid-twentieth-century Buenos Aires, stuffed with the enormous variety of the morning's fruits—the afternoon's detritus—of Latin America's largest publishing industry. With over seven hundred different Spanish-language newspapers and magazines together with sixty-seven dailies and periodicals in Yiddish, Arabic, Russian, Japanese, Armenian, Greek, German, and a host of other languages, all competing for readers' attention, the sheer volume and variety of publications could easily overwhelm any curious pedestrian.[1] As two foreign journalists working at the English-language *Buenos Aires Herald* in the 1940s remarked, "the newsstands of Buenos Aires have for years offered a bewildering assortment of newspapers printed locally in such a babel of languages that I never did learn to recognize more than a third of them, let alone read them."[2] Earlier visitors to the city like Georges Clemenceau and Vicente Blasco Ibáñez highlighted the technological complexity and wealth of the periodical press, proclaiming newspaper institutions like *La Prensa* and

La Nación the embodiment of an obviously vibrant and optimistic Argentine modernity.[3]

The rise of the Buenos Aires press in the first decades of the twentieth century marks more than a simple quantitative expansion of publishing capacity. In Argentina, as in many other parts of the world, newspapers underwent a dramatic transformation from their roots in the partisan publications of the mid–nineteenth century to emerge as a qualitatively distinct new means of social communication. The twentieth-century press, though forged in the heat of the previous century's political agitation, was shaped less by formal partisan disputes than by a rapidly expanding market of readers and advertisers. In this new world of commercial journalism, explicit identification with a specific, politically inscribed circle of readers acted less to guarantee an audience than to constrain a newspaper's potential market. Overt partisan militancy increasingly ceded to "general interest" reporting and class-based cultural appeals in the ceaseless effort to attract what appeared an ever-expanding readership.

This transformation implied an important refashioning of the whole network of relationships that constituted the Buenos Aires press. Where partisan political engagement and journalism practice had been intimately intertwined in the nineteenth century, the proprietors and journalists of the new press professed their autonomy from the vagaries of explicit partisan interests and— most emphatically—state power. Drawing on the rapidly expanding and increasingly diverse market of readers and advertisers, the owners of the commercial press forged a new relationship not only between political society and the newspaper industry, but between individual newspapers and their readership. Press and public increasingly faced each other as commodities, their relationship driven less by partisan militancy than by the more mundane forces of market exchange. In the process, Argentina's commercial newspapers became a particularly complex amalgam of journalistic types: the "objective" reporting of the independent press—independent of both state power and organized political factions—allegedly mirrored reality, while editorialists sought at once to reflect and shape the interests and opinions of Argentine society as a whole.[4]

At the same time, the institutional structure of the press increasingly reflected the general contours of the Argentine economy. Not only did newspaper production necessitate progressively greater investments in imported capital goods and inputs like technologically advanced rotary presses, newsprint, and ink, but the transformation of the press demanded a reworking of newspaper relations of production. In the Buenos Aires of the mid-1920s, the politician-proprietors of nineteenth-century journalism, who had founded newspapers as "combat posts" in the defense of private economic and political interests, had largely given way to journalistic entrepreneurs whose primary business interests sprang from the newspapers themselves. As the ranks of politician-proprietors ceded to newspaper capital proper, the press's rapid economic development and increasing technological complexity, as well as the growing thematic diversity of newspaper content, demanded a corresponding expansion of the ranks of wage earners specialized in different aspects of newspaper composition, production, and distribution. By 1930, Argentina's commercially insignificant partisan press of the nineteenth century had become an economically powerful, capital-intensive, newspaper *industry* employing thousands of wage-earning journalists, printers, managers, and distributors.

This emergence of a new kind of press carried with it a rising dissonance between idealized conceptions of the social role of journalism and the commercial practices of the modern Argentine newspaper industry. The press's juridical bases centered upon an understanding of newspapers as vehicles of citizen participation in an idealized public sphere, with the press as a whole acting as a fourth estate alongside and balancing the other representative institutions of republican governance. This conception, firmly rooted in nineteenth-century liberalism, held the economics of newspaper operations as incidental. Indeed, newspapers had rarely proven profit-making ventures in the course of the nineteenth century, and economic self-sufficiency was usually as surprising as it was short-lived.[5] Yet, by the 1920s, not only had newspaper proprietors begun to wring spectacular wealth from an activity that for ideological reasons lay beyond the margins of the Argentine commercial code, but the commercial transformation of the newspaper industry had left the relationship between the ideological bases of journalism practice, press-related jurisprudence, and the actual functioning of the newspaper industry increasingly strained. The multiple fissures that had begun to open in the Argentine newspaper industry in the course of this transformation were precisely what would fuel the press conflicts of the 1930s and, ultimately, of the Peronist years.

The Legal Environment of the Argentine Press

The ideological roots and legal precedents of Argentine journalism are tangled with ambiguities more pronounced and more complex than the dominant, romanticized view of national press history allows.[6] Rather than marking an abrupt and total rupture with an emphatically statist colonial political philosophy, the initial moves to create what would become the Argentine national press retained crucial aspects of the previous views of the realm of state prerogative, and thus of the relationship between the state and the means by which information is created and distributed. Both the Argentine press and early press law necessarily emerged in a moment in which, as Jorge Myers has argued, "the principal ideological traditions that have shaped the political vocabularies of the twentieth century . . . had still not achieved a full crystallization."[7] Indeed, in the chaotic first years of the republic, ideological clarity often served only to limit the range of options open to those attempting to establish a new political order in the wake of the dissolution of the old. Even if the Constitution of 1853 created a more stable juridical basis for journalism practice, the charter also incorporated new elements of uncertainty. Not surprisingly, each of the multiple parties to twentieth-century press conflicts could find ample raw material and historical precedents for their arguments by invoking the nineteenth-century ideological, institutional, and juridical beginnings of the national press.

Based as much in the immediate political exigencies of national state formation as in the realm of private political expression, the Argentine press's moment of birth embodies these profound ambiguities. While informational hand-copied *gazetas* circulated in Buenos Aires even before the city became the seat of a new viceroyalty in 1776, commercial print journalism began with the appearance in 1801 of *El Telégrafo Mercantil, Rural, Político, Económico e Historiográfico del Río de la Plata*.[8] The first regular periodical of the republic, however, had its origins as an integral part of the nascent national state: at the behest of the ruling junta, the *Gazeta de Buenos-Ayres* published its first issue under the direction of Mariano Moreno on June 7, 1811. Though the junta explicitly created the *Gazeta de Buenos-Ayres* not as a vehicle of private expression but as the mouthpiece of a still fragile provisional government in the midst of the violently contentious process of breaking the colonial link and fashioning a new state, Argentine journalists have long held the paper's appearance as the birth of the national press and Moreno as the nation's first journalist.[9] Invocations of Moreno as the archetype of the Argentine journalist thus carry with them a legacy with an equivocal relationship to the antistatist conceptions of journalism practice that would become hegemonic later in the century.

The junta decree that laid the juridical basis for national press law similarly maintained a degree of ambivalence between the realm of private prerogative and the public tasks of state formation. Still, well into the twentieth century newspaper editors would point to the first two articles of the junta decree of April 22, 1811, as establishing the press as outside the realm of legitimate state regulation:

> Article 1. All bodies [organizations] and private persons of whatever condition and state they might be, have the freedom to write, print, and publish their political ideas, without need for any license, revision, or approval prior to publication, under the restrictions and responsibilities expressed in the present decree.
> Article 2. All present press courts, as well as the censorship of political works prior to their publication, are hereby abolished.[10]

The decree declared the individual action of publishing at once a "barrier against arbitrary actions by those who govern," a source of public education, and "the only path to arrive at knowledge of true public opinion." In this way, the junta decree established a latitude of publishing freedom that broke the restrictions enforced by the Bourbon colonial regime and promoted a significant democratization of public debate regarding the formation of what would become the postcolonial state.

However, the same decree restricted in important ways this freedom of private citizens to publish. If the decree did not require authors to sign their articles, it did insist that publishers record the authors' identity so they could be held accountable in case of denunciations for acts of libel and licentiousness, writings that contradicted "public decency and good customs," and any other "abuse of freedom of the press." Similarly, article 6 asserted the necessity of prior censorship by ecclesiastical authorities with regard to writings on religious topics, while other articles of the decree loosely prohibited the "abuse of freedom of the press" and the publication of writing that was libelous, licentious, or contrary to public decency. To enforce these elements, a "Supreme Junta of Censorship" with ecclesiastical participation, established by article 13 of the decree, stood ready to "assure freedom of the press and contain at the same time its abuse."[11] Deán Gregorio Funes, author of the decree, justified these measures before the junta, explaining that "the liberty [*libertad*] to which the press has a right is not in favor of licentiousness [*libertinaje*] of thought."[12]

Initial formulations of the juridical norms surrounding the Argentine press, then, embodied a blend of interpretations on the parameters of the press and the realm of state competence with regard to the circulation of information and opinion. On the one hand, the decree legally recognized the existence of a print public sphere, at once open to the participation of all residents of the rebellious territories and free from prior censorship.[13] At the same time, however, the decree limited legitimate debate to "political ideas," leaving discussion of questions of public morality open to official censorship and effectively ceding control over legal print debate on religious matters to the clergy precisely *because* of its vested interest in upholding certain aspects of Catholic doctrine. This latter element of the decree was hardly inconsequential, especially in an environment in which struggles over the nature and form of political authority as well as the rights and limits of republican citizenship—and thus also of the relationship between state and church—were becoming increasingly contentious.[14] Essentially, even as the junta set the basis for a political press that could serve as a forum of political debate among an emerging political elite, it also retained the monitoring and regulation of the press within the legitimate realm of state *and* church activity. Not until 1821 and 1822, a decade after the junta's initial decree, did authorities in the province of Buenos

Aires enlarge the realm of the rights of private citizens to publish by enacting a set of laws affecting both the press and the process of secularization.[15] The decree of April 1811 and its subsequent revisions thus stood together with the junta's creation of the *Gazeta de Buenos-Ayres* as an amalgam of disparate influences: the statist and Catholic legacy of Spanish colonial rule; emerging bourgeois conceptions of the separation of public and private rights; and the practical demands of erecting a new political order in the ashes of the old.[16]

If continued revisions of the April 1811 press decree reflected, for the most part, a trend toward expanding the legal latitude allowed in the press, they also represented a more pragmatic attempt to create a legal framework that authorities could actually enforce. This liberalization, however, proved short-lived. In May 1828, the Manuel Dorrego regime in the province of Buenos Aires sharply curtailed the right to "attack state religion" through the press and prohibited the use of satire to criticize the public actions and private "defects" of "any individual" under penalty of heavy fines.[17] The rise of Juan Manuel de Rosas as governor of the province of Buenos Aires—with vast authority over both the province as well as the United Provinces of the Río de la Plata as a whole—only strengthened restrictions on the press. Indeed, while the Rosas dictatorship continued to allow some semblance of a public sphere, publishing became subject to increasingly tighter legal and de facto state and quasi-state control.[18] The most vibrant press opposition to the Rosas regime, in fact, came from the journalism practice of writers who, like Domingo Sarmiento and Bartolomé Mitre, attacked the government from beyond the reach of the *rosista* state while in exile in Chile, Uruguay, and Bolivia.[19]

Only the Unitario victory over Rosas at the battle of Caseros in 1852, together with the broader ascendancy of a more coherent political liberalism in the Río de la Plata and beyond, allowed a new and ultimately more stable juridical framework for the operation of the Argentine press. Delineating the relationship between state and press in a far clearer fashion than previous attempts, Argentine lawmakers devoted article 14 of the 1853 constitution to the question of public expression through the press, while the subsequent addition of article 32 in 1860 further limited the capacity of the federal government to impose restrictions on publishing activities. Together, articles 14 and 32 of the constitution addressed the positive and negative aspects of the ideal press-state relationship: article 14 stood as a positive definition of citizen rights with regard to publishing, while article 32 embodied a conception of the role of the press as necessarily free of state restriction.

Yet the drafters of the new constitution also attempted to reconcile a basic contradiction that Sarmiento himself had asserted plagued the functioning of the press in any republic: "without complete freedom of the press there can be neither liberty nor progress. But with it one can barely maintain public order."[20] To address this, not only did the drafters of the constitution allow provincial authorities significant latitude in determining local press law, but in doing so they also unlinked the rights of individuals to publish from the broader laws restricting libel and other aspects of the content of expression. In drawing a distinction between the private prerogative of citizens to publish and the public right of individuals to be protected from certain kinds of written attacks, the drafters of the new constitution sought to strike a new balance between the operation of a highly politicized press and broader political stability.

Article 14 of the 1853 constitution established that "all inhabitants of the Confederation enjoy the following rights in conformity with the laws that regulate their exercise; that is: . . . to publish ideas through the press without prior censorship."[21] Based on the draft constitution of liberal ideologue Juan Bautista Alberdi in his *Bases y puntos de partida para la organización política de la República Argentina,* the article guaranteed freedom of the press in its positive and universal sense: as a *freedom for* the expression of thought through the press, ostensibly open to use by all inhabitants of the republic regardless of citizenship, political affiliation, ethnicity, or gender. Article 32, added in 1860 as the province of Buenos Aires rejoined the Confederation, reinforced the terms of the earlier article by declaring that "the Federal Congress will not dictate laws that restrict the freedom of the press, nor establish federal jurisdiction over that freedom."[22] Born as a concession to inhabitants of the rebellious province who feared President Urquiza's attempts to stifle the opposition press, article 32 defined press freedom in its negative form: as *freedom from* the dictates of state authorities. The Constitution of 1853 thus effectively placed press freedom in the realm of natural rights, both universally valid and prior to the constitution itself, while at the same time explicitly limiting the actions of the federal government with regard to the functioning of the press.

Still, while establishing the right of private individuals to exercise freedom of expression through the press, both articles contained ambiguities that helped shape the particular environment in which the Buenos Aires commercial press would grow. First, though article 14 declared the right to publish without prior censorship, it did so only "in conformity with the laws that regulate [its] exercise," despite Alberdi's more unequivocally antistatist inclinations.[23] Until the 1930s, for the most part, these laws remained restricted primarily to offenses stipulated in the Argentine Penal Code that might be committed through the press: *calumnia* (libel), *injuria* (insult), and *desacato* (contempt of a public official).[24] By holding the authors of published works answerable for offenses as subjective and murky as *injuria* and *desacato,* the qualifications drafted into article 14 thus established the possibility that press activity could, in fact, remain subject to legitimate state penal action despite constitutional prohibitions against prior censorship. As a result, the federal legal and legislative battles surrounding the press prior to the 1930s centered primarily upon the proper definitions and limits of violations of the Penal Code committed through the press.²⁵ The possibility of litigation for these offenses—and the concrete cases of such litigation—marked a clear and constant limit to the role of the press within the emerging Argentine public sphere.

Second, article 14 did not guarantee freedom of expression, but rather a more limited right to publish "through the press" without prior censorship. Article 32 would reinforce this by focusing explicitly on *libertad de imprenta*, perhaps most accurately translated as the medium-specific "freedom of print" or "freedom of the printing press." The national constitution, then, did not endorse a blanket right of Argentines to express themselves by any means, and in this Argentine constitutional law remained consonant with that of countries like Chile, Switzerland, and Belgium.²⁶ Nor did the 1853 constitution establish the right of *libertad de prensa* (freedom of the press), with its institutional and ill-defined quasi-corporate connotations, even if that expression did come into common usage at least by the late nineteenth century. These issues transcended simple semantics and left newer media like radio, audio recording, and film in an indeterminate position vis-à-vis constitutional law by the time of their growing importance in the 1920s.²⁷

This qualification of the right of expression by means of the press, finally, reinforced a corollary to article 32: if the federal Congress could not dictate laws preempting the exercise of expression through the medium of print, provincial legislatures remained bound only by the provisions of article 14. The subsequent federalization of the Argentine capital in 1880, then, effectively established multiple juridical universes for the national press: one in each of the Argentine provinces, where article 14 and the various press laws of provincial legislatures held sway; and another in the sparsely populated, peripheral National Territories together with the densely populated Federal Capital (the city of Buenos Aires proper), which fell under the administration of the federal government. In the city of Buenos Aires, then, any moves toward state regulation of the press would effectively clash with the constitutional constraints of article 32, and restrictions on the press remained far more controversial and difficult to establish—provided that the affected parties and their allies were powerful enough to mount a legal challenge. As a result, provincial journalists often found opposition to the actions of local officials much more problematic than did journalists in the city of Buenos Aires, even in periods of "intervention," or direct rule by the federal government. Small, usually Left and labor publications of the Argentine capital, on the other hand, often did not have the means for legal defense against closures and harassment of dubious constitutionality, nor could they easily recover economically from quasi-legal police-imposed suspensions.²⁸

The 1880 federalization of the city of Buenos Aires, by separating the nation's most prosperous and populous city from the country's most powerful province, effectively resolved many of the more contentious issues facing the federal nature and geographical balance of powers of the Argentine national state. With the relative subsiding of large-scale social conflict that the measure secured, the most pressing impediment to the rapid expansion of the Argentine economy receded. The subsequent economic boom, and the generation of unprecedented prosperity for many in the port city, provided an environment in which commercial newspapers could serve at once as catalysts and beneficiaries of an increasingly vibrant national economy.

At the same time, the creation of the Federal Capital also established a juridically and economically privileged territory for the emergence of the commercial press. The emergence and spectacular expansion of the Buenos Aires newspaper industry thus owes as much to a growing acceptance of the antistatist elements of Argentina's liberal Constitution of 1853 as to the federalization of the national capital. This combination, coupled with the subsequent rise in the public influence of newspaper owners that it helped engender, allowed the negative interpretation of press freedom—as freedom from state regulation—to emerge as dominant, while the positive right of publication became increasingly displaced from private individuals to become a broader, quasi-corporatist, institutional right of "the press." In the process, Buenos Aires newspapers themselves became integral elements of the liberal institutional and ideological hegemony that played such a crucial role in their emergence.[29] Indeed, it is the rupture of that hegemony in 1930, with the military coup of September serving as both catalyst and symptom, that would ultimately undermine the broad consensus that had developed regarding the ideal character of the Argentine press.

The Structural Transformation of the Argentine Press

The rapid expansion of the press in the final decades of the nineteenth century, in fact, came coupled with a marked change in the practical character of journalism practice and the nature of newspaper institutions. If the explicitly political and bitterly polemical writing of the anti-Rosista exiles served as the foundation for Argentine journalism in the wake of Caseros, it is this latter tradition of *periodismo faccioso* (factional journalism) that would eventually give birth to the nation's modern commercial press.[30] Yet the dramatic economic and demographic changes of the Argentine fin de siècle entailed a quantitative and qualitative transformation of the Buenos Aires press that differentiated the twentieth-century commercial newspapers far more starkly from their predecessors. By the 1920s, a nineteenth-century press focused on partisan militancy had become Latin America's largest commercial newspaper industry.

Indeed, the Argentine press in the years between the fall of Rosas in 1852 and the federalization of Buenos Aires in 1880 formed an integral part of the often violent confrontations over the final character of the Argentine state.[31] More than a simple extension of political activity, the practice of journalism was intrinsically political, with the separation between time dedicated to writing and time dedicated to state activities determined less by individual interest than by fluctuations in a given faction's access to state power. Thus, journalist-politicians like José Hernández viewed newspapers like *El Nacional Argentino* together with the ballot box as a single "battlefield," and competition for readership as an appeal to the mobilizing potential of ideas. For Hernández, journalists simultaneously gave voice to and guided public opinion, while the journalist himself served as a kind of precursor to a more sophisticated political leader that had yet to appear unequivocally.[32] Similarly, Bartolomé Mitre found in *La Nación Argentina* a "combat post" to defend his factional interests, and in journalism practice more generally a place for tactical retreat from more literal battlefields.[33]

It is precisely out of this tradition of factional journalism that two of the twentieth century's more important Argentine commercial newspapers emerged. Both *La Prensa* and *La Nación* had their origins in the final conflicts over the status of Buenos Aires and the nature of Argentine federalism. Yet both newspapers would survive and prosper well after those conflicts had subsided, in large measure due to their owners' embrace of key elements of the less factious *journalism of opinion* and *objective journalism* models—models that, in many ways, presented themselves as historical possibilities only with the subsiding of those conflicts and the establishment of liberal hegemony.[34] This transition, together with the concomitant emergence of a market more than capable of economically sustaining a set of commercially oriented newspapers divorced from specific political factions, ushered in a period of journalism in Buenos Aires in which polemical stances became increasingly subordinate to newspaper business interests.[35]

The commercial transformation of the Argentine press has received scant attention from historians precisely with regard to the newspaper that would become Latin America's most economically powerful in the first half of the twentieth century: *La Prensa*. The appearance of *La Prensa*, founded by José C. Paz, on October 18, 1869, marked an important step in the creation of a new style of Argentine journalism. In the first issue, Paz immediately declared his intention to move beyond the practices of factional journalism to create a paper that would always maintain an "independence" from political factions, resting instead on a broader reading market. Rather than signaling a "mercantile motive," Paz declared, *La Prensa*'s engagement with the market would remain restricted to that needed to allow the editors to "be genuine interpreters of public opinion."[36] Indeed, even the layout of Paz's paper, with its physical separation of opinion, information, and advertising, revealed a move to more general notions of the press as a vehicle of both commerce and expression.[37]

Any embrace of the more modern journalism of opinion and "objective" journalism models continued to rest uneasily with the still prominent role that force played in the resolution of political disputes. This became clear with Paz's participation in a rebellion against the presidential succession of Nicolás Avellaneda in 1874. Upon joining the rebellion, Paz decried the relative powerlessness of the press itself against the "political caudillos" dominating the country and suppressing "public opinion." In this situation, Paz wrote, "the word of the press is impotent.... What should be done in this case? Honorable and patriotic journalism knows no other temperament than to trade the pen for the sword."[38] Thus, despite the subsequent consolidation of *La Prensa* as the country's premier commercial daily and preeminent example of the potential of new kinds of journalistic practices and institutions, this transition was neither immediate nor entirely unequivocal. As would become apparent in the course of the 1930s, the tradition of factional journalism never entirely vanished in Argentina, even if it did remain largely submerged beneath the commercial strategies of the major dailies.

Claims to economic independence for the paper, however, were more than mere assertions. Indeed, the Paz family newspaper established a market position that gave it an unprecedented autonomy vis-à-vis not just Argentine political society, but even the rural landed interests with which the paper's editors continued to identify. If the Paz family maintained a broad identification of the national interest with that of the rural oligarchy, *La Prensa*'s exclusive control by a single family rather than a political faction made it at once unpredictable and more effective as a representative of the long-term interests of that class as a whole.

Perhaps just as strikingly, by the 1920s a *La Prensa* monopoly on classified advertising insulated the paper's owners from economic dependence not just on any political faction or social class, but on any single group of business advertisers as well. These thousands of classified advertisements, which covered the first five to twelve pages of the newspaper, extended the public of *La Prensa* well beyond the upper-class and educated middle-class readership that editors almost exclusively addressed in the paper's editorials.[39] *La Prensa* achieved an average circulation of over 250,000 copies daily in 1927, growing to over 380,000 daily and nearly 500,000 for the Sunday edition by 1946, while its pre–World War II record stood at 745,894 copies on January 1, 1935.[40] This rapid rise in circulation necessitated a division of labor and level of capital investment that was in stark contrast to the artisanal production of nineteenth-century newspapers. In fact, by early 1946 *La Prensa* employed 1,698 persons and had consumed twenty-six thousand tons of imported newsprint the previous year—the scarcity and high price of newsprint due to the world conflict notwithstanding.[41] Despite the political troubles the paper faced in the subsequent Peronist years, its circulation only continued to climb and the ranks of journalists, printers, and other staff at the paper to swell.

The tremendous wealth generated by *La Prensa* brought with it a rearticulation not only of the relationships between newspapers, market, and political society, but of that between the Argentine press and foreign news organizations.

Indeed, *La Prensa* even played a key role in changing the character of international news agencies. In January 1919, editor and proprietor Ezequiel Paz contracted the services of Scripps's struggling United Press, which had only months earlier lost its contract with *La Nación*. When, six months later, the United Press—and thus *La Prensa* in Argentina—broke the story of the signing of the Versailles Treaty, Paz signed a full contract with the agency.[42] *La Prensa*, which already maintained an extensive system of correspondents in Europe and Latin America, effectively merged its foreign service with that of the United Press. The paper began paying up to U.S. $550,000 per year to the news service, an amount that one former United Press journalist would later call "probably the largest sum of money that any newspaper in the world paid to any news-gathering organization."[43] Extensive coverage of Italy and Spain for *La Prensa*—the countries of origin of the majority of Argentina's immigrants—essentially acted as a subsidy to the expansion of the news service in Europe, since the detailed information and analysis gathered at Ezequiel Paz's behest remained property of the United Press for subsequent distribution to the rest of the agency's clients.[44] Paz's demand that the service give special attention to the Arica-Tacna dispute between Chile and Peru in 1925 further boosted the fortunes of the agency, and by the end of the year the once struggling United Press served 95 percent of the business available on the continent.[45] This intertwining of the Argentine paper and the Washington-based United Press became extreme: between 1920 and 1930, *La Prensa* essentially underwrote the expansion of what would become one of the world's more important news agencies, and the Paz family's newspaper continued as the United Press's single largest client until the paper's expropriation in 1951.

Its high circulation made individual issues of *La Prensa* an integral if ephemeral part of the urban landscape, while the *La Prensa* building itself stood as an imposing monument not just to the wealth the paper generated but to the broader social, cultural, and political pretensions of the Paz family. Designed by Parisian-trained architects Alberto Gainza and Carlos Agote and finished in 1898, the large, ornate building stands on the Avenida de Mayo, the long avenue anchored on either end by the seats of the national Executive and the national Congress, respectively. Just meters from the Plaza de Mayo, the *La Prensa* building shares a common wall with the offices of the mayor of the Federal Capital. The building's cupola held what would become the paper's emblem: a three-thousand-kilogram French sculpture of an Argentine Marianne—the personification of the republican virtues of Reason and Liberty—standing with extended arms, carrying both a large lantern and a copy of *La Prensa*.[46] The spatial message of the Paz family is clear, and often found itself explicitly articulated in the pages of the paper: *La Prensa* stood as an equal and independent fourth branch of the Argentine state itself, illuminating and watching over the workings of the other branches.

Fig. 2 The *La Prensa* offices, 1938.

Fig 3 Statue to be placed atop *La Prensa* offices.

In addition to housing *La Prensa*'s newsrooms, the building held an "Industrial Chemical Clinic" for agriculturists and merchants, medical and legal clinics open to the public, an extensive library, a restaurant, rooms for fencing and billiards, a theater, and a large banquet room.[47] Following his visit during the Argentine Centennial celebrations in 1910, former French prime minister Georges Clemenceau wrote,

> The building is one of the sights of the city. Every department of the paper is lodged in a way that unites the most perfect of means to the end in view. Simplicity of background, a scrupulous cleanliness, comfort for every worker therein, with a highly specialized method that gathers together all the varied workers on the staff to direct them toward their final end and aim, namely, promptness and accuracy of news. With all this there are outside services, such as a dispensary, so complete it would need a specialist to catalogue it, and suites of apartments that are placed at the disposal of persons whom the *Prensa* considers worthy of honor. I confess that I thought less luxury in this part of the building would have been more to the taste of the poor distinguished men who are lodged there, since a comparison with their own modest homes would be wholly to the disadvantage of the latter.[48]

La Prensa was the most technologically and stylistically modern of the Buenos Aires newspapers in the first decades of the century, and the paper's building itself seemed to embody the promise of an unbounded, elegant, and self-confident Argentine modernity.

La Prensa's closest journalistic peer also grew out of the tradition of factional journalism to become one of Latin America's premier dailies, even if it did not attain the same degree of commercial success as the Paz family paper. On January 4, 1870, less than three months after the birth of *La Prensa*, *La Nación* appeared under the direction of former president of the republic Bartolomé Mitre. Although it had been preceded by *La Nación Argentina*, originally Mitrista but now the political mouthpiece of a competing faction of the Partido Liberal, Mitre announced that the new paper would differ from that paper in more than politics: the first issue of *La Nación* carried the subheading "A General Interest Newspaper," proclaiming a break from the journalistic model of the partisan press and the embrace of a broader journalistic program.[49]

With national unity at least provisionally secured and the bases of a stable political order emerging, Mitre ostensibly abandoned the overt factionalism of *La Nación Argentina* to place *La Nación* within the French model of *journalism of opinion*—as a supporter not of immediate and personal political interests, but as caretaker of the long-term stability of oligarchic liberalism. In the paper's first editorial, "New Horizons," Mitre wrote, "The great conflict has finished. . . . *La Nación Argentina* was a [means of] struggle. *La Nación* will be a [means of] propaganda. . . . . With the nationality founded it is necessary to propagate and defend those principles in which it is inspired, the institutions that are its basis, the guarantees that it has created for all, the practical ends it seeks, [and] the moral and material means that must be placed at the service of those ends."⁵⁰ Yet, like *La Prensa*, *La Nación* remained tied to the political aspirations of its founder, who led the 1874 revolt against Avellaneda, and to those of its subsequent owner, Emilio Mitre, who headed the Mitrista Republican Party.⁵¹ Prior to the establishment of a broad consensus on the institutional arrangements of the Argentine state—achieved only in the years subsequent to the 1880 federalization of Buenos Aires—the broader political environment of the republic still seemed to militate against the emergence of the kind of journalism that both Mitre and Paz perhaps prematurely envisioned.

It was precisely the contentious nature of this continued practice of factional journalism that brought Socialist Party founder Juan B. Justo to leave the paper's staff in 1896, later denouncing *La Nación* for "reserving its energy to defend the vileness of the Mitrista camarilla."⁵² Not until Emilio Mitre's death in 1909, in fact, did the directors of *La Nación* establish the paper's autonomy from partisan and factional politics in a less ambiguous fashion. The moment proved ripe for such a move, as the series of electoral reforms that culminated with the expansion of effective suffrage under Roque Sáenz Peña in 1912 not only provided an alternative to insurrection for dissident sectors of the Argentine political class, but also signaled a broadening of that class itself.⁵³ In the new political environment, Jorge and Luís Mitre, the paper's new coproprietors, quickly distanced *La Nación* from narrow partisan affiliation in order to extend the paper's reach to this increasingly heterogeneous Argentine political class as a whole.

This transformation of *La Nación* from an organ of Mitrismo proved as successful as it was ambitious: resting on an expanding market of readers and advertisers, the Mitres positioned the family paper to act as a "tribunal of doctrine," ostensibly impartial to the immediacies of partisan politics while maintaining a "political-pedagogical" mission directed at the entirety of the Argentine elite.⁵⁴ Under Jorge and Luís Mitre, then, editorialists at the paper publicly proclaimed their role as a sort of collective organic intellectual of the nation's ruling class, pragmatically reworking the abstractions of liberal ideological principles in changing practical circumstances in order to guide the Argentine economic and political elite.⁵⁵ Rather than self-consciously occupying the "combat posts" of factional politics or viewing journalistic activity as a stepping-stone to concrete political action, the journalists at *La Nación* instead claimed that they could effectively, in the words of Ricardo Sidicaro, "view politics from above." This rearticulation of the web of relationships between journalism practice, market, and state would situate the Mitre family paper as an effective ideological-institutional guardian of the long-term viability of an Argentine social order that had emerged from the export boom of 1880–1910.

Unlike *La Prensa*, with which it shared the same journalistic model and liberal-conservative orientation, and despite its greater ideological flexibility,

La Nación did not attract an audience far beyond the upper-class and professionals addressed in its pages. It never reached the circulation levels of La Prensa, selling approximately 210,000 copies daily (317,500 on Sundays) by 1935 and, despite slowly increasing sales during World War II, finishing 1945 with an average circulation about 150,000 copies short of the Paz family's newspaper.[56] Yet the inability of the Mitre family's paper to match the growth of La Prensa—whose monopoly on classified advertising guaranteed an ever-increasing, multiclass readership—did not signal a commercial failure for La Nación: the paper still finished the war with the sixth-highest circulation in Latin America, outselling its nearest non-Argentine peer by 10,000 copies daily.[57] The contrast with La Prensa was also reflected in the comparative architectural modesty of the paper's offices. While still close to the geographic center of national political power, the relatively staid offices of La Nación were several blocks away on San Martín Street, the heart of the country's financial district, only moving to the commercial Florida Street in 1929.[58]

If the phenomenal growth of La Prensa brought with it a particularly intimate relationship with the United Press, La Nación similarly became closely allied with a United States–based news organization. Jorge Mitre had originally signed a contract with the United Press in 1916 order to bypass the French news agency Havas, which held the rights to the South American market under the terms of the international wire service cartel. Mitre, however, attempted to expand his own news service in Latin America at the same time, and eventually broke his contract with the United Press in 1918 in a dispute over the ownership of collected information. The conflict between La Nación and the United Press worked to the detriment of the former, especially as La Prensa began to throw its economic weight behind the rapidly expanding agency. Mitre's abandonment of the United Press in favor of the more established and powerful Associated Press thus linked La Nación with a news service less dependent upon the paper's continued satisfaction, especially in comparison to the services rendered to La Prensa by United Press. Still, La Nación became the Associated Press's gateway into the South American news market, and the offices of the Mitre family's paper also served as the regional offices of the Associated Press. The relationship between La Nación and the Associated Press only grew more intimate in the wake of the formal dissolution of the wire service cartel in 1934—a process that the Argentine papers did much to facilitate.[59]

Where La Prensa and La Nación represented the journalistic high-water mark of Argentina's "serious" press in the first half of the twentieth century, the proprietor and journalists of the newspaper Crítica fervently embraced the whole range of possibilities that the medium of commercial journalism presented. Founded by the Uruguayan émigré Natalio Botana in September 1913, the evening paper dramatically changed the practice of journalism in the country, and its abrasive, sensationalistic character is as intimately linked to its historical moment of origin as the more staid, reasoned styles of the Paz and Mitre family newspapers are linked to their moments of origin. Within a decade of the paper's founding, Botana himself also became the most spectacular and controversial example of a new social type: the journalistic entrepreneur, whose conspicuous wealth and enormous social influence flowed not from landed interests or political patronage, but from the practice of journalism itself.[60] Indeed, although *La Prensa*'s economic power and international stature were unrivaled among the Argentine press of the first half of the century, *Crítica*'s unique character, and the vast web of anecdote and legend surrounding Botana, still loom largest in the Argentine popular imagination.[61] In quite unexpected ways, it was Botana's great success in creating an aura around *Crítica* as the voice of the urban popular classes and embodiment of utopian aspirations for egalitarian democracy that placed the paper at the center of the many of the press conflicts after 1930.

The same national political opening that prompted Jorge and Luís Mitre to abandon the vestiges of *La Nación*'s entanglement with factional politics created much of the impetus for the founding of *Crítica*. Botana, a working journalist, launched the paper in the wake of the 1912 Sáenz Peña Law's expansion of suffrage, a moment when national political life suddenly became significantly more relevant to a much larger section of the population.[62] *Crítica*, Botana announced in the paper's first issue, would "repudiate the old practice of the fourth power"—that is, the "petulant" use of journalism to advance the interests of a specific political faction—and instead would remain "without program, but with ideas."[63] If the Mitre brothers sought to create in *La Nación* a forum of debate and guidance for the nation's political class as a whole, Botana similarly intended to create an organ that would shape broad political worldviews. Unlike *La Nación*, with its self-conscious appeals to the nation's political class, however, *Crítica* would engage the now effectively enfranchised and rapidly growing urban middle and working classes. Through *Crítica*, Botana sought to make the Argentine press—or at least his newspaper—a factor in the new age of mass politics. The direction he took implied a dramatically new journalistic style and set of journalism practices.

Yet the director's intention of using the paper as the vehicle for organizing the urban popular classes into a base for a disparate array of conservative political forces left *Crítica* at a serious competitive disadvantage with respect to its already well-established conservative evening rival *La Razón*. The difficulty of success for Botana's project only seemed confirmed as the Sáenz Peña Law resulted not in the unlikely scenario of mass affirmation of liberal-conservatism, but in the rather predictable ascent of the tremendously popular Radical Party leader Hipólito Yrigoyen to the presidency in 1916. As Sylvia Saítta has convincingly shown, the particular model of factional journalism that Botana initially sought to follow—ironically, one so eclectic and independent that it remained without the financial backing and guaranteed public of any organized political faction—simply did not generate the revenue needed to sustain a viable newspaper in what had become a capital-intensive and fiercely competitive industry.[64] That Botana adopted this strategy in the midst of the First World War, with its predictable spike in the price of imported newsprint, ink, and machinery, only aggravated the situation for the evening paper.[65]

In the course of the 1920s, however—what one *Crítica* journalist called the paper's "romantic period"—Botana transformed *Crítica* from a failing mouthpiece of "popular conservatism" into Latin America's most widely read evening newspaper, and a stylistically innovative and politically influential daily.[66] Through shrill editorials, sensationalistic crime investigations, a heavy emphasis on graphic material, and the latest and most complete sports reporting, Botana reshaped the newspaper to capture readers among ever-increasing sectors of the population.[67] The pages of *Crítica* also became a vehicle of ceaseless self-promotion, in which the paper's journalists proclaimed *Crítica* and its young, bohemian journalists—the "muchachada de *Crítica*"—central protagonists in the very news the paper carried. Natalio Botana held no pretension of dispassionately viewing "politics from above," while *Crítica* reporters proudly rejected the model of an objective journalism divorced from the subjectivity of the journalist.[68] Political opinions, cultural assertions, and open subjective biases thus dramatically shaped the paper's format, appearance, and content. Indeed, not until the mid-1930s—well beyond the period of Saítta's study—did *Crítica* regularly carry a separate "opinion" section, and even then commentary remained interspersed throughout the paper's articles and graphic materials. Combined with a new commitment to the speed of news reporting, this strategy proved remarkably successful: by the middle of the 1920s *Crítica* had surpassed the circulation of its evening rival *La Razón* to become the third most widely read paper in Argentina.[69] By decade's end, *Crítica* had ceased its frequent moves around the city and established itself, with the most powerful rotary presses, in a suitably modern Art Deco building on the country's passageway of political power, the Avenida de Mayo, and its circulation had exceeded that of *La Nación*, behind only *La Prensa*.[70]

The tremendous influence of *Crítica*, its sensationalist style, and its economic success have given Natalio Botana's paper a presence bordering on the mythical in the Argentine popular memory. The figure of the Citizen Kane–like Botana himself also continues to hold a particular place in memories of the 1920s and 1930s, maintained by the anecdotes and memoirs of numerous *Crítica* journalists as well as the thinly disguised Botana character in Leopoldo Marechal's epic novel *Adán Buenosayres*.[71] Regardless of the veracity of stories of Botana's use of *Crítica* as a tool for extortion (of matchmakers who did not include the correct number of matches in each box, or breweries whose product was over 95 percent water), the image of Botana as a flamboyant and powerful man circulated widely. That the *Crítica* owner had managed to expand his power to include other media only increased the sense of that power: where other film studios could threaten to withhold advertising from newspapers as a means of ensuring favorable reviews, the Botana-owned Baires Film studio had the added recourse of *Crítica* crusades against competitors who printed "questionable" criticism of its films. Such tactics seem to have ensured the critical acclaim of the studio's releases—as well as bolstered Botana's self-cultivated reputation as a local blend of Hearst and Al Capone.[72]

Botana's mansion in Don Torcuato, just outside the Federal Capital, resembled that of a younger, more avant-garde Hearst; it included a spectacular mural by Mexican painter David Alfaro Siqueiros.[73] The reaction of Chilean poet Pablo Neruda, who visited Don Torcuato with Federico García Lorca, is typical of the mix of fascination and unease that the aura surrounding Botana and his newspaper inspired:

> We were invited one evening by a millionaire like those that only Argentina or the United States could produce. This was a rebellious and self-taught man who had made a fabulous fortune with a sensationalist newspaper. His house, surrounded by a tremendous park, was the incarnation of the dreams of a vibrant *nouveau riche*. Hundreds of cages of pheasants of all colors and all countries bordered the road. The library was filled only with extremely old books that he bought by cable in the auctions of European book collectors and was large and full. But more spectacular was that the floor of this enormous reading room was covered totally with panther furs sown together to form a gigantic cover. I knew that the man had agents in Africa, Asia, and the Amazon destined exclusively to collect the skins of leopards, ocelots, phenomenal cats, whose spots now shone under my feet in the ostentatious library.... This is how things were in the house of the famous Natalio Botana, powerful capitalist, who dominated public opinion in Buenos Aires.[74]

With the emergence of *Crítica*, the Buenos Aires press completed its transformation into a powerful commercial newspaper industry, and it was Botana the journalistic entrepreneur—the embodiment of capital—who most spectacularly and unequivocally replaced the politician-proprietors of the nineteenth-century model of the press.

The establishment and evolution of *La Prensa, La Nación,* and *Crítica* exemplify the complexity and journalistic variety in the structural transformation of the Argentine press from the modest economies of newspapers dedicated to the practices of factional journalism to the modern commercial press. Yet a host of other dailies also successfully competed for readership in Buenos Aires. Some of them would at times exceed *La Prensa, La Nación,* and *Crítica* in sales, but only occasionally would any surpass any of the three major dailies in influence or independent economic clout.

Of the major dailies, perhaps none suffered as many shifts in ownership and orientation prior to the crises of the 1930s and 1940s as *La Razón*. Founded in 1905 by Emilio B. Morales as a commercial newspaper independent of the nation's political factions, *La Razón* was the nation's leading evening newspaper until its eclipse by *Crítica* in the early 1920s. Morales sold the newspaper to the conservative journalist José A. Cortejarena in 1911, and after Cortejarena's death the paper became the property of his widow, Helvecia Antonini, who delegated the direction of *La Razón* to a host of different journalists and administrators. This instability in the newspaper's top management lent *La Razón* an increasingly amorphous market identity precisely as Natalio Botana consolidated that of *Crítica*, eroding at once *La Razón*'s base readership and its financial viability. By 1935 *La Razón*'s daily circulation stood at only 81,000— still large by contemporary Latin American standards, but a fraction of the over 250,000 copies of *Crítica* that *porteños* purchased each afternoon.[75] Ironically, the financial weakness of *La Razón* ultimately made the paper exceedingly valuable in the 1930s. The paper's sudden reemergence by the end of the decade reveals not only the degree to which the Argentine commercial press had become independent of state power and political factions in the previous decades, but just how decisive—and lucrative—the rearticulation of the relationship between state and press could prove.

On May 14, 1928, Buenos Aires' first tabloid-sized daily appeared. Founded by the English immigrant Alberto Haynes, who had lain the foundations of the multimedia empire Editorial Haynes with the magazine *El Hogar Argentino* in the first years of the century, *El Mundo* had an immediate impact on journalistic practices in Buenos Aires.[76] The physical size of the paper made it easier to read on the rapidly growing city's crowded public transportation. Under the guiding principle that "what is good, if brief, is twice as good," *El Mundo* carried national and international news stories synthesized in clear, simple articles, while editorials also remained short.[77] Reporting and editorials also tended to mask any political sympathies in order to appeal to as wide an audience as possible—*El Mundo* was, a frequent heading to its inside pages proclaimed, "the newspaper that aspires to be read in all homes." The paper carried a variety of sections: theater, international news, film, literature, the lottery, "for women and the home," and for children. Instead of the haphazard arrangement of the equally diverse content of *Crítica*, however, *El Mundo* readers found well-organized, consistently placed thematic sections. *El Mundo* became successful immediately, with daily circulation climbing to over 200,000 by 1935 and increasing by another 100,000 before the end of World War II.[78] While *Crítica*'s rise came at the cost of *La Razón*, however, the growth of *El*

Mundo had a very different impact on the newspaper landscape: with a price of five centavos—half that of the other major dailies—the Haynes paper tended less to draw readers away from the established press than to entice new ones or those who bought it as an *additional* paper. As a result, *El Mundo* generally escaped the kind of internecine polemics that permeated much of the popular press.

Among the major Argentine newspapers only *Noticias Gráficas* emerged directly from within the multiple crises unleashed in the 1930s. The paper (in its first month called simply *Noticias*) appeared on June 10, 1931, as an attempt by *La Nación*'s Jorge Mitre to occupy the gap in the evening market left by the suspension of *Crítica* after the military coup of September 6, 1930. At first a tabloid largely in the style of *El Mundo,* the paper benefited from conflicts within the administration and newsroom of the "new" evening paper *Jornada,* a thinly disguised *Crítica* surrogate. Alberto Cordone, director of *Jornada/Crítica* during Natalio Botana's exile in Uruguay, joined the staff of *Noticias Gráficas* in September of 1931, bringing with him thirty colleagues.[79] *Noticias Gráficas* quickly adopted the format of *Crítica* virtually in its entirety. The resurrection of *Crítica* proper in February 1932, however, placed serious strains on *Noticias Gráficas,* as increased competition in the newspaper marketplace together with strong attacks from the pages of *Crítica* eroded *Noticias Gráficas*'s readership. Despite renouncing his post at *La Nación* in favor of his brother Luís, Jorge Mitre failed to create a newspaper financially independent of *La Nación*. Through much of the decade Jorge Mitre continued to pass *Noticias Gráficas*'s bills for electricity, rent, newsprint, and other expenses to *La Nación*—much to the dismay of the morning paper's shareholders.[80] Businessman José Agusti finally rescued the paper from complete financial collapse in 1938 and remained as the proprietor and director of *Noticias Gráficas* until the daily came under Perón's control in 1947. If *Noticias Gráficas* remained financially precarious for the entirety of its existence, its circulation nonetheless rivaled that of *Crítica:* in 1935 the paper's three daily editions averaged 250,000 copies, and 270,000 copies in 1945.[81]

The federalization of Buenos Aires in 1880 inaugurated a transformation of the city's press unrivaled within Latin America, a process that only accelerated with the expansion of suffrage via the electoral reforms of 1912. Argentines were already among the world's greater per capita consumers of newspapers, and the rapid growth and prosperity of Buenos Aires would make it exceptional in absolute terms as well. In 1928, the only three Latin American newspapers that consistently maintained daily circulation in excess of 150,000 copies were published there: *La Prensa, Crítica,* and *La Nación*.[82] Even *La Razón,* battered by competition from *Crítica* for evening readers, outsold its nearest non-Argentine peer, Río de Janeiro's *A Nôite,* by 10,000 issues daily.[83] The gap only widened as the world economic crisis of the 1930s pushed still more Argentines into the Federal Capital and surrounding suburbs. By 1935, the city of Buenos Aires boasted just under 2.5 million inhabitants and had five daily newspapers—*Crítica, Noticias Gráficas, La Prensa, La Nación,* and *El Mundo*— each consistently selling well over 200,000 copies daily. Outside of Buenos Aires, only *A Nôite* maintained that circulation level. The total circulation of Buenos Aires dailies exceeded that of both Los Angeles and San Francisco, California.[84] On the eve of the February 1946 elections that brought Perón to the presidency, the Buenos Aires newspaper market stood at nearly triple that of its nearest Latin American peer, Mexico City, with the city's residents purchasing more newspapers than those of Río de Janeiro, São Paulo, Santiago de Chile, and Mexico City *combined*.[85]

By the late 1920s the emergence of the commercial press had created a set of institutions that far exceeded in economic complexity and wealth anything that the drafters of the 1853 constitution might have imagined. The Argentine press of the nineteenth century, rooted in a tradition of factional political conflict and intimately tied to those wielding or aspiring to wield state power, had become something quite different: a capital-intensive, technologically advanced, and market-dependent commercial newspaper industry with millions of readers.

The Press as Newspaper Industry

The rapid expansion of the press in the early twentieth century not only created a quantitatively distinct set of institutions, it also engendered a profound qualitative shift in the nature and social significance of journalism. The press's divergence from the model of factional journalism signaled a new relationship between individual newspapers and the public, one mediated by the market and in which political affinity receded in importance in favor of a broader set of appeals to potential readers. The growth of a newspaper market also carried with it a significant change in the relationship between political society and the press: by the 1920s, the owners of the nation's premier newspapers had become largely autonomous from the factional politics and even the social classes that marked their origins. At the same time, the industrialization of the press demanded a rearticulation of newspaper relations of production, with the hand-cranked printing presses manned by nineteenth-century politician-journalists giving way to enormous mechanized rotary presses under the guidance of wage-earning printers producing the texts of increasingly specialized working journalists. More than the development of a new style of journalism, then, the emergence of the commercial press implied a profound reworking of the press's entire network of relationships.

Where political militancy linked reader and newspaper in the tradition of factional journalism, the relationship between the commercial press and the public was mediated by a more complex amalgam of factors. By the 1920s, the appeal of the most widely read newspapers of the Argentine Republic lay less in explicitly polemical political and economic journalism that addressed the concerns of an audience segmented by partisan militancy than in more general reporting and editorials that engaged the political, work, sport, leisure, social, and cultural concerns of increasingly broad sectors of the population. Sensationalism, melodrama, and the incorporation of photographs and other graphic material in the daily press sought the attention of popular-class readers, while the physical layout and page size of newspapers like *El Mundo* facilitated the incorporation of reading into the routine of the urban middle- and working-class daily commute.[86] In the place of specific factional sympathy, then, a more stable—and more sweeping—set of political, class, gender, cultural, and ethnic markers grew in prominence as newspaper directors aimed at generating a committed readership.

The factional newspaper's role as public forum for partisan debate also increasingly ceded space to a more powerful form of publicity. If Argentines together consumed far more newspapers than their regional peers in the first half of the twentieth century, those living in the Argentine capital also absorbed greater quantities of a much more sophisticated set of classified and display advertising. Not only were residents of the Argentine capital considerably wealthier and more literate on average than other Latin Americans in the first half of the century, but a 1920 U.S. Department of Commerce study declared Buenos Aires "an oasis in the advertising desert" and "so far in advance of all other cities of South America in advertising development as to be in a class by itself."[87] Exposure to classified and display advertising became an integral and unavoidable part of the newspaper reading experience, in effect "educating" readers as consumers and producers even as it served as a conduit for the incorporation of consumer demands into the market.[88] Commercial publicity—the "poetry of Modernity," in the words of Henri Lefebvre—together with the breadth of newspaper reporting thus helped shape the city's rapid economic transformation in the first decades of the century.[89]

Such changes signaled a fundamental shift in the practical nature of the relationship between press and public. Where nineteenth-century factional newspapers had ideally served as participatory media for communication among political militants, the scale of the twentieth-century commercial press placed newspapers before the public less as an accessible forum for expression than as an item of consumption. Similarly, even as press owners competed to sell ever-increasing numbers of newspapers to a growing public, they also competed to sell advertising space to businesses. With the relationship between press and public increasingly mediated not by political exchange but by market exchange, the practice of journalism assumed an additional role that press critics would soon declare threatened to overwhelm all others: that of delivering the attention of consumers to the goods and services offered by businesses. The press by no means ceased to serve as a forum of public debate; the penetration of the commodity form in the relationship between newspaper and reader, however, placed expression through the press in a new key.

The technological imperative imposed by this fiercely competitive newspaper market also fundamentally changed the character of press production techniques, and with it the relations of production within the newspaper industry. Where José C. Paz and Cosme Mariño printed the first issue of *La Prensa* themselves with a hand-driven rotary press, by 1935 the paper's 1,050-horsepower presses stood two stories high and forty-six meters long.[90] *Crítica* updated its presses to the latest Hoe Superspeed upon Botana's transfer of the paper's facilities to Avenida de Mayo 1333. In singular *Crítica* fashion, the paper's journalists boasted that the extraordinary publishing capacity of the machine more than compensated for the nearly year-long process of its assembly: "with a single hour of continuous publishing the Hoe rotary can encircle the city in a belt of newspapers."[91] In a poem dedicated to the new rotary, poet and *Crítica* journalist Raúl González Tuñón even found inspiration in its seemingly boundless technological modernity, proclaiming it a "song of steel" and "the heart of Buenos Aires."[92] *El Mundo* and the other major newspapers of the city maintained similar installations. For newspaper proprietors, access to capital goods and

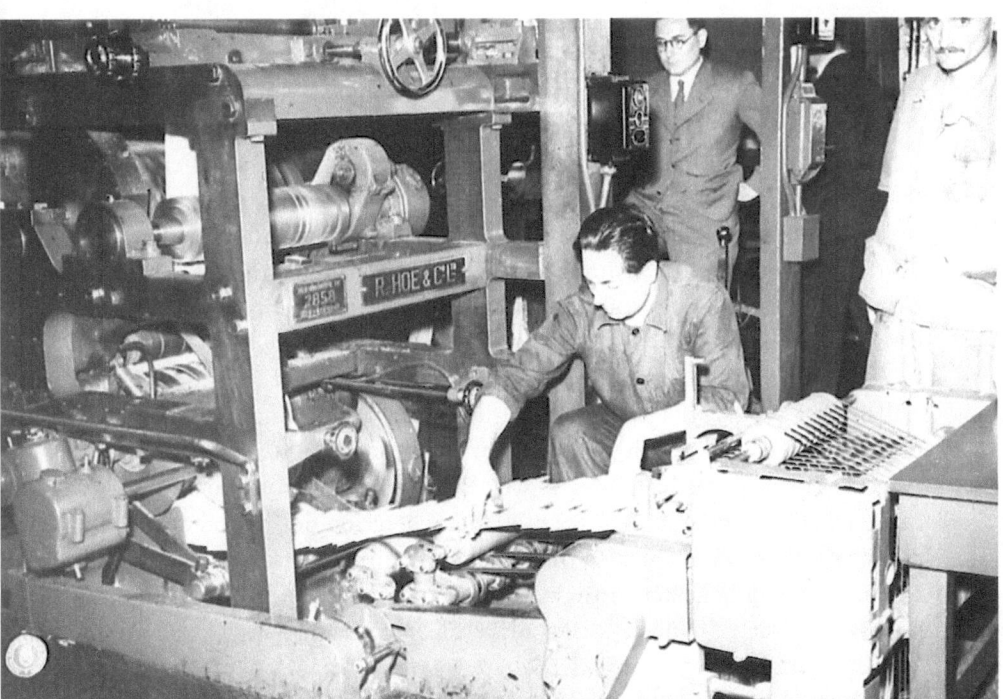

Fig. 4 Printer at a Hoe printing press, November 1941.

Fig. 5 Printers at work in *La Prensa*, October 1924.

industrial inputs of ever-increasing cost and sophistication was not only an indicator of the power and progressive nature of their papers; it proved absolutely essential to the survival of their enterprises.

This industrialization of the newspaper production process implied not only the growing complexity of the press's division of labor, but the emergence of capitalist relations of production—and class conflict—in the newspaper industry. Prior to the establishment of *La Prensa* and *La Nación*, printers had already begun the process of unionization, eventually creating the Federación Gráfica Bonaerense (FGB) for the typographers of the Federal Capital and Greater Buenos Aires in 1907. By 1922, when members of the Argentine Socialist Party gained effective control of the union, the FGB maintained a strong presence among the 350 printers employed with *La Prensa*, and had made inroads at the other major dailies as well.[93] Similarly, news vendors (popularly called *canillitas*) unionized in 1920 as the Federación de Vendedores de Diarios.[94] Less than two years later, the *canillitas* mounted a bitter strike against *La Razón*, which only hastened the decline of the evening paper. After the first *canillita* death at the hands of strikebreakers from the right-wing Liga Patriótica, Botana confidante Eduardo "El Diente" Dughera organized protective caravans to cover vendors in what had become a virtual war among evening newspaper distribution networks.[95] When the strike ended nearly ten months later,

Fig. 6 News vendors prepare *El Mundo* for distribution, mid-1930s.

not only had the vendors' union achieved broad recognition, but *Crítica* had emerged as the country's dominant evening paper and "El Diente" had become the "undisputed boss" of what remained the dangerous business of newspaper sales.[96]

The emergence of the commercial press also profoundly altered the relationship between proprietors and journalists, and between Argentine intellectuals and the market. Where politician-journalist-proprietors of the nineteenth-century press like Bartolomé Mitre had given way to journalism entrepreneurs like Natalio Botana, the newsroom itself also became filled with wage earners. In an environment of growing demand for texts of all kinds, the commodification of journalism practice, as Ángel Rama has observed, allowed intellectuals far greater latitude in their relationship to state power and political factions.[97] It did, however, subordinate many of them to the demands of newspaper proprietors and the commercial logical of the newspaper industry. If *Martín Fierro* author José Hernández, in the era of factional journalism, had viewed the journalist as a "precursor to the political leader," by the 1920s journalism had become an activity that at best could serve as a source of inspiration, avenue of opportunity, and economic subsidy for writers and artists; at worst, newspapers simply provided a meager paycheck in exchange for long hours and the subordination of writing to the demands of editors and the whims of the market.[98]

Indeed, the enormous success of many dailies depended in great measure upon the array of truly impressive literary talent that gravitated toward the practice of journalism. Many of Argentina's most important writers of the 1920s and 1930s came to work for Botana's *Crítica,* including Jorge Luís Borges, Roberto Arlt, Raúl and Enrique González Tuñón, Leopoldo Marechal, Edmundo Guibourg, Ulyses Petit de Murat, and Pablo Rojas Paz. Borges's direction of *Crítica's Revista Multicolor de los Sábados* in 1933 and 1934, a brief but memorable period, also made the sensationalist daily a literary rival of *La Nación:* in addition to the writings of Borges, Petit de Murat, Enrique González Tuñón, and Uruguayan novelist Juan Carlos Onetti, the supplement carried Borges's translations of international figures like O. Henry, H. G. Wells, and George Bernard Shaw.[99] Similarly, Nicaraguan poet Rubén Darío reached his fame while writing for *La Nación,* the Cuban poet and revolutionary José Martí served as a correspondent at the paper from 1882 to 1891, and novelist Eduardo Mallea directed *La Nación's* literary supplement in the 1930s and 1940s.[100] Even the editorial writing that appeared in the paper tended to better that of *La Prensa* in expressive quality and intellectual subtlety, and *La Nación* at different times boasted regular editorialists of the caliber (and disparate political views) of Joaquín V. González, Leopoldo Lugones, and Alberto Gerchunoff.[101]

Despite the glorification of the bohemian lives of journalists in the course of the 1920s—especially those of the literary figures associated with *Crítica*—the newsroom was a place of long hours and generally poor pay. In his memoirs of his time at Botana's newspaper, Roberto Tálice, who joined the paper, like many of his colleagues, while in his mid-teens, recounts that not only did his wages cover a small room in a boardinghouse and little more, but "*Crítica* has made us into fakirs." Tálice even credited the omnipresence of drug use among the paper's journalists less to bohemian experimentation than to the more pragmatic demands of their work routine: "Although it pains me to recognize it," Tálice would later write, "many attribute the miracle of such great resistance to sleep and alcohol to the little envelopes of cocaine, sometimes vials, containing a gram dose of the purest *Merk.*"[102]

The experience of Tálice, as well as that of other journalists, embodies a profound shift in the nature of writing as a social practice. The commodification of journalistic labor, though less stark than that of printers' and newspaper vendors' labor, rested uneasily with the cultural nature not just of the poetry, short stories, and novels of newspaper employees like Raúl González Tuñón, Jorge Luís Borges, and Roberto Arlt, but with the content of newspapers themselves. In his 1933 *Radiografía de la pampa,* Ezequiel Martínez Estrada denounced the particular form that the commodification of writing took within the newspaper industry, where authors became subject to the commercial demands of advertisers and found their individual expression brutally subsumed within the collective enterprise of the newsroom. Little remedy existed for the situation, however, since "having nothing to eat is worse. . . . Those intellectuals free of the politics of the press businesses are destroyed at the root."[103] Novelist Leopoldo Marechal, even more dramatically, evokes the merging of anonymous journalistic labor with the machinery of industrial newspaper production in the "journalists' hell" of the imaginary city of Cacodelphia. There, in a printing room inspired by the author's time at *Crítica* and *El Mundo,* journalists jump headlong into the rotary presses, only to have the machines crush, print, fold, and "vomit" them as hybrid, commodified newspaper men (*hombres-diario*).[104] Even the paper's "man on the street" readers could not escape the alienation that formed an integral part of the commercial newspaper industry, with "ten pages full of ignominy" consuming leisure time better dedicated to family and introspection.[105]

Still, the division of labor in the newsroom and the commodification of journalism practice remained more ambiguous than the broader class divisions in the newspaper industry as a whole. Rather than forming independent trade unions, journalists in the city of Buenos Aires formed the mutual aid society Círculo de la Prensa in 1896, with *La Nación* founder Bartolomé Mitre himself serving as first president.[106] For decades the Círculo remained under the explicit tutelage of newspaper proprietors: Ezequiel Paz of *La Prensa* and Luís Mitre of *La Nación* alternated in the presidency of the organization until the 1920s, when they ceded to an alternation of their respective paper's editors and administrators.[107] In addition to providing health, unemployment, and burial benefits to members, the organization served as an effective lobbying organization for the corporate interests of the newspaper industry. Thus, not only did the Círculo de la Prensa act as a watchdog regarding press issues—which, until the 1930s, remained largely confined to denunciations of censorship and harassment outside the Federal Capital—but the group pushed for greater professionalization and training among journalists.[108] This latter project bore fruit under the aegis of the Universidad Nacional de la Plata and the Círculo's sister organization, the Círculo de Periodistas de la Provincia de Buenos Aires, with the founding of the country's first formal journalism school in 1935.[109]

This dual push toward the independence of commercial newspapers from factional politics and the professionalization of journalism practice, however uneven it remained, corresponded to a substantive shift in the journalistic philosophy of owners of the "serious" press. Ezequiel Paz of *La Prensa* most forcefully articulated the characteristics of an objective journalism model, which declared accuracy of information, the absence of journalists' subjectivity, and the clear separation of fact and opinion as the hallmarks of a proper press: "To inform with exactitude and truth; to omit nothing which the public has a right to know; to use always an impersonal and cultured form [of address] without prejudice to the severity and force of critical thought; to abandon rumor . . . to affirm only that which one has firm conviction from proof or documentation."[110] Similarly, journalists should remain vigilant about the insertion of opinion into reporting; otherwise they would "invade" the territory—physically demarcated in the pages of the paper—of opinion-driven editorials.[111] Together with the sharp distance from formal state imperatives guaranteed by the Argentine constitution, the pages of the press would provide the necessary information through which ordinary citizens might judge the acts of government.[112]

Where adherence to this objectivist model of journalism reinforced the market relationship between press and public by emphasizing the consumption of accurate information as a right of citizenship, Paz maintained an equivocal stance with regard to the editorial pages of *La Prensa*. "The daily press," Paz argued in 1920, "must represent public opinion." Yet Paz continued with an important qualification: "public opinion is the general criterion in exercise of the right to judge, as much of the result as of the appropriateness of the management of issues of common order." Public opinion depended upon a rationality, "impartiality, serenity, and culture" that the *La Prensa* owner maintained stood above "the rough vocabulary of the working-class neighborhood [*arrabal*], which pretends to be democratic, but is nothing more than the result of intransigence and ignorance."[113] Two decades later, Ángel Bohigas, vice-director of *La Nación*, similarly argued against the validity of the press's direct appeals to a popular readership, since "the journalist should try to make his page get to the thinking classes of the country, to those who carry greater weight in the elucidation of affairs of public interest."[114] Through the "healthy civic propaganda" of *La Prensa*'s editorial pages and *La Nación*'s "elevated mental level," the owners and directors of the "serious press" explicitly sought to shape public opinion, an aim that stood in tension with similarly explicit assertions of the press as a virtually unmediated *expression* of the broader opinion, elevated or not, of the general public.[115] Similarly, Ezequiel Paz's claims that the press represented public opinion as a whole rested uneasily with Paz's simultaneous dismissal of the subjective views of working-class readers.

The proprietors and editors of *La Prensa* and *La Nación*—and, by extension, the leadership of the Círculo de la Prensa—embraced a vision of the press and the social role of journalism firmly rooted in nineteenth-century liberalism, but with important modifications. In this libertarian conception of the press, the negative aspects of press freedom as enshrined in the Argentine constitution—in which the press would remain free from state interference—received special emphasis; like their counterparts in the United States and Britain, proponents of the "serious press" repeatedly elevated the press as "a 'Fourth Estate' in the government process."[116] Yet, in its positive aspects, the conception of press freedom articulated by the proprietors of *La Prensa* and *La Nación* had undergone a crucial transformation. In both cases, the constitutional principle of the right of publication as a component of citizenship remained rhetorically powerful even as the scale of the commercial press—and the scale of the polity—eroded the practical possibilities of a universally participatory daily press. The rights of citizenship through the press instead increasingly centered upon the public's information consumption, with the ideal of the "informed citizen" largely eclipsing notions of the universality of rights of expression. As a consequence, the accuracy and impartiality of information together with claims to represent public opinion faithfully—however ambiguous they remained alongside Ezequiel Paz's exclusionary, class-based qualifications—became pivotal elements of legitimacy for the "serious press."

Of the major Argentine dailies in existence prior to 1930, *Crítica* diverged most markedly from this journalistic model. The name of the paper and the slogan below its masthead—"God set me upon your city like a horsefly on a noble horse, to bite it and keep it awake. (Socrates)"—announced a sharp watchdog role for Botana's newspaper, and the constant campaigns against certain public figures served in good measure to reinforce that perception. Yet the cult around the paper and its bohemian "gang of boys" (*muchachada*) exalted the notion of the journalist and newspaper that found little common ground with the ideals set forth by Ezequiel Paz. On the contrary, not only did *Crítica* journalists self-consciously portray themselves as committed and active participants in the news they were reporting, but, as often as possible, *Crítica* and its journalists were the news itself.[117] Botana and his staff similarly sought to create a relationship, even a complicity, between reader and paper based not on rationality and appeals to elite culture, but on an emotional identification of *Crítica* and its journalists with the culture, poverty, and language of the urban popular classes. More than a newspaper, *Crítica* was "the hand for the fallen, the support for the widow and the orphan, the paternal hand for children, and the defender of the innocent."[118]

If Ezequiel Paz could claim *La Prensa* as a faithful representative of public opinion only by dismissing as irrelevant the language and interests of a significant portion of that public, Botana sought discursively to dissolve the boundaries between *Crítica* and the very public Paz discarded. In reassuring readers that commercial success would not change their "friendship," the journalists at *Crítica* went beyond asserting that they "thought with the mind of the people" to cultivate an affective identification between the paper and the urban popular classes.[119] Upon the move to Avenida de Mayo 1333, the paper's journalists blurred any substantive distinction between the popular reading public and what had become a significant commercial enterprise: "If at some time you need the loyal advice or help of a friend, come to CRITICA as if to a common home, assured that the doors of our house will only be closed to domination, abuse or injustice. *Reader and newspaper, we form, in sum, a single thing:* an immense journalistic entity that lives of the people and for the people and in which thousands and thousands of men collaborate. Consider yourself a kind of 'shareholder' in this singular Sociedad Anónima Popular that is CRITICA."[120] Where the proprietors and directors of *La Prensa* and *La Nación* viewed their papers largely as shapers of elite opinion and dispensers of the information needed for the proper practice of individual citizenship, Botana upped the ante: *Crítica*'s legitimacy rested upon assertions that it was nothing less than the voice, the democratic embodiment—as chaotic as that might prove—of the urban popular classes in the public sphere.

The Coming Crisis

This notion of *Crítica* as an expression of the collective citizenship of the urban popular classes represented a particular—and particularly lucrative—solution to a fundamental dissonance that the industrialization of the press and the concomitant expansion of political participation had created: by the 1920s what the press *was* had shifted dramatically; notions of what the press *should be* had changed little. On the one hand, the set of relationships between journalists, newspapers, and public had become increasingly mediated by commercial exchange rather than participation and representation, while the very scale and capital-intensive nature of the Buenos Aires newspaper industry exceeded what nineteenth-century Argentine liberals might have conceived. On the other, the underlying ideological and juridical bases of journalism practice had remained centered upon a conception of the press as the privileged forum for the public expression of opinion. How could Argentines exercise their rights of expression through the press in a socially meaningful way if the means to do so remained beyond their reach? Could the affective bonds between *Crítica* and its audience and the supposedly rational link between the so-called serious press and its public effectively create a truly representative public sphere? Did the rights of citizenship in relation to the press rest solely upon the right to consume accurate information? In short, who embodied the rights of the press: journalists, proprietors, or members of the public?

Yet self-proclamations of Botana's paper as the collective voice of Argentine workers rested on more than the pervasive use of the underworld *lunfardo* dialect in the pages of the paper, the distribution of sewing machines from the newspaper's offices, or *Crítica* campaigns in defense of Sacco and Vanzetti or striking news vendors. No less than the more explicitly liberal journalistic philosophy behind *La Prensa, La Nación,* and the Círculo de la Prensa, *Crítica*'s claims also rested upon the continued viability of a broad consensus around the utopian notions of egalitarian, democratic representation that they invoked. Ironically, it would be *Crítica* itself that would figure among the chief instigators of the 1930 constitutional rupture that put that consensus to the test.

Indeed, the multiple crises of the 1930s would witness a serious erosion of the political and economic liberalism upon which the entire spectrum of the Buenos Aires commercial press rested. Although the industrialization of the Argentine press had created a newspaper industry whose economic complexity and internal divisions surpassed anything imaginable by the drafters of the 1853 constitution, these contradictions remained largely latent in the 1920s. As competing conceptions of the proper relations between state and civil society gained ground in the following decade, however, the liberal ideological hegemony that undergirded traditional press relations with the national state came under concerted and direct attack from powerful sectors of Argentine society. At the same time, growing class tensions within the journalism profession—a manifestation at once of the press's industrial transformation as well as of the more general elevation of social conflict in Argentine society—would ultimately prove difficult to contain within the logic of a mutual aid society model that did not differentiate between newspaper proprietors and working journalists. The entire network of relationships that constituted the "fourth estate" underwent a profound transformation in the first decades of the twentieth century; the political and ideological maelstrom of the 1930s would only begin to lay bare the deep fissures in those relationships that this process had engendered.

JOURNALISM AND POWER IN THE IMPOSSIBLE REPUBLIC

> The appearance of a newspaper should be an occurrence of interest in society... precisely because a newspaper forms part of nothing less than the "power of the state," of those tacit powers of the state.
> —**Senator Matías Sánchez Sorondo, June 7, 1934**
>
> Journalism can never be a function of the state.
> —*La Nación*, **October 7, 1933**

The military movement that ended the presidency of Hipólito Yrigoyen rode a broad wave of support. For months the Yrigoyen government had failed to respond to the first devastating moments of a world economic crisis that threatened to undermine the foundation of the political opening that had brought his party to power fourteen years earlier. At best, the agonizing disarray of the administration only seemed to confirm the dangerous ineptitude of the Radical Party's Yrigoyenist wing; at worst, it signaled the ultimate consequences of an inherently decadent political liberalism that right-wing Argentine Nationalists had denounced since the 1910s.[1] Sectors of the military, Nationalists, Anti-Personalist Radicals, Conservatives, rival factions of Socialists, and, perhaps most vocally, Natalio Botana and *Crítica*, formed a common front for the ouster of the aging president. On September 6, 1930, the first military coup in modern Argentina met little resistance.

The breadth of the political convergence that toppled Yrigoyen, however, belied the depth of agreement surrounding the goals of the "September Revolution." For de facto president General José F. Uriburu and his closest allies, the movement was to be more than a simple change of administration. They viewed the chaos of the final year of Yrigoyen's government as the disastrous but logical culmination of the 1912 Sáenz Peña Law's expansion of suffrage and thus as an indication of the need to transform Argentina's "individualist democracy" into a corporatist-inspired "functional democracy."² Convinced of the inevitability of their own victory, the de facto authorities held elections in the province of Buenos Aires in April 1931, only to find far too many Argentines unprepared to jettison constitutional liberalism in favor of the corporatist vision advocated by Uriburu. Even worse, provincial voters seemed unwilling to abandon en masse the party of Yrigoyen. The electoral defeat quickly and publicly splintered the anti-Yrigoyen alliance that had brought the military to power. Having revealed their own lack of public support, the de facto authorities called national elections, and, in February 1932, Uriburu passed the presidential baton to his rival, General Augustín P. Justo, a coconspirator in September 1930.³

The failure of the Ubriburu experiment reveals that if, as Mariano Plotkin and others have shown, a prolonged crisis of liberalism had permeated the country since the late 1920s, that crisis was as ambiguous as it was profound.⁴ The shattering of a liberal consensus that had buoyed Argentine political and economic life since the 1880s did little, in itself, to establish the legitimacy of competing projects like that of Uriburu and his allies. In addition, the stubborn refusal of the Radical Party and its popular base to accept the fall of Yrigoyen as a terminal defeat collided with the equally determined coalition of forces united by little more than a shared resolve to block the Radical's full resurgence. This impasse found a curious solution: a liberal democracy sustained through thinly veiled and repeated electoral fraud.⁵ By 1935, even the defeated Radicals had resigned themselves to participation in what Tulio Halperín has called an "impossible republic": one whose political order, for its own continuity, "saw itself obliged to systematically violate the principles invoked as its source of legitimacy."⁶

The survival of constitutional liberalism as the normative basis for the Argentine political order after 1930, however, owes as much to the ideological breathing room ceded by liberalism's own malleability as it does to the failure of rival political projects. Indeed, core conceptions of liberalism retained their broad appeal and political utility not despite, but *because of* their sustained modification by a set of basic pressures: government attempts to generate popular acquiescence to authoritarian and semiauthoritarian rule; the increasing appeal of expanding state power as a pragmatic response to the world economic crisis; repeated attempts by the political Right to forge an alternative project; and the heightened class tensions that accompanied the country's rapid economic reorientation. A wounded liberalism staggered on as the dominant language of the political sphere and the republic's guiding political philosophy, owing much of its resilience to its own rearticulation, equivocal transformation, and regular transgression in practice.

These convulsions of the social order with which the Argentine commercial press was linked from birth sent shock waves throughout the press's entire network of relationships. The rapid expansion of the Buenos Aires press in the previous decades had placed the newspaper industry at the heart of social communication and the generation of public consent, while the shattered political consensus and disintegrating party structures of the 1930s made the press increasingly valuable as an instrument in factional disputes. Yet changes in public attitudes toward the relative legitimacy of journalism, together with a generalized—and well-founded—public suspicion of the political process, precluded a simple resurrection of the factional press. The power of the commercial press as a shaper of public consciousness, unlike that of its nineteenth-century counterpart, rested in good measure on its perceived autonomy from specific factional struggles. Nonetheless, by the late 1920s, the consolidation of the commercial press had created the conditions for a new and potentially more effective model of factional journalism: now, instead of politicians delivering a convinced public to a newspaper on the basis of shared partisanship, powerful commercial dailies could deliver a reading public—convinced or not—to politicians. As a result, when sections of the mass commercial press became tightly linked to specific political factions in the impossible republic, the links were on a far grander scale than those of the previous century's factional press, and based on a markedly different network of relationships between journalists, newspaper proprietors, public, and politicians.

For the press as a whole, the growing acceptance from across the political spectrum for an expansion of state power to meet the multiple crises of the 1930s clashed with key elements of the traditional consensus around press rights and prerogatives. The brief experience of corporatist dictatorship under General Uriburu brought a sudden imposition of an unexpected, if temporary, level of state restrictions on the commercial press. The replacement of that dictatorship by a sham democracy did little to guard the press's underlying juridical principles from constant threat. At the same time, the continued periodic invocation of the state of siege, with its suspension of constitutional guarantees, made official censorship a factor in the newsrooms of all the major Buenos Aires dailies.[7] While these states of siege were, by definition, exceptional and temporary responses to immediate crises, moves to permanently alter the juridical foundations of state-press relations also emerged in the course of the 1930s. Although both a legislative attempt by right-wing senator Matías Sánchez Sorondo and an executive decree of President Justo failed in the face of fierce resistance, the implications were clear: the traditional interpretation of the constitutional guarantees regarding the press that had made the Federal Capital so amenable to the emergence of Latin America's largest commercial newspaper industry faced serious challenges.

Finally, the newspaper industry's continued expansion placed even greater strain on traditional liberal conceptions of journalism practice and the nature of newspaper institutions. In the course of the 1930s, the growing class divide within the newsroom suddenly emerged into the open just as labor militancy rose and the Argentine Congress became more willing to entertain worker demands. Following the surprising congressional approval and equally unexpected presidential veto of a newsworker pension law, tensions between journalists and newspaper proprietors became impossible to contain within the mutualist Círculo de la Prensa. Working journalists around the country organized a national confederation, beginning the process of transforming provincial mutual aid societies into labor unions. In the Federal Capital, however, the proprietor-dominated executive committee of the Círculo de la Prensa reversed course, leading to a split in the organization and the creation in Buenos Aires of the most militant of the new journalist unions.

Taken together, the persistent crises unleashed in September 1930 profoundly shook the foundations of the Argentine commercial press. Though often appearing little more than the product of broader ideological and political change, the tensions that permeated the Argentine press's entire network of relationships in the 1930s also marked a surfacing of fundamental conflicts created by the commercial development of the newspaper industry since the 1880s. Far from a linear process, the forging of new relationships between the commercial press and political factions, together with clashes over the nature of the press and the social role of journalism, set a series of precedents and left a web of unresolved tensions. Ambiguous, intricate, and profound, these press conflicts would ultimately prove crucial to the Peronist transformation of the newspaper industry in the following decade.

The New Partisan Press

While the Argentine commercial press stood out among its Latin American peers for the immensity of its circulation levels, it had also attained an equally notable independence from specific political factions. The political upheavals of 1930 to 1943, however, seriously eroded the distance between political actors, important sectors of the newspaper industry, and institutions of the Argentine state. President Augustín P. Justo (1932–38), head of the governing Concordancia coalition's uneasy alliance of Conservatives, Anti-Personalist Radicals, and members of the newly formed Independent Socialist Party (PSI), created not only a fictitious democracy, but a sympathetic "independent" media apparatus. Himself partyless and lacking an autonomous and organized base of popular support, Justo looked to the enormous power of the commercial press as a mechanism for both generating public consent around his administration and disciplining his political rivals. In the process, he and his associates created a web of hidden connections between political power and media power that only become all the more entangled with the rise of Peronism after 1943.

Ironically, the process through which a new, and very different, version of factional journalism emerged coincided almost precisely with the symbolic consolidation of *Crítica* as a successful commercial newspaper. In mid-1927, the transfer of the newspaper's offices to Avenida de Mayo 1333 coincided with a series of conflicts with the printers of the Socialist-dominated Federación Gráfica Bonaerense.[8] When, in the midst of Socialist calls for a boycott of *Crítica*, a dissident group of Socialists left the party to form the Partido Socialista Independiente, Botana not only lent extensive coverage to the PSI's founding congress, but threw the full weight of his paper behind the new organization.[9] More an example of the enormous political latitude that the vast circulation of his paper allowed him than of any subservience to the still tiny political apparatus of the PSI, Botana's support remained within the kind of independent political endorsements common within the commercial press—though set in *Crítica*'s typically hyperbolic and strident journalistic voice.

It is only in the wake of Yrigoyen's victory in the presidential elections of 1928 (in which he enjoyed *Crítica*'s backing) that Botana began to tie the fate of his paper to the triumph of a particular political project.[10] As the government of the seventy-eight-year-old president faltered, *Crítica* began a spectacular series of personal attacks against Yrigoyen and his followers, painting the president as senile, isolated, and deaf to open calls for insurrection.[11] More tellingly, Botana himself became a key figure in the negotiations between civilian conspirators like Independent Socialists Federico Pinedo and Antonio De Tomaso and rival military leaders Generals Justo and Uriburu, while the offices of *Crítica* began to fill with political and military figures on the eve of the uprising.[12] The call for general civilian mobilization in support of the uprising came through the sirens and loudspeakers at the newspaper's offices on the morning of September 6, 1930, where, despite police attempts to block the newspaper's distribution, printers smuggled issues of *Crítica* to waiting vendors.[13] The central role that *Crítica* and Botana played in the ousting of Yrigoyen was lost on no one: the paper had increased its average circulation to over 350,000 for the month of September, with descriptions of the actions of Botana and the *Crítica* journalists during the course of the "Revolution" providing much of the paper's copy.[14] In the public parades celebrating Uriburu's presidential oath two days later, firefighters stopped in front of the *Crítica* offices to sing the national anthem.[15]

The tension between the conspirators of September emerged into the open just over a month after Yrigoyen's fall, when PSI leaders openly called for a quick return to constitutional rule.[16] *Crítica* endorsed the call, and tested the limits of official censorship when journalist Luís María Jantus denounced police procedures against dissidents. In reporting Jantus's subsequent exile, the paper informed readers that the state of siege prohibited further comment but that "the people should judge" the incident.[17] Not surprisingly, on November

15 *Crítica*'s Paris correspondent, Edmundo Guibourg, warned Natalio Botana that "the police of Buenos Aires are hungry for you" and that Leopoldo Lugones Jr., head of the police's section of Political Order, embodied a particularly dangerous threat.[18] Botana's own refusal to ally himself with the de facto government by accepting Uriburu's offer of Argentina's Parisian embassy further aggravated the tense relationship between the powerful newspaper owner and the regime, and, in particular, between Botana and acting minister of the interior Matías Sánchez Sorondo.[19]

Though opposition from the pages of *Crítica* remained muted due to the state of siege, even simple characterizations of Uriburu's proposed corporatist reforms as "disquieting" had a significant effect.[20] Provisional authorities privately credited the "waning enthusiasm for the September Revolution" among the general public to the actions of the "opposition press," and clumsily sought to counter those effects through state propaganda.[21] Yet, as Uriburu and his corporatist allies succumbed to pressure from General Justo, the Independent Socialists, and *Crítica,* as well as a host of other social forces, and called elections in the province of Buenos Aires for the following April, animosity only mounted.

Botana had now become personally involved in factional politics to a startling degree, while the circumstances of the Uriburu regime's retreat from power made his—and *Crítica's*—commitment irreversible. On April 15, 1931, Antonio De Tomaso penned an article in the paper declaring the electoral defeat of the government in the province of Buenos Aires earlier that month and the subsequent annulment of election results a clear sign of the regime's lack of popular support.[22] In response, Sánchez Sorondo ordered the suspension of *Crítica* for forty-eight hours and that of the Independent Socialist Party paper *Libertad* for ten days, threatening to make those closures permanent.[23] *Crítica* essentially ceased comment on local politics in favor of coverage of events in Spain, the growing importance of tango in Paris, and ambiguous political cartoons lamenting the retreat of democracy around the globe.[24] Still, Sánchez Sorondo's resignation from the cabinet three weeks later only made the situation for Botana more complicated: as his final act, the minister of the interior followed through on his threat and decreed *Crítica's* indefinite closure.[25] Immediately, the federal police detained Botana, his wife, Salvadora Medina Onrubia de Botana, and scores of *Crítica* journalists, while Leopoldo Lugones Jr. himself raided the newspaper's offices in search of incriminating documentation.[26] After three months of prison at the hands of Lugones—an experience the officer ensured was far more traumatic for the *Crítica* owner's wife than for Natalio Botana himself—the Botana family left for exile in Spain.[27]

Sánchez Sorondo expected the closure of *Crítica* to at once eliminate the most vocal opponent of the regime among the major commercial dailies and send a chilling message to the rest of the press. Instead, the measure placed

Botana's daily directly in the hands of Uriburu's principal rival, General Justo. In the confusion surrounding his detention, Botana managed to ensure the survival of his paper by transferring legal ownership to his political allies. Federico Pinedo—who together with Antonio De Tomaso had emerged as the ideological force behind Justo—received the stock certificates for the *Crítica* publisher Sociedad Poligráfica Argentina, and Justo immediately assumed the presidency of the company, placing De Tomaso and Pinedo on the board of directors.[28] The move, which legally made *Crítica* the property of figures too powerful to persecute, saved the paper from oblivion.

It also, for the first time since Emilio Mitre's death in 1909, placed the ownership of a major Buenos Aires newspaper directly in the hands of a presidential contender. On August 8, 1931, the Sociedad began to edit *Jornada,* a thinly disguised *Crítica* surrogate, setting the "new" newspaper directly at the service of General Justo's presidential campaign. *Jornada,* in addition to painting the retired general as a man of "great civilian spirit," launched a series of attacks on Justo's rivals, the Alianza Civil's Lisandro de la Torre and Nicolás Repetto.[29] The characterizations of the candidates of the Alianza, however, reveal the role that *Jornada* played in the Justo campaign strategy: rather than portraying the Alianza candidates as incompetent, the paper repeatedly warned abstentionist Radical Party supporters that de la Torre intended to extinguish Radicalism and taunted supporters of the Socialist Repetto that the vice-presidential candidate had lost his leftist credentials.[30] In the absence of an extensive, organized political apparatus, *Jornada* served at once as a vehicle of communication for the Justo campaign as well more specifically as a tool for mobilizing the Buenos Aires popular classes around the candidacy of the general. Unlike the papers of the nineteenth-century political press, *Crítica* had a long-established, relatively loyal mass audience that Botana had cultivated for over a decade; *Jornada* sought to deliver that public to General Justo.

Only on February 20, 1932, when Justo assumed the presidency and lifted the long-running state of siege, did *Crítica* proper—and Natalio Botana—return to the streets of Buenos Aires. *Crítica* continued as a mouthpiece of President Justo, Minister of Agriculture Antonio De Tomaso, and, after mid-1933, Minister of Economy Federico Pinedo until well after the Justo presidency ended in 1938. As the decade progressed, not only did *Crítica* remain a reliable bastion of support of the Concordancia government, but Botana himself served the Justo administration in even less transparent ways. In early 1933 Natalio Botana served as Justo's informal ambassador to both Franklin D. Roosevelt and William Randolph Hearst, lobbying for U.S. support of Argentine trade negotiations with the British Empire.[31] When opposition senator Enzo Bordabehere was assassinated on the chamber floor in July 1935, Botana and Justo sought to push the news from the headlines by launching a *Crítica* campaign to create a popular cult around tango singer Carlos Gardel, who had died the previous month in an airplane crash in Colombia. "Natalio understood it," his son Helvio would later recall; Gardel "was the symbol of happiness, of criollo purity adequate to oppose the moment of discredit and deception that shook the republic."[32] A year later, Botana facilitated—at Justo's behest—a bribery scandal that successfully tainted several members of the opposition Radical Party who had only recently ended their electoral abstentionism to participate in the fraudulent democracy.[33]

Crítica served as President Justo's connection to a set of urban social classes far better organized by the opposition Radical, Socialist, and even Communist Parties than by members of the Concordancia coalition, and it necessarily did so from a decidedly leftist political position. Alongside paeans to Pinedo's economic policies lay denunciations of Mussolini and Socialist-Realist drawings exalting Argentine workers as the true producers of the country's wealth and national progress.[34] In addition, the paper continued to employ prominent members of the Argentine Communist Party like Ernesto Giudice, Cayetano Córdova Iturburu, Raúl González Tuñón, and José Portogalo—ironically, even as the Justo government continued a policy of repression against the Party. Botana also set his newspaper firmly behind the Republican cause in the Spanish Civil War, organizing fundraising for the Spanish government through Crítica, employing Spanish exiles as contributors, and sending Communist Party members González Tuñón and Córdova Iturburu as special envoys to the Republic.[35] Thus, despite the clearly conservative orientation of the Concordancia government and its neutrality on issues like the Spanish Civil War, Crítica served to associate President Justo and the economic policies of Federico Pinedo with the more left-leaning and antifascist positions that held sway among the Buenos Aires popular classes.

To dismiss such positions as merely opportunistic, or as a manipulation of Botana by Justo, however, runs contrary to the volumes of anecdotes affirming Botana's genuine commitment to antifascism and other popular causes.[36] The exact nature of Botana's relationship with President Justo, Federico Pinedo, and Antonio De Tomaso is far from clear, and the dearth of documentary evidence that might illuminate that relationship is no accident: the uncertainties surrounding Crítica ownership and finances, after all, had shielded the paper in 1931 and 1932. Indeed, the effectiveness of Crítica as a mobilizer of passive support for the Justo administration rested in good part upon the opaqueness of Botana's personal relationship to the president, and thus on the believability of Crítica as a voice with, at the very least, great autonomy from the government. The reading public does not appear to have purchased Crítica in ever-increasing quantities throughout the decade of the 1930s because of the paper's support for Justo. Judging from the manner in which editors allocated space in the paper and the repetition of certain topics, Crítica continued to solidify its readership base through variations of its usual material: its early coverage of breaking stories; sensationalistic crime reporting; campaigns around popular causes like support for Republican Spain; attention to labor disputes; attacks on rival newspapers; and exaltation of the paper itself as a living embodiment of the urban popular classes. The relationship between Botana, Justo, Pinedo, and De Tomaso was symbiotic, with *Crítica* delivering a popular audience to a sector of the Concordancia coalition and Botana receiving in turn an unparalleled political access to a powerful group of public officials with whom he genuinely sympathized both personally and ideologically.

This convergence between the agendas of Botana, Justo, Pinedo, and De Tomaso is also evident in another *Crítica* function that came into prominence after February 1932: the public disciplining of President Justo's Concordancia "allies." Within the Concordancia's alliance of Conservatives, dissident Radicals, and Independent Socialists, it was clearly the Conservatives of the province of Buenos Aires, who had rebaptized themselves the Partido Demócrata Nacional (PDN), that wielded the most extensive political machine. Justo's exclusion of prominent Buenos Aires Conservatives from his cabinet in favor of PSI members like De Tomaso and dissident Radicals like Leopoldo Melo left the president in a potentially awkward situation vis-à-vis the Concordancia's most powerful political organization. In his own conflicts with the governor of the province of Buenos Aires, Conservative Federico Martínez de Hoz, Justo could not rely on the support of an organized political apparatus; instead, he depended on the selective use of executive power and on divisions within the PDN that might work in his favor.[37] It is precisely in attempts to foment these divisions and weaken the PDN's power within the Concordancia that Botana's and Justo's interests again converged, and in which *Crítica* proved particularly useful.

A long series of unrestrained and even sensationalistic denunciations against police brutality and torture under the Uriburu regime—especially at the hands of the Botanas's jailer, Leopoldo Lugones Jr.—occupied much of *Crítica*'s pages in the first months of the Justo government.[38] Yet attacks against a prominent member of the Concordancia itself ultimately carried with them more far-reaching consequences not just for Botana, but for the Argentine press as a whole. Uriburu's former minister of the interior Matías Sánchez Sorondo had become a powerful senator for the province of Buenos Aires in the same elections that brought Justo to the presidency. Uneasily ensconced as an informal bridge between the PDN and the far-Right Nationalist movement, the senator sought to push his party, in which he was one of the more prominent figures, to embrace the kind of protofascist political projects of which he had become increasingly enamored. Sánchez Sorondo's formal break with the PDN and the Concordancia came precisely because of his resistance—literally alongside the brownshirted Legión Cívica Argentina—to Justo's ouster of Governor Martínez de Hoz in early 1935.[39]

Botana's own role in provoking such divisions within the PDN were, at the time, notorious. As Natalio Botana's son recalls, the *Crítica* owner's belligerence toward Sánchez Sorondo "was a personal problem" as much as it was political.[40] Beginning in mid-1932, *Crítica* carried a long-running series of caricatures of the senator with exaggerated nose and pointed ears, labeling him the "Gravedigger" for his role in Uriburu-era repression and condemning what the paper claimed—accurately—was the senator's increasing fascination with Italian Fascism. In addition, the paper ran numerous denunciations of Sánchez Sorondo's association with the Legión Cívica Argentina, claiming that the group intended to attempt a "Revolución Fascista" that would place the senator at the head of an Italian-style dictatorship.[41] Botana even used this rumored fascist putsch as a reason to excoriate the "serious press" for propagating the "venom of skepticism against the present institutional situation" through its admittedly tepid criticism of electoral fraud, and for failing to report news of the fascist plot.[42]

At the same time, Botana also ran a series of articles against the senator's business interests that would eventually create significant legal troubles for the *Crítica* owner. Beginning in mid-August 1932 and running through the end of the following month, *Crítica* carried five stories proclaiming the grocery chain Almacenes Reunidos Sociedad Anónima (ARSA)—on whose board sat not only Sánchez Sorondo, but General Uriburu's son Alberto Uriburu—a "trust" and the profits its owners reaped "ill-gotten."[43] In the same pages, the paper's caricaturists added a series of advertisements parodying the senator's grocery stores, with slogans like "ARSA: Where your peso is worth less" and "Buy today, because the municipal inspectors are about to close our doors!" and a fake promotion proclaiming that all customers would receive a coupon redeemable for public employment "once our owner Matías Sánchez is dictator."[44] The tactic echoed past *Crítica* public campaigns, but with an important difference: now, attacks on the ARSA were not extortionate, but designed purposefully to discredit the whole range of activities of a specific political figure.

Botana's success in fomenting divisions within the PDN as a means of weakening powerful rivals to Justo, Pinedo, and De Tomaso often sat uneasily with the simultaneous necessity of maintaining cohesion within the Concordancia as a whole. The directness and vehemence of some *Crítica* attacks occasionally threatened to turn the paper into more than a mere counterweight to Justo's more organized rivals. After several such incidents, Antonio De Tomaso wrote to President Justo, "I spoke for a long time with Botana. I told him of your displeasure. Today there will be an article saying that the harmony of the [Concordancia's] leaders has been established."[45] In the same message De Tomaso reaffirmed Botana's desire "to be at the service of the government" and relayed to the president Botana's request for better information from the federal police.[46] Perhaps even more importantly, the attacks on Sánchez Sorondo's

ARSA brought a well-publicized series of calumny cases against Botana, for which the *Crítica* owner at one point stood condemned to five and one-half years in prison and $43,900 in punitive damages.[47] The cases against Botana not only threatened the *Crítica* owner with stiff legal penalties, but served as an ongoing headache for Botana, Justo, and Pinedo in the mid-1930s.[48] Botana's actions against Sánchez Sorondo, then, threatened to envelope rival Concordancia figures, either directly or indirectly, in the kind of legal disputes that might weaken not just Conservatives, but the cohesion of the Concordancia as a whole.

Crítica was by no means the only commercial newspaper with close ties to the government, even if it did lie at the center of President Justo's media strategy. As Natalio Botana's legal problems mounted, President Justo and Federico Pinedo began exploratory discussions with a number of journalists and newspaper proprietors regarding the creation of a "neutral" commercial newspaper closely tied to the government. One plan submitted by two journalists at *El Mundo* called for massive state advertising subsidies to create a new "independent" newspaper that "at no time would use the expression 'supported by the government,'" but would clearly serve the interests of General Justo.[49] Although the journalists did not explicitly state from where the "great amount of capital" needed to launch the paper might come, they did propose that at least two-thirds of the newspaper's operating costs come in the form of sustained government advertising. In this way, the projected paper might maintain the kind of productive infrastructure that would allow it to "orient the people in the midst of the enormous political disorientation that reigns," bringing them toward the kind of "cleansed" Radicalism that Justo ostensibly represented.[50]

Though Pinedo and Justo rejected the offer, their reasons for doing so are revealing of the tensions inherent within this particular model of partisan journalism. Although both men understood that maintaining the appearance of objectivity and independence was crucial to gaining readers' confidence and establishing the legitimacy of a newspaper, they found investing in a new paper with no preexisting readership too risky and expensive.[51] What's more, Pinedo pinpointed a potential problem with the arrangement that a decade later would gravely afflict Juan Domingo Perón in his own initial dealings with newspaper owners: "The proposal fails . . . in the base itself, since even if it were viable, its authors offer no serious moral guarantee to back their agreements. A newspaper destined to fulfill an official government function could only be possible by giving its direction to a man of absolute confidence, or better, an ideological confidant of the general."[52] The proposal did bring Pinedo to suggest that at some point in the future a more selective official daily "might become necessary in order to bring the presidential word not to the great public, which doesn't matter, but to specific sectors."[53] Thus, President Justo had a clear idea not only that any journalistic ally must remain closely tied to himself through political affinity (as was clearly the case with Botana) or, perhaps, near absolute economic dependence, but that the kind of broad public appeal of a newspaper like *Crítica* did not necessarily lend the government legitimacy with potentially more influential sectors of Argentine society.

The proposal by the *El Mundo* journalists also did not prosper, in part, because a far better prospect soon presented itself. In 1935, Helvecia Antonini de Cortejarena, proprietor of *La Razón,* approached Minister of Economy Federico Pinedo for help in managing the paper's mounting debt and fending off an administrative intervention in the newspaper by an increasingly intrusive group of creditors.[54] The end result was a complex relationship between Pinedo, Justo, and Ricardo Peralta Ramos (son-in-law of the paper's owner) mediated through the recently created Central Bank and a handful of other state agencies. While, as Ronald Newton has observed, "no one knows the full story" of *La Razón*'s connections with different national and international political groups, it is clear that President Justo and Federico Pinedo became far more involved in the internal affairs of the newspaper than most suspected.[55]

For Justo and Pinedo, control of *La Razón* raised the prospect of privileged access to a reading public that differed sharply from that of *Crítica*. In their internal evaluation of the newspaper—based, it appears, on information assembled by Peralta Ramos in mid-1935—the drop in circulation that had resulted from *La Razón*'s competition with *Crítica* in the 1920s had nonetheless left a potentially prosperous (if dangerously indebted) business.[56] While the circulation of the paper had fallen to approximately 81,000 copies daily, advertising had increased, signaling, the author of the evaluation concluded, that *La Razón* remained attractive to advertisers because of its readers' "undoubted acquisitive power."[57] An established paper with name recognition, a sizable middle- and upper-class readership, and an existing advertising base appealed to Pinedo and Justo for precisely the reasons that the *El Mundo* journalists' project failed. A detailed financial study of the newspaper also seemed to suggest that, with administrative trimming and debt relief, *La Razón* could quickly become an important newspaper once again.

The recovery of *La Razón* depended largely upon an investment of "approximately three and a half million pesos" in order to "pay individual creditors, [and] acquire machinery and newsprint," as well as a more general rationalization of the newsroom—including barring Cortejarena's widow from any decision making at the paper.[58] Together with a pressing debt of $2.5 million that *La Razón* still owed the Banco Hipotecario—headed, since 1933, by former *Crítica* administrator and Botana confidant Enrique Noriega—the newspaper required a combination of investment and debt relief at a level approximately equivalent to twice *La Razón*'s entire cost of production for the period March 1935–March 1936.[59] By late 1936, Pinedo and Justo had paid the paper's creditors and seen to the purchase of new machinery to modernize *La Razón*'s format and printing capacities by drawing funds from the Pinedo-created Central Bank, leaving a $5 million debt frozen in the bank's Instituto Movilizador de Inversiones Bancarias.[60]

Through the Central Bank, President Justo and Federico Pinedo essentially purchased favored access to *La Razón*'s audience. Yet the value of the paper depended in large degree not on its overt identification with the president, but with the maintenance of *La Razón* as a plausibly independent newspaper. A Justo and Pinedo *La Razón* would remain flexible in its political orientation, much as *Crítica* remained, as a means of both expanding its circulation and generating reader confidence: "Without becoming oppositional, the newspaper should have its freedom of opinion. . . . *La Razón* should praise the good works of the government and criticize it in the appropriate cases. A political newspaper is never a commercial success. The orientation should be made intelligently and in agreement with the editors."[61] Indeed, the political latitude granted *La Razón* allowed the paper's newly appointed director and ostensible "primary shareholder," Ricardo Peralta Ramos, to assume a stance that would both minimize conflicts with *Crítica* and appeal precisely to that public that rejected *Crítica*'s workerist and protopopulist style. The two papers essentially divided the evening market along political lines, with *Crítica* intransigently anti-Fascist and even pro-Soviet in international matters and *La Razón* openly supportive of the Italian, Spanish, and German Fascist experiments.

Both papers, of course, painted President Justo in a sympathetic light consonant with these divergent political stances and in ways that appealed to *Crítica*'s and *La Razón*'s distinct reading publics. Rumors—most likely true—would later suggest that this arrangement corresponded less to the political tendencies of Peralta Ramos than to the "coaching" given him by Botana.[62] Regardless, *La Razón*'s editorial embrace of international fascism marked a sudden but lucrative turn for Peralta Ramos: in August 1935 the paper had denounced Stalin and Hitler as essentially equal, but in May 1937 *La Razón* published a special issue entitled "Resurgent Germany," supposedly edited at Goebbels's Berlin offices, for which the director allegedly received as much as $1 million.[63] Few familiar with the paper could deny that *La Razón*'s political line followed its funding sources.

The transformation of *La Razón* proved incredibly successful. Thanks to the paper's capital improvements and layout modernization, circulation steadily increased beginning in 1937. By 1945, *La Razón* had more than fully recovered from its financial crisis ten years earlier to achieve a circulation of 238,000 and had come to control eighteen radio stations across the country.[64] While some might attribute this resurgence to the journalistic genius and administrative acumen of Ricardo Peralta Ramos and editor Félix Laíño, clearly other important factors had also came into play. Peralta Ramos owed—literally—the conditions for much of *La Razón*'s remarkable comeback to President Justo, Federico Pinedo, and the Central Bank that they had created.

La Razón's success, however, was also President Justo's. Bereft of a coherent political apparatus, General Justo depended in part on the support that a sympathetic media voice might generate. That both *Crítica* and *La Razón* had long-established, successful traditions of interpellating sociologically and ideologically distinct sectors of the Argentine public granted the Justo administration positive exposure across the political and class spectrum. This transformation marked neither a simple return to the hyperpoliticized factional journalism of the previous century nor a mere expansion of the still vital tradition of political journalism embodied in newspapers like the Socialists' *La Vanguardia*, the Yrigoyenist *La Época*, or the Nationalist *La Fronda* and *Crisol*. The importance of *Crítica* and *La Razón* for the Justo administration resided neither in their overarching ideological consonance with General Justo nor in their utility as a forum for the elaboration of specific political principles to be embraced by Concordancia militants. Neither *Crítica* nor *La Razón* stood as unequivocal and explicit mouthpieces of Justo and his closest allies; the diametrically opposed political stances of both papers on a host of issues only bolstered the appearance of an editorial independence that was not altogether fictitious even as it lent greater weight to their convergence in support of the agenda of key figures of the Concordancia. Unlike the organs of traditional partisan journalism, *Crítica* and *La Razón* proved valuable as vehicles for generating popular acquiescence to the semiauthoritarianism of the Concordancia governments precisely insofar as both papers outwardly adhered to the models of journalistic autonomy that had come to dominate the commercial press prior to 1930, and that continued as normative within the newspaper industry. More than a mere weapon in factional struggles, then, this new version of partisan journalism also served the much broader mission of generating both active and passive consent for the regime among broad swathes of Argentine society.

President Justo's media strategy significantly altered the network of relationships between political power and media power that had emerged over the previous three decades. The web of economic, legal, and political threads that linked Natalio Botana and President Justo and the complex financial ties that made Ricardo Peralta Ramos dependent on the continued goodwill of administrators at the Central Bank remained at once confusing and largely opaque to the reading public.[65] This was no accident: the legitimacy and effectiveness of this new form of factional press rested precisely upon public perceptions of an autonomy that, in the final instance, proved only slightly less illusory than the democratic principles that the Concordancia repeatedly invoked but continually violated. In this, the sympathetic media apparatus assembled by General Justo—at the time unprecedented in its scale—would serve as an important precursor to a far more extensive, ambitious, centralized, and disciplined quasi-state media project that helped the consolidation of Peronism a decade later.

State Power and the Commercial Press

If the relationship between political factions and sectors of the Argentine commercial press changed abruptly with the military coup of September 1930, a broader transformation facilitated that shift: the expansion of the regulatory powers of the Argentine state. In its most obvious manifestation, the Uriburu regime's invocation of extraordinary state-of-siege powers of censorship limited the actions of the commercial press on a scale not seen since the previous century. But the closure of *Crítica* had also inadvertently solidified the connections between General Justo and that newspaper. The subsequent creation of the Central Bank and its Instituto Movilizador, similarly, gave Justo a new and powerful mechanism for the creation and maintenance of a set of friendly newspapers.

Uriburu's sweeping but temporary use of state power for censorship and Justo's surreptitious use of the Central Bank also coincided with attempts to take a series of permanent, institutional steps intended to change fundamentally the relationship between the Argentine state and the press as a whole. These moves did not always prove successful. Such initiatives do, however, reveal the increasing tensions between an ideological environment characterized by a growing consensus around the beneficial potential—even necessity—of new forms of state activity, and the operation of a commercial press whose juridical basis, professional ideology, and public legitimacy had long rested on the antistatist elements of Argentine liberalism.[66]

The first of these measures emerged precisely as public enthusiasm for the Uriburu regime began to wane. Crediting this erosion of popular support to the government's failure to completely contain the actions of opposition newspapers, Lieutenant Colonel Emilio Kinkelín, the secretary of the presidency of the provisional government, created the "Sección Prensa" under his own authority.[67] Kinkelín defined the Sección Prensa's overriding mission as the "channeling of public opinion toward the high purposes of [the provisional government]" by disseminating the opinion of "the people's leaders in order to detract from all tendentious propaganda that seeks to diminish the merit of the works being done after the revolution."[68] Rather than a mere mechanism for the enforcement of censorship, then, the new institution had multiple functions that went beyond purely negative attempts to restrict newspaper content. In effect, Kinkelín sought to make the Sección Prensa a state agency of public opinion formation, a task ostensibly reserved for—but far too important and delicate to be entrusted to—the private organs of the fourth estate.

The Sección Prensa's range of activities proved surprisingly wide. Sección staff monitored newspaper content throughout the republic, responding to the relative lack of "predisposition of the big newspapers to lend their columns" by planting articles in smaller but friendly newspapers in direct response to press criticism of government officials.[69] In addition, the Sección Prensa used radio programming to boost support for both the provisional government and the candidacy of General Justo in the elections of November 1931, broadcasting musical auditions from the Teatro Colón opera house and taking advantage of the intervals between performances to "give civic and moral advice."[70] The Sección also employed a team to distribute leaflets and fliers from cars and to post murals denouncing the failures of the Soviet Union and lauding the ways in which the provisional government had protected the Argentine worker from immigrant competition.[71] More ominously, the Uriburu-era press monitors also elaborated memoranda on the internal operations of at least one Buenos Aires newspaper, *Noticias Gráficas*, detailing the political tendencies of its editors for use in extraofficial arm twisting. In handwritten margin comments, a reader of the memo—presumably Lieutenant Colonel Kinkelín—asks if the paper's director, Alberto Cordone, holds any accounts at the Banco Nación and remarks that assistant editor Armando Casarino would soon lose his post in the Buenos Aires municipal administration, presumably for his association with the "newspaper of the *peludista* [Yrigoyenist] revolution."[72]

While the Sección Prensa did continue to function well into the Justo period, it appears to have done so with diminishing institutional coherence. Occasionally operating under the title "Oficina de Prensa," the institution continued to monitor the commercial press, producing broadly informative memos on the daily coverage of specific newspapers.[73] In addition, in early 1934, staff within the institution developed a project for an "anti-Marxist" campaign designed to weaken the electoral strength of the Socialist Party in pending parliamentary elections. The campaign was to include murals reminding Argentines that "Socialism Is Semitic in Origin" and pronouncing Marxism the "opiate of the people."[74] Yet the decree that Justo administration auditors prepared for the permanent establishment of the Sección Prensa never materialized.[75] By 1937, even the Uriburu-era centralization of government advertising distribution—crucial for generating a coherent strategy of favoring some media over others—fell by the wayside.[76] If the Concordancia governments appear to have allowed the Sección Prensa to fall into administrative oblivion, the project would see a sudden resurrection with the end of those regimes: the ideas and motivations that had led to the establishment of the Sección Prensa would reemerge in a far more powerful, durable, and coherent form in its post-1943 successor, the Undersecretariat of Information and the Press.

Kinkelín's creation of the Sección Prensa responded as much to the immediate political demands of defending the provisional government as to that regime's broader embrace of a statist, antiliberal, corporatist solution to the particular crisis facing the Argentine nation.[77] In the same way, a mid-1934 push by Senator Matías Sánchez Sorondo to legislate a new relationship between state and press embodied an impulse to blur the normative boundaries between public and private and between state and civil society. Sánchez Sorondo, however, also now understood just how complex and ambiguous the crisis of liberal hegemony that had established those boundaries remained: as Uriburu's minister of the interior, he was the one who had inadvertently hastened the demise of the corporatist experiment by promoting the regime's ill-fated April 1931 electoral gamble. Rather than an unequivocal frontal assault on traditional conceptions of press autonomy, then, Sánchez Sorondo presented his bill For the Protection of the Press largely as a defensive measure, couched—however ambiguously—in terms of the liberal political order. Nonetheless, like the ultimately more timid media project of Emilio Kinkelín, the bill embodied a starkly corporatist view of the national state as the ultimate arbiter of social communication, with the private press standing as a corporate entity whose overriding mission was to serve as buttress to the state itself.

Sánchez Sorondo had ostensibly designed the proposed legislation not to create a new press, but to "protect" the existing press from its own degeneration. Sections of the Argentine press, he argued, had fallen prey to *"gangsters* [sic] of journalism" who used their newspapers to promote "the envy and resentment of the poor against the rich, of servants against their *patrones,* of the governed against the governing."[78] Unlike *La Nación* and *La Prensa,* which had forged the "courageous . . . spirit of Argentine journalism," this scandal-driven press had become a serious "factor of social corruption: it corrupts the facts, it corrupts ideas, it corrupts consciousness."[79] Rather than restricting the "honest" press, which fulfilled "an irreplaceable social function," the projected law would instead inhibit the "extortionary periodicals . . . the filth that must be cast away."[80]

In this sense, Sánchez Sorondo claimed the bill largely as a return to the state regulatory powers promoted by Deán Funes and the first junta in the press proclamation of April 1811, powers which—in the words of Funes—would prevent the degeneration of "liberty" into "licentiousness."[81] Much of the bill, in fact, centered on bolstering the enforcement for violations of the Penal Code committed through the press and setting stiff mandatory sentencing for these offenses.[82] Under the projected law, directors and proprietors would explicitly register their ownership of specific periodicals with the recently established Registry of Intellectual Property and become jointly responsible with journalists for the criminal content of any articles appearing in their periodicals. As a means of ensuring that periodical proprietors could remain economically capable of paying fines, the bill also required that a "demonstration of financial capacity" accompany the periodical's registration.[83] In addition, not only did the bill specify strict fines and prison sentences for violations, it also opened the possibility for judges to order the immediate closure of periodicals whose directors had run afoul of the law more than five times, a sanction that would be both permanent and obligatory upon further violation.[84]

While the bill For the Protection of the Press contained a series of measures that essentially toughened enforcement of the Penal Code, Sánchez Sorondo's own statements to the Senate in presenting the project revealed a far more ambitious attempt to rearticulate state-press relations. The project's title announced an inversion of dominant conceptions of press freedom by positing the state not as the primary threat to the proper functioning of the press, but as its guardian. For Sánchez Sorondo, the rapid expansion and immense political and ideological power of the press had allowed newspaper owners to impose their own self-interested understanding of the "inviolability" of the press as normative. This situation had set the stage for the emergence of a set of newspapers that took shelter in this situation only to remain "permanently at auction, ready to turn themselves over to the highest bidder." The resulting rise of "rags" (*pasqines*) not only threatened to debase the press by marrying its influence and power to the nefarious forces of social degeneration, but threatened to strip journalism practice of its lofty philosophical and literary attributes, making it instead merely a "means of earning a living."[85] The threat to the press, then, did not come from the state, but from the unregulated development of the newspaper industry itself in an environment of generalized social decay that only state power could reverse.

Sánchez Sorondo's remarks also betrayed his own understanding of the bill as part of a broader corporatist push against liberal conceptions of the divisions between state and civil society and between public and private that stood at the heart of Argentine press jurisprudence. The senator continually referred to the press as a coherent corporate entity—even as a medicalized body itself—announcing that he intended to "defend the rights [*fueros*] of journalism, protecting its dignity" from the "cancer of scandalous and immoral journalism which corrodes its entrails." Nor did Sánchez Sorondo shy away from invoking the logical consequences of this conception of the press: if the "rights of journalism" were less the rights of individuals to express themselves by means of the press than corporate rights reserved for clearly defined press institutions, those institutions in turn were integral elements of the ultimate repository of the national will. A newspaper, the senator argued, "forms part of nothing less than the 'power of the state,' of those tacit powers of the state. As a result, the creation of a part of power cannot be a matter of individual will."[86] The publicness of the privately owned fourth estate, in effect, made its proper role clear: as an institutional manifestation of social power, the press should be collapsed within the ultimate instrument of government. Perhaps even more explicitly, Sánchez Sorondo openly proclaimed that the Nazi German press law of December 1933 embodied precisely the kind of law "that I would like to see practiced in our country" and provided a template for the realization of Deán Funes's aspirations regarding Argentine journalism.

Beyond the more ambitious goals of fundamental reform, however, Sánchez Sorondo also had more practical and immediate matters in mind. Not only were sections of the Buenos Aires press engaged in a web of litigation for more than a year prior to the bill's introduction, but the senator himself was a litigant against the journalistic figure with the most actions against him: Natalio Botana. By the time that Sánchez Sorondo introduced his legislative project, Botana already faced a sentence of over five years in prison for the ARSA cases alone, and he still had pending charges against him filed by the director of the National Penitentiary, various police officers, the owner of the Nationalist paper *Crisol*, and the German ambassador in Buenos Aires, among others.[87] Botana had evaded orders for his arrest by taking an "extended business trip" to Montevideo, further antagonizing his opponents. In an act of defiance, Botana took the unusual step of running a signed letter from himself to Emilio Kinkelín on the front page of *Crítica* just days before Sánchez Sorondo presented his bill in the Senate. Botana unleashed a long stream of accusations against Kinkelín, taunting him with a torrent of anti-Semitic slurs and questioning the sincerity of his transformation from a "mercenary of Hebrew banking" into "the Goebbels of creole Nazism."[88] Regardless of whether it expressed his own anti-Semitism, Botana's letter was a clever provocation at the height of the litigation storm: to bring charges against the *Crítica* owner for calumny, Kinkelín could only argue that there was in fact no international Jewish conspiracy, effectively forcing him to deny publicly the validity of a key element of the brand of Argentine Nationalism that he had so fervently embraced.[89]

Clearly frustrated with the slow pace and ineffectiveness of judicial actions against Botana, Sánchez Sorondo seems to have tailored his bill to silence *Crítica* specifically. Botana's representatives claimed before multiple courts that the litigants had not established his ownership of *Crítica*, arguing that the paper belonged to the anonymous consortium Buenos Aires Poligráfica—Botana, in effect, *might not* be the newspaper's owner after all. Together with a string of other arguments and the aid of President Justo, Botana's representatives delayed rulings and channeled appeals into the hands of "friendly" judges, tactics that would eventually allow the *Crítica* owner to avoid legal consequences.[90]

Even if Sánchez Sorondo claimed the bill was a stand on impersonal, general principles, many of its articles are transparently direct responses to the legal maneuvers that had allowed Botana to evade court rulings. In addition to making the closure of *Crítica* obligatory due to the multiple violations of the Penal Code of which Botana already stood convicted, the bill would strip Botana and Justo of their ability to obfuscate the paper's ownership: articles 3 and 10 required that periodical owners register their names and addresses and that any change in ownership status be filed with the Registry of Intellectual Property.[91] Despite Sánchez Sorondo's own denial that his personal situation influenced the proposed legislation, at least two of his fellow senators thought otherwise. Francisco Correa remarked that many senators supporting the bill had in mind "the name of a particular newspaper," and reminded them of their own prior association with *Crítica* by placing into the record an October 1930 speech delivered by right-wing senator Benjamín Villafañe in praise of Natalio Botana.[92] Alfredo Palacios, likewise, told the Senate that while in committee Sánchez Sorondo had referred to the bill's article 5 as limiting newspaper ownership to "native Argentines"—effectively proscribing the naturalized Botana—even though the actual text of the article only limited ownership to citizens.[93]

Though in the end the proposed Law for the Protection of the Press never reached President Justo's desk, this failure was far from certain. Palacios led the charge against the measure in the Senate, arguing that article 32 of the constitution prohibited the Congress from even considering such legislation.[94] The Círculo de la Prensa also protested the measure as unconstitutional, adding that its passage would "restore, from a dark era of Argentine life, measures born in the heat of tyranny"—a clear reference to the Rosas press restrictions.[95] Such dissent, however, remained far from unanimous. Perhaps most surprisingly, editorialists at *La Nación* seemed amenable to some aspects of the bill despite their earlier intransigent rejection of the German press law from which Sánchez Sorondo drew much of his inspiration.[96] While the Senate approved the measure with some modifications, the bill, due to the combined opposition of the Círculo de la Prensa, *La Prensa, La Nación* (however ambiguous), and Socialist members of the Chamber of Deputies, died without debate in the lower house. The bill did serve as a model for short-lived press laws in the provinces of Santa Fe (1937) and La Rioja (1941), and, more than ten years later, for the proposed reforms of at least one Peronist congressman.[97] More importantly, the fact that the projected Law for the Protection of the Press achieved the visibility that it did is testament to just how shaky the consensus around the liberal foundations of the press had become; on the other hand, the measure's eventual failure confirmed the lack of attractive alternatives to those foundations.

The death of the bill, however, did not mark the final move to alter press jurisprudence permanently. Just weeks after the bill's Senate approval, an incident involving international news agencies in Argentina inspired a second attempt to rework the Argentine press's legal standing vis-à-vis the state, this time in the form of an executive decree. The original impetus for the decree was a series of articles published in Chile's *El Mercurio* regarding the opening of the October 1934 Eucharistic Congress in Buenos Aires. Penned by United

States journalist T. P. Farrell, a correspondent with the United Press in Buenos Aires, the articles carried not just spectacular factual inaccuracies, but exaggerated stereotypical distortions—including the masses of poor Indians and gauchos in the streets of Buenos Aires—all of which came as an affront to Argentine "national dignity" when they appeared in the pages of *El Mercurio*.[98] The Argentine Ministry of the Interior immediately contacted its Chilean counterpart over the incident, and the ministry expelled Farrell from Argentina by month's end.[99] The perceived seriousness of the issue even led the Executive Committee of the Círculo de la Prensa to take the unusual step of recommending that only Argentine journalists, or at least journalists who "identify with the life of this country," be allowed to send local news by cable.[100] The Ministry of the Interior investigation, however, revealed the incident as a curious example of journalistic practice. Farrell had actually sent the articles by airmail two weeks *prior* to the opening of the Eucharistic Congress, and had planned to cable any necessary modifications before their publication. Once the Congress commenced, however, Farrell apparently found himself "with too much work" to send corrections.[101]

Nonetheless, the focus of Argentine authorities remained fixed on the international wire services. Following the investigation of the incident, on July 13, 1935, President Justo issued an executive decree even more stringent than Sánchez Sorondo's proposed Law for the Protection of the Press. The measure established that the Dirección General de Correos y Telégrafos would collect signed copies of all outgoing wire transmissions and store them for three years. In addition, Argentine authorities would hold the directors of news organizations legally accountable for the veracity of the information transmitted. The decree also demanded that all news organizations transmitting cables beyond the national borders deposit up to $50,000 in the National Bank as a guarantee against potential infringements of the new law.[102] Like the Sánchez Sorondo bill, then, the Justo decree sought in part to establish accountability within the newspaper industry for publication content, and placed that responsibility directly upon the shoulders of newspaper proprietors and directors.

The measure also threatened to set the pace of information flow between Argentina and the outside world back by decades. Faced with stiff opposition from the Argentine commercial press and the U.S. news agencies, Justo immediately suspended the decree's implementation pending further investigation.[103] Even with the subsequent delay of the Justo administration in reaching any final decision on the legality and convenience of the measure, editorialists at *La Nación* pronounced that "the decree is dead" less than a month after its announcement.[104] By the middle of September, the opposition to it bore fruit: Justo revoked the "absurd decree" in its entirety, though his repeal reasserted that outgoing cable transmissions bear the signature of newspaper owners or their delegates.[105]

Both the Sánchez Sorondo bill and the Justo decree sought to rework the juridical boundaries of the relationship between state and press, but their proponents' arguments for doing so were sharply different. Unlike the Conservative senator's bill, President Justo's executive decree was not inspired by corporatist aspirations for a statist absorption of civil society. Instead, it marked the extent to which the economic underpinnings of the Argentine commercial press had broadened, entangling themselves with the economic infrastructure projects of an Argentine state itself in rapid expansion. Not surprisingly, this intertwining of press and state activities set the stage for precisely the type of legal ambiguities embodied in the Justo measure. The decree's justifications for state intervention in the transmission of news by cable lay not just in the larger interests of protecting the nation from the consequences of false news sent abroad, but in the fact that "such information uses the communications services run by the state or under its vigilance, and [the state] is thus involuntarily serving as a vehicle for that information's dissemination."[106] Rather than a corporatist-inspired attempt to chip away at the autonomy of civil society, the Justo measure rested upon something far simpler: a recognition of the economic expansion of both the Argentine state and the commercial press itself, a transformation that had *already* refashioned the relationship between state and press in practice.

Where the supporters of the Law for the Protection of the Press had sought to undermine the liberal ideological underpinnings of journalism practice, its failure reflected a broader phenomenon of the Argentine 1930s: despite the shattering of the liberal consensus, no comparably powerful alternatives had yet emerged. Justo's invocation of more pragmatic principles in his press decree would ultimately prove more powerful, precisely because he tended to sidestep ideological confrontation. Even though they ultimately failed, both measures, together with the initial creation of the Sección Prensa, signaled the existence of multiple fissures within and around the newspaper industry, which would only become more pronounced over the following decade as the regulatory activities of the Argentine state grew, the corporatist tendencies of sectors of the Argentine military reemerged, and political polarization increased. It is precisely out of these struggles within and around the newspaper industry that Peronist media policies would take shape.

"Workers of the Pen"

Attempts to rework the relationship between state and press revealed the weakening political consensus regarding the social role of journalism as an integral element of the broader crisis of Argentine liberalism. Yet a parallel dispute also emerged from within the ranks of working journalists themselves over the nature of their profession. By the mid-1920s, the commercial transformation of the Buenos Aires press had created a newspaper industry whose economic and social complexity the proprietor-journalists of the nineteenth-century press could scarcely have imagined. While the rapid growth of the Buenos Aires newspaper industry after 1880 had fundamentally altered relations of production in the newsroom, no corresponding transformation had occurred in journalists' professional ideology nor in national labor law.

In the course of the 1930s, however, the ambiguous position of journalists within the broader array of Argentine social classes—an ambiguity bolstered by conceptions of "the press" as an internally coherent set of institutions and of journalism as a strictly cultural activity—sat increasingly uneasily with both the rising social demands of working journalists and the growing willingness of state officials to recognize those demands as legitimate. Class conflict in the heart of the newspaper industry—the newsroom—became increasingly difficult to contain within the confines of mutual aid societies like the Círculo de la Prensa. By the end of the 1930s, then, a distinct understanding of journalism practice as a form of wage labor had emerged alongside notions of journalism as an exclusively cultural activity. Tensions between normative conceptions of the press as a public forum and the self-evidently private, commercial nature of the newspaper industry reflected a fissure between working journalists and newspaper proprietors that would only deepen with the rise of Perón.

This fissure had first become clear in 1919, when the journalists of the newly formed Sindicato de Periodistas y Afines mounted a strike against *La Prensa* over the right to unionize. For its organizers, the strike signified a profound questioning of their professional self-image. As one of them, Octavio Palazzolo, would later recall, "we journalists had reached a turning point, asking ourselves for the first time what we were within the social body. Salaried workers? Did we constitute a special class, as some intellectuals claimed?" Working journalists, Palazzolo recognized, by no means had agreed upon the answers to those questions, even if for him the class status of his colleagues remained clear: "On one side were those who, puffed up with vanity, continued feeding the legend of the completely disinterested journalist, Quixote-like, heroic, who lived only to spread ideas; on the other side were those of us who had risen above that magnificent pretext [to see that we were] destined to collect hunger for a salary, to enrich the businesses or enable the luxuries of some director-proprietor."[107] Even when printers of the Federación Gráfica Bonaerense joined the journalists, however, the strike failed dramatically and the journalists' union disintegrated. Still, at least three of the participants in the action, journalists Octavio Palazzolo and José Gabriel and printer Sebastián Marotta, would play important roles in press labor relations in the coming years.[108] Though clearly premature, the *La Prensa* strike raised the possibility that the growing class divisions within an increasingly complex newspaper industry might produce not only rising journalist discontent, but coordinated labor actions involving different social groups within the newspaper production process.[109]

Newspaper proprietors overwhelmingly rejected suggestions that, as Palazzolo and the other strikers of 1919 argued, romantic notions of journalism practice as a purely cultural activity did little to hide the capitalist nature of the commercial newspaper industry. Instead, they maintained that newspaper finances remained peripheral to the press's true function as a vehicle of citizenship, expression of public opinion, and check on state power. Proprietors and editorialists at *La Prensa* and *La Nación* maintained this stance well into the Peronist years. Even Natalio Botana could assert that *Crítica* was not in fact a commercial entity, though for him that was less a statement of principle than a means of claiming that the paper's relationship with its public was one not of cold commodity exchange, but of sentimental affinity.[110] This anticommercial element of journalism discourse drew its strength from a conflation of journalism's normative cultural, political, and representative character and assertions regarding the actual functioning of the newspaper industry. Claims that the press *was not* a commercial entity precisely because it *was not supposed to be* remained an integral component of press legitimacy but began to unravel with increasing speed in the 1930s and 1940s.

The world economic crisis of the 1930s brought the question to the fore as growing state economic interventionism inevitably affected an Argentine newspaper industry intimately linked to the world market. In December 1933, the Círculo de la Prensa appealed to Minister of the Economy Pinedo for an exception to new foreign exchange controls, declaring that since local news organizations by necessity imported virtually all of their newsprint, ink, machinery, parts, photo plates, and wire services, the new rates would effectively devastate the press. More importantly, they argued, "a newspaper is not, by definition, a commercial enterprise. . . . In truth, it is a public service" and therefore should remain exempt from "economic" laws.[111] The regulatory gestures made by Matías Sánchez Sorondo and President Justo, similarly, rested in part on claims that the reality of private newspaper economics had begun to collide with claims of journalism's public social function.

This recognition by state officials of the newspaper industry's economic character overlapped with growing pressure from many working journalists to gain recognition of their roles as salaried workers. In fact, just as the Argentine Senate considered the Sánchez Sorondo bill For the Protection of the Press, the Chamber of Deputies debated legislation establishing a retirement fund for journalists and printers. The measure, which responded to a concerted effort by members of the Círculo de la Prensa beginning in the mid-1920s, finally reached the Congress after members of the organization's executive board appealed personally to President Justo in mid-1932.[112] In August of that year,

Justo's minister of the interior, Leopoldo Melo, submitted draft legislation for a joint journalist-printer pension law, a version of which received preliminary approval by the Congress's lower house in September 1934.[113] The Senate also approved the measure, adding a single modification at the behest of the Federación Gráfica Bonaerense.[114] The bill was approved unanimously by the lower house in June of the following year.[115]

The pension law, however, met with concerted resistance. Even before legislative approval, posters began to appear around the city denouncing the law as contrary to the interests of Argentine workers.[116] Opposition only intensified after approval, with several newspaper owners supporting dissident printers in lobbying for a presidential veto of the measure. Luís Ramiconi, the Socialist head of the FGB, sent a public letter to President Justo denouncing the campaign, proclaiming it a product of "industrialist" manipulation of transient labor organizations that had never volunteered their own suggestions for the modification of the bill.[117] The situation also revealed a tension within the profession that would only increase in the coming years: claiming health and family reasons, the Círculo de la Prensa's president, Juan José Navarro Lahitte (editor in chief [Secretario General] of La Prensa) and treasurer, Alfredo Calisto (also of La Prensa) suddenly resigned their positions just as the bill left Congress.[118] Ezequiel Paz also took the unusual step of refusing to print the Círculo de la Prensa's declaration in defense of the pension law in the news section of La Prensa, accepting it only as a $5,000 paid advertisement.[119] President Justo did, in fact, veto the law on July 8, arguing that the "last-minute" inclusion of printers in the bill introduced serious complications for its implementation—even though the minister of the interior, Leopoldo Melo, had included printers in his draft legislation submitted to Congress nearly three years earlier.[120] That less than a week later Justo delivered the executive decree regulating the use of wire services only compounded the array of tensions that had begun to build within and around the newspaper industry.

Nonetheless, the legal precedent that newspaper proprietors feared in the legislation—the classification of newsworkers as employees of commercial enterprises—soon came from the courts. In two separate decisions in mid-1935, federal judges ruled in favor of Manuel Sofovich and Oscar di Leo, who had begun litigation for dismissal without compensation against the owners of Noticias Gráficas and La Prensa, respectively.[121] Both decisions rested upon a determination that journalists did, in fact, qualify as employees under the recently revised Argentine Commercial Code, an expansive interpretation of the new law that remained consistent with other rulings in the course of the 1930s.[122] In the case against Ezequiel Paz, Judge Eduardo Broquen rejected defense assertions that the La Prensa owner did not qualify as a merchant (comerciante) under the Code since his newspaper was nothing more than a means of propagating news. According to the judge, La Prensa was "a periodical in which the ingenuity and intellectual labor of many people is done for the advantage of those who own the periodical. And when we add to this that a good part of the newspaper is notoriously reserved for paid advertising, one cannot doubt that the activity has as its end, in addition to whatever higher motive, the idea of procuring a profit. [This is] the essential element of an act of commerce." *La Prensa*, Broquen concluded, was "clearly a mercantile establishment."[123]

Even if the judges who handled these cases and the subsequent appeals remained hesitant to classify journalists unequivocally as workers, the implication of the rulings was clear: the newsroom could not remain somehow aloof from the more general division between labor and capital that had come to dominate the newspaper industry. Luís Praprotnik, one of the Círculo de la Prensa's more prolabor Executive Board members, argued before the organization that the decisions confirmed the basic equivalence of newsworkers that President Justo had denied by his veto of the journalist and printer pension law. For Praprotnik, the rulings brought "journalists or intellectual workers," administrative employees, and printers to "the same level of juridical equality" before newspaper businesses, setting broader solidarity within the newspaper industry on a much firmer legal footing. Perhaps more importantly, Praprotnik maintained, the new Commercial Code and the court rulings "open unsuspected horizons . . . for a future labor organization of newsworkers" to which government officials would have no choice but to grant legal standing.[124]

For many journalists the Círculo de la Prensa's inability to guarantee enactment of the pension law demonstrated the need for just such an organization, while the ambiguity of subsequent court rulings on the status of journalists under the Commercial Code lent the issue even greater urgency. Following a series of contradictory judicial decisions in the city of Córdoba, the Executive Board of the Círculo de la Prensa de Córdoba invited its sister organizations around the country to attend a National Congress of Journalists to be held in that city in mid-1938.[125] In an open letter, the journalists from Córdoba enumerated a preliminary agenda for the meeting that, in avoiding "the formulation of purely lyrical questions without practical ends," would instead lay the basis for legislation and other actions that "might elevate the moral and material level of the journalist." Rather than simply lobbying for "press issues," the Córdoba journalists proposed five basic items for the Congress to consider: the establishment of a national federation of journalists; the legislative approval of a journalist's statute to regulate working conditions within the profession; the passage of a law granting life and disability insurance for journalists; the creation of a national registry of journalists; and the establishment of a standardized pay scale.[126] The Executive Board of the Buenos Aires Círculo de la Prensa embraced the proposal, adding that in addition to considering the issues of retirements, pensions, and a professional statute, the Congress should also consider the broader issue of freedom of the press in the country.[127]

On May 24, 1938, the Círculo de la Prensa de Córdoba published an official statement welcoming the delegates from around the country. The message set the tone for the meeting, stressing the fundamental importance of proper working conditions for the nation's journalists. "Without any justification," the declaration read, "some still speak of the 'beautiful bohemian life of journalism,'" a notion that only insulted "the most respectable intellectual workers that society has today" in its anachronistic denial of journalism's transformation with the emergence of the modern newspaper industry.[128] Instead, the Congress would "break with these nineteenth-century concepts, proper to the extinct romantic and decadent poets, in order to place the guild [gremio] front and center."

The participants in the Congress did indeed address the workplace issues that had become increasingly urgent for the nation's journalists. While initial discussions centered on the establishment of June 7 as "Journalist's Day" in commemoration of Mariano Moreno and the broader importance of freedom of the press, delegates quickly engaged the central issue. The Córdoba delegates had prepared a framework for a "Collective Contract of Journalistic Labor," which was overwhelmingly embraced by the Congress as a whole. In presenting the draft, Ernesto Barabraham justified the measure as a response to an historical shift in the nature of the press, declaring that "times have modified the structure of the daily press. Publicity, the rapidity of information, the great circulation levels have all transformed the bastions of the ideal, of reason, and of law into vast commercial enterprises."[129] For Barabraham, the structural transformation of the press into the modern newspaper industry had made "the demands of the proletariat" far more relevant to the "workers of the pen," those "intellectual workers" who engaged in journalism practice as paid employees.

Like Matías Sánchez Sorondo, Barabraham argued that the Argentine state had a fundamental role to play in the functioning of the press, but for completely different reasons than those proposed by the proto-fascist senator. The complexity of the modern press's division of labor, the journalist maintained, made the once private nature of journalist-proprietor contracts a public matter, as only the state could guarantee the consistent enforcement of general labor laws. In the increasingly common disputes between working journalists and newspaper proprietors, the state was the only entity capable of defending the "workers of the pen."[130] The delegates in attendance did more than approve the draft: they also established the Argentine Federation of Journalists (Federación Argentina de Periodistas—FAP) as a national labor union that would lobby to make it law.

This dual assertion of a class divide in the newsroom and the state's potentially benevolent role vis-à-vis the press raised the possibility of greater soli-

Fig. 7 Octavio Palazzolo addresses the founding meeting of the Federación Argentina de Periodistas, Córdoba, 1938.

darity within the profession, but nonetheless precipitated a fissure between journalist organizations. The Círculo de la Prensa of the Federal Capital—the nation's largest—had sent a particularly active delegation to the Córdoba meeting, including the organization's president from 1936 to 1938, *La Nación*'s Juan Valmaggia. Despite the Círculo de la Prensa General Assembly's approval of the society's entrance into the newly founded FAP—whose first secretary general, Octavio Palazzolo, came from the Círculo's own executive board—the relationship between the two organizations quickly deteriorated. The return of *La Prensa*'s Navarro Lahitte to the Círculo's presidency in mid-1938 introduced an element hostile to the turn toward labor unionism that membership in the Federation signified. In a particularly contentious meeting of the Círculo de la Prensa executive board in September 1938, Navarro Lahitte proposed the organization's withdrawal from the FAP on the grounds that the Círculo's statutes prohibited any limits on its autonomy.[131] The argument proved extraordinarily awkward: not only had Valmaggia and the other Buenos Aires delegates welcomed the formation of the FAP at the Córdoba meeting, but the agenda for the gathering had met with explicit approval from the Círculo de la Prensa in its letter accepting the invitation from Córdoba. The journalist Congress had received ample and sympathetic coverage in the Círculo de la Prensa's own publications.[132] For Palazzolo, this drive to override the Círculo's General Assembly and withdraw from the FAP responded to the continued "hegemony" of proprietor interests within the mutual aid society; Navarro Lahitte's opposition to the labor union, Palazzolo noted, curiously corresponded to the position held by the owner of *La Prensa*, the newspaper where Navarro Lahitte worked.[133]

The contentious withdrawal of the Círculo de la Prensa from the FAP dealt a serious blow to the journalists' labor federation, while giving the national organization a particularly complex character. Journalists in the Federal Capital interested in pursuing association with the Federation found themselves obliged to form a new FAP affiliate from the ground up.[134] Octavio Palazzolo, who had advocated a class-based journalist organization for over a decade, made clear that the new Asociación de Periodistas de Buenos Aires (APBA) differed sharply from the service-oriented mutual aid society that had deserted the FAP: "in one the union concept would prevail; in the other, mutualism. In the Círculo de la Prensa, medical treatment, medicine and tombs [panteón]; in the Asociación de Periodistas, union struggle, purely and exclusively."[135] By contrast, most associations from the Argentine interior had affiliated themselves with the FAP nationally while preserving their own mutualist inclusion of working journalists and local director-proprietors. The situation thus compounded the class ambiguities of professional journalists with a geographic tension: the journalists of the APBA unequivocally viewed their organization—and, by extension, the FAP—as a labor union standing against newspaper capital; organizations from the interior tended to retain a greater heterogeneity of membership and ambiguity of class identification.

Two factors nonetheless brought the FAP and Círculo de la Prensa together for the time being. In mid-1939, journalists succeeded in pressuring Congress and the executive to enact a journalist pension law—this time, without printers.[136] The rush to adequately capitalize the pension fund within the five-year period stipulated by the new law brought the rank and file of both organizations together as journalists sought to monitor the compliance of newspaper proprietors. The reemergence of concerted state censorship also worked to diminish tensions within the profession by presenting journalists and proprietors with a common problem. Just over a week after the Japanese attack on Pearl Harbor brought the world conflict to the Americas, Argentine president Ramón Castillo declared the nation once again under a state of siege. This suspension of constitutional guarantees placed special restrictions on the national press, as the Federal Police came to monitor periodicals for any content inconsistent with the official position of neutrality in the global conflict.[137] Several of the more daring commercial dailies and political periodicals subsequently faced intermittent suspension and harassment by the Federal Police.[138] As a result, delegates to the Third Congress of the Federación Argentina de Periodistas, held in July 1942, spent more time addressing the pressing issue of state sanctions against journalists and newspaper institutions—one of the Círculo de la Prensa's traditional functions—than they did debating either the still-shaky pension law or the FAP's goal of a statute regulating professional employment.[139]

This greater coincidence of efforts, however, could not surmount now-established institutional divisions. If the struggles surrounding the pension law had united the rank-and-file members of both organizations in common cause, it had by no means mended the deep mutual suspicion that continued to dominate within the leadership of the FAP and the Círculo de la Prensa. Nor did the common threat of censorship mend the rift: in late 1942, an overture by FAP president Leandro Reynés to the Círculo de la Prensa proposing that both organizations coordinate appeals for the lifting of the state of siege met with a polite rebuff from the Círculo's president, *La Prensa*'s Adolfo Lanús.[140]

The Círculo de la Prensa's abandonment of the FAP and the subsequent creation of the APBA revealed that not only had class tensions in Buenos Aires newsrooms become too complex to contain within the context of the journalists' mutual aid society, but these disputes were also now impossible to ignore. The institutionalization of the split between those who emphasized the class character of the newsroom's division of labor and those who maintained a more traditional view of the press's internal organization would prove too difficult to overcome in the near term. In the 1930s, a dual fissure had emerged within the commercial press's network of relationships, one that divided journalists among themselves, and working journalists from newspaper proprietors. These fundamental disagreements over nothing less than the nature of journalism practice and the juridical status of newspapers as institutional entities—at heart, disputes over what the press *was* and what the press *should be*—had done much to dissolve illusions of unity within the press; as the decade drew to a close, these tensions remained far from resolved.

The Commercial Press and the Authoritarian Turn

The invocation of state-of-siege powers, however, had also revealed the Castillo regime's clear weakness. General Justo's successor, President Roberto Ortiz, had failed to bring legislation through Congress that would have limited press commentary on the international conflict, while Castillo himself, who had assumed the presidency due to Ortiz's diabetes-induced blindness, lacked even the limited democratic credentials of his predecessor.[141] The early 1940s, in fact, found the nation still caught in the worsening crisis of political legitimacy brought on by the military coup of 1930 and deepened by over a decade of electoral fraud and political corruption. Castillo's attempt to impose a particularly unpopular conservative politician as his political heir in the elections of 1944 opened the possibility that members of the Argentine political class would call upon the military—the ultimate guarantor of national politics since 1930—to validate the most blatant case of electoral fraud to date. If Castillo assumed a particularly hard line with regard to the daily functioning of the Buenos Aires press, that censorship was an increasingly necessary part of a political project in clear disarray.

It also signaled the weaknesses of the media strategies adopted by both the de facto regime of Uriburu and the fraudulent democracy of General Justo. Neither positive efforts to create a new form of factional journalism and quasi-state media apparatus nor negative attempts to legislate new constraints on publishing had managed to fully reshape the relationship between press, state, and the leaders of different political projects. Similarly, despite the best efforts of FAP members, they still had not achieved the goal that constituted the union's very reason to exist: the legal recognition of journalists as workers. Yet the 1930s had witnessed the first serious, sustained challenges to traditional liberal conceptions of the press and the social role of journalism since the 1880s. That these challenges came not just from those wielding state power but also from those located in the heart of the press's institutional structure only revealed the potential severity of the newspaper industry's incipient crisis of legitimacy.

The ouster of Castillo by the military in June 1943 would inaugurate a period of political and social transformation more far-reaching than even its protagonists expected. Within the context of the dramatic reworking of the relationships between state and civil society, the emergence of newly powerful social sectors and heightened factional political competition, the ruptures within the press's network of relationships in Buenos Aires, which had suddenly become a matter of public dispute in the course of the 1930s, would only deepen. Out of these conflicts over the nature of the press and the social role of journalism, together with increasingly fierce factional struggles for access to the power of journalism, Peronists would ultimately fashion a dramatically new media project.

PART 2

THE TRIUMPH OF SILENCE

> [It is necessary] to consider the social function served by the press as an activity of public interest and to proceed, therefore, with its adequate regulation.
>
> **—Decree 18.407, December 31, 1943**

For the second time since the world crisis began in 1930, the city of Buenos Aires filled with the sounds of sporadic gunfire, tanks, sirens, and marching soldiers while thick smoke poured from burning buses and streetcars. Jubilant civilians occupied the Plaza de Mayo, embracing passing soldiers in appreciation and rushing the entrance to the Casa Rosada in excitement. Yet the success of the military coup of June 4, 1943, depended less on these open displays of force and spontaneous civilian support than on what was neither seen nor heard publicly. In contrast to the deft political maneuvering of General Justo, Castillo had embraced clumsy political fraud, open corruption, and increasing repression, exhausting whatever tenuous democratic legitimacy the Concordancia governments might have enjoyed in the 1930s. As troops began to move against his government, President Castillo stood bereft of even rhetorical defense of his right to govern. "It was the triumph of silence," wrote one *La Nación* journalist: the active silence of the secret GOU military lodge that had organized the coup, and the passive silence of the regime's would-be defenders.[1]

The coup marked the final dissolution of a political arrangement in agonizing disarray even as it opened possibilities for a profound transformation of Argentine politics. By the time he had begun to prepare the path for his even more unpopular successor, Castillo had not only undermined the ability of the Concordancia to govern, but he had inadvertently granted broad de facto legitimacy to virtually any military faction that might engineer his removal from power. As a result, few failed to embrace the call for political renewal issued by the new authorities, even if Argentines remained sharply divided on why that renewal was needed and what it implied. For supporters of liberal democracy, the problem lay not in the Argentine state's nineteenth-century institutional structures, but in their abuse and disregard by government authorities; the ouster of Castillo was a necessary step toward the restoration and honest implementation of the Constitution of 1853. For right-leaning opponents, the corruption of the Castillo regime and growing political polarization were not the cause of the nation's political and social degeneration, but mere symptoms of liberalism's inherent decadence.[2]

The majority in the newspaper industry placed themselves firmly in the former group. With their professional practice already tightly restricted, scores of journalists detained, and newspapers repeatedly suspended and intervened, the editors and journalists at most Buenos Aires commercial dailies greeted the military movement with guarded optimism. For them, Castillo's removal from power opened the possibility of reversing the inroads made by official censors and the police into what journalists regarded as their exclusive competence: public opinion formation. The new regime's promise of a swift return to full constitutional rule implied the definitive end of state intervention in press operations and the lifting of the state of siege. The conspirators of June 4, then, seemed ready to perform a necessary task in protecting the "free press" from state interference. As a result, early military assertions of devotion to constitutional principles largely met with the press's enthusiastic approval, as did the de facto government's project of "cleansing" tainted and untrustworthy elements from the political class.

Yet if official pronouncements in the days and weeks following the coup provided ample rhetorical fuel for optimistic speculation by newspaper editors and journalists, the new government's actions belied the military rulers' avowed constitutionalist tendencies. In its first six months, the new regime enforced the terms of the state of siege—including restrictions on the press—even more strictly than Castillo, while its prohibition of the Buenos Aires underworld *lunfardo* slang necessitated the creation of radio-friendly alternative versions of popular tangos.[3] Newspaper closures and the vigilance of government censors only increased as the de facto government became more entrenched. Viewing the armed forces as the only national institution untainted by the corruption of the previous thirteen years, the military regime consistently positioned the state as a barrier between a fragile social order and the "indiscretion of the journalist."

Rather than simply restoring the constitutional rule that many in the newspaper industry had hoped would follow quickly, the military coup would ultimately open a new chapter in Argentine history. As the regime consolidated, the growing marginalization of "democratic" military officers in favor of members of the nationalist GOU placed state power behind a new, dramatically different political project. Stopgap measures aimed at controlling the press during the proclaimed national emergency gave way to concerted efforts to create permanent "harmony" between state officials and the press, as part of a broader attempt to transcend all social conflict and organize the nation along corporatist lines. Growing government intervention in information production and distribution sought to bind the press to a political project designed not just to overcome the immediate crisis of Argentine democracy, but fundamentally to refashion the country's social and political institutions.

The regime's architects largely failed in these attempts to integrate the press into this broader project by force: as problematic as it had become, the continued broad hegemony of traditional liberal conceptions of the nature of the press, the social role of journalism, and the relationship between the state and this key institution of civil society nonetheless worked against the military's vision of an acclamatory or even silent press. The repression exercised by the military against broad sectors of the press, furthermore, tended to draw journalists and newspaper owners together, dampening the newsroom conflicts of the previous decade. By depending on a level of coercion that could not be sustained without ultimately damaging the regime's legitimacy, central elements of the de facto government's media project simply proved inadequate for any long-term political project. Still, the experience of the first nine months following the coup of June 1943 did lay the basis for a much more profound, sophisticated, and effective rearticulation of state-press relations in the coming years.

"Patriotic Collaboration" and the Integrative Function of Journalism

Hopes that the June coup would provide the necessary springboard to a democratic restoration did not depend solely on perceptions, based on its actions to that point, that the new regime would reverse the dictatorial and pro-Nazi tendencies of the government it displaced. In fact, pronouncements by the coup's visible leaders seemed to confirm that they sought a return to the full reign of the Constitution of 1853 and, by implication, a withdrawal of the state from the nation's newsrooms. Within this context, calls for press cooperation in a short-term "cleansing" of political society appeared less an unequivocal subjugation of the newspaper industry than a temporary collaboration between the power of journalism and the power of the state aimed not at the final dissolution of liberal Argentina, but at its revival.

In this sense, the initial pronouncements of military authorities were encouraging for journalists and newspaper proprietors alike. On the morning of the coup, the provisional president of the republic, General Arturo Rawson, declared from the balcony of the Casa Rosada that the army had "taken to the streets not precisely to make a revolution, but in order to fulfill constitutional precepts. The constitution gives [the armed forces] the duty of protecting order and defending [the country's] institutions. The institutions were not being respected."[4] Even Rawson's removal from power just twenty-four hours later would not hinder the optimism of those who sought a quick return to institutional normality. General Pedro Ramírez, Rawson's successor, enjoyed significant democratic legitimacy: only days before, the Radical Party had secretly offered Ramírez, then Castillo's minister of war, its backing in the upcoming presidential elections as a means of ensuring military compliance with clean suffrage. Castillo's response, the immediate and humiliating dismissal of Ramírez, had at once prompted the coup and validated Ramírez's democratic credentials.

In the days following the coup, the editorial staffs of *La Prensa* and *La Nación* sought to reinforce the regime's proclaimed liberal democratic intent. Writers at *La Prensa* argued that the republic already possessed "the sure resource to find its orientation in these story days": the constitution, which codified "the institutions of the fatherland."[5] Similarly, editorialists at *La Nación* remarked that "public opinion has duly noted" the new authorities' initial declarations of respect for constitutional rule and sought to discourage any modifications to the charter by the regime.[6] The editors of both papers, then, addressed the military government and the upper spheres of the national elite with a dual message: not only had the regime's spokesmen assumed the correct posture in announcing their constitutionalist intentions, but violation of this democratic promise would prompt the rapid evaporation of public support and make impossible the regime's proclaimed goal of national unity.

Moreover, *La Prensa*'s editorialists insisted that public debate on the questions of government, as antagonistic as it might become, provided the best solution to the fundamental problems of the country and would be the most productive form of "collaboration" with the new regime. This dialogue would bypass the discredited and corrupt political parties and find its natural home in the primary organ of political communication and public opinion formation: the press. Yet this hardly constituted a call for generalized public debate. The weakness of Argentine democracy and the root of the present crisis, the paper's editorialists claimed, lay in the failure of those "who are intellectually above the general level" to participate more assertively in social decision making, ceding ground instead to "the demagogues, the greatest plague of this century."[7] Rather than providing a forum open equally to all citizens, the editorialists at *La Prensa* clearly implied, the power of the press should now allow Argentine professionals to make felt "the natural gravity of their superiority"; and military authorities would be wise to heed their advice.[8]

The journalists and directors of *La Nación* and *La Prensa*, of course, knew of the conflicting ideological currents within the armed forces. In fact, much of the praise of liberal tendencies within the government was a thinly veiled attempt to bolster moderates in an increasingly uncomfortable balance of pro-

Allied "democrats" and pro-Axis "fascists" in the de facto government. Both papers, however, retained the cautious stance that they had assumed with the imposition of the state of siege eighteen months earlier, dutifully reproducing government manifestos and refraining from unauthorized commentary. The staff of *Crítica* appeared even more wary of provoking the new regime's ire: the paper's director, Raúl Damonte Taborda, briefly took refuge within the Uruguayan embassy until the military government had fully stabilized.

Such caution was not unwarranted. On June 6, the regime closed the Argentine Communist Party newspapers *La Hora* and *Orientación*, detaining fourteen editors and journalists; only General Rawson's removal from the de facto government saved *La Hora*'s director from summary execution.[9] The pro-Allied periodicals *Nueva Gaceta* and *Argentina Libre* suffered similar fates, while authorities suspended the principal newspaper of the city of Mendoza, *Los Andes*, for having strayed from official accounts of the military uprising.[10] In the morning hours of June 8, President Ramírez signed a communiqué authorizing civilian and military authorities to detain immediately all those who propagated rumors or released "alarmist or tendentious" news.[11] The message such moves sent could not be clearer: the restrictions of the state of siege still held, and the new government would enforce them with vigor.

Although the closures of periodicals and detentions of journalists in the immediate aftermath of the coup were well within the regime's state-of-siege powers, a fundamentally different discourse regarding the social role of journalism quickly emerged from inside the military government. In remarks to reporters just days after the coup, the new minister of war and a leading figure within the GOU, General Edelmiro J. Farrell, presented a conception of the press that would become increasingly important as his own power grew. General Farrell proclaimed the press a necessary ally of the regime, since it "is, undoubtedly, a guide orienting public opinion in the judgment of the work that the armed institutions are carrying out," and the means by which official actions could come to the attention and "appreciation of the people."[12] More than a simple affirmation of the press's social-communicative function, the pronouncement affirmed Farrell's break with ideas of the press's independent and even inherently antagonistic relationship to the state. Instead, the minister of war suggested, the power of journalism and the power of the state should work together to ensure the success of the military's "cleansing" mission.

In Farrell's vision of this process, however, the press would act as a clearly subordinate partner. Echoing the notions of Sánchez Sorondo during his term as Uriburu's minister of the interior (1930–32), Farrell called on the press to lend its "patriotic collaboration" to the military regime; in effect, the press should facilitate a fluid and undistorted flow of communication from a military government bereft of an organized political base to the general public, and guide it toward a favorable view of the new government. This did not imply, however, that the press might play an active role in orienting the regime. Farrell left little doubt that he envisioned the press's flow of communication as unidirectional: "[the press's collaboration] does not appear indispensable to inform the men of arms of their correctness or error."[13] Even political debate circumscribed within the Argentine elite—the kind encouraged in the pages of *La Prensa*—would find little sympathy among the new authorities. Blurring the dividing line between state and press, the general saw the press as an agent whose primary task was bolstering the hegemony not just of the general social order, but of this regime in particular, integrating the general population into the political project of the armed forces as passive supporters. Thus, in addition to imposing tighter constraints on reporting and expression, members of the regime's dominant current also began to envision a state-press relationship sharply at odds with the traditional liberal conception of the power of journalism as a check on the power of the state.

Ironically, such clearly antiliberal views of the press as the public relations extension of a nascent "revolutionary" state allowed for significant slippage between Farrell's discourse and many journalists' own ambiguous conceptions of their profession. Praising the minister of war's "exact insight into the sense of the function of Argentine journalism," one *La Nación* contributor claimed that Farrell's notions of the proper relationship between state and press were rooted in the constitution, which had "placed [the press] in the same field as state institutions."[14] Instead of the press being a subordinate instrument of state power, as Farrell clearly envisioned, the power of journalism resided alongside the state power proper, and by the press exercising its critical function, its "constructive labor contributes powerfully to the betterment of government practices." That the minister of war recognized this, the editorialist disingenuously asserted, marked a clear demonstration of the provisional government's fundamentally "democratic character."[15] A few weeks later, in a piece titled "The collaboration of the press," another *La Nación* editorialist offered an even more adventurous reading of Farrell's statements. The author took pains to distinguish between factional journalism and "those newspapers consecrated exclusively to the defense of the public interest, with impersonal ends and in the name of doctrinal principles." While the former had presumably become sullied by the political corruption of the past decade, the latter "have as their duty a work of transcendental convenience in republican life, and *are the most authorized interpreters of the national spirit.*"[16] Like editorialists at *La Prensa*, then, those at *La Nación* seemed willing to abandon blanket assertions of citizens' rights of expression in favor of a public discourse restricted largely to those in control of the "serious press." Hovering above politics, this press should assume its place alongside the military as an untainted institution, collaborating not simply in the integration of the general population into the de facto government's political project, but in the shaping of that project itself.

Such wishful thinking notwithstanding, "the triumph of silence," the victory of that which refuses to communicate its identity and intentions, of the unknown, was also the defeat of the liberal journalist. Extremely opaque and contradictory in their ideological pronouncements, Ramírez and his cabinet certainly did not look for guidance in the "public opinion" expressed in the pages of the commercial press, regardless of how distinguished, disinterested, and supportive those who expressed that opinion might be. Instead, the new regime presented the general public with a rapid series of sweeping measures and provincial interventions while tightening controls on the expression of dissent. That the primary driving force within the government was now the hermetic GOU—the nationalist military lodge of whose very existence many were still uncertain—served only to complicate matters. That the staff of *La Nación* had hit closer to the mark regarding the nature of the new government in its succinct early characterization of the military coup only became clearer as the months wore on, leading many Argentines to refer to the military regime as simply the "Revolution of Silence."[17]

In fact, the political discourse of journalists at both *La Nación* and *La Prensa* became increasingly ambiguous in the wake of the coup, as a combination of the state-of-siege restrictions and general support of the regime's actions dampened editorial critique. *La Prensa* editorials fully backed government measures designed to eliminate corruption within the existing political parties, and even insisted that promised elections should not take place until that process had reached its conclusion. Echoing military justifications for the seizure of power, editorialists argued that only the "pure" citizens who remained unstained by cases of corruption could legitimately govern.[18] Those at *La Nación*, similarly, saw the "cleansing" of public administration and the political parties as "unavoidably necessary."[19] Both papers covered official events extensively, dutifully reproducing government communiqués while continuing to obfuscate criticism of official policies using the same tactic they had invoked while addressing General Farrell's pronouncements on the press: the abstract praise of opposing principles.[20]

Crítica proved most directly amenable to the intentions of the de facto regime. Rather than echoing the call from *La Prensa* and *La Nación* for greater participation of the "most apt" in a broad debate over the future political direction of the country, the paper's editors instead urged readers simply to trust the new authorities. The first editorial following the coup—prudently published only after Ramírez had formally taken office—exhorted readers, in the paper's stylized populist fashion, to "have faith" in the new authorities: "Workers, soldiers, merchants, students, men of the cities and countryside; hardworking builders of the nationality in the thousand anonymous forms of constant and daily effort; Argentines, all of you, in whose hearts might dwell anxiety and uncertainty: history is being made and it is time to have faith. . . . Let us have confidence in the men that assume the enormous labor of reviving the republic."²¹ Reflecting the conception of the press elaborated by the minister of war, *Crítica* director Raúl Damonte Taborda, ever sensitive to the shifting balance of political power, placed the paper fully in line with the demands of the new regime.

Yet the staff of *Crítica* did more than simply editorialize support of the cleansing of the political system begun by Ramírez. Before the month's end, the paper ran a (likely invented) series of short interviews with lawyers, politicians, bakers, construction workers, students, and teachers, providing a consistent voice of praise from all social classes.²² Damonte Taborda's paper wildly applauded federal intervention in the province of Buenos Aires and the resulting displacement of Governor Rodolfo Moreno and the notoriously corrupt mayor of Avellaneda, Alberto Barceló, demonizing both men despite their having been close associates of *Crítica* founder Natalio Botana.²³ General Farrell's denunciation of the work of the dissolved anti-Nazi parliamentary Investigative Commission on Anti-Argentine Activities also found an amplified echo in the paper, as editorialists drew a sharp division between the commission's early work under the presidency of Damonte Taborda and its "decadence" under that of Socialist Juan Antonio Solari. Clearly at the behest of Damonte Taborda himself, *Crítica* inexplicably found Moreno and former minister of the interior Miguel Culaciati (then under arrest) guilty of the commission's unnamed failures.²⁴

Perhaps more importantly, *Crítica* served as a reliable link between the government's increasingly prominent pro-Axis figures and the broad spectrum of working- and middle-class Argentines set firmly behind the Allies. Unequivocal denunciations of the Axis powers, of course, remained prohibited under the terms of the state of siege, yet reporting and editorial comments remained firmly sympathetic to the Yugoslav guerrillas, the Soviet Union, Britain, and the Spanish Republican government-in-exile. The edition of July 4, 1943, even included a special section dedicated to the independence of the United States and the beginning of a series on U.S. history, while the fall of Mussolini became yet another opportunity for the reaffirmation of *Crítica*'s supposedly "unsullied" antifascism.²⁵

Through constant praise and reinforcement of the regime's supposedly democratic character, constitutionalist intentions, and (often dubious) struggle against reactionary and corrupt forces at home, the antifascist credentials that founder Natalio Botana had earned for the paper were spent in bolstering the legitimacy of a government whose fascistic tendencies were becoming increasingly clear.²⁶ A caricature by Eduardo Alvarez in early July 1943 concisely stated the paper's stance vis-à-vis the growing power struggle within the de facto government. General Ramírez, seated behind the presidential desk and pointing to a portrait of "Gravedigger" Matías Sánchez Sorondo—the familiar

Justo-era *Crítica* caricature—remarks, "That portrait darkens the panorama of June. We have to get rid of it."²⁷ For *Crítica* readers the message was clear: just as *Crítica* had stood with General Justo against Sánchez Sorondo and other local admirers of Italian Fascism, so would it back President Ramírez against those same forces. Similarly, sycophantic adhesion to Ramírez and his cabinet—not an easy feat, considering that neither the president nor his ministers were terribly charismatic—placed national authorities before *Crítica*'s working-class audience in the most favorable context possible. *Crítica*, in essence, would serve the military government much as it had served General Justo a decade earlier: not as the voice of the urban popular classes, but as the regime's connection to the *chusma* (rabble).

Now, however, *Crítica*'s service as a public-relations agent of the de facto government had little to do with any personal or ideological affinity between the paper's owner and state officials. Instead, Damonte Taborda's practical adherence to Farrell's call for the press's "patriotic collaboration" was motivated by a complex ownership dispute involving the Botana heirs, only recently aggravated by a series of unexpected deaths. Following Natalio Botana's fatal automobile accident in August 1941, the intricate web of property titles established through *Crítica*'s official publisher, Buenos Aires Poligráfica, became a tangle as the Botana family wrangled for control. On February 6, 1943, at the behest of Raúl Damonte Taborda—husband of Botana's daughter Georgina—a federal court took control of the paper after allegations of fraud and illicit association led to the arrest of interim director Eduardo Bedoya and Botana's son Helvio.²⁸ Damonte Taborda's moves against his rivals proved well timed: just three weeks earlier, the Botana brothers' primary protector and the man who undoubtedly stood at the center of Buenos Aires Poligráfica, General Justo, died suddenly of a stroke, following his wife by only two weeks.²⁹ *Crítica*'s web of ownership titles did not come undone; with General Justo no longer an obstacle, Raúl Damonte Taborda now sought simply to cut through the knot.

Under the protection of President Castillo himself, Damonte Taborda assumed effective control of *Crítica* in the name of both his wife and his mother-in-law by virtue of a 5 million–peso loan from the Central Bank's Instituto Movilizador, leaving Botana's sons, Jaime and Helvio, fighting the seizure of the paper in the courts.³⁰ At the moment of the military coup of June 1943, *Crítica* remained technically in the hands of the judges, but with a new twist: having lost the protection of Castillo, Damonte Taborda now depended upon the goodwill of the de facto government to maintain control of the paper. Should *Crítica* suffer yet another of its habitual closures, Raúl Damonte Taborda would surely lose the paper, and with it not only his most powerful political weapon, but his livelihood. Even the *Crítica* campaigns against Natalio Botana's associates Alberto Barceló and Rodolfo Moreno in the weeks following the June coup responded as much to Damonte Taborda's drive against the Botana sons and other Buenos Aires Poligráfica shareholders as they did to the de facto government's campaign against powerful politicians.[31] When ownership of *Crítica* passed definitively into the hands of Damonte Taborda and his associates in November of 1943, the military regime had a new trump card to ensure the paper's cooperation: the money used to buy the remaining shares of Buenos Aires Poligráfica (now rebaptized simply Publicaciones, S.A.) had come in the form of a 10.4 million–peso official loan.[32] With a new slate of enemies and with the noose of debt around his neck, *Crítica*'s new owner would place few conditions on his paper's "patriotic collaboration."

The Limits of Patriotic Collaboration

While substantive differences regarding the press's proper role in the process underway emerged almost immediately after the coup, the ideological contest over the social role of journalism remained relatively subdued in the regime's early months. In the short term, potentially contentious new rules were not needed; members of the military government retained sufficient legitimacy simply to impose limitations on less cooperative elements of the commercial press through the terms of the existing state of siege. Larger economic and political changes, however, began to reveal the de facto regime's growing distance from even an authoritarian form of liberalism and, as a result, from traditional liberal conceptions of the nature and role of the press. As the scope of the regime's political project broadened, the limits of press "collaboration" with the military government became increasingly apparent.

State actions regarding the press continued to find justification in official assertions of their exceptional, temporary nature. In early August, minister of the interior Colonel Alberto Gilbert issued the executive power's first official, detailed statement of the regime's view of the proper relationship between state and press in the new circumstances. In a circular sent to all federal interventors (provincial governors appointed by the central government), Gilbert instructed them to maintain the same criteria regarding the press as held by the national authorities. Ironically, the instructions corresponded more closely to the conceptions of the press enunciated in the columns of *La Prensa* and *La Nación* than to those elaborated by the minister of war in the first days of the government. In practice, however, the press entered a period of uncertainty whose only twentieth-century precedent lay in the early days of the Uriburu dictatorship.

Rather than the strict model of the press as a conduit for communication from above, Gilbert maintained that the press actively mediated a bidirectional flow of communication between the government and the general population: the "criticisms, insinuations, and suggestions" in the articles and editorials of the press, he declared, served the essential function of "signaling problems and solutions, and enlightening the authorities and the people on the convenience or necessity of reforming, bettering, or broadening services." Gilbert admonished the federal interventors that "under no circumstances should the procedures of the 'directed press' or prior censorship be attempted." Interventors instead must always respect newspapers' status as "mouthpieces of public opinion" whose "educational social function" played an indispensable role in maintaining the "good harmony of [the country's] inhabitants and citizens."[33] Essentially, Gilbert seemed to endorse the traditional liberal conception of the press's function in terms virtually identical to those repeatedly employed in both La Nación and La Prensa.

Yet each endorsement of this liberal conception of the press carried a strong corresponding qualification. Gilbert instructed the interventors to make journalists aware that their prerogatives had natural limitations and corresponding responsibilities: "the rights of each begin and end where those of others end and begin," he warned. Interventors should convince journalists to adjust their commentary to accord with "the educational social function of the press [and] the circumstances of the world conflict." Thus, crime reporting, criticisms of foreign nationalities, governments, political figures and social arrangements, as well as any reporting that might "deform the healthy sentiments of the people" or incline against the "labor of culture which the state sustains," must remain seriously curtailed. Similarly, the "indiscretion of the journalist" should not extend to "excessive criticism" of state functionaries: "[Journalists], like all inhabitants of the country, have the right to discuss with liberty and with frankness the actions, decisions or directives of government; but . . . the constitutional guarantees and privileges, which protect our free governments, are irreconcilable with insult [*injuria*] and slander [*calumnia*] directed at the agents of power and with appreciations that are purely insidious, inflammatory, harmful, or mortifying for popular culture or education, institutions, or persons."[34] Interventors should handle violations of these requirements through persuasion of the offending party; failing this, or in cases of repeated or "intolerable" violation, the minister of the interior deemed more extreme measures acceptable.

In effect, the circular amounted to an elaborate reiteration of the terms of the state of siege that concerned the press, blended with a discourse of press freedom—and corresponding responsibility—reminiscent of Sánchez Sorondo's failed 1934 Law for the Protection of the Press. Like both of these measures, Gilbert's instructions to the federal interventors left them ample room to maneuver: not only did "corrective measures" against journalists and newspapers remain ultimately acceptable, but the fundamental distinction between "freedom of opinion and the press" and the "deceptive vice of license" remained as purposefully malleable as ever.[35] The dual discourse of the minister of the interior fully justified expanded state restrictions on the press, maintaining that such intervention corresponded to purely circumstantial factors—the world conflict, the anticorruption program of the government, and the threat of civil war at home—while remaining consistent with, and even protecting, the underlying force of the constitution. Despite Gilbert's invocation of a liberal intent constrained by a dangerous situation, the regime's practical limitations on the scope of press activity increasingly corresponded less to the uncertainty of the moment and more to the exigencies of a political and ideological project that began to reveal itself as far more daring than many first assumed.

The commercial press of Buenos Aires, of course, emphasized the constitutionalist elements of Gilbert's discourse. *La Nación, Crítica,* and other papers of Buenos Aires—along with the Argentine Federation of Journalists and the Círculo de la Prensa—praised the minister's instructions to the interventors as a necessary step in curbing the "excesses" committed against the press in the provinces. Editorialists at *La Nación* maintained that the establishment of common criteria among provincial interventors and the federal government regarding the latitude of reporting and commentary in the press—which they apparently found in Gilbert's nebulous guidelines—eliminated the uncertainty surrounding journalists' professional activity, and demonstrated that journalists could, in fact, reconcile the critical function of the press with the restrictions of the state of siege and "the limitations imposed by culture."[36]

Despite its purposeful vagueness, Gilbert's circular, as the regime's first official pronouncement on the press, did open the possibility of criticizing the military government for its own inconsistencies. The editors of *La Prensa,* partially shielded by the cultural weight of their daily, cited it selectively to attack more explicitly the rising authoritarianism of the Ramírez government. They praised the minister of the interior, asserting that the circular "corresponds to the traditional Argentine concept of the press and is inspired in the clear prescriptions of the National Constitution, which has consecrated freedom of the press as one of the firmest and broadest conquests of our form of government."[37] Yet *La Prensa*'s habitually vague and selective praise of official pronouncements now gave way to concrete examples of government failure in current practice: application of the criteria on the national level, they insisted, would undercut the prohibitive and open censorship currently operating under the auspices of federal interventors in the provinces of Tucumán, Mendoza, and Entre Ríos.[38] For the first time, specific denunciations of state policies toward the press surfaced in a newspaper of national importance. The "patriotic collaboration" of the directors of *La Prensa* began to show clear signs of strain.

This erosion of *La Prensa*'s support for the regime, however, was not solely—or even primarily—based on the issue of censorship. Instead, the paper's open dissent was a reaction as much in the military's increasingly statist economic policies as to the continued imposition of the state of siege. Within three weeks of seizing power, the military government had lowered and then frozen urban rents, fixed food prices, intervened in food distribution to combat speculation, and raised wages.[39] By early August, the regime had initiated a systematic program of state-driven economic growth through military mobilization and the promotion of industry. The Ramírez government also decreed a 20 percent reduction in rural rents—particularly alarming for the directors of *La Prensa*, who maintained close ties to Buenos Aires landowners—and began a series of interventions in transportation, gas, and other public utilities.[40] Clearly, the scope of the military regime's political agenda extended far beyond a simple "cleansing" of a decidedly corrupt political system or even the simple generation of popular support; instead, sectors within the de facto government appeared increasingly intent on a much broader reworking of the nation's economic and social structure and a dramatic rearticulation of the relationship between state and civil society.

The directors of *La Prensa* responded to what they perceived as this incipient all-encompassing political project with an equally totalizing assertion of the coherence and interpenetration of the entire spectrum of individual "rights" now under attack. State censorship and the limitations on individual prerogatives of property formed part of a more general—and dangerous—shift in the balance between public and private, a process that threatened to undermine at once the constitutional rights that citizens of the republic ostensibly enjoyed and the prosperity that sustained the nation. Citing Juan B. Alberdi, the embodiment of nineteenth-century Argentine liberalism, the editors of *La Prensa* linked freedom of the press with all other bourgeois liberties: "'Paralyze freedom of thought, which is the supreme and culminating face of this multiple liberty, and with just that you make impossible freedom of conscience or religion, political freedom, the freedoms of industry, commerce, circulation, association, of publication, et cetera.'"[41] Thus, while refraining from considering newspapers as mere commodities subject to market exchange, the editorialist nonetheless argued that the complete interpenetration of the rights of expression through the press and the private rights of property meant that state infringement upon one necessarily limited the other. In terms that tested the limits of the state of siege, he concluded by signaling the gap between the regime's continued liberal rhetoric and its actions: "liberty in theory is sarcasm if it is taught to a people subjugated in practice."[42]

If state intervention in the functioning of the market threatened to hinder the general prosperity of the nation, a *La Prensa* editorialist argued on another occasion, restrictions on the functioning of the commercial press also threatened the stability of this government. While the power to see the obstacles inherent in modern society certainly resided in individuals and government officials, this vision became clouded in the obscuring shadows cast by press restrictions. "The action of the independent press," the editorialist insisted, "can be called the action of light," and its absence left government officials in darkness.[43] Press denunciations, in fact, had instigated the "cleansing" process of the current government's anticorruption campaign, the central—and hardly unwarranted—justification of the regime's domestic political policies. Without the effective information gathering of an active and critical journalistic presence in the country, the regime risked grossly misjudging the political environment in which it operated. In an ironic inversion of the press's role as public watchdog over the state, the editorialist maintained that officials should accept the criticisms of an independent press as the unavoidable cost of observing the general population.

More importantly, the legitimacy of the regime and the legitimacy of the press remained inherently intertwined. By censoring opinion and information in the press, argued the *La Prensa* editorialist, the military government inadvertently undermined itself. "It is sufficient that the people know that a certain limitation [on the press] exists for the general environment to become populated by rumors. Those of malicious intentions . . . put into circulation versions [of events] that are false and even highly improbable, which do more harm to a government than the most violent attacks in a regime of freedom. To the incredulity of the people they answer: 'It is true. Believe it. The newspapers cannot speak.'"[44] Censorship, then, while a tempting expedient, had a triple negative effect: it hindered government officials from monitoring impasses within society, leaving them blind to potential flashpoints; it removed an outlet for the channeling and dispersion of discontent; and, by weakening the authority of the press as a reliable and moderating source of information, it boosted the legitimacy of less controllable—and usually hostile—voices as the genuine bearers of the truth.

The author's assertion that "these reflections do not carry any implicit complaint or demand" and that they instead corresponded solely to "desire for the public good" remained ambiguous at best.[45] Almost immediately after the coup, in fact, a combative clandestine press had stepped in to denounce government violations of the sovereignty of the University of Buenos Aires—where left-wing student organizations carried significant political weight—as well as to provide news on labor and political actions by members of the Socialist, Radical, and Communist parties.[46] The frustration of the Federal Police over its failure to combat underground periodicals effectively even brought the regime to edit an "official clandestine newspaper" in the hope that the appearance of distance from the government would lend legitimacy to its support for the authorities and attacks on the opposition.[47] Information production and distribution was clearly beginning to escape the control of traditional channels and to reside increasingly with those who threatened a less predictable—and potentially more radical—reworking of Argentine society. The growing political polarization that the emergence of the clandestine press signaled could hardly have comforted the directors of either *La Prensa* or *La Nación,* who still largely backed the Ramírez regime's policies as the safest means of ensuring a stable return to constitutional normality and "responsible" democratic politics.

More ominously, however, domestic and international events led to a strong rightward shift in the government that had serious consequences for the large commercial newspapers of the city of Buenos Aires as well as those of the interior. Admiral Saturnino Storni, the clearly pro-Allied minister of foreign affairs, contacted U.S. secretary of state Cordell Hull in early September with an offer to break diplomatic relations with the Axis powers provided that the United States agree to end its arms embargo against Argentina. What might have proved a significant victory for moderate elements within the regime in their thinly veiled power struggle against proto-fascist officers instead turned to near-total defeat when Hull not only rejected the offer, but did so publicly. In the resulting cabinet crisis, Storni and other moderates left the government. The new cabinet became increasingly dominated by the men of the GOU and their civilian allies: General Edelmiro Farrell became vice president; the notoriously anti-Semitic author Martínez Zuviría (Hugo Wast) assumed the head of the Ministry of Justice and Public Instruction; and a month later General Luís Perlinger became minister of the interior, replacing Gilbert, who had taken Storni's place in Foreign Affairs.

The shift in the cabinet had immediate consequences for the national press. The respected Socialist Party paper *La Vanguardia,* briefly suspended in August for denouncing the government intervention against the Unión Ferroviaria and La Fraternidad railway unions, was again closed for emitting "imprudent and exaggerated appreciations that disorient and confuse public opinion."[48] In mid-October, the minister of the interior, General Perlinger, closed the country's vibrant ethnic press. Though Greek, Hungarian, Lithuanian, and Spanish papers ceased to exist, it was the simultaneous closure of Jewish newspapers that the United States media—and President Roosevelt himself—saw as absolute and final proof of the Ramírez regime's fascist and pro-Axis character.[49] To the dismay of the editors of *La Prensa* and *La Nación,* the most important newspaper of the interior, Rosario's *La Capital,* suffered a twenty-four-hour closure for its reporting of the Storni-and-Hull affair.[50] As tensions with Brazil reached fever pitch and practice bombing raids and air defense drills sent tracer bullets into the sky of a blacked-out Buenos Aires, journalists' and newspaper proprietors' illusions of an end to the state of siege and a return to the dictates of the constitution all but vanished.[51]

Even the traditional safety valve of the Círculo de la Prensa, so effective as a behind-the-scenes lobbying force for newspaper directors and journalists during the 1930s, began to show signs of serious strain. On September 8, Federal Police confiscated the sixth edition of the popular Buenos Aires daily *Noticias*

Gráficas in retaliation for its interpretation of Italian surrender, and ordered the paper closed until further notice.[52] Days later, the director of the newspaper, José W. Agusti, found himself arrested on charges of fraud. *Noticias Gráficas* reopened, only to suffer another suspension three weeks later for following the publication of an article in praise of the paper's still-detained director.[53] Early gestures by Círculo de la Prensa president Adolfo Lanús and secretary Mauricio Bornand (both from *La Prensa*) for the reopening of *Noticias Gráficas* met with silence from the Ministry of the Interior.[54]

By mid-October, with *Noticias Gráficas* still closed and Agusti imprisoned, the Círculo de la Prensa faced a near rebellion from several of its members employed at the newspaper in frustration over the organization's impotence. *La Nación*'s Alberto Gerchunoff, a highly respected journalist and vice president of the Círculo, responded that, quite simply, circumstances did not permit further action: the authorities, beyond denying that Agusti's detention had any relation to his profession as a journalist, had imposed a wall of bureaucratic indifference.[55] The mutual aid society that linked journalists and newspaper owners and had long provided an institutional channel for press relations with the government had become increasingly ineffectual in stemming the tide of newspaper closures. Gestures by the journalists' labor union, FAP, met with similar official stolidity.[56]

As internal opposition grew, the Ramírez regime swung further to the right, largely abandoning even heavily conditioned pronouncements that state censorship might remain limited by broader constitutional principles. Instead, the military government imposed increasingly inflexible restrictions on reporting. Government circulars in late September and October directly prohibited any reporting of events relating to students, the resignation of university professors, or labor actions, unless the news came directly from government offices. Not only could newswriters no longer editorialize on official actions regarding the press, but news of censorship itself was now censored.[57] Conciliatory pronouncements of adherence to traditional liberal conceptions of the social role of journalism became superfluous as state efforts vis-à-vis the media rested increasingly on coercion.

By the end of the year, direct editorial comment within the increasingly narrow parameters accorded press commentary evaporated together with spaces for institutionalized dissent. The final days of December saw a massive police sweep across the country, in which over forty newspapers faced closure for having published various kinds of extraofficial information. Unable to directly comment upon the situation facing the press, newsworkers turned again to the journalist-proprietor alliance in the Círculo de la Prensa as a means of appealing directly to the regime. Yet, in the increasingly tense circumstances, the de facto government simply ignored the organization's protests. In a gesture that symbolized the increasing government dismissal of the existing press's legitimacy, Círculo president Adolfo Lanús's letter to Ramírez protesting the newspaper closures did not even reach the presidential office; a secretary of the Casa Rosada returned the note for addressing the general simply as "Señor Presidente de la Nación" rather than the correct "Excelentísimo Señor Presidente de la Nación."[58] Even this, however, did not mark the height of the bureaucratic indifference of which Alberto Gerchunoff had complained earlier: the note, sent on December 29, was not returned until January 12, by which time circumstances facing the press had changed dramatically.

The Bureaucratization of State-Press Relations

The drastic measures toward the press taken in late December reflected not only the regime's rapidly growing concern with the flow of information, but also the expansion of state agencies designed to control it. As the military leaders turned sharply to the right with the September cabinet reshuffling, GOU officers and other nationalists within the government sought to refashion the existing set of relationships between state and civil society more extensively. This extension of the military regime's political project could hardly leave the national press untouched. The commercial press as a whole had proven itself ideologically suspect and practically unreliable as a vehicle for any transformation that went beyond a simple "purifying" of previously existing political arrangements. Similarly, although the press formed an integral part of the set of institutions to be transformed, neither newspaper proprietors nor journalists seemed prepared to surrender their relative institutional autonomy en masse.

Regime policy regarding the commercial press thus took a dual course at year's end. First, the de facto government dramatically expanded direct state production of information as a means of more dependably influencing public perceptions. Attempting to guarantee a more uniformly acclamatory press, in the final hours of 1943 the military government took the additional step of placing the force of law—by executive decree—behind its desire for press "collaboration." Combined, the measures gave national authorities an unprecedented degree of influence over the political and ideological orientation of the national press, in effect implementing by force the vision of the social role of journalism espoused by General Farrell and other nationalist officers.

The most visible step toward creating an effective state media apparatus came in late October 1943, when Ramírez signed a decree creating the Undersecretariat of Information and the Press (Subsecretaría de Información y Prensa).[59] Headed by Colonel Héctor Ladvocat, the new Undersecretariat in turn depended upon the resurrection of the Secretariat of the Presidency—with the rank of Ministry—headed by the openly pro-Axis colonel Enrique P. González. The creation of the Undersecretariat marked a clear attempt to revive the media tactics of the proto-fascist Uriburu regime of 1930 to 1932. In fact, the Undersecretariat was not formed from the ground up, but upon the foundation of the Oficina de Información—the heir of Uriburu and Kinkelín's Sección Prensa—which since the June coup had already centralized instructions to the media regarding censorship policies. Yet its creation marked a far more systematic and sustained expansion of state action proper into the media, both in censorship and information production.[60] The sweeping vagueness of the area of competency of the Undersecretariat of Information and the Press ("all which is relative to the exercise of publicity activities and information in general") provided a less than subtle hint as to the powers that Ladvocat would wield.[61] With its mission further refined by presidential decree two weeks later, the Undersecretariat took on the "intensification of the relations of the press with the public powers," the "organization of state propaganda," and the promotion of Argentine cinema and newsreels. In a capacity reminiscent of that desired by General Justo a decade earlier, the Undersecretariat would also collaborate "in the activities of foreign agencies and correspondents in order to impede the diffusion abroad of news or commentary prejudicial to the prestige of the nation." Finally, through a relatively unnoticed measure that would have dramatic consequences, the executive power extended to the new Undersecretariat the responsibility of assuring the adequate supply of newsprint and fresh film, "intervening as necessary in order to achieve their adequate distribution."[62]

The creation of the Undersecretariat coordinated—and dramatically expanded—state monitoring and restriction of the press under the terms of the state of siege. As with its precursor, this purely negative responsibility formed the counterbalance to a positive task: the Undersecretariat would act as the state's own means of "guiding and orienting public opinion." Now the Argentine state would work to "assure the dignity of the right to the free expression of ideas," not merely on a case-by-case basis through the courts, or—in times of national emergency—through the police, but through the executive power's systematic, active, and permanent intervention in the actual creation of information. In effect, the Undersecretariat would act as the regime's ideological arm, "contributing to the defense and the exaltation . . . of the culture and moral and spiritual values of the Argentine people" in a way that the mass-circulation press—corrupted by cosmopolitan liberalism, in the view of the officers of the GOU—simply could not.[63]

The measures creating the Undersecretariat of Information and the Press reflected the most statist practical conception of the role of the press since the onset of the crisis of Argentine liberalism, surpassing even the most ambitious proto-fascist visions of Matías Sánchez Sorondo in the mid-1930s. Modeled as much on the Italian Sottosegretario per la Stampa e Propaganda as on the institutionally flimsy Sección Prensa, the new Undersecretariat unabashedly blurred the division between state and press, and, as such, formed part of a broader effort to expand state activities into areas traditionally considered the domain of civil society.[64] With this active state intervention, as at once censor, coordinator, and direct producer, in the "means of meaning production," the Undersecretariat essentially embodied the channel for top-down social communication envisioned by General Farrell in the early days of the regime.

That the Undersecretariat shifted the "right to the free expression of ideas" from the private, individual realm to that of public authority would hardly be lost on the defenders of traditional liberal views of the nature of the press and the social role of journalism. Still, reactions to its creation in the Buenos Aires commercial dailies remained muted due to the government's recent increased vigilance over the press as political tensions with Brazil and the United States grew. That reporting on the Undersecretariat's formation would be monitored by officials from the Undersecretariat itself also surely worked to guarantee that editorial responses remained "dignified."

Again, *Crítica* most closely embodied the government vision of the press's role: a sympathetic interview with Colonel Ladvocat in *Crítica* essentially restated the decree in narrative form, making the dry text of a government proclamation palatable and intelligible to the general public. Ladvocat denied any intention to subordinate journalists to the dictates of the government, arguing that he did "not seek an unconditional press, but a serene press."[65] Ironically—though it was clearly a result of the ownership dispute—the traditionally histrionic *Crítica* largely remained loyal to the regime's ideal: a commercial newspaper flexibly subjugated to the dictates of the regime on all issues of importance.

However, not all journalists greeted the creation of the Undersecretariat so warmly. Editorialists at *La Nación* seized upon statements regarding the wartime press made by Kent Cooper, the director general of the Associated Press—with which the paper maintained intimate ties—to make furtive comments on both the creation of the Undersecretariat and the growing restrictions on the press. Strict censorship, an editorialist argued, lay at the heart of the current world conflict, risking rather than securing the social harmony that its proponents sought to protect. "One can define the degree of civilization of a country by the degree of spontaneity shown in its newspapers. The lack of this liberty initiates a sort of blindness that endangers peace among peoples and invariably leads to a situation of continuous danger. The effect of this absence of fresh air is equally perturbing in the internal existence of a nation."[66] Growing state intervention in the functioning of the press, the editorialist implied, was beginning to weaken an essential safeguard to both national security and the long-term stability of the Argentine social system, potentially stripping Argentina of its status as a civilized nation.

Writers at *La Prensa* also seized upon abstract statements made abroad to deliver an even more systematic critique of the Undersecretariat.[67] Not only did censorship negate public rights of expression through the press, but the centralization of this authority in the national executive power, rather than in the local civil courts, violated both federalism and the constitutional separation of powers. Even more basically, the power of the press simply did not figure among those that the Argentine public had delegated to its government; that the Constitution of 1853 did not include information production among state attributes effectively barred it from engaging in the activity. "Thus, because the press is an element of sovereignty expressly excluded from all official intervention in its exercise, it is an instrument of government that is, equally, in the hands of all the inhabitants of the republic, but not in the official powers. It is an instrument of government that does not serve to order, to legislate, to judge cases nor to apply punishment; but it does serve to orient, to guide, to understand, and to communicate from one to another."[68] The power of the press was indeed an integral part of the "state," the writer argued, but only in the broadest sense of the latter term—that is, as an element of the entire scope of institutions that sustained the orderly evolution of Argentine society along liberal lines.

In a final rhetorical flourish, the writer concluded that "the history of the Argentine people is the history of its liberties. The history of Argentine liberties is the history of the Argentine press."[69] Since "all the inhabitants of the republic" held the power of the press equally, "the press" constituted the very subject of national history. The Undersecretariat of Information and the Press thus not only contradicted the fundamental charter of the nation on multiple levels, it confirmed that the state itself—not merely this particular regime—constituted the gravest menace to the proper functioning of the fourth estate. More fundamentally, in curtailing the press, the actions of the Undersecretariat constituted nothing less than a threat to the Argentine people as a whole.

If members of the regime overestimated Argentines' enthusiasm for state control of information, the editorialists at *La Prensa* responded with obvious hyperbole. Assertions that the power of the press rested "equally in the hands of all the inhabitants of the republic" invoked liberalism's promise of egalitarian democracy, obfuscating the private and capital-intensive nature of the newspaper industry. The prerogatives of an abstract and idealized "press" and a reified, homogeneous "public" became coterminous, transforming the press from a mere forum for the expression of public opinion to the embodiment of public opinion. Yet, beyond dissolving the practical aspects of a press effectively controlled by the few into this collective utopian vision, the claim sat uneasily with the paper's own record: just months earlier, *La Prensa* editorialists had argued for limiting the scope of the public participation in the public sphere and conditioning the expression of opinion on "knowledge and aptitudes."[70] This rhetorically powerful conflation of "press" and "public," then, nonetheless remained divorced from the unambiguous elitism of *La Prensa*'s editors, the commodification of journalism practice, and the property relations of the industrial press. It would also soon collide with the momentous social change just beginning to stir as newly empowered sections of the Argentine public called on *La Prensa* to embody in practice the ideal press-public relationship its editorialists had articulated so forcefully.

In fact, the formation of the Undersecretariat of Information and the Press marked the beginning, rather than the culmination, of the regime's attempts to refashion the relationships between state, press, and civil society. In a sweeping series of decrees issued on the final day of 1943, the de facto authorities carried the statist impulse significantly further. Ostensibly due to the failure of the "cleansing" process to eliminate internal corruption, the executive power dissolved all political parties in the country.[71] Religious education in Argentina's highly secular public school system also became mandatory. The New Year's decrees marked a broad and unprecedented attempt to rearrange permanently the national state–civil society relationships in Argentina.

One decree in particular placed tight new restrictions on the press, seeking to link the nation's newspapers more closely and strictly to the Argentine state and, thus, to the political project of the GOU. Ironically, decree 18.407 embodied a notion that newspaper proprietors—particularly those of both *La Nación* and *La Prensa*—had trumpeted since well before the constitutional rupture of 1930: that the press was an institution operating in the public interest. Where newspaper proprietors saw this as a justification for their refusal to abide by the Argentine Commercial Code, however, the architects of the military regime viewed it as a sign that, as with other public services, the practice of journalism fell within the state's scope of regulatory activity.[72]

At the same time, decree 18.407 also brought the first systematic legal pronouncement of the increasingly commonsense notion that newspapers served a general economic function in society, as the advertising in their pages proved central to the daily flow of commodities. The promulgators of the decree, in essence, announced their intention to resolve the potential conflicts between the public, cultural aspects of journalistic activity and the economic function of newspaper publicity. In addition to fulfilling the high mission of guiding public opinion, "the press participates in commercial activity and facilitates the realization of transactions between individuals, linking in this way numerous private interests that tend to exert pressure to the point in which they dominate [the press's] authentic mission. . . . *It is the duty of the state to assure the press the normal realization of its activity and to watch over the dignity of the right of the free expression of ideas,* avoiding that its exercise be impeded by mercantile interests."[73] Echoing the directors and editorialists of *La Nación*, *La Prensa*, and even Damonte Taborda's *Crítica*, the decree recognized "the social function served by the press as an activity of public interest," but drew an opposite—though just as logical—conclusion: instead of barring state intervention, the communal concern expressed in the press begged for the state to oversee "its adequate regulation."[74]

The argument amounted to a clear reversal of the assertions of the liberal newspaper proprietors, directors, and editors. Yes, the decree stated, the press did serve an exalted "authentic mission"; but the public interest held in the pure functioning of the press was in danger of becoming malignantly privatized by the indecorous influence of the commercial activities in which newspapers participated. Rather than a menace to the "right of free expression of ideas," the state—the repository of collective sovereignty and ultimate arbiter of national interest—was instead its primary defender. In this way, the decree marked a significant turn in the relationship between state and press. By elevating the issue of the interaction between the press and the broader economic life of the nation, the decree inched toward a new formulation of the character of the national press as it existed in practice. The assertion that the press "participates in commercial activity" remained for now somewhat ambiguous; only later would the regime declare newspapers inherently commercial enterprises. The New Year's press decree, as the first tentative legislative recognition of the newspaper industry's economic role, revealed the ideological key to reconciling still-powerful liberal conceptions of the press with the regime's growing corporatist impulse: only the state could protect the public role of journalism from hostile forces and restore the purity of a press that commercial activity had sullied in practice.

Despite the ambiguity of the decree's characterization of the relationship between the economic and cultural functions of the press, the requirements of the new law imposed dramatic new requirements on newspaper institutions. As part of the effort to ensure that "mercantile interests" did not obstruct the journalist's mission, decree 18.407 required that actuarial books of newspapers and wire service organizations conform to the standards of the Commercial Code. The Undersecretariat of Information and the Press also established an official registry, obliging the country's news organizations to provide the name and addresses of the directors, proprietors, and all employees, as well as an itemized account of the sources of all income, clearly indicating funds of foreign origin. Journalists convicted of homicide or manslaughter lost the right to exercise the profession, as did, significantly more ominously, "those who engage in activities contrary to the general interests of the nation, of morality, of good customs, or who disturb public order."[75]

In a series of requirements reminiscent of General Justo's ill-fated 1935 measure, the decree added to the systematic bureaucratic oversight of the press already in place through the Undersecretariat of Information and the Press. Directors, proprietors, and journalists became jointly responsible for the content of any news article or editorial published in their periodical. In order to ensure proper compliance, all commentaries were to carry either the author's name or an officially registered pseudonym. Employees of the Undersecretariat of Information and the Press—itself expanded and more coherently organized in a parallel decree that day—also found the monitoring of media content simplified: signed copies of commentary and news wired abroad were to be deposited with the Undersecretariat within four hours of transmission. Yet another decree issued on December 31 compelled newspaper publishers to submit fifteen copies of each edition to the Undersecretariat.[76] The intended outcome of both press decrees was double: not only would bureaucratic vigilance of the press become more methodical and enforcement of restrictions more systematic, but the measures would also greatly boost the Undersecretariat's effectiveness as an information-gathering agency for government officials.[77]

Taken together, the New Year's Eve decrees also effectively ended hopes for a swift return to constitutional normality. The regime had not only strengthened the restrictions on journalism established under the state of siege, it had codified them as law.[78] Beyond the clear legal ramifications, the shift carried significant symbolic implications as well. The state of siege, by definition, corresponded to exceptional circumstances and was remedial in character. Since the June coup, military leaders had claimed that the dangerous situation in which the country found itself—surrounded by a world conflagration and bordering on local civil war—necessitated these unusual measures; ultimately, the stabilizing effect of the restrictions themselves, together with continued military tutelage, would help pave the way for a return to constitutional democracy. With the "cleansing" of Argentine political life and the lifting of the state of siege (which, if the regime were to claim success, must come at some point), the reasons for constraints on the press would vanish, and with them the constraints themselves. The press decrees, however, threatened a permanent, unconditional normalization of state intervention in the functioning of the press. In effect, the state of siege became thoroughly institutionalized and the relationship between state and press fully bureaucratized.

The subsequent publication of the decrees on January 5, 1944, engendered a systematic campaign by the Buenos Aires press and journalist organizations for the measures' immediate retraction. Luís Mitre, director-proprietor of *La Nación*, immediately defended the consistency of his paper since its foundation, asserting that the editorial line would remain unchanged despite the new circumstances. In particular, Mitre dismissed the relevance of decree 18.407's differentiation between proprietors, directors, and journalists. The personnel of *La Nación*, he argued, enjoyed a quasi-spiritual "moral unity," in which editorialists "know how to interpret the thought of the direction."[79] Since *La Nación* effectively acted as a single collective subject, the decree's threat to hold all responsible for the content of the paper posed no particular menace, Mitre asserted. The owner of *La Prensa*, Alberto Gainza Paz, similarly returned to the paper's first issue for its liberal-positivist statement of purpose: "Truth—Honor—Freedom—Progress—Civilization."[80] The proprietors of both *La Nación* and *La Prensa* thus at once denied the legitimacy of the measures while defiantly refusing to recognize that the New Year's decrees would in any way alter the daily functioning of their newspapers.

Even the editors of *Crítica*, who in waves of editorials flooded the political class with charges of corruption—transparently at the behest of the regime—eventually turned against decree 18.407.[81] In terms strikingly similar to the liberal discourse characteristic of *La Prensa* rather than the populistic discourse usually found in the paper's commentary, the editors began to attack the press decree.[82] Damonte Taborda's motivations to break ranks with the regime, of course, went beyond any adherence to traditional liberal conceptions of the role of journalism: not only did the property and income declarations undermine his ownership strategy, but the severity and permanence of the measure surely caused him alarm. In a political climate of increasing instability, such sweeping state powers for disciplining the press could quite easily fall into the hands of one of Damonte Taborda's many adversaries. Should *Crítica*, a newspaper with a long history of bumpy relations with authorities, face another series of closures, loss of the paper to his rivals—or even official confiscation—was not only possible, but increasingly likely.

The most energetic protest, however, came from the Círculo de la Prensa, which again acted as a channel for a more direct communication of journalist and proprietor collective dissent. In a letter to Ramírez on behalf of the organization, Adolfo Lanús argued that the New Year's press decree explicitly violated the Constitution of 1853: "the right to publish ideas in the press without prior censorship" (article 14); and the inability of the Federal Congress to dictate restrictive press laws on the national level (article 32).[83] Now, however, the Círculo protests met with something more ominous than "bureaucratic indifference": Secretary of the President Enrique González ordered Lanús arrested in his home province of La Rioja on charges of contempt of a public official.[84] The regime, it increasingly appeared, would have little patience for any expression of dissent.

Toward a New Politics

A combination of changing national circumstances and news organization resistance, however, would ultimately leave decree 18.407 null in practice. On January 15, an earthquake leveled the city of San Juan, creating a virtual black hole into which state resources and bureaucratic energy seemed to fall endlessly.[85] The devastation caused by the tremor had a threefold effect on state-press relations and the implementation of the press decree: coverage of the quake pushed all else off the pages of the newspapers; the public outpouring of solidarity in facing the crisis softened criticisms of the regime; and the three-month-old Undersecretariat of Information and the Press found itself increasingly occupied with the propaganda aspects of the relief effort. The decree's thirty-day deadline for news organizations to fully register and open their books to the government came and went with little compliance, yet without government reprisals.

A political tremor of far-reaching proportions followed just over a week after the San Juan quake. Following the abrupt "discovery" of a Nazi spy ring in the country, the Ramírez regime broke diplomatic relations with the Axis powers on January 26. Yet the rupture with Germany and Japan actually originated not in any "violation of Argentine sovereignty," but in an attempt to intensify relations with the Axis: the "Nazi spies," in fact, were government agents. Hindered in the rapid expansion of the military by a U.S. weapons embargo, Ramírez had sent a covert mission to Berlin with the hope of arranging a weapons deal with German agents. When British intelligence captured one secret agent, Ramírez had no choice but to break relations or face the consequences of public revelation of the mission.[86] The shock waves of the abrupt departure from Argentina's neutralist stance reached the highest levels: within three weeks the still little-known Juan Domingo Perón had engineered the removal of President Ramírez, Secretary of the Presidency Enrique P. González, and Minister of Foreign Affairs Alberto Gilbert from the governing junta.[87] Almost immediately, Perón revealed himself as the driving force within the new government.

General Edelmiro Farrell's subsequent rise to the presidency signified far more than a mere change of personnel within the cabinet. The authoritarian project of the de facto government in many ways had reached a turning point, with restrictions on opposition to the regime essentially maximized through the New Year's series of decrees. Simple repression, however, had limits; the stifling of dissent effectively created the illusion of silence while doing little to promote the regime and much to undermine its long-term legitimacy.

The growing power of Juan Domingo Perón, however, signaled the emergence of a far more sophisticated political project, one that joined the suppression of political opponents with an unprecedented pragmatic search for an extensive base of support among broad sectors of the national population. The genesis of Peronism, a movement that would ultimately mark the dissolution of old political and social allegiances as much as the creation of new ones, immediately shook the complex web of professional and political identifications and relationships that made up the Argentine newspaper industry. Proprietors and working journalists alike would see the press change dramatically as the "triumph of silence" gave way to the rising cacophony of early Peronism.

JOURNALISM AS LABOR POWER

What interests journalists is that we are finally recognized as possessing the same right to demand better working conditions as all [other] workers.

—Octavio Palazzolo of the Argentine Federation of Journalists

We consider it the greatest and most prejudicial of errors any attempt to consider the journalist an intellectual worker.

—Alberto Gainza Paz, *La Prensa,* **February 22, 1944**

In the first months following the coup of June 1943, the government of General Ramírez had found its primary source of legitimacy in the profound public discontent with the political corruption of the preceding thirteen years. Yet, by defining their overriding mission as the cleansing of political life, the military leaders had undermined the validity of an indefinite perpetuation of the government: either they succeeded in this dubious task and retreated to the barracks as promised, or they attempted to maintain their hold on power, implicitly admitting failure. Without a new course and a redefinition of goals, then, the longevity of the military regime depended more on enforcing passive silence than on generating active consent among the general population.

The emergence of Colonel Juan Domingo Perón as the regime's clear protagonist within the newly reconfigured cabinet was an implicit acknowledgment that the clumsy authoritarianism of the military regime had reached its limits. Perón, more than any other government figure, not only perceived this contradiction between the regime's contingent legitimacy and the military leaders' greater, unstated aspirations, he began to envision the solution to the predicament: the creation and maintenance of an active base of support for the military government through a sweeping program of social reform. Although initiated in November 1943 following Perón's appointment as head of the then innocuous National Labor Department, this significantly more ambitious project deepened substantially with Ramírez's ouster in late February of the following year.

If the New Year's press decree embodied these tensions between the repressive program of the regime and its failure to generate positive support among influential sectors of the population, the circumstances of its abrogation three months later exemplify the course that Farrell and Perón charted through this impasse. In attempting to normalize what were by definition exceptional measures taken in exceptional circumstances, decree 18.407 mandated passivity rather than organized consensus for the regime, and, as a consequence, served as much to provoke as to silence dissent within the national media. On March 28, 1944, however, Farrell revoked the decree, replacing it with a fundamentally different measure that signaled a new approach to state-press relations.

Decree 7.618/44, the Journalist's Statute (Estatuto del Periodista), far from systematizing stringent prohibitions on reporting, instead established strong government assurances of concrete improvements in journalists' working conditions. With the simultaneous abrogation of decree 18.407, censorship once again became a temporary emergency power of the state. The focus of permanent state intervention in the functioning of the press, in turn, suddenly shifted from an ominous vigilance over newspaper content to a positive enforcement of social justice for newsworkers. Journalists greeted the measure with a fervor that quickly extended to the decree's sponsors within the military government. Censorship alone had opened the regime to claims that its authority rested solely upon the power of coercion; now, however, the military government sought to generate the active support of the direct producers of press content.

Despite its profound impact on the internal workings of the newspaper industry, the Journalist's Statute has appeared as little more than a footnote in the historiographies of Argentine labor, the press, and law. Such inattention to the material and professional-ideological conditions of journalism practice is hardly unique to considerations of the Argentine press, as several historical studies of newsworkers in the United States attest.[1] This oversight has much to do with journalists' professional ideology and the nature of journalism itself; in fact, ambivalent perceptions of journalistic activity as labor formed an integral part of the conflict surrounding the statute. Thus, while the political environment in which the press functions has received media historians' ample attention, the human relational context of the newspaper production process more often than not remains curiously opaque.[2] Similarly, the comparatively small number of journalists, together with their relative social mobility and educational level, has marginalized working journalists from the extensive studies of Argentine labor history. Lodged in the interstices of both media and labor studies—though clearly important to both—Argentine journalists, their working conditions, and the meaning assigned to their labor have tended to receive little more than cursory glances from historians.

In its unequivocal identification of journalists as wage workers, the new Journalist's Statute struck to the core of traditional liberal understandings of journalism practice and marked, as would become clear in the coming years, a decisive step in reworking the ideological underpinnings of the national press. By extending collective bargaining rights to journalists, the Argentine state explicitly recognized reporters as workers above all else. Suddenly, the newspaper industry's network of internal productive relations and broader socioeconomic structure became a recognized, legitimate element in public discourse on the nature of the press and the social role of journalism practice. The ideological innovations of the Journalist's Statute, though not fully apparent at first, would become clearer as Peronism gained greater momentum. Ultimately, Peronists would draw upon the statute's legal redefinition of what the press *was* together with variations of more traditional notions of what the press *should be* to lay the ideological basis for the expropriation of La Prensa at the height of the movement's power.

More immediately, the statute effectively drove a wedge between working journalists and the owners of the national press. While the new statute's extension of significant material and symbolic gains to newsworkers gave many journalists ample reason to back the de facto government despite the continued official harassment of their colleagues, adversely affected newspaper proprietors mounted a thinly veiled attempt to render the measure null in practice. By providing powerful economic and ideological incentives for the two key sectors of the newspaper industry to take opposing stances vis-à-vis the project advanced by Perón and Farrell, the new decree brought the newsroom's latent class tensions to the surface and channeled them into the broader, rapidly changing political process. At both an abstract ideological and a practical political level, the notion of "the press" as a coherent social subject—an important element in traditional journalism discourse—became increasingly difficult to sustain. The fissure between working journalists and newspaper owners, which had opened in 1919 and had been growing steadily since the mid-1930s, quickly became a chasm, and the military state stepped in to arbitrate the very conflicts that government officials hoped to foment.

From Mutual Antagonism to Mutual Advantage

Perón embraced the aspirations of working journalists almost immediately, an early indication not just of the importance he would assign to the media, but of his divergence from the military regime's essentially suppressive approach to civil society. In fact, the Journalist's Statute formed part of the first tentative series of labor measures enacted within eight months of the founding of the Secretariat of Labor and Social Welfare (Secretaría de Trabajo y Previsión— STP), the National Labor Department's new, more powerful successor.[3] Reasons for this early inclusion in the secretary of labor's social project are not at all difficult to imagine. Railroad workers, another group of laborers included in this first wave of reforms, played a crucial role in the broader economic life of the country due to their pivotal position in the physical circulation of commodities. Journalists similarly occupied a key position in the production of two intimately related "commodities" central to the launching of any political and social project: information and ideology. Thus, where decree 18.407 sought to silence the media through the menace of systematic repression, the Journalist's Statute brought the enticement of material advantage to those actually charged with the daily task of creating newspaper content. Perón, in effect, intended to use class divisions in the newsroom not just to fracture opposition within the press, but to gain the active sympathy of a crucial sector of those whom he clearly saw as the direct producers of ideology.

Yet following media scholar Pablo Sirvén's assumption that the statute was essentially the product of Perón's calculated decision to "play the card of capturing press workers" means neglecting a decade of sustained efforts by many journalists to promote the extension of labor rights to members of their profession.[4] After the 1935 court rulings classifying journalists as employees under the Commercial Code, Círculo de la Prensa spokesman Luís Praprotnik, using language strikingly similar to that of the 1944 Journalist's Statute, had declared the need for state regulation of newsroom labor. In an extensive article in the organization's *Boletín Oficial,* Praprotnik warned that "generally sterile and unproductive" class conflict in the newsroom threatened to become more acute unless the state specifically promoted the "peaceful and harmonious combination of . . . capital and labor."[5] Similarly, those present at the 1938 founding congress of the Argentine Federation of Journalists had made the implementation of a professional statute for journalists the new union's primary objective.[6] Subsequent meetings of the organization had only confirmed this aspiration even as divisions within the profession and congressional inaction continued to frustrate their efforts. As with most other sectors of the labor movement, for journalists the primary novelty in Perón's ascent was neither a sudden emergence of class tensions where there had been none, nor an increased threat to their professional sovereignty. Instead, they found themselves unexpectedly faced with a powerful state official sympathetic to their agenda. Press workers, in large measure, had good reason to believe that it was in fact they who were "capturing" a government official.[7]

Not surprisingly, then, the immediate impulse for what became the Journalist's Statute came not from Perón, but from several correspondents assigned to the Casa Rosada in response to the lobbying efforts of newspaper owners.[8] In mid-October 1943, Colonel Héctor Ladvocat, the newly appointed undersecretary of information and the press, received a letter from a group of newspaper proprietors asking for the termination of the still-unenforced 1941 law granting retirement benefits to journalists. Ladvocat casually mentioned the proprietor petition to a group of journalists following government news, who in turn informed the *El Mundo* Casa Rosada correspondent and former FAP president Octavio Palazzolo. Within days the newspaper proprietors' strategy backfired: Palazzolo agreed to work together with Ladvocat in drafting an extension of the pension law, to be later enacted by government decree. A week later, a joint statement by the FAP, the Asociación de Periodistas de Buenos Aires (APBA—the FAP's Buenos Aires affiliate) and the Círculo de la Prensa dismissed proprietor objections, declaring that "authentic journalists of Argentina" supported the retirement law.[9]

This limited goal of maintaining existing retirement legislation, however, was quickly overshadowed by the prospect of more far-reaching gains as the military regime suddenly became more receptive to the aspirations of labor. Before Ladvocat and Palazzolo could begin work on the decree, Juan Perón became head of the National Labor Department, radically expanding the options available to unionized journalists. At the urging of members of the FAP and the APBA and through the efforts of the journalist and long-time Perón friend Oscar Lomuto, Palazzolo gained an interview with the new functionary, along with Helvio Casal Cabrera and Marcial Rocha de María of *Crítica*. The three journalists urged Perón to extend their retirement law, underscoring not only its importance to the material well-being of newsworkers, but also its symbolic value as the only concrete legislative gain working journalists had made in several decades of struggle. Palazzolo told of the success that the FAP had had in organizing journalists at the national level, explaining to Perón that "what interests journalists is that we are finally recognized as possessing the same right to demand better working conditions as all [other] workers."[10] Then, taking the opportunity to communicate the union's broader agenda, he added that journalists were interested in having a professional statute, a formal regulation of working conditions in the profession.

Perón's response to Palazzolo's comments far exceeded the expectations of any of the three journalists: "If you are in a position to do so, prepare the project [for the Journalist's Statute] and in just a little while, when the decree is issued that will replace this department with the Secretariat of Labor and Social Welfare, come to see me. Come to see me *two days after* I have taken charge of the Secretariat."[11] The speed with which Perón appeared prepared to move on the statute—beyond the obvious initial energy of a new government minister—grew out of a nascent media savvy totally lacking among his colleagues. Journalists, after all, would be "shaping public opinion" regarding his Secretariat's subsequent actions. At the same time, Perón's novelty on the national scene, combined with his bureaucratic distance from the government agencies charged with the task of disciplining journalists, mitigated his association with a regime widely perceived as hostile to the journalists he was now courting. For both Perón and the journalists the advantages of alliance were clear: the colonel could quickly ingratiate himself and the military government with the only national organization of journalists, and the FAP could deliver to its members concrete and long-sought material gains.

Still, despite both Perón's and Palazzolo's interest in advancing as quickly as possible, the project encountered significant delays. In mid-December, Palazzolo, accompanied by members of the FAP and the APBA, submitted a draft of the projected statute directly to the secretary of labor. If Perón seemed anxious to fulfill the journalists' aspirations, however, the bureaucracy that he inherited apparently did not share his enthusiasm. Almost immediately, the project disappeared amid the shuffling of a bureaucracy long accustomed to obstructing and moderating labor legislation, only to surface as nine separate drafts after passing through the hands of the Secretariat's lawyers. Perón even confessed to Palazzolo that he was unaware of the cause of the delays, after approaching several of the Casa Rosada correspondents to ask if they had abandoned the project for some reason.[12] Only the direct intervention of the secretary of labor himself, and the personal attention of the head of Social Welfare, Juan Bramuglia, pulled the project through the bureaucratic labyrinth in early February 1944.

The Journalist as Worker

While the elaboration of the Journalist's Statute marked the first steps toward forging a new relationship between Colonel Perón and working journalists, it also profoundly and immediately altered the relationship between the Argentine state and a central institution of civil society. The statute initiated a process of state intervention in the press by which government functionaries mediated not circumstantial disputes between state and press, but the mundane conflicts that formed a normal part of class relations in the newsroom. Relatedly, the Journalist's Statute unequivocally lent the force of law to definitions of the nature of the press and journalistic practice that many working journalists had already embraced, but that nonetheless remained contentious within the profession as a whole: namely, that newspapers were, in practice, commercial enterprises and journalists were wage workers. By juridically defining newspapers as profit-oriented entities and the relationship between journalists and proprietors as that between labor and capital, the statute introduced institutional and ideological innovations that were both sweeping and immediate.

The changes that the Journalist's Statute would introduce into the complex relationships between the Argentine state, journalists, and newspaper owners, in fact, preceded the final approval of the new law. In mid-February, with the legal draft of the document prepared, the secretary of labor and social welfare named a commission drawn equally from journalist organizations and newspaper proprietors to determine the statute's final form. Over a period of ten days, representatives of the FAP, the APBA, and the Círculo de la Prensa, together with the ownership of five newspapers, met at the offices of Perón's Secretariat to debate the details of the measure, with officials from the Secretariat mediating the talks. Journalists and proprietors from the city of Buenos Aires dominated the commission: Octavio Palazzolo (FAP) and Óscar Ares (APBA) most forcefully pressed the demands of journalists against attempts by José W. Agusti (*Noticias Gráficas* and *Córdoba*), Raúl Damonte Taborda (*Crítica*), and Ricardo Peralta Ramos (*La Razón*) to derail the proceedings. *La Prensa*'s Alberto Gainza Paz refused to acknowledge the commission's legitimacy.[13]

The debate, however, coincided with rumors of an imminent cabinet shakeup, and newspaper proprietors delayed consideration of the statute in the hope that a new government might shelve or even reject it. When the administration did change, however, it was in a manner that favored the promulgation of a statute even more sympathetic to the aspirations of journalists: the resignation of Ramírez revealed Perón as the dominant force within the new government. Not only would the statute move forward, it now became clear, but Perón's increased power meant that the regulations of the Journalist's Statute would see strict enforcement.

The Journalist's Statute became law by decree just two weeks after General Edelmiro Farrell assumed the presidency. In a short ceremony held at the Casa Rosada, the new president symbolically presented a formal copy of the decree to the FAP's oldest member, journalist Ernesto Muello, who in turn called on Octavio Palazzolo to address those gathered. Palazzolo's words are indicative of a new attitude toward the de facto regime among a growing number of journalists, shaped in great part by Perón's new prominence: "Thanks to the intelligent comprehension and to the spirit of justice that motivates the secretary of labor and social welfare, Colonel Perón; to the almost heroic collaboration of Doctor Bramuglia, director of social welfare; and to the clear sense of social justice of the present government, we journalists have been able to make this conquest. . . . It is also the result of the struggle of our journalist's union, whose aspirations have been manifest in [our] different national congresses."[14] The material and symbolic gains enshrined in the Journalist's Statute, Palazzolo suggested, did not come from attempts by a dictatorial regime of dubious legitimacy to co-opt newsworkers. Instead, the Journalist's Statute was the product of a quarter century of effort by journalists fortuitously converging with the sudden appearance of a government that recognized the justice and legitimacy of their struggle.

If Palazzolo saw the ceremony as the culmination of a much longer effort, for Farrell's cabinet the ceremony signified something quite different. The president, after all, literally and symbolically handed the new statute to the journalists. In addition, the secretary of labor and social welfare was not the only cabinet member in attendance. The presence of General Perlinger, the hard-line minister of the interior who had overseen the police sweeps directed against journalists just months before, likely served a dual purpose: that Perlinger might mitigate journalists' understandably negative feelings toward the Ministry of the Interior through his association with the new decree; and, more ominously, that Perlinger's presence might remind journalists that an uncompromising, ever-present stick remained should Perón's carrot prove inadequate. In a clear reminder of who had jurisdiction over journalists, Farrell expressly noted that he had requested the attendance of the minister of the interior since the new decree was "in relation to the press."[15] The photo that *Crítica* carried of the ceremony in this sense is quite revealing. Farrell, dressed in civilian suit and tie, is flanked on his right by the uniformed Perlinger, rigid and unsmiling, hands behind his back. To Farrell's left stands a jovial Perón, briefcase in hand (perhaps it contains yet another of the busy minister's many projects?). Bramuglia, smiling and clearly at ease, stands beside Perón.[16]

Just as revealing, newspaper proprietors were not invited to the ceremony despite their participation in the statute's elaboration. Officially, this was due to Farrell's reluctance to interfere with proprietors' busy schedules, but Octavio Palazzolo hinted at the true reason when he pronounced, "Mr. President: you have given us an instrument of peace in which the social program of this government is realized: to create and maintain the harmony between capital and labor. If at some point it becomes a weapon of war, that will not be our fault."[17] Rhetorically, the owners of the nation's newspapers also benefited from the statute's alleviation of what Praprotnik had called "destructive class conflict" in their institutions; in practice, however, the statute contained little to advance the goals of proprietors. Just one article of the Journalist's Statute, in fact, represented an important concession to the interests of newspaper owners, though it was indeed crucial: article 66 declared the total abrogation of the New Year's press decree (18.407).[18] Regardless of official pronouncements, then, members of the regime did perceive the statute, at least partially, as a means of dividing opposition within the press and at the same time incorporating the nation's journalists into an ambitious social project.

If Palazzolo's warning that the statute might at some point become a weapon in a heightened class struggle in the newspaper industry revealed a full awareness of proprietor hostility to the measure, it also recognized the degree to which journalists were the primary beneficiaries of the new capital-labor "harmony" in the newsroom. Journalists fell into ten clearly delineated categories under the Journalist's Statute, each with a minimum monthly wage set in accordance with a three-tiered classification of employing periodicals.[19] Further wage increases of 5 percent would become effective every thirty-six months.[20] To reinforce the strength of the salary increase and in an attempt to expand the total number of positions open to the nation's journalists, the statute also limited the formal workweek to thirty-six hours (no limit had previously existed) and deducted overtime from the following week's hours.

This combination of higher wages and a shorter workweek had an impact as beneficial for working journalists as it was contrary to the interests of newspaper proprietors. For example, the evening paper *Noticias Gráficas*, provisionally classified as category two, immediately raised salary payments to journalists by 33 percent under the statute; the increase would top 64 percent by October 1945, following the paper's reclassification as category one in April of that year.[21] Owners of economically more powerful newspapers like *Crítica* saw even greater growth in journalists' wage payments, not only because their classification as category one periodicals demanded steeper salary increases, but also because they distributed these higher wages to more employees.[22] For working journalists, the financial advantage of the new regulations went beyond the new pay structure. In addition to rapidly rising wages, the advent of the thirty-six-hour workweek opened the possibility for newsworkers long accustomed to extended hours to hold positions at more than one newspaper or, alternatively, to seek additional employment in the rapidly expanding public sector.

At the same time that it granted journalists more favorable pay and working hours, the statute stabilized employment for journalists by making employer dismissal of newsworkers both difficult and costly. Only conviction of serious crimes, physical or mental disability, prolonged or repeated absences, serious or repeated disobedience in the workplace, and poor performance by "apprentice" reporters qualified as legitimate grounds for dismissal, and union membership was specifically prohibited as a cause for termination.[23] In addition, the statute placed any termination in accord with the still unenforced judicial rulings of the 1930s, requiring employers to give one month prior notice for dismissal as well as severance pay equal to half of one month's salary (at the new pay scale) for each year of employment.[24] Newspaper proprietors faced even stiffer penalties for dismissing journalists in anticipation of the statute's promulgation: in a last-minute addition to the measure, journalists discharged between January 1, 1944, and December 31, 1945, became entitled to the equivalent of six months of wages plus one month's salary per year of employment—again, all calculated under the statute's higher wage levels.[25] Retroactive to the beginning of 1944 and lasting for two full, extremely eventful years, these provisions made it nearly impossible for newspaper proprietors to dismiss journalists for economic, political, or even work-related reasons. In a crucial period of rapid national economic transformation, newspaper owners suddenly faced a sharp curtailment of their ability to control important aspects of the economic fortune of their businesses.

If the Journalist's Statute brought concrete, sweeping reforms to the working conditions of professional journalists, its importance for the ideological foundations of the Argentine press were no less profound. Decree 18.407 had tentatively recognized the press's intervention in the daily course of commerce; the Journalist's Statute, in turn, categorically identified news organizations themselves as commercial entities. In the course of the 1930s, the traditional view of the press as a purely cultural institution designed for the individual exercise of democratic citizenship had already shown signs of strain together with the democratic liberalism upon which the notion rested. With the Journalist's Statute, however, the conception of the newspaper as at once cultural and economic, expression and commodity, became both widely accepted and an integral element of the press's legal status. This recognition of the newspaper industry *as industry* and the practice of journalism as an economic activity also clearly situated the press within a much broader social discourse articulated by state functionaries and, in particular, by the secretary of labor. In promoting the workplace demands of journalists, the statute explicitly declared that the newspaper industry—indeed, the newsroom itself—was divided, like the rest of Argentine society, into two mutually antagonistic camps: labor and capital.

Editors, proprietors, and even journalists of the Argentine commercial press traditionally spoke and wrote of individual news organizations and the institution of "the press" in anthropomorphic terms. Such discursive constructions of newspaper institutions as internally coherent, harmonious, and unified entities went beyond linguistic convenience and served to mystify the broad array of individual and collective interests personified in those institutions, to mask conflicts within the press, and to allow newspaper proprietors to present their own interests and goals as those of the profession as a whole.[26] State policy historically reinforced this perception: government measures tended to address an undifferentiated "press" and, in turn, adversely affected the entire spectrum of those involved in the newspaper industry. As a result, previous government interventions, like decree 18.407, tended to strengthen rather than undermine solidarity and the identification of interests between journalists and proprietors.

Yet the Journalist's Statute, unlike decree 18.407, explicitly addressed the press not as a unified object, but as an institution fraught with internal divisions. Regardless of the innate "moral unity" of proprietors and staff proclaimed by the directors of papers like *La Nación*, the statute recognized not only that newspapers were not individuals, but that the actual human relations within those institutions were inherently antagonistic.[27] That the Journalist's Statute declared journalists rather than proprietors the direct producers of the "knowledge, thought, and spirit" of the press as well as the source of the newspaper industry's material and cultural wealth, together with the dramatic material gains accorded to journalists, made recognition of the divisions within the press more than merely formal: the measure drew the enthusiastic support of journalists and the resolute defiance of newspaper owners.[28]

The Journalist's Statute, in fact, proposed a fundamentally different relationship between the national state and the press, in which, consistent with the Farrell-Perón regime's corporatist vision, the Argentine state would act as the fulcrum of class equilibrium in the newspaper industry. The statute placed the Secretariat of Labor and Social Welfare in charge of enforcing the wage increases and other benefits to journalists enshrined in the decree, and extended to the Secretariat the power to impose stiff and progressive fines for any employer violations. Employee grievances saw resolution through a special labor court in which the secretary of labor and social welfare had the final word.[29] Similarly, a special commission drawn from the FAP and proprietor representatives, presided over by a delegation from the Secretariat, would examine all questions related to salary and working conditions not addressed in the statute.[30] Officials of the Secretariat of Labor and Social Welfare even became the final arbiters in determining who might exercise the profession: disputes over admission to a new national registry of journalists fell to another FAP-proprietor commission, in which the secretary of labor held the deciding vote in case of deadlock.[31] Even though the denial of registration appeared quite difficult, the fact that the Secretariat itself also maintained the registry and issued journalists' identification cards gave state officials greater bureaucratic oversight of professional journalists.

This new form of state intervention in the functioning of the press, however, was based as much on the public nature of journalism practice as on the state's emerging role as mediator of social conflict. Class conflict, the Journalist's Statute made explicit, permeated the newsroom and formed an integral part of the set of relationships that constituted the modern press. Crucially, the importance of the press as a public medium of ideology creation demanded state "harmonization" of those relationships. According to the statute's preamble, the press's public character made it vital to national interests—in Farrell's and Perón's corporatist conception, an integral part of the state itself—and the mediation of newsroom class tensions a duty of the national state: "the press, as a cultural manifestation and expression of public opinion . . . , and as an industrial and commercial organization, being, as it is, *part of the State itself,* is equally interested in elevating the standard of living of the fundamental factors of its production—the journalists. . . . In that way [the press] truly works for the greatness of the nation."[32] State intervention in the newspaper industry in the form of labor regulation and the mandatory arbitration of labor disputes did not threaten the press, the creators of the statute affirmed; it protected the "true mission" of journalism and journalists as agents of public expression.

The statute, then, not only facilitated a rearticulation of the complex set of relationships between newsworkers and newspaper proprietors, it also fundamentally and immediately altered the status of the press vis-à-vis the Argentine state. The long-term implications of this shift were threefold. First, the juridical classification of news organizations as commercial entities opened the newspaper industry—like any other area of the Argentine economy—to state regulation of labor, newsprint, and other productive inputs. Coming at a time of increasingly broad acceptance of the legitimacy of state economic interventionism, this fundamental shift in the legal status of the commercial press would have consequences in the coming years that would prove far greater than were apparent in 1944. Second, the statute drove not only a figurative wedge between newspaper proprietors and working journalists, but an institutional one: the Secretariat of Labor and Social Welfare. Beyond recognizing the preexisting reality of class struggle in the newsroom, Perón's Secretariat entered the newsroom not as a temporary, circumstantial factor, like the state censors, but as an integral part of the relationship between newspaper proprietors and journalists. Finally, unlike the Undersecretariat of Information and the Press, already a contentious part of newsroom life, this particular state presence acted not as censor, but as protector of journalists' material interests.

For many working journalists, the notion that any state involvement in the functioning of the press necessarily compromised press freedom and restricted the practice of journalism no longer held; the work of the Secretariat of Labor and Social Welfare now gave a clear indication to the contrary. For newspaper proprietors, the statute's erosion of their prerogatives in what they considered the private realm of their papers' newsrooms only confirmed the dangers and illegitimacy of state intervention in the workings of the press. Although disputes between working journalists and newspaper proprietors over the nature of the press, the meaning of journalism practice, and the proper relationship between state and press were not creations of Perón's Secretariat, the Journalist's Statute made these more abstract issues of the press's ideological foundations suddenly urgent, practical, and impossible to ignore.

"Enemies of the Profession"

If members of the FAP, the APBA, and the Círculo de la Prensa actively participated in the elaboration and promotion of the Journalist's Statute, the reaction of newspaper proprietors to the project was overwhelmingly—and predictably—negative. Despite Perón's proclaimed intention of "harmonizing" the relationship between journalists and newspaper proprietors, the statute, by recognizing the existence of class conflict in the newsroom, brought antagonisms brewing since the 1930s suddenly to the surface. The conflict surrounding the statute, in fact, resembled a typical labor-capital dispute much more than most proprietors seemed willing to concede; proprietors, in their efforts to derail, weaken, and nullify the measure, inadvertently bolstered journalists' militancy and sense of the statute's necessity. For many newsworkers, the primary threat to their profession no longer necessarily came from the national state, but, as some journalists began to argue, from newspaper proprietors themselves.

Just prior to the enactment of the Journalist's Statute, heightened censorship and official harassment prevented a complete journalist-proprietor split by presenting both parties with a common threat: the military government. By early February 1944, a campaign by *La Nación, La Prensa, Crítica*, and other papers to win the full abrogation of the New Year's decrees dominated editorials—coinciding, surely not by chance, with a leak of the text of the proposed Journalist's Statute.[33] The Círculo de la Prensa of the province of Tucumán even initially refused to consider the statute at all, advising both Perón and the FAP, of which the organization was an affiliate, that any potential material advance for journalists was rendered null by the government's continued violation of freedom of the press.[34] Alberto Gerchunoff and Mauricio Bornand, negotiators for the Círculo de la Prensa of the city of Buenos Aires, similarly found themselves torn between supporting the statute and lobbying for the elimination of press restrictions.[35] The combined pressure of proprietors and journalists, Perón's ascent in the regime, and international criticism of the still-unrecognized Farrell government's vigilance over the press ultimately forced the addition to the statute of article 66, which repealed decree 18.407. A clear point of contention among journalists with regard to the statute was thus removed.

For the owners of the country's newspapers, the revocation of decree 18.407 did not make the Journalist's Statute more palatable. Still, opposition to the measure appeared only in the most muted of forms in the commercial press. *Crítica*, despite its enthusiastic support for other measures of the Secretariat of Labor and Social Welfare, gave tepid coverage to Farrell's presentation of the statute and did not address the event editorially. A commentator at *La Nación*, in turn, praised the "satisfactory repeal" of decree 18.407 contained in the new measure's article 66, adding only that "free journalism should act with no other limitation than that of the general laws, and with no form of official involvement either in its public services or its internal workings [*régimen interno*]."[36] Nor did other editorialists explicitly endorse the Journalist's Statute; the pages of the commercial newspapers would not become the primary battleground in the growing conflict between newspaper proprietors and journalists with regard to the measure.

La Prensa marked the clear exception. In a lengthy critique published while the joint proprietor-journalist commission considered the statute, Alberto Gainza Paz objected not just to particular terms of the proposed measure, but to the bases of the statute itself: the twin notions of journalistic activity as labor and newspapers as commercial enterprises. Gainza Paz dogmatically insisted that the labor-capital dichotomy, while perhaps valid in other areas of social life, bore absolutely no relation to the reality of the newspaper industry and the "exalted mission of the press" as a central element of the public sphere. "We repudiate any conception that does not coincide with the [press's] mission of public good," he declared, "and any attempt to take from the newspaper its character as a tribunal of government to assign it that of a profit-making business or industry."[37]

If the newspapers, because of their normative character as public fora, simply could not be commercial institutions, Gainza Paz declared, journalistic activity could not be equated with wage labor. "We deem it the most gross and prejudicial of errors any attempt to consider the journalist as an intellectual worker. 'Worker,' by definition, is the paid manual laborer: the machinist who can [do his work] in any factory; the bricklayer where there is a building to build.... The journalist has no affinity with the worker due to his condition as an intellectual."[38] Journalists could not "possess the same right to demand better working conditions as all other workers," simply because they were not, in fact, workers; misguided attempts to "diminish the intellectual status of the journalist in benefit of some *dark unionism*" could not change this.[39] The intellectual character of journalism practice, Gainza Paz maintained, required "innate" skills and "moral attributes that are not always necessary or evident in other professions." In effect, the journalist stood not within the broader context of Argentine social classes, but rather above society, as a "spectator and censor . . . , as a man of the world and also of government." The journalist was not a "worker of the pen," but something immeasurably more honorable: an intellectual.

The relationship between journalist and proprietor, then, had nothing to do with the relationship between labor and capital that might exist in other fields. Instead, journalists were bound to "their" newspapers by a set of affective bonds that transcended economic interest or obligation, not by a wage. Dedication to the "dissemination and triumph" of his ideas, Gainza Paz maintained, gave the journalist's activity "a spiritual and ideological seal, and obliges him to be where he should be, where others think and feel as he does. For that reason we believe in the intimate and inseparable connection of the journalist with the newspaper. That newspaper is not one of many, but rather is his newspaper, matching his temperament, his ideas and ideals, and for which he gives the best of his life and fervor."[40] Revealingly, in Gainza Paz's formulation newspaper proprietors—the actual personifications of capital in the press industry—remained invisible, vanishing in the harmonious collective subjects embodied in their newspapers. How could the statute serve to better a relationship *already* based on the voluntary and affective bonds of an intimate spiritual, ideological, and temperamental affinity?

For Gainza Paz, the statute's threat to the press and its extraneousness to the proper relationship between journalists and proprietors indicated more than the "dark unionism" of some journalists. The true motive for the statute, Gainza Paz declared, was revealed in a passing reference, in an early draft of the statute, to the Italian and French precedents: to make the Argentine press the "instrument of a totalitarian state."[41] The means by which the nation's journalists might become simple "state functionaries" as in Fascist Italy, or "bankrupted by demagoguery" as in Third Republic France, lay in the Secretariat of Labor and Social Welfare's registry of professional journalists. Through the registry, ostensibly designed to ensure the proper allocation of pensions and benefits, the state held veto power over those who participated in the profession. Registering officially in order to practice journalism, as the statute required, amounted to asking government permission to exercise the fundamental freedoms of work and the press; Alberdi, Gainza Paz reminded his readers, had already explained that "to ask for permission to be free is to confess oneself a slave."[42] Far from an assurance of social justice for those who practiced the profession, Gainza Paz maintained, the Journalist's Statute was an unequivocal and purposeful erosion of the press's independence. The American Society of Newspaper Editors quickly applauded his "courageous" stance.[43]

In some measure, as would become clear in the coming years, Gainza Paz was correct: the incorporation of journalists into the political and social project of the regime did alter the state-press relationship in ways not always conducive to journalists' intentions for the profession. Yet the arguments of *La Prensa*'s owner, and his concrete actions in later years, hardly worked to avoid this outcome. First, the archetypal relationship between journalist and newspaper that Gainza Paz presented hardly resonated with the common experience of the vast majority of the country's working journalists—at least since the turn of the century. At *La Prensa,* as well as many other less economically powerful newspapers, even editorialists received compensation "by the centimeter" of text; the "ideas and ideals" for which Gainza Paz expected the true journalist to "give the best of his life and fervor" figured, in fact, in the coarsest form of commodity exchange.[44] The *La Prensa* proprietor's insistence that the statute would bring about journalists' proletarianization thus amounted to a transparent reversal of cause and effect in newsworkers' perceived reality. Gainza Paz's denial of the statute's legitimacy and his criticism of "dark unionism," similarly, convinced few journalists that his arguments were not ultimately based in his economic self-interest. Finally, few would hesitate to remark that Gainza Paz's rejection of the notion that newspapers bore any resemblance to commercial enterprises found its clearest counterexample in his own enormously lucrative, advertisement-laden newspaper.

Still, Gainza Paz's open criticism of the Journalist's Statute remained the exception among newspaper owners. Rather than the pages of the nation's commercial dailies, the main venues for proprietor response to the project would be the Joint Commission examining the statute and the newsroom itself. Most ominously, the early leak of the project by the United Press brought its first victims in the city of Córdoba in early February, as newspaper proprietors around the country began to discharge employees in preparation for the statute's promulgation. The reprisals and layoffs appear to have stopped only with the last-minute inclusion of article 67, the statute's final article, which imposed exceptionally strong penalties on employers for dismissals made between January 1, 1944, and December 31, 1945.[45]

Similarly, José Agusti, a proprietor's representative on the Secretariat of Labor and Social Welfare's statute commission, attempted a series of delays and "secret" amendments to the project, earning himself on one hand the surprising classification of his *Noticias Gráficas* as category two—despite its being Latin America's fourth-largest newspaper—and on the other the epithet "greatest enemy of the profession" among some members of the FAP.[46] Journalists also accused Raúl Damonte Taborda of calling upon seemingly endless legal chicanery (*chicanas*) to impede first the statute's approval, then the classification of *Crítica* as category one, and, finally, the full implementation of the new pay scale.[47] The vast majority of newspaper proprietors also resisted the statute's pay increases, with even the more prosperous papers holding to the pre-statute pay scales until the official classification of news organizations became effective in June. Ironically, Gainza Paz again marked the exception: the proprietor of *La Prensa* conceded immediately—and logically—that his paper would fall into category one and began compensating journalists accordingly from the date of the statute's enactment.[48]

Divided Solidarity

Gainza Paz's early, unhesitating compliance with the Journalist's Statute did little to allay the growing tensions between many of the country's journalists and newspaper proprietors. In fact, the form and tenacity of proprietor opposition confirmed for many journalists not just the need for the statute, but also the fundamental divergence of interests between labor and capital in the newspaper industry. Still, the breach between journalists and proprietors was neither absolute nor the sole division within the profession; working journalists themselves differed over the social, political, and ideological implications of the Journalist's Statute, and Perón's growing power more generally. Torn between their identification with both the working class and "the press," the nation's journalists began to feel more urgently the contradictory effects of the social transformation underway.

Again, the primary obstacle to journalists' unequivocal alliance with the regime resided in continued—and increasingly severe—punitive state actions against news organizations and individual journalists. *La Prensa*, the government's harshest media critic, became a special, highly visible target. Just ten days before issuing the Journalist's Statute, the Farrell regime suspended the United Press in Argentina for carrying news that the Argentine navy was preparing to act against the military government.[49] Although the closure lasted just eighteen days, the move dealt a major blow to the agency since not only was Argentina a major market for the UP—*La Prensa* was the agency's single largest customer in the world—but Buenos Aires served as the organization's South American headquarters.[50]

The closure, however, had as much to do with the political exigencies of the regime as with the content of UP's reporting. Faced with the refusal of the United States to recognize his government, Farrell apparently sought, unsuccessfully, to convince UP officials to intervene on his behalf with the State Department in exchange for lifting the closure.[51] In addition, Argentine officials likely saw the closure of the United Press as a prelude to the rapid expansion of a properly Argentine news agency, ANDI (Agencia Noticiosa Argentina, S.A.). While the action against the United Press did bring journalists at other news organizations to act with greater self-censorship, it failed to achieve the broader goals: the Farrell regime remained unrecognized, and the ambitious ANDI project collapsed almost immediately. Surprisingly, the closure also only barely interrupted the flow of UP cables to *La Prensa*, as the agency temporarily managed to reroute its news flow from Buenos Aires to Montevideo, passing news to *La Prensa* by cable and courier.[52] It did, however, have a long-term effect on the functioning of the news organization in Argentina, with the UP moving to decentralize its operations in South America. It also brought *La Prensa* to contract the services of Reuters for the first time, following the British ambassador's suggestion to the agency head that they supply the service free of charge to the paper for the duration of the crisis. With the lifting of the closure of the UP, Gainza Paz began a regular contract with the British agency, no doubt at least partially in an effort both to protect *La Prensa* from further interruptions in cable service and to broaden alliances with foreign news organizations.[53]

On April 26, just three weeks after the Argentine government lifted the closure of the United Press, *La Prensa* itself ceased to appear. The previous day, in a comparatively staid commentary on "Savings in the Municipal Hospitals," a *La Prensa* editorialist ostensibly overstepped the bounds imposed by official censors, providing the regime with a justification for action against its most prominent critic. The paper suffered its first closure since its founding seventy-five years earlier. Five days later *La Prensa* reappeared, running an extensive response to the original editorial penned by functionaries of the General Direction of Sanitation and Public Assistance; officials from the Undersecretariat of Information and the Press permitted no further commentary. Ironically, in the midst of the closure, the courts finally acquitted the president of the Círculo de la Prensa and editorialist with *La Prensa*, Adolfo Lanús, accused in January of "disrespecting" then-President Ramírez.[54]

The closure of *La Prensa*, together with the strong police presence in the paper's newsroom to supervise its reappearance, had a dampening effect on journalists throughout the country.[55] Local commentary on the five-day suspension of one of the world's more powerful newspapers remained limited by the continued state of siege; only the official decree of the closure and the direction of sanitation's correction appeared in the national press.[56] A more cautious attitude prevailed in the newsrooms in the coming months, and even the traditionally candid criticisms of government policy in the pages of *La Prensa* softened.

The action against *La Prensa* also brought Luís Mitre to tighten internal censorship at *La Nación*. Immediately after the paper published an abstract opinion piece warning against the dangers of demagoguery, Mitre penned an apology to President Farrell, assuring the general that author Mila Forn de Oteiza Quirno had "surprised [his] good faith" in submitting such a clearly impertinent article. The text of the letter appeared on page 1 the following day, together with the assurance that the author of the offensive text would no longer write for *La Nación*—even though, ironically, such ideological offenses did not qualify as grounds for dismissal under the Journalist's Statute.[57] The brief episode reveals the conditions under which much of the Argentine press had begun to operate: not only did strict internal censorship prevail in the *La Nación* newsroom, but Mitre appeared willing to act publicly as the censor himself.[58] Even the regime's lifting of all newspaper closures in early August— a move clearly made in response to growing U.S. pressure against the supposedly "Nazi-fascist" regime—had little impact on the functioning of the press as a whole, since the state of siege still held.[59]

By October 1944, then, Argentine journalists faced an awkward situation vis-à-vis the military government, and particularly with regard to that government's most dynamic figure. On the one hand, working journalists had achieved extremely important material gains by virtue of Perón's activities as secretary of labor and social welfare. At the same time, Perón's growing dominance within the regime had neither eased government-imposed censorship nor slowed the continual flow of journalists through the nation's jails. With Perón now occupying the offices of vice president and minister of war as well as secretary of labor, and clearly dominating other cabinet posts, journalists could no longer so easily separate the repressive and social reformist sides of government press policy. Where journalists had once viewed Juan Perón as marginal to the regime's repressive apparatus, the colonel now unequivocally stood at the center of the entire range of the regime's policies. In March, employees of the suspended United Press had felt that they could find sympathy from Perón for their situation; by midyear, it had become obvious that any action affecting the press could not occur without his prior approval.[60] Dissociating the government's labor policies from the broader political project advanced by Farrell and Perón became more difficult to sustain, straining journalists' unity.

Journalism, Citizenship, and the State

The fifth annual congress of the Argentine Federation of Journalists met in this charged atmosphere. That the union now met under vastly changed legal circumstances and in the wake of the unexpected triumph of their maximum program would guarantee an eventful FAP congress. Yet the combined effects of the shifting ideological context of journalism practice, the heightened militancy of the FAP, continued proprietor opposition to the Statute, and relentless state censorship would make this first national meeting of journalists since the enactment of the Journalist's Statute uncharacteristically tumultuous. *La Vanguardia*, the Socialist Party newspaper, at which many FAP and APBA members worked, had remained closed by government decree since April, despite the regime's lifting of most other suspensions.[61] Equally problematic, the Radical Party politician, director of *La Unión* (Entre Ríos), and *Crítica* contributor Silvano Santander sent his greetings to the FAP delegates, sarcastically apologizing for his absence from the proceedings; as a member of the union's executive committee, Santander should have attended the congress but instead found himself incarcerated in Villa Devoto.[62]

While the enthusiasm of the more vocal journalists from Buenos Aires for explicit tactical alliance with the Farrell-Perón regime would not prove entirely persuasive, the APBA members' influence within the FAP brought many of their colleagues along in practice. In fact, the logistical and administrative details of the 1944 FAP congress itself reveal the solidity of the journalist union's good relations with the government. The meetings took place not in the locale of an allied union, as they had in previous years, but in the administrative heart of the emerging Peronist project: the offices of the Secretariat of Labor and Social Welfare.[63] In addition to the FAP delegates, a roster of prestigious and politically symbolic guests attended the inaugural session of the congress: the minister of the navy and interim minister of the interior, Alberto Teisaire; the director of social welfare, Juan A. Bramuglia; the general director of social action and director of welfare for railroad workers, Lieutenant Colonel Domingo Mercante; and other functionaries of the Secretariat of Labor and Social Welfare.[64]

To prolonged applause, Perón delivered the meeting's key opening address. The secretary of labor and social welfare placed the roots of the Journalist's Statute precisely in the practical situation of class divisions within the newsroom, describing the "tremendous contrast between some businesses that are too rich and journalists that are too poor."[65] Pointing to government investment in the press in the form of official advertising, infrastructure support, and customs benefits—"a real state subsidy," he declared—Perón argued that it was only logical that the state should ensure that its expenditures benefited those who actually created newspaper content, rather than being to the exclusive benefit of proprietors.[66] Like General Justo a decade earlier, then, the secretary of labor argued that the de facto intertwining of the economic elements of the national state and the national press ensured the legitimacy of state intervention in the functioning of the press.

Perón diverged from Justo's precedent, however, in setting out to the assembled journalists his own view of how the press should best function. If the Journalist's Statute brought the force of law to a previously unrecognized ele-

Fig. 8 Perón addresses the Fifth Congress of the Federación Argentina de Periodistas, Buenos Aires, October 20, 1944.

ment of what the press *was*—a set of commercial institutions—it nonetheless remained ambiguous on what, in fact, the press *should be*. In his address, Perón presented a characterization of the "essential function of the press" that, revealingly, melded corporatist conceptions of representation, authoritarianism, and liberal notions of the press's function as a "fourth estate" monitoring the branches of government. Echoing Gainza Paz, Perón declared the criticism of state actions a central element of the press's social role, arguing that governments could survive neither the "uniform and directed praise" of inept state practice nor "the wave of silence, indifference, rumor, and ridicule" that accompanied strict censorship.[67] The regime would continue to oppose, however, "arbitrary invocations of freedom of expression which hide campaigns destined to confuse and disorient public opinion."[68]

Still more ambitiously, Perón continued by invoking the role that journalists might play not merely as actors within the arena of public expression, but as conduits for the expression of the whole range of the Argentine public. In this sense, Perón argued that journalists had a duty to create a press that would serve as a mirror of the public's opinion, rather than simply as a public expression of private opinion. The true social role of journalism, Perón declared, was the *"authentic expression of the collective feelings and thoughts"* of the public.[69] The journalist thus "has the inexcusable duty to collect the clamor of the street, of the factory, and of the countryside if he wants his judgment to be something more than the personal expression of a commentator—whose opinion we do not underestimate, *but which we cannot accept as a reflection of popular sentiment.*"[70] The proper social role of journalists, then, was less as individual writers than as facilitators of a social conversation. Communication should flow not just vertically between populace and state or between the small, powerful political and economic elite and the mass of the population, but horizontally across *all* sectors of society. Perón thus exhorted journalists to seek actively the inclusion of *all* of "the public" in their articulation of "public opinion," balancing the disparities in social power that traditionally plagued the press; otherwise, claims that the press voiced anything but the thoughts of individual journalists and, above all, the private interests of newspaper proprietors, advertisers, and investors would remain empty.

For Perón, then, the gap between long-standing promises of formal citizenship (full and equal membership in "the public") and the fact of social inequality might be bridged not just by the social justice policies of the state, but in the pages of the daily press. Rather than negating individual rights of self-expression, Perón emphatically expanded them to include the collective social right of expression and positive representation in the media. Indeed, the roots of this demand for broad media representation lay within the discourse of the commercial press itself, even as it responded to the crisis of representative democracy unleashed in the 1930s: constantly interpellating its readers as equal members of "the public" whose opinion it expressed, how could the commercial press fail to include the voices of what were undeniably large sectors of that public? If universal access to the means of expression remained a practical impossibility in the modern press, the role of journalists was to serve faithfully as conduits for the exercise of collective expression and to represent selflessly the entirety of the polity in the public sphere. Thus, even as formal political citizenship remained repressed, Perón declared the mission of the press that of serving as a vehicle for the collective articulation of aspirations and interests of the Argentine public.

For Perón, it was not the state, but the private "political interest" and "economic interest" of certain businesses and "social sectors"—in short, capital and its allies—that were the primary threat to the press's role as embodiment and representation of public opinion's true diversity.[71] The potential instrumentalization of this discourse as a means of dismissing criticism emanating from the press, however, remained latent, and the possibility remained years distant that accusations against newspaper owners for impeding the true function of the press as a vehicle of collective expression and representation might lead to serious legal action. Similarly, the true importance of Perón's appeal to journalists to serve as the conduits for the Argentine popular sectors' articulation of interests and aspirations would only become obvious twelve months later, when the polarization between the "mouthpieces of public opinion" and an increasingly large and powerful sector of the public itself became a chasm bridged only by violence.

Through the course of the three-day FAP meeting, however, journalists quickly became conscious of the potential for polarization within their own profession, as disputes emerged surrounding not just the particular national political juncture, but the changing conceptions of the nature of journalism itself. A sharp division arose on the first full day of the congress, pitting those who saw the social changes inaugurated by the regime—and, in particular, the Journalist's Statute—as far outweighing the military government's authoritarianism, against those who maintained a more traditional view of the nature of the press and the social role of journalism.

Not coincidentally, the vocal adherents of both tendencies shared a further difference: those who gave broadest support to the social transformation underway belonged to the FAP's Buenos Aires affiliate, the APBA, while the traditionalists came from the province of Santa Fe.[72] This geographic separation also reflected a latent class division within the union, making debate between the two groups that much more heated. The APBA, after all, had emerged as the response of working journalists to the inordinate influence of newspaper proprietors within the *porteño* Círculo de la Prensa; the large and influential Círculo de la Prensa de Rosario, on the other hand, simply affiliated with the FAP in 1938, leaving its multiclass, mutual aid society structure intact. The conflicting agendas of journalists of the APBA, who had participated directly in the elaboration of the Journalist's Statute, and those of the Círculo de la Prensa de Rosario revealed the divergent allegiances of journalists alternatively to the national working class and to "the press" as a coherent, quasi-classless whole.

At no point during the congress did this divergence become clearer than late in the evening of October 21. A simple motion to send greetings to *La Prensa* on the paper's seventy-fifth anniversary met with the staunch opposition of journalists from the city of Buenos Aires. What for the Rosario representatives amounted to a simple homage to "the institution that is *La Prensa*, as a mouthpiece of public opinion ... [and as] a defender of the principles of our national constitution" struck the APBA delegates as a capitulation to the maximum representative of capital in the newspaper industry. Journalist Santiago Senén González reminded his colleagues of Gainza Paz's assertion of the FAP's "dark unionism," adding more fundamentally that "we have taken a position with regard to these [newspaper] businesses since the statute came out, and we face them in a position of struggle." Oscar Ares of *La Razón* similarly argued that the class solidarity of working journalists at this moment of tension within the industry—and even in Argentine society as a whole—precluded any possibility of solidarity with the directors of *La Prensa* or any other newspaper: "The newspaper *La Prensa* has opposed the [journalist pension law], the statute, and all other victories of our union. It has never had a line of conduct with regard to our problems. Since [the coup of] June 4 *La Prensa* has not had a line of conduct; *La Prensa* and *La Nación* have disillusioned us as instruments that might have guided national opinion. And we say these words: *La Prensa* is simply a commercial instrument that is seventy-five years old!"[73] Offended, the delegates from Rosario threatened to abandon the congress, agreeing to stay only when the presiding officers—also from the province of Santa Fe—called an immediate vote on the issue. The motion passed, despite the vocal protests of Octavio Palazzolo and other APBA delegates.

The incident placed in stark relief the consequences of the ideological transformation underway within the profession. Domingo Varea of the Círculo de la Prensa de Rosario "could not permit" assertions of *La Prensa*'s purely commercial character, maintaining that the paper's record in "defending freedom of the press, individual rights, and our constitutional system" deserved the union's recognition.[74] He argued that the greeting applied to all those who worked at the paper, without distinction—in effect, to *La Prensa* as a collective subject. For Oscar Ares and Santiago Senén González, in contrast, any praise of *La Prensa* as a whole amounted to an explicit endorsement of the man who dominated the organization: Alberto Gainza Paz. The particularly acute level of class struggle within the newspaper industry, they argued, demanded a consistent, unyielding solidarity among working journalists; the primary threat to the profession came not from state repression, but from the continued ideological and material hegemony of newspaper proprietors.

Furthermore, a thinly veiled corresponding political rupture had begun to emerge within the organization. Varea's praise of *La Prensa*'s adherence to the tenets of traditional Argentine liberalism as enshrined in the Constitution of 1853 indicated a clear support for Gainza Paz's opposition to the military government. For the Rosario journalist, the regime's undemocratic and repressive character far overshadowed in importance any supposed conflict of class interests within the profession. Senén González and Ares, however, implicitly endorsed the current government in denying the legitimacy and coherence of the *La Prensa* editorial line since, precisely, the coup of June 4, 1943. The two competing conceptions of the regime and its relation to journalists remained only partially reconcilable: both tended to concede that the Farrell-Perón government remained clearly dictatorial, but for the Buenos Aires journalists, the regime's social policies clearly mitigated its political inadequacies.

The previous day, during his report on the events leading to the elaboration and enactment of the Journalist's Statute, Octavio Palazzolo had made an even more explicit and far-reaching apology for journalists' strategic alliance with military authoritarianism. Yes, the current regime did embody certain characteristics inimical to the political ideals of journalists and detrimental to the practice of the profession; but, he explained, the suspension of constitutional guarantees may have been the only solution to the political and social morass into which the country had descended. Without the military's breaking of the bottleneck caused by over a decade of unrepresentative, thoroughly corrupt government administration, the Argentine state simply would not have responded to journalists' concerns within the foreseeable future. "I maintain that if we had waited to achieve this victory [the Journalist's Statute] until we had a normal government, elected not by means of a fraudulent semblance of democracy, but by the truth of the ballot box . . . ; if we had waited for the [existence] of a legislature, also clean; this statute, this first regulation of journalists' labor, who knows when and how it might have become a reality. Perhaps twenty-five years later, which is the normal process in our country for each one of the social laws."[75] The current regime's suspension of the exercise of fundamental elements of political citizenship was, given the nature of its predecessors, not a novelty; that state officials went against powerful economic interests for the benefit of less powerful sections of Argentine society was.

Yet Palazzolo went further still, questioning whether legislation favoring journalists might have surfaced at all under constitutional democracy. If the corruption of Argentine political life that had characterized the republic for over a decade had forestalled the implementation of social legislation, many such projects would have remained thwarted even under a "clean" constitutional government. In the particular case of labor legislation for journalists, the overwhelming power of newspaper owners easily negated liberal assertions of individual equality in political representation: "We are not so stupid as to fail to realize that legislators and political leaders cannot escape the 'influence of printed paper,' an influence which we know well. Few would dare to confront the journalism businesses by supporting a law like we currently have in our statute."[76] Neither the power of the press nor the power of the vote resided equally in the hands of all Argentines; for Palazzolo and others the saving grace of the military regime resided in the understanding that its most disturbing characteristic—authoritarianism—might just prove the only mechanism that could empower the otherwise disenfranchised.

The Journalist's Statute and the Coming Transformation of the Argentine Press

With the advent of the Journalist's Statute, the fundamental shift that began to take hold within the professional ideology of press workers in the course of the 1930s became irreversible. By the end of 1944, many influential journalists increasingly identified themselves as workers—not just in abstract political sympathy or class background, but in their present position in the process of production. In addition, that the Journalist's Statute lent force of law to this notion even as it recognized newspaper organizations as commercial enterprises brought important and long-sought material benefits. Perhaps not surprisingly, then, an important sector within the profession increasingly saw the actions of newspaper capital as the primary menace to the exercise of their profession, even as a branch of the national state established itself as a permanent mediator of the network of relationships that formed the press.

This self-identification of journalists with the politically ascendant working class, together with growing political polarization on the national level, began to carry with it a corollary that would become increasingly divisive: support for Juan Domingo Perón. In addition to the broader questions of the nature of the press and the social role of journalism that the Journalist's Statute brought to the fore, the close ties that the FAP leadership had begun to cultivate with the government remained a source of controversy. *La Prensa* journalists in the city of Córdoba, for example, withdrew from their union en masse in protest against the very statute designed to benefit them, while the Círculo de la Prensa de Rosario disaffiliated from the FAP immediately following the October congress.[77] Still, by early 1945, it had become clear that the Journalist's Statute had begun to "Peronize" not just the mechanics of productive relations in the newsroom and journalists' understanding of the nature of their professional activities, but also, more tentatively, the political sympathies of a growing sector of journalists themselves.

Ultimately more crucial for the future of the Argentine press, however, the Journalist's Statute carried with it a decisive modification of the juridical understanding of the nature of the newspaper industry and the social role of journalism. The explicit classification of newspapers as commercial enterprises—apparently little more than a belated recognition of the Argentine press's transformation in the twentieth century—opened the press to further government regulation as statist economic policies continued to gain ground. Despite the repeal of decree 18.407, the need to "balance" cultural and economic factors in order to protect the press's "genuine mission" as a conduit of social citizenship remained implicit in the Journalist's Statute's preamble, and explicit in Perón's assessment of the legitimate exercise of the power of journalism.

Thus, three clear justifications for future state intervention in the newspaper industry began to carry greater ideological weight: to ensure that commercial interests should not overwhelm the normative role of the press as a forum of public opinion and source of reliable information; to guarantee socially just conditions of production and fair competition, as with any other industry; and, finally, to defend labor, capital, and consumers from crises of production and distribution wrought by internal bottlenecks or external shocks. This vision of the state as defender—of the "true press" from commerce; of journalists from proprietors; and of smaller news organizations from more powerful ones—would soon become the central element of the Peronist discourse of the nature of the press and the social role of journalism. With the Journalist's Statute, this conception found its first concrete, broadly accepted, and enforceable expression.

Ironically, the recognition of commercial journalism's economic character combined coherently with traditional liberal portrayals of the role of the press. Gainza Paz himself, in his dogmatic repudiation of "any conception that does not coincide with the mission [of the press] as a public good . . . and designates it a profit-oriented business," inadvertently put forth a logical corollary that would come to haunt him in the coming years: if a newspaper should at any point become "a profit-oriented business or industry," it would thereby abdicate the "genuine mission of the press," and with it any claims to constitutional guarantees. State action, then, could conceivably provide greater protection for the press as a vehicle for the public exercise of citizenship than the deleterious, corrupting effects of the market or the narrow interests of private newspaper proprietors. In his comments at the October 1944 congress of the FAP, Oscar Ares prophetically revealed the degree to which the emerging discourse of the press-as-commerce had begun to gain legitimacy: his dismissal of *La Prensa* as "simply a commercial instrument" foreshadowed exactly the arguments used against the paper in congressional expropriation proceedings over six years later. More immediately, the notion that newspapers should embody the diversity of public opinion and represent the public as a whole would prove central to the strained relationship between press and vast sectors of the Argentine public in the coming twelve months.

The Journalist's Statute, by drawing attention to the underlying contradiction in the commercial press's dual cultural and economic function, marked a crucial shift in the evolution not just of the relationship between state and press in Argentina, but of dominant ideas of what the press is and what the press should be. This shift carried with it the potential to broaden citizen access to the means of communication substantially by definitively placing questions of property and economic power within the competence of media jurisprudence. Yet this socially democratizing possibility was surprisingly compatible, it would soon become clear, with expanding legal powers for authoritarian-minded government officials vis-à-vis the commercial press. It was precisely this tension between democratizing potential and political authoritarianism that would come to dominate state policy toward the press—and much of Argentine political life—in the coming years.

SCENES FROM THE PRESS WARS

> *Crítica*, after this, has disappeared from Argentine journalism. Its pistol-packing scribes, its criminal directors, its assault bands will be cleaned up by the police. Its machines have been left totally destroyed, and the front of the building says good and loud what the struggle was. The people will never again be shot in the back.
>
> —*La Época*, **October 18, 1945**

Few moments are as pivotal in modern Argentine history as the evening of October 17, 1945. The forced resignation of Juan Domingo Perón from the government and his subsequent detention by military officials on October 12 laid bare the fragility of the sweeping social transformation inaugurated less than two years earlier. As millions of Argentines mobilized in the early hours of October 17 to demand Perón's release, it became clear that the Farrell regime had succeeded beyond expectation in building a popular base; ironically, however, it also became clear that this support remained contingent precisely upon the presence of Perón himself within the regime. The unexpected success of the working-class mobilizations of October 17 in gaining the release of Perón changed the balance of power within the nation, earning labor an unprecedented protagonism. It also set the stage not just for a continuation of the social reforms that had begun under the aegis of the Secretariat of Labor and Social Welfare, but for their deepening under a constitutional Peronist regime. The crisis that had spurred that mobilization, however, also revealed important weaknesses in Perón's approach to the media.

The dramatic events surrounding October 17, 1945, quickly became the center of political ritual for what now became the Peronist movement proper, and have justly received more attention from scholars of Argentina than those of any other single date.[1] Still, few have addressed more than anecdotally that evening's most violent episode: the siege of *Crítica*.[2] As demonstrators dispersed after Perón's emotional address from the balcony of the Casa Rosada, a large crowd made its way thirteen blocks down the Avenida de Mayo, where it stopped in front of the *Crítica* offices. In a confrontation that lasted nearly three hours, demonstrators laid siege to the building with Molotov cocktails and machine guns before finally forcing their way into the offices and setting fire to the *Crítica* machine room. When the exchange of gunfire between demonstrators, the police, and the building's defenders finally ended, two men lay dead, nearly forty people were wounded, and forty-seven *Crítica* employees were detained.[3] The paper's director, Raúl Damonte Taborda, was already en route to Montevideo. The evening also left *Crítica*, the Spanish-speaking world's most innovative and widely read evening newspaper, moribund.

Despite the ferocity of the fighting at Avenida de Mayo 1333 and the extent of destruction caused by the onslaught on *Crítica*, historian Daniel James is the only scholar to seriously consider the nature and meaning of attacks on newspaper offices on October 17 and 18, albeit primarily in reference to worker mobilization in and around the city of La Plata, capital of the province of Buenos Aires.[4] As James argues, beyond reasons of political enmity, demonstrators saw the press, together with the universities, as the quintessential redoubts of a cultural and symbolic power exercised over and against them. In attacking newspaper offices, then, workers "attempted to assert their own symbolic power and the legitimacy of their claim for representation and a recognition of the social relevance of working class experience, values and organization within the public sphere."[5] This "secular iconoclasm" of pro-Perón demonstrators thus responded not just to the political stance of the Argentine press, but also to its clear failure to articulate faithfully the broader aspirations of the nation's popular classes in its pages. That evening's attacks on the press, then, signaled a symbolic rejection of private and exclusive control over the means of social communication, an unraveling of press claims of universal representation, and a dramatic assertion of demands for working-class access to expression through the press. In good measure, the siege of *Crítica* was a particularly explosive product of the stark disjuncture between long-standing ideas of what the press *should be* and what the press *was* in practice, and, more generally, between the egalitarian, utopian promises of Argentine liberalism and the fact of social exclusion.

While violence against much of the press on the evening of October 17 remained largely symbolic and cathartic, however, the siege of *Crítica* was that and something more. Not only did both protesters and *Crítica* defenders use deadly force, but the 3rd Regiment of the Infantry was prepared to use artillery against the building if its occupants did not surrender.[6] The degree of violence unleashed in this case clearly moved both qualitatively and quantitatively beyond a symbolic struggle over the nature of representation within the media and access to publicly meaningful expression; protesters seemed intent not just on undermining the paper's "cultural and symbolic capital," but on destroying its physical capital and its ability to operate. In this, they proved surprisingly successful. We are also left with a simple but unanswered question: why *Crítica*? If the actions against the press on October 17 amounted to assaults on the institutions of elite cultural power, *La Prensa* would seem a more logical target: that paper was more consistently and unequivocally against not just Perón, but the government's whole reform program; the paper and its owner were unapologetically oligarchic and cosmopolitan; and the *La Prensa* offices stood adjacent to the Plaza de Mayo, the center of the evening's gathering, while the *Crítica* offices stood more than a kilometer away. What explains, then, the fact that *La Prensa* received only insults and stones, while *Crítica* received devastating physical and symbolic violence from which it never fully recovered?

The targeting of *Crítica* is central to understanding the evolution of state-press relations in the military period and had important ramifications for the subsequent transformation of the commercial press. No single factor, of course, explains the events at the paper's offices on the night of October 17, which arose from a confluence of the broader social changes of 1944 and 1945, the particular role that *Crítica* played in Argentine journalism, and the political ambitions of the paper's owner, Raúl Damonte Taborda.

In just under two years, the reformist program of the military regime had substantially altered many Argentines' expectations with regard to the rights of citizenship, class relations, and the proper functioning of the nation's political and cultural institutions. The military's responsiveness to workers' social demands had raised the possibility that the egalitarian impulse of Argentine liberalism had run aground not *despite* procedural democracy, but because constitutional democracy permitted entrenched interests to preserve their social power—an argument that FAP activist Octavio Palazzolo embraced.[7] With pressure mounting for a return to constitutional rule, supporters of the regime's social policies faced a new dilemma: would a constitutional democracy sustain the redistribution of social power that the Argentine military had begun, or would it simply turn the clock back on workers' gains? As a result, abstract questions of who and what constituted the "public"—and, by implication, who embodied the rights of the press—became both viscerally political and increasingly urgent as 1945 progressed.

As World War II drew to a close in Europe, the Argentine commercial press threatened to become a battlefield—at times quite literally. In the rapid polarization of that critical year, the directors and editors of the major commercial dailies shifted from tentative support of the de facto regime to nearly unanimous intransigent opposition; vast sectors of the Argentine population, however, moved in precisely the contrary direction.[8] By October 1945, the growing gulf between the dominant representatives of the Buenos Aires press and the public they claimed to represent had become an unbridgeable chasm. In no case was this disjunction between an already internally divided press and an increasingly polarized public more acute than with regard to the newspaper whose legitimacy and journalistic character rested on claims that it embodied the voice of labor and the dispossessed: *Crítica*. That this crisis presented a fundamental challenge for the traditional role of the Buenos Aires commercial press is clear; but it also placed in stark relief the failure of the Farrell-Perón regime to resurrect the media strategy that a decade earlier had served General Justo so well. More importantly, the crisis revealed the inadequacy of established forms of press relations for what would become the New Argentina.

Crítica and the Convenience of Reflecting Popular Sentiment

If the social reforms and sweeping prolabor measures served to counterbalance the politically repressive elements of the military regime, Farrell and Perón similarly began to take a new approach to state-press relations in mid-1944. Even as the state-of-siege censorship restrictions remained in place to quiet opposition, Perón began a conscious campaign to mobilize active support within the press. The regime's success in generating sympathy among working journalists had been more than apparent not just with the FAP's understandable embrace of the Journalist's Statute, but with the enthusiastic reception that Perón himself received from journalists at the union's annual meeting in October 1944. Even if journalists created newspaper content, however, it was those on the other side of the newsroom's class divide that ultimately controlled the overall political tendencies of the commercial press; Perón understood that newspaper proprietors, even more than journalists, held the key to the construction of a media that would fulfill the needs of the de facto authorities.

Just as working journalists moved to back Perón through a combination of conviction, material interest, and fear, some owners of the Buenos Aires commercial press found a similar set of reasons to lend support to the increasingly personalist regime. Contrary to current belief—extrapolated from the ferocity and uniformity of press opposition in mid-1945—the military government and Perón did enjoy the support of significant elements of the Buenos Aires commercial press. Rather than directly challenging the ownership of the commercial dailies as he would years later, Perón gained this backing by forming a set of mutually beneficial alliances with owners and editors that, in the short term, gave his political and social project an unprecedented media presence. While these alliances had clear and obvious inspiration in the relationship between General Justo and Natalio Botana in the 1930s, however, the situation now was significantly more complicated. Not only did Perón lack a pivotal economic stake in his allies' newspapers, but his social policies had institutionalized class divisions in the newsroom in a way that empowered working journalists, not owners. This quintessential Perón stratagem of currying favor with both labor and capital in not entirely transparent fashion, together with his failure to place his newspaper allies in a dependent position, held fairly predictable consequences: it was precisely his allies among the proprietors who would figure among Perón's most vociferous opponents as the regime began to crumble in mid-1945.

Like Justo, Perón made *Crítica* the center of his media strategy. Yet the national press as a whole, while falling far short of mirroring "public opinion" in the ideal sense proposed by the de facto authorities, did show important signs of articulating support for the broader project of the Farrell-Perón regime. Unlike editorialists at *La Prensa*, who dogmatically continued to sustain the liberal triad of property rights, individual liberties, and constitutional rule, those at *La Nación* initially approved of certain elements of state economic interventionism, especially with regard to labor legislation.[9] Perhaps more significantly, *La Nación* editorialists intervened directly in the diplomatic row unleashed by Perón's famous June 1944 La Plata speech, in which the new minister of war asserted that only a strong military could guarantee Argentine peace and security. Calling U.S. State Department denunciations of the address as fascist-inspired a "grave error of interpretation," the editorialists entered into a lengthy, analytic defense of Perón.[10] Two days later, as the diplomatic crisis grew increasingly serious, the paper's editorialists expanded that defense to include the whole government, arguing that "the lack of [diplomatic] recognition [of the Farrell regime] is inexplicable, given the characteristics of the government. It is not totalitarian, but Argentine, since it is imbued with the spirit of San Martín. . . . Moreover, in the social order it does not proceed with criteria that are fascistic, but democratic."[11]

Coming less than two months after the retraction of and public apology for the Mila Forn de Oteiza Quirno "demagoguery" article, this negation of the regime's "totalitarian/fascistic" character and endorsement of its "democratic" social criteria seemed to contradict Luís Mitre's direct experience with the government; and the rigor of his point-by-point defense of Perón's speech far exceeded in competence, energy, and international respectability anything offered by the Ministry of Foreign Relations. Thus, even if the support of "oligarchic" newspapers like *La Nación* only occasionally became more than tepid, circumstantial, and passive, when it did it lent the regime a significant positive media presence both within the country and beyond. When combined with the continually expanding activities of the Undersecretariat of Information and the Press—now directed and increasingly staffed not by military officials, but by experienced professional journalists—and the goodwill generated by the Journalist's Statute, this support in certain measure offset the military government's continued imposition of censorship and incarceration of journalists.[12]

La Nación's upper- and educated middle-class readership, while valuable to the overall stability of the regime, did not constitute the core of the population whose support Farrell and Perón saw as crucial to the success of their project. The audience of Crítica, on the other hand, did. Not only could this paper reach the urban popular classes to a greater degree than any other commercial daily, but Crítica also ostensibly embodied the kind of ink-and-paper mirror of society that Perón had invoked as a model of journalism practice in his speech before the FAP in October 1944. In fact, while the directors of La Nación and La Prensa repeatedly asserted that their papers acted as "mouthpieces of public opinion," for the directors of Crítica, the paper was an "expression of popular feeling."[13] This phrase and the claims it reflected came much closer to Perón's conception of the role of journalism in its assertion of a less rational, more direct, affective and sentimental link with the popular classes.

Furthermore, the populist impulse that had guided Natalio Botana and the paper's directors since the day of Crítica's founding in 1913 consistently led them to present the newspaper not merely as *for* the urban nonpropertied classes, but *of* them.[14] Even in the midst of the ownership disputes that followed Botana's death in 1941, Crítica journalists managed to retain the paper's image as the primary voice within the commercial press of the greater Buenos Aires multitude. Through a variety of discursive strategies that included informal opinion polls, letters, interviews, the regular use of the *lunfardo* street dialect, and a constant exaltation of the journalists themselves as street-wise, the directors of Crítica constructed an image of the paper as a genuine embodiment of "the popular." The directors of Crítica, more than those of any other commercial newspaper, could convincingly claim that their paper spoke not merely *to* Perón's target audience of urban workers, but *as* that public. If any of the Buenos Aires dailies suggested that the citizenship rights of the nation's popular classes included the right to positive representation and access to the commercial media, it was Crítica. What was largely, though certainly not completely, a marketing strategy envisioned by Botana also legitimated egalitarian, collective access to expression through the press as an integral element of Argentines' rapidly changing expectations with regard to the nation's institutions.

Not since Jorge Mitre's creation of Noticias Gráficas in the Uriburu years had Crítica faced any significant rival as the primary representative of the urban popular classes.[15] Yet the long-cultivated aura of Crítica as directly linked to the public had been weakened and tarnished, though by no means ruined, by Botana's dealings in the 1930s and Damonte Taborda's even more crass manipulation of the publication since early 1942. Juan Domingo Perón, however, held a dual advantage over the paper that virtually assured his supremacy in the minds of *Crítica*'s audience: not only could he express himself without concern for overstepping the limits imposed by government censors, but, as secretary of labor and social welfare, he could make concrete advances toward the socially just order that *Crítica* journalists could only propose. Thus, together with the clear pro-Perón sympathies of many *Crítica* journalists as a result of his social policies, the position of the paper with respect to the regime appeared virtually preordained. How could *Crítica* maintain its legitimacy and market distinction as the voice of the working class if it did not applaud the redistributive policies that so positively affected its core readership (and that the paper had historically promoted)? At the same time, *Crítica*'s place within the Argentine press gave the newspaper an undeniable value for the architects of the military regime: since the influential, populist paper was such an important link to the working class, how could Farrell and Perón not employ it for their political and social project?

If compelling reasons of journalistic character made a *Crítica*-Perón association both logical and mutually beneficial, a variety of more obscure motives assured the cooperation of the paper with the military regime's key member. *Crítica* director Raúl Damonte Taborda had lent his support to the de facto authorities in the early months of the regime in large measure as a means of ensuring his control over the disputed newspaper. At the same time, market considerations and the desire to preserve *Crítica* as the supposed quintessential voice of the urban nonpropertied classes made opposition to the economic and social reforms of the regime unwise and out of keeping with the historical character of the paper. Yet the long-term aspirations of Colonel Perón soon presented Damonte Taborda the politician with a possibility at least as enticing as full, uncontested ownership of *Crítica*: the vice presidency of the republic.

In September 1944, the military authorities—now clearly under the direction of Perón in his triple role of secretary of labor and social welfare, minister of war, and vice president—began a series of attempts to court Radical Party politicians as a means of both broadening the regime's political base and preparing the military for a sympathetic electoral exit. Repeated overtures, significantly, did not win the backing of Amadeo Sabattini, the powerful precoup governor of the province of Córdoba and the UCR's most likely presidential candidate. Yet Perón's persistence did bring a core group of lesser Radical Party figures like Juan I. Cooke, Armando Antille, and J. Hortensio Quijano into alliance with the military authorities. In addition, more minor figures like Eduardo Colóm, owner of *La Época,* and Emilio Cipolletti, the head of *Crítica*'s political section, proved themselves not only loyal Peronists, but key supporters of the movement's leader in the coming years.[16]

Of these Radicals, the most important figure to bend toward the regime was arguably Raúl Damonte Taborda, national deputy for the city of Buenos Aires from 1938 to 1943. Damonte Taborda not only brought his paper into line with the military government from its earliest days, but he also quickly developed a close relationship with Perón and his mistress, Eva Duarte, to whom he tended to give expensive presents.[17] Beyond the clear advantages of alliance with Perón, Helvio Botana, Damonte Taborda's exiled brother-in-law, later attributed the *Crítica* director's collaboration with his powerful associate as much to a predilection for the supernatural as to political opportunism. This enthusiasm peaked following a reading of Perón by the Egyptian psychic Badú, whom Damonte Taborda had taken under his wing:

> In Perón [Badú] saw the makings of a great [political] conductor. He would be a great Argentine leader and his declarations would spread throughout the world. Perón modestly expressed his lack of ambition and the impossibility that such predictions could come true notwithstanding any opportunities that might present themselves.
> ... Raúl left with great enthusiasm since he was Perón's candidate for the vice presidency, due to the fact that within the political plan a Radical was needed, and Sabattini had rejected [Perón's] proposals of union.[18]

Despite the apocryphal nature of the story, the scenario is not unimaginable: not only did an undercurrent of such "esoteric" belief run through segments of the Argentine political class, but *Crítica* itself had an unusually strong connection with spiritualism through Natalio Botana's widow and Damonte Taborda's mother-in-law, Salvadora Medina Onrubia de Botana.

Whether his reasons for alliance with Perón were supernatural or practical—or both—by May 1945 Damonte Taborda had suddenly managed to accumulate all outstanding shares of the *Crítica* publishing company to become the paper's sole proprietor, but he soon found himself touring Brazil, the United States, and Great Britain as Perón's informal ambassador—much the same service that Natalio Botana had provided for General Justo a decade earlier.[19] Similarly, Emilio Cipolletti, who acted at once as Damonte Taborda's personal secretary, Salvadora Medina Onrubia de Botana's legal aide, and *Crítica*'s national political editor and primary Casa Rosada correspondent, had formed a close relationship with Perón, presumably with Damonte Taborda's encouragement. For Perón, however, Cipolletti would ultimately perform an even wider variety of tasks of far greater importance, serving successively as the military government's interventor of the earthquake-racked province of San Juan, as president of the state oil company YPF, and finally as head of the Undersecretariat of Information and the Press.[20]

While *Crítica* functioned as an important avenue of communication between the regime and the general population from the early days of the military government, by the first anniversary of the coup the paper had become more unequivocally promotional. In a clear departure from the normal tone of the paper, the unmistakably fascistic aesthetics of the massive July 9, 1944, military parade, with its iron condor and Nazi-like hanging banners of the Argentine flag, earned both *Crítica*'s enthusiastic support and an editorial praising the military as the true protectors of national sovereignty.[21] Perhaps more effectively, Damonte Taborda also served government interests by deploying *Crítica* in its area of greatest strength: the destruction of public figures. From late June through July of 1944 (and intermittently thereafter), the paper engaged in a campaign against businessman Otto Bemberg, the target of a government tax-evasion investigation.[22] In the sensationalist style of the paper, the reporters claimed that the naturalized Argentine threatened national security because of his interest in the coal industry, was in the process of organizing a monopoly of the nation's natural resources, and frequently assaulted *Crítica* photographers.[23]

With the developing alliance between Perón and Damonte Taborda, however, praise for the regime in general quickly gave way to more decidedly personal support for the government's dominant figure. On November 22, 1944, *Crítica* carried three full pages of laudatory information celebrating the accomplishments of the Secretariat of Labor and Social Welfare. Alongside the official portrait of Colonel Perón, the paper proclaimed that national independence hero "San Martín, worker, should be our goal" and recast the military coup of 1943 not as the negative reaction to a fraudulent political arrangement, but as a positive movement of social liberation: "Given that Argentina has still not achieved the social state that it deserves, we must take the movement to establish it as historically necessary. The revolution of June 4 promised the realization of that social justice, and its fruition will bring posterity to consider it a revolution inspired by San Martín [*revolución sanmartiniana*]; that is, effected with the selflessness that characterized the actions of the Liberator."[24] Declaring the coup a "justified revolution," *Crítica* left little room for doubt as to the place Perón should occupy in the political imagination of the Argentine people: in the editorial accompanying the articles, Perón appears as the fitting descendant of San Martín, Moreno, Rivadavia, Urquiza, and Sarmiento. Thus, where the Nationalists saw in Perón and the military government a resurgence of the spirit of nineteenth-century dictator Juan Manuel de Rosas, *Crítica* placed the colonel firmly within the Argentine liberal, democratic tradition. Perón, the paper would have its readers believe, stood as the only living member of the Argentine liberal pantheon, and any seeming coincidence between government figures and the authoritarian Rosas amounted to an incomprehensible misinterpretation.[25]

This and subsequent reworkings of national history served an important purpose: not only did denials of the clearly fascistic aura surrounding the military government allow *Crítica* writers to reconcile support for Perón with the newspaper's long-standing antifascism, but they also sought to make Perón more palatable to those local and foreign political forces that defined themselves as hostile to authoritarianism. Editorials like "Fascist Argentina," which declared the national Right moribund due to its inability to "bear the climate of liberty and democratic morality" that Perón had supposedly ushered in, allowed journalists to resurrect the paper's virulent antifascism of the 1930s while remaining within the bounds set by the Damonte Taborda–Perón alliance.[26] Declarations that article 14 of the Constitution of 1853 acted as a "poison" to the Nationalist Right, similarly, implied that the open criticism of the press had played a crucial role in the imminent demise of local fascism and that the regime did, in fact, protect freedom of the press.[27] By early 1945, *Crítica* editorialists deemed Perón the only government figure worth quoting, and then only to prove that the colonel spoke not the language of rosista nationalism, but that of his liberal conquerors at Caseros.[28] That the discursive reconstruction of Perón as an inheritor of Argentina's liberal traditions would ultimately prove unconvincing mattered little in the first months of the year; Damonte Taborda had made the paper Perón's greatest champion within the mass press.

Argentina's declaration of war on the Axis on March 27, 1945, provided a temporary respite from the contradictions of supporting both liberal democracy and the government led by Perón. Five days before the government decree, *Crítica* broke the usually hermetic seal surrounding government policy making and unequivocally declared that the popular will—long expressed by the paper itself—demanded war on *nazi-fascismo:* "'Monsieur tout le monde' is our [average] man on the street. It is he who, from the minute that they appeared, has been at war against Nazism and Fascism. And he will continue [to be at war]. Those are his sentiments, and they are the sentiments that CRITICA has interpreted for the last twenty years."[29] If *Crítica* consistently interpreted the "man on the street's" clear understanding of the threat posed by fascism, however, it remained confused by the attitude of the leaders of the opposition to the government. The editorialists declared that in congressional votes on the question of war against the Axis prior to June 1943, "one of the Radical groups, that of Córdoba, vacillated and left in order to miss the vote; at the same time, all of the Nazi press proclaimed in the streets their hate for our institutions; and that Nazi press received official advertising from Radical governments like that in Córdoba."[30] For *Crítica* readers, the message was clear: where Perón had suppressed the Nazi-fascist press and now stood on the verge of war against the Axis, it was the opposition—especially former Córdoba governor Amadeo Sabbatini, who had repeatedly rebuffed Perón's overtures—that had not only maintained an inconsistent stance, but had even aided economically the cause of fascism.[31] Thus, while opposition figures continued to denounce the supposed Nazi-fascist nature of the regime, it was they, *Crítica* editorialists intimated, who had colluded with the Axis.

The declaration of war on the Axis also signaled the final passage from Perón's search for a broader base of support for the military regime to a more explicit preparation for the military's electoral exit and his own presidential campaign. In March and April, *Crítica* gave solid coverage to Perón's repeated and unequivocal denials of his presidential ambitions—a relatively transparent form of suggesting that popular moves were underway to "draft" the supposedly reluctant colonel as candidate for an electoral continuation of the reformist regime.[32] It was in April and the following months, however, that Damonte Taborda's newspaper would move beyond veiled attacks on figures of the opposition and unconvincing proclamations of Perón's antifascist, liberal-democratic credentials to support Perón's presidential ambitions more directly and effectively.

In the Argentine fall of 1945, the intimacy of the connection between state officials and the press suddenly became more obvious in the commercial press than it had ever been in the previous decade. In mid-April, Damonte Taborda began ceding a daily section of *Crítica* to transparently official news of Perón's Secretariat of Labor and Social Welfare. Entitled simply "Secretaría de Trabajo y Previsión," the advertising-free pages carried articles chronicling the advances that labor continued to make under the military government. Yet, while ostensibly boosting *Crítica*'s stature as the "voice of the people" for its attention to labor issues, the articles inevitably highlighted not worker resilience, but the benevolence of state tutelage and the sincerity of the only figure whose photograph consistently graced the section: Juan Domingo Perón.

The tone of the articles is hardly surprising; after all, even if *Crítica* journalist (and future Peronist) Alberto Rudnitzky was ostensibly in charge of the section, it was likely not current *Crítica* staff members who wrote it, but rather the growing number of professional journalists at the Undersecretariat of Information and the Press.[33] Lieutenant Colonel Domingo Mercante of the Secretariat of Labor and Social Welfare lobbied other newspaper proprietors to include the section in their dailies as well, with compensation corresponding to each paper's established advertising rate. José Agusti, owner of *Noticias Gráficas*, publicly dismissed criticisms of his own acceptance of the official propaganda, claiming that funds received from Mercante paid for the space occupied by legitimate advertising and was not a form of coercive subsidy to the paper. Agusti also made the unsubstantiated assertion that *La Prensa* and *La Nación* also regularly ran the Secretariat's propaganda—presumably in exchange for money.[34]

If "Secretaría de Trabajo y Previsión," which ran daily in *Crítica* well into August, ostensibly presented relevant working-class information to the paper's readers and provided a representative voice for labor in *Crítica*'s pages, it also served Damonte Taborda's far less selfless interests. The Secretariat of Labor and Social Welfare paid advertising rates for the extensive space used by the section. Perhaps more crucially, however, it also boosted the *Crítica* proprietor's political fortunes by helping to position Damonte Taborda's supposed running mate as the only figure capable of carrying the military's social policies forward into a constitutional regime.

That the declaration of war on the Axis effectively lifted the state-of-siege proscription on direct and specific criticisms of Hitler and Mussolini, furthermore, placed this laudatory material from the Secretariat of Labor and Social Welfare in direct line with a renewed rhetorical onslaught against fascism. Yet, while *Crítica* journalists and editorialists resurrected stories of the paper's confrontations with Hitler, Mussolini, and their diplomatic representatives and consistently denounced the horrors of the Italian and German regimes, they also began a succession of attacks on the local Right.[35] Coinciding with the appearance of "Secretaría de Trabajo y Previsión," journalists at the paper began a serial history of the Nationalist Right, entitled "Life, Passion and Death of Argentine Nationalism: On How a Group of Resentful People Dreamed of Governing the Country." In twenty installments, *Crítica* attacked the figures of the Argentine Right, particularly the Alianza Libertadora Nacionalista (ALN), declaring them poor imitations of Hitler and Mussolini, ideologues of an oligarchy in its death throes. By presenting discussions of the Nationalist Right exclusively in the past tense and by unequivocally declaring the movement "dead," the authors effectively dismissed the local Nationalists as a continuing influence on the present regime. If the local fascists were politically "dead," how could the still vital Perón possibly figure among their ranks?

Exalting Perón's reformism while attacking the authoritarian Right in which he found much of his inspiration, of course, served to distance Perón from a political sector whose support was virtually guaranteed but whose visible presence in the Peronist camp had now become a liability.[36] Yet this strategy would ultimately prove untenable, and the difficulty of maintaining this dual adherence permeated the text of *Crítica*. In declaring the consistency of its opposition to fascist authoritarianism, for example, the paper's journalists presented *Crítica*'s long history of suspensions as evidence. But in so doing they belied the notion that the military government had proven particularly liberating for the press and undermined claims that military authorities—Perón being the most prominent—had respected civil liberties more generally.[37] That declarations of Perón's liberal, constitutionalist intentions surely rang hollow for any readers who saw political liberalism as crucial undoubtedly deepened this tension.

When the collapse of fascism in Europe seemed to doom the Argentine experiment in military authoritarianism, the dual discourse in the pages of *Crítica* became untenable. With the military regime's days apparently numbered, Damonte Taborda found compelling reason to abandon his support for

Perón during what appeared to be his inevitable and politically fatal fall from grace. The Egyptian psychic Badú's confession to Damonte Taborda that he in fact "saw" great futures for *all* military men as a matter of convenience only served to seal Perón's fate in the eyes of the *Crítica* owner.[38] *Crítica*, the commercial daily that had most effectively supported Perón, that appeared the most committed to working-class ascendancy, and whose journalistic character seemed to lend the power of journalism to the urban popular classes through its incorporation of working-class language and issues, would soon figure among the most vehement critics not just of Perón, but of his followers in the general population.

Popular Nationalism, Class, and Public Opinion

If the coming end of the war in Europe made the military's need for identification with the Allies and liberal democracy more urgent, it also invigorated an opposition long bereft of unity. For the opposition, the perception, which had grown steadily since the mid-1930s, that Argentine politics replicated world confrontations now seemed to approach its logical culmination: with the impending victory of the Allies, the parallel triumph of Argentine liberals and leftists over the "Nazi-fascist" military regime appeared only a matter of time. Political disputes in Argentina, it appeared, had little to do with anything particularly Argentine; the country served simply as another battleground in a world war whose outcome was now clear.

The Argentine situation, however, would prove vastly more complicated. If Perón's political reinvention in the pages of *Crítica* as, at heart, a supporter of liberal democracy remained unconvincing, the paper's glorification of the military government's social achievements carried greater weight, in large part because those accomplishments were both far more real and far more popular. As a result, even if opposition discourse placed the struggle in terms of international politics, the key issue for supporters of Perón remained the consolidation and extension of the concrete social gains and the symbolic national-popular advances that had come not through the workings of the traditional Argentine political parties, but through the labor unions and Perón himself. For them, Perón had emerged from and addressed Argentine issues. The Argentine public thus increasingly found itself divided into two mutually hostile camps: those who viewed the current military period as no more than an "exceptional" intrusion of foreign-inspired authoritarianism into the country's essentially liberal democratic historical trajectory, and those who viewed the military government, and Perón in particular, as the unquestionably Argentine guarantors of social justice and the redeemers of a lost national and popular sovereignty, regardless of outward political forms.

That the Argentine opposition found its most potent rhetorical weapon in the identification of its own struggle with that of the nearly victorious Allies carried serious implications. In fact, the opposition's almost exclusive emphasis on equating Perón and the military with the *nazi-fascismo* now on the verge of worldwide defeat—and itself with the victorious liberal democracies—has rightfully figured in virtually all of the literature on the emergence of Peronism as a key element in Perón's eventual triumph. In the Argentine winter of 1945, the Buenos Aires commercial dailies reinforced this identification and, in the process, helped to create a discursive space in which the press appeared less an institution representative of all sectors of the nation and more the ideological weapon of foreign interests and a local oligarchy set on reversing the social reforms of the military regime. With the country increasingly divided along class lines, and with the commercial press overwhelmingly in the hands of an internationalist, liberal opposition, declarations that the press acted as the "mouthpiece of public opinion" and "reflection of popular sentiment" bore only a tenuous resemblance to reality. This proved especially awkward for *Crítica*, a newspaper whose existence centered on its close identification with a public that remained staunchly loyal to Perón.

For newspapers like *La Nación*, *La Prensa*, and later *Crítica*, as well as other commercial papers like *Noticias Gráficas*, *La Razón*, and *El Mundo*, this identification with U.S. and British interests proved as much structural as ideological and circumstantial. Even before World War I, both *La Nación* and *La Prensa* had tended to devote at least as much attention to international events as to occurrences in Argentina. Technological and business changes in the 1920s only served to reinforce this predisposition: as the Associated Press and United Press gained lucrative contracts with *La Nación* and *La Prensa*, respectively, news from Europe and the United States became not only more readily available, but increasingly immediate and affordable. The onset of the Second World War deepened this tendency, as a journalistic and economic preference for the U.S. and British wire services, a political bias toward the Allies, and an increased demand for news of the war pushed coverage of more quotidian local events from the pages. That both papers maintained strong institutional and economic links to North American news organizations further fueled the drive to provide news articles of foreign origin, especially those that favored the Allied cause.

At the same time, the imposition of the state of siege in December 1941 made local political reporting increasingly problematic. Notwithstanding the subsequent efforts of the Undersecretariat of Information and the Press, the paucity of material on important national events at once acceptable to official censors and press opponents of the regime only accentuated the tendency to rely on coverage of the compelling international conflict. State-of-siege restrictions, similarly, made critical editorial commentary on local politics increasingly risky. The solution which many editors found to this inability to report and comment on national events lay in the regular use of what Ricardo Sidicaro has called "editorial by proxy": the use of reporting and commentary on foreign events to address local issues indirectly, or the reprinting of foreign press items on Argentina.[39] The tendency to engage in the tactic increased as pressure on the regime grew. For example, in June *La Prensa* dedicated articles on the immediate postwar period in Europe to the issue of freedom of the press, and devoted extensive coverage and commentary to declarations by U.S. figures on the topic.[40] Such commentaries clearly carried implications far more local than a literal reading might imply, and formed part of a tactical response to government monitoring of the press.[41] At the same time, however, the constant use of foreign examples—especially regarding the issues of democracy and freedom of the press—also served to present the Argentine commercial press as responding not to local public opinion, but to the political demands of the United States, Western Europe, and their local allies.

If the attention of the major commercial dailies centered increasingly on the United States and Western Europe, foreign powers appeared to embrace the Argentine commercial press in return. The circumstances surrounding the final days of the war in Europe worked to place the traditional liberal understanding of the nature of the press within the set of foreign demands on Argentine sovereignty. The Argentine government's signature of the Act of Chapultepec in April—together with the March declaration of war on the Axis, a necessary condition for Argentina's insertion in the postwar world—carried with it obligations "to eliminate, as soon as possible after the end of the war, the measures of censorship . . . that have been necessary in times of war."[42] Similarly, in a letter to U.S. president Truman reprinted in *La Prensa,* the Union of Democratic Action, cochaired by Eleanor Roosevelt, placed the "immediate establishment of freedom of the press" at the top of its list of requirements for Argentine membership in the inter-American system.[43] In language clear to its Argentine audience, one *La Nación* editorialist evoked the civil conflicts of the nineteenth century while playing to both regime and opposition preoccupation with Argentina's international image, remarking that "it is easy to judge a nation by the freedom that its press enjoys. In the present times, it is a sign of political civilization."[44] State intervention in the functioning of the press—especially controls on newspaper content—quickly became a barometer by which the local and international opposition to the military regime could quantify the Argentine government's authoritarianism.

Censorship, opponents of the regime declared, amounted to a transparent attempt to hide the government's lack of support within "public opinion." Journalists at the *New York Times,* in an editorial widely republished in the Argentine press, declared that "the attempt by the Argentine government to hide its actions through the censorship of the news that is received or transmitted implies a greater sense of insecurity than that which it would like to admit: almost all observers believe that if the Argentine people were given the freedom of elections, the present government would not remain in power longer than the time necessary to count the votes."[45] Restrictions on the press were, in effect, restrictions on the public whose voice it embodied. That a public might exist beyond that represented in the commercial press would only become apparent as the military regime reached its breaking point in October.

This strong linkage between state policies toward the press and foreign demands on the de facto government soon became even more dramatically explicit: the regime's most unequivocal declaration of its commitment to lifting newspaper content restrictions and ending newspaper closures came not from the mouth of Perón or the minister of the interior, Alberto Teisaire, but from the newly arrived U.S. ambassador to Argentina, Spruille Braden. According to Braden's much-repeated account, Perón had sent Oscar Lomuto, acting head of the Undersecretariat of Information and the Press, to assure the ambassador that foreign correspondents in Argentina would no longer face restrictions and that the Argentine government stood prepared to guarantee "complete freedom of the press for all journalists whether of American [U.S.] or other nationality."[46] What Perón and Lomuto understood as a confidential discussion, however, appeared in that evening's press; Braden, hardly the most diplomatic of diplomats, had held an informal conference immediately upon Lomuto's departure, implicitly presenting Perón's agreement as a conciliatory measure not to the Argentine press, but to himself as representative of the United States.[47]

The form of the announcement, as much as the substance of Lomuto's assurances regarding the press, sent shock waves through the Argentine opposition and at the same time even more explicitly tied the disputes surrounding the press to foreign demands on the regime. An editorialist at the Socialist Party paper *La Vanguardia*, a harsh critic of the government, declared the event an insult to national dignity yet placed the blame firmly on Perón, calling the incident a "demonstration of how dangerous it can be to try to govern on the margin of the law."[48] Historian Félix Luna, then a young opponent of Perón, would later remark, "It was the first time in the history of Argentina that a foreign ambassador assumed the role of protector of the rights of [the country's] inhabitants. The government had to swallow the insult. And the opposition became jubilant; with such a guarantor the definite possibility of preparing the offensive with all available resources seemed affirmed."[49]

The degree to which Braden (for many Argentines then and now, the embodiment of U.S. imperialism) managed to make the defense of the Argentine commercial press his own is startling; a week earlier the military government had already formally ended all newspaper suspensions and made new closures more difficult.[50] It had done so not as the direct result of foreign pressure, but in order to diffuse tensions within the FAP, where both pro-Perón and anti-

Perón journalists had combined forces to threaten a labor action on the Day of the Journalist (June 7) in protest over a spate of newspaper closures.[51] But even press reactions to the subsequent release from prison of *La Vanguardia*'s director, Américo Ghioldi—reactions that themselves revealed a clear loosening of press censorship—were overshadowed by Braden's sensational announcement.[52] Compared to the U.S. ambassador's actions, the more immediate local pressures have long since faded from the popular, and even academic, memory of the period.

If demands regarding restrictions on the press seemed to place the commercial newspapers of Buenos Aires in league with foreign interests in the country, this collusion only appeared confirmed by a wealth of circumstantial evidence. Despite *La Prensa*'s closer ties to the U.S. embassy and information agencies, British ambassador David Kelly remembers that by mid-1944 he could essentially set the reporting agenda at the paper, which "became ready always both to insert and to give prominent publicity to whatever I personally requested them to feature," and gave at least one leading story to a speech made by his wife.[53] Similarly, Ambassador Braden flaunted his close personal relationship with *La Prensa*'s Alberto Gainza Paz, the newspaper proprietor who most embodied intransigent opposition to Perón and who most dogmatically denied even the possibility of public support for the regime.[54]

In late June and early July, two U.S. correspondents in Argentina known for their critical reporting on the regime took refuge in the U.S. embassy in an arguably exaggerated response to anonymous threats; the dispatches about their plight, in which they portrayed themselves as little less than war correspondents in the heat of battle, figured prominently in the Buenos Aires press in the form of relayed United Press and Associated Press cables.[55] Spruille Braden even sought to allow journalists to use diplomatic code for subsequent cable transmissions, while U.S. newspapers declared the Argentine regime dangerously authoritarian.[56] In one of an increasing number of public events, Braden appeared as guest of honor at a Círculo de la Prensa luncheon just days after the organization had endorsed a demand for a return to constitutional normality; the conspicuous absence from press reports of the usually profuse direct quotation of his comments provides some indication of just how damning of the regime the outspoken ambassador's remarks surely were.[57] That the U.S. ambassador was rapidly emerging as de facto leader and champion of the Argentine opposition placed Perón's adversaries on a collision course with nationalist sentiment in the country.[58] Braden's embrace of the cause of the commercial press would, in the end, have the same consequences as his embrace of the broader opposition: it gave the appearance of smothering press autonomy and compromising newspaper claims to represent national public opinion.

At least as important for the fate of the opposition, however, was the growing slippage between denunciation of the regime's authoritarian practices and hostility to the whole set of social reforms that it had launched. In mid-June, a broad coalition of Argentine capital, the so-called *fuerzas vivas*, published a "Manifesto of Commerce and Industry" which explicitly blended calls for the return to constitutional democracy with even stronger denunciations of the "climate of distrust, provocation, and rebelliousness" created by the growth of union power.[59] *La Prensa*'s Alberto Gainza Paz, who had most consistently linked the issues of liberal democracy, freedom of the press, and the inviolability of private property, now saw a less ambiguous stance from his colleagues at *La Nación*. In June, editors at *La Nación* criticized state price controls as harmful to the "workingmen" who had signed the Manifesto, and went so far as to declare that proposed mandatory profit-sharing arrangements would not be acceptable even if they were to come not by decree, but from a reconstituted, democratic Argentine Congress.[60] A return to the constitution, the editorialists at *La Nación* made clear, implied a return to the primacy of individual property rights. Thus, in the wake of the Manifesto of Commerce and Industry, *La Nación*, *La Prensa*, and other commercial newspapers would increasingly equate the impending democratic transition with the reversal of Perón's social reforms and a lifting of state economic intervention. Major representatives of the opposition, then, openly aligned themselves with Argentine capital and left little doubt that the demise of the regime would signal the dismantling of a social project of clearly broad popular appeal.

For working journalists, the Manifesto and the growing hegemony of capital and its immediate allies within the opposition movement threatened to further divide the profession. The FAP leadership, meeting in its annual Congress less than two weeks after the publication of the Manifesto, found no way of maintaining unity other than by declaring its disagreement with "the social, political, and economic content of the polemic between the *fuerzas vivas* and the Secretariat of Labor and Social Welfare."[61] In the coming months, as the Argentine public's political polarization grew, the FAP repeatedly proclaimed its independence from the contending bands, avowing only that the solution to the political impasse and to the serious problems facing the press and press workers lay in a return to constitutional normality.[62] With believable rumors in the air that a meeting between several newspaper owners and government officials had focused as much on rescinding the Journalist's Statute as on lifting censorship, the journalist union's leadership found it difficult to divorce the political demands of the opposition from the reversal of the whole set of social reforms that Perón had inaugurated—including those affecting journalists themselves.[63] As a result, the leaders of the FAP and its affiliates assumed a position only slightly different from that of most other Argentine labor leaders: unable to fully adhere to what they assumed would be the "winning band" without dividing the union and forfeiting its defense of the concrete advances it had recently made, they sought to assure that the journalists' organizations at least did not identify with the losing band.[64]

The Manifesto of the *fuerzas vivas,* together with the increasingly explicit political activities of Spruille Braden, marked a watershed for the internal politics of the military regime, after which political polarization became both more pronounced and more rapid. By late June, even ambiguous expressions of praise for the social policies of the military virtually vanished from the commercial press, leaving the dry, mandatory communiqués from the Undersecretariat of Information and the Press as the only proregime voice in the press of mass circulation. With the Buenos Aires commercial newspapers nearly unanimously arrayed against the regime's dominant and most popular figure, the growing chasm between the press and those broad sectors of the public that supported Perón became more apparent each day. The lifting of the nearly four-year state of siege in early August, designed as a concession to the opposition and a first step in the return to electoral democracy, served only to embolden both the political opposition to the government and the anti-Perón editorialists and journalists of the commercial press.

Perón's response to the growing press campaign against the government remained consistent with his earlier explanation of commercialism and the exclusivity of newspaper ownership as the root causes of "distortions" in social communication. In September, as the opposition was set to begin what many thought would be a final push against the government, the minister of war warned of the press's "low and ruinous propaganda designed to provoke disorder and anarchy for the benefit of interests foreign to the nation."[65] "A part of the press," Perón declared, "the corrupt and bought [*venal y paga*], is at the service of those wretched schemes against order and tranquility, daily spreading a disfigured social and political panorama in order to confuse public opinion. To this end they falsify and twist the facts, the circumstances, and the goals of the government."[66] The sudden and "curiously unanimous" press campaign against the government thus found its explanation not in any justified opposition to the regime or understandable impatience with the transition to constitutional rule, but rather in a veritable seizure of the primary means of social communication by powerful local and international interests. Far from serving as a voice of "public opinion," then, the commercial press stood against the true national public.

Such declarations carried significant explanatory power within the growing movement of workers who backed the secretary of labor and social welfare. As Peronist labor militant Ángel Perelman would later remark, echoing Perón's October 1944 address to the FAP,

> We came to realize that the "public opinion" of our country reflected nothing but private opinion, or, better said, the opinion of interest

groups—small or large—while workers, who for their number and for their importance in the Argentine economy constituted the true public opinion, had no means to express themselves. In this way, opinions heard in Argentina between 1944 and 1945 regarding the government, Perón's union policies, and Perón himself were the opinions of groups that did not represent the national and popular interest, while [those who did represent the national and popular interest] had neither form nor means of expressing themselves. And having neither form nor means of expressing themselves, they did not constitute "public opinion."[67]

The Buenos Aires commercial press, rather than collecting the "clamor of the street, of the factory and of the countryside," increasingly appeared to Peronists as the exclusive realm of a wealthy and antinational sector set on reversing the social reforms of the preceding years.

The political polarization of mid-1945, then, starkly revealed the practical absence of popular access to expression through the press and collective representation in the media precisely as the Argentine working class began to emerge as a major political protagonist. The right of freedom of the press—a universal individual right in the liberal conception—appeared suddenly and transparently in practice as the exclusive privilege of those with a tight hold on the nation's means of social communication. That the commercial press maintained a virtually unanimous intransigent opposition to the regime—suspiciously like that of certain foreign interests—belied claims of the press's fully representative, and even national character. After all, how could a press truly representative of public opinion remain so united regarding an issue on which the public was so clearly divided?

To those looking to dismiss the press, then, the growing conflict provided ammunition for claims that commercial newspapers like *La Prensa* operated less as genuine "mouthpieces of public opinion" or "reflections of popular sentiment" and more unequivocally as the propaganda apparatus of an unsavory alliance between foreign interests and the local oligarchy. In an address to a mass gathering of the CGT in mid-July, Perón made the linkage explicit: arrayed against the social policies of the government, he declared, stood "powerful enemies" that included "the *fuerzas vivas,* [and] the newspapers paid for by the *fuerzas vivas* and other forces even less responsible."[68] Days later, an officially sanctioned leaflet distributed near the U.S. embassy similarly proclaimed, "Al Capone in Buenos Aires? Unconfirmed reports lead one to suppose that a personage similar to Capone [Braden] is operating in this ... city of Buenos Aires trying to blackmail the country. The Círculo de la Prensa, the Rural Society [Sociedad Rural], and stock exchange are helping him. Beware: details at the Bank of Boston."[69] As the regime began to unravel in the face of opposition mobilizations, this growing gulf between "press" and "public," as well as popular demands for representation in the pages of the "organs of opinion," would place *Crítica*, the newspaper whose long-standing claim of embodying popular sentiment would become suddenly and shockingly meaningless, literally in the sights of pro-Perón forces.

The Press as Battleground

At 11:00 on the evening of July 24, a small explosive device detonated at the entrance to the offices of the Círculo de la Prensa.[70] Coming just a week and a half after Braden's much-publicized visit and only days after the leaflet accusations of the Círculo's collusion with Braden and the *fuerzas vivas*, the explosion, which left only some shattered glass in the building's foyer, was clearly intended as more symbolic than physically destructive. Editorialists at *La Prensa* attributed the attack to the obvious antigovernment inclination of press reporting, yet saw it as a signal that the growing conflict in Argentine society had taken a new, inescapable turn and carried with it an assured conclusion:

> Material aggression is the logical and inevitable outcome of this process that, now as in all periods of history, is defined as the expression and synthesis of an eternal struggle: on the one side, ideas at the service of liberty; on the other, uncontrolled violence without visible direction or certain object.
> This experience teaches, nonetheless, . . . that in that eternal struggle triumph always belongs to the spirit, whose light grows and gains greater intensity the more rudimentary are the desires to extinguish it.[71]

If, as we know, the *La Prensa* writers erred spectacularly in suggesting the inevitability of Perón's defeat, the explosion at the Círculo de la Prensa did provide a clear signal that "attacks" against the press would no longer remain confined to official censorship and bureaucratic harassment.

The conflicts surrounding the Argentine commercial press, in fact, grew in frequency and ferocity as the military government's hold on the country became increasingly tenuous. The offices of *Crítica, La Prensa, La Nación,* and *La Razón* became obligatory stopping points in the competing mass mobilizations that shook the Argentine capital as World War II—and with it, many assumed, the period of military rule—drew to a close. Between shouts for and against the Allies, for and against democracy, and for and against Perón, bottles, sticks, and paving stones smashed the windows of several commercial newspaper offices. As serious as the attacks became, however, none matched the fury that demonstrators would unleash on *Crítica* on the evening of October 17.

If *Crítica* had bent most explicitly to the will of Perón and military authorities, in the Argentine spring of 1945 this suddenly changed. In what doubtless seemed a wise decision at the time, Damonte Taborda began to distance himself and *Crítica* from Perón as the regime's days appeared numbered.[72] Damonte Taborda proceeded cautiously, with *Crítica* giving prominence to Perón's and labor's responses to the Manifesto de las Fuerzas Vivas; further disparagement of the Manifesto even formed the center of the now larger section dedicated to the "Secretaría de Trabajo y Previsión."[73] For over a month, not a single formal editorial appeared in *Crítica*. Only in the final days of June did any indication of discontent with the regime surface in the pages of the paper, in the form of calls for the release of political prisoners.[74] Not until August 8, with the long-awaited lifting of the continuous state of siege, did Damonte Taborda begin to bring *Crítica* into line with the rest of the Buenos Aires commercial press by lending greater coverage to the now-emboldened opposition. Once again, *Crítica* editorialists stepped up attacks on the far Right. It is revealing that even after the end of official censorship the paper's editorials and coverage refrained from direct, unequivocal confrontation with the government: it appears that for Damonte Taborda the lifting of the state of siege signaled less a resurgence of press freedom than a measure of uncertainty about the future of his primary political associate.

The unconditional surrender of the last Axis power, Japan, in mid-August, the continued activities of Spruille Braden, and the further polarization of the Argentine public made Perón's and the military's hold on the country increasingly tenuous, despite the incorporation of Radical Party civilians into important cabinet posts just two weeks earlier.[75] By late August, *Crítica* editorialists had moved from derisive reports about Nationalist supporters of the regime to the unequivocal declaration that "the people feel defrauded" by the military government in place since June 4, 1943.[76] Damonte Taborda inaugurated an increasingly direct attack on the regime a week later, in a clear reprisal of *Crítica*'s role in the wake of the Uriburu dictatorship over a decade earlier: under the bold headline "This occurs in Buenos Aires, in 1945. Forty-three documented cases reveal the existence of a veritable Gestapo," the paper carried three full pages of dramatic denunciations of torture at the hands of the Special Section of the Federal Police.[77] The following day's editorial contained the provocative claim that the tenacity of the recent use of torture against political prisoners had less in common with any Argentine precedent than it did with practices at Buchenwald, Belsen, and Dachau.[78] The implications of such rhetorical flourishes meshed with the larger opposition discourse surrounding the government, and could hardly be lost on the regime or its opponents: the opposition would accept only the "unconditional surrender" of the Nazi-fascist regime, and shouts of "Nuremberg" at opposition demonstrations left little doubt that trials would surely follow.[79]

In mid-September, as the opposition prepared its massive "March of the Constitution and Liberty," *Crítica* editorialists began to attack Perón personally and directly. The issue of September 15 marked the final, unequivocal break between Damonte Taborda and Perón: alongside scathingly worded editorial challenges to the minister of war for his comments on the "corrupt and bought" press appeared news of the beginning of war crimes trials in Germany.[80] To make the implications even clearer, the issue also featured excerpts from a speech by Spruille Braden under the provocative title "The war will only end when there are no Fascist strongholds, declared Braden. He addressed the dangers of the present hour in [the] America[s]."[81] Just days later, a *Crítica* editorialist ridiculed the growing comparison of Perón with former president Hipólito Yrigoyen articulated by dissident, pro-Perón members of the Radical Party: Yrigoyen was a "leader," as was his present heir, Enrique Mosca, the writer asserted; Perón was nothing more than an "insignificant . . . small-time local chief [*cacique lugareño*]."[82] Finally, news of Perón's detention by the military junta on October 12 appeared in *Crítica* under the simple title "He no longer constitutes a threat to the country."[83]

If Damonte Taborda's rupture of his alliance with Perón brought *Crítica* into alignment with the rest of the Buenos Aires commercial press, the change in the newspaper's political stance was most likely brought about by simply giving freer rein to journalists in the newsroom. The strong presence of Communist journalists at *Crítica* dated to the mid-1920s and continued through the 1930s, despite the anti-Communist policies of Natalio Botana's personal friend and Buenos Aires Poligráfica shareholder President Augustín P. Justo. In 1945, several of the Party's more prominent members worked in *Crítica*'s newsroom, including Raúl Larra, Eduardo Giudice, Paulino González Alberti, José Portugal, Nicolás Olivari, Raúl González Tuñón, Héctor P. Agosti, Cayetano Córdova Iturburu, and Rodolfo Puiggrós.[84] Previously limited to attacking the Nationalist Right and lauding the Allies, these journalists now found themselves able to directly attack the "Nazi-fascist" regime at home. Beyond easing *Crítica*'s political transition, however, the widely known presence of Communist journalists introduced a complicating factor into pro-Perón denunciations of the paper: to anti-Communists, *Crítica* was not merely beholden to foreign interests, but aligned with the Soviet Union, a fact obvious from the prominent display of the Soviet and Yugoslav flags in *Crítica* crowd photos.[85]

Crítica's long history of opposition to fascism, its support of the Allies, and the strong presence of Communist journalists in the newsroom made the newspaper an obligatory point of gathering for demonstrators either celebrating or denigrating the Allied victory in World War II; it also made *Crítica* the scene of two important acts of violence that provide a direct antecedent to the events at the paper on October 17. On May 8—ironically, at the height of the paper's support for Perón—the *Crítica* staff displayed flags of the members of the United Nations on the balcony above the paper's Avenida de Mayo entrance in celebration of the unconditional surrender of Nazi Germany. The presence of the Soviet flag alongside the Argentine clearly disturbed several Nationalist protesters, who, together with the police, demanded that the Soviet flag be removed. In the ensuing confrontation, at least one person was killed, and police arrested retired major Ernesto C. Carreras, *Crítica*'s business manager, for "sowing confusion" in the paper's report of the incident.[86] Only direct appeals to the minister of the interior by Miguel Fulle, head of the Círculo de la Prensa, brought his release from the prison at Villa Devoto.[87]

The surrender of Japan and the end of World War II proved even more violent for *Crítica*, as an accelerating political polarization regarding the military government and the intensifying sense that Argentine "democrats" stood on the verge of their own victory over local "Nazi-fascists" combined with the paper's growing opposition to Perón. According to reports in *Crítica* and *La Nación*, on the evenings of August 14 and 15 about 150 progovernment protesters, including many conscripts and soldiers, shouting "Death to Democracy" and "Viva Perón," repeatedly attacked the evening paper with bottles, rocks, and gunfire.[88] After several failed attempts to set the *Crítica* building on fire on both nights, protesters burned hundreds of copies of the paper seized from delivery trucks. When police finally intervened by closing off adjacent streets and placing armed guards from the Infantry at the building's entrance, two lay dead: twenty-three-year-old Nationalist Eduardo Crocco and the "democratic" minor Alberto Beltrán.[89] The offices of the two other opposition papers located on the Avenida de Mayo, *La Prensa* and *La Razón*, in contrast, ended both nights with only minor damages.[90]

If editorialists and reporters at *La Nación* and *Crítica* assigned blame to the extreme Right and soldiers, however, the chief of police filed a quite different report:

> The clear goal of perturbing order and producing disturbances held by certain groups of known Communist affiliation could be seen. This became manifest in the horrible attack carried out from the newspaper *Crítica*, from whose balconies bottles with inflammable liquid and other heavy objects were thrown against a group of demonstrators that at 9:40 p.m. yesterday marched down the Avenida de Mayo. This brazen assault produced the justified indignation of those present, among them some soldiers who found themselves there by chance, and left as a tragic result two dead and many wounded. Some enraged demonstrators, as an act of reprisal, overturned a truck owned by the newspaper *Crítica* and set fire to the printed material it contained.[91]

Rather than an unprovoked assault by bands of "Nazi-fascist" soldiers, then, according to the government version of events the blame lay squarely with Communist agitators, in particular those journalists at *Crítica* who had supposedly moved from attacking the government and its supporters with words to more deadly forms of assault. Regardless of whether journalists or pro-Perón demonstrators initiated it, however, by mid-August the violence surrounding the newspaper *Crítica* had moved beyond the symbolic.

The reimposition of the state of siege on September 25, following a failed coup attempt by General Rawson, brought a new wave of state and quasi-state actions not just against *Crítica*, but against the Buenos Aires press as a whole. With threats of civil war as a backdrop, the Federal Police detained scores of journalists, newspaper directors, and proprietors, including Alberto Gainza Paz.[92] The extremity of police actions against the press, combined with the clearly emboldened ranks of opposition journalists, led to an act unimaginable just months earlier: at the suggestion of *Noticias Gráficas* journalist Bernardo Verbitsky, the entire board of directors of the Círculo de la Prensa cut short an emergency meeting and immediately marched to the offices of the chief of police, where they confronted en masse Minister of the Interior Hortensio Quijano.[93] The action brought the release of several journalists and proprietors who the minister found were not "implicated" in the Rawson uprising, and it also signaled a new, more direct and energetic activism of the Círculo.[94] A similar police sweep two weeks later following press attempts to report the death of an antigovernment demonstrator in Plaza San Martín brought an even more dramatic and unprecedented demonstration of press solidarity: in protest, the proprietors of *El Mundo, Crítica, Clarín, La Razón, El Día, Hoy,* and *Noticias Gráficas*—a broad range of Buenos Aires commercial dailies—refused to publish.[95]

If the three-week period between the Rawson uprising and Perón's detention proved chaotic for the Buenos Aires commercial press as a whole, at *Crítica* matters appeared even more serious. Upon news of General Rawson's uprising, the Special Section of the Federal Police raided the newspaper's offices; the discovery of several rifles, a machine gun, and seventy-three Molotov cocktails led authorities to detain a number of journalists and, again, the paper's manager, Ernesto Carreras.[96] The Ministry of the Interior closed the paper for the remainder of the month.[97] Upon its reopening in October, *Crítica* journalists produced only three heavily censored issues before a second police raid and occupation again closed the paper.[98]

On October 12, *Crítica* reappeared with an issue dedicating extensive coverage to events at the newspaper itself. While written in the paper's sensationalistic tone and making no mention of Damonte Taborda's previous alliance with Perón, the articles concerning events from September 26 through October 11 ring true with subsequent circumstances surrounding *Crítica* and other Buenos Aires papers. Following the closure and police occupation of the paper on September 26, armed pro-Perón groups once again attacked the building, apparently causing significant material damage in what one *Crítica* journalist called Perón's attempt to "pulverize" the paper's productive infrastructure.[99] Failing this, the journalist reported, Minister of the Interior Quijano began a maneuver to "capture" *Crítica* with the aid of official advertising and the newspaper's pro-Perón journalists. Quijano conditioned any reopening on *Crítica* once again moving within the Peronist orbit: "[The naming of] a new director 'satisfactory' to both parties, who would be the journalist [Orestes] Confalonieri, and the elimination of various members of our personnel in administration, direction, and the newsroom. To the opportunist journalist—transformed in 'ersatz' director—should be given an annual contract signed and validated before the minister of the interior. [The paper] could then receive twenty million pesos for the future electoral campaign."[100] Despite warnings that refusal to accept the offer would mean the paper's indefinite disappearance, Damonte Taborda hesitated and then rejected the offer of reassociation with Perón. In fact, the *Crítica* owner's delay in responding to the demands was itself an answer: within four days of the paper's October closure, Perón found himself obliged to resign all of his posts within the government; his subsequent detention by the junta seemed to confirm the end of his political career. On October 11, the Ministry of the Interior lifted all sanctions against the newspaper, and the following evening—several Peronist reporters less—*Crítica* reappeared.[101]

Even before Perón supporters took to the streets on the afternoon of October 17, then, *Crítica* surely occupied a unique place both in the general media landscape and in the political imagination of a sharply divided public. An avowedly democratic supporter of the military government since Perón's ascent, the paper had suddenly become rabidly anti-Perón, now turning *Crítica*'s particularly jarring form of political attack against the colonel by consistently labeling Perón and his backers "Nazi-fascists" and denying the existence of any popular support for the regime. The offices of *Crítica*, just as importantly, had not merely been the target of impromptu vandalism as had those of *La Nación*, *La Prensa*, and *La Razón*; instead, confrontations between progovernment protesters and the paper's "Communist" staff and supporters had turned violent on several occasions prior to October 17, leaving a total of three people dead. Finally, *Crítica*'s proprietor and staff themselves had widely publicized the recent attempts first to "pulverize" the paper's productive apparatus and then to impose a renewed Perón-*Crítica* alliance. *Crítica*, a newspaper whose image and market position was built on decades of self-portrayal as the unmediated expression of working-class opinion in the public sphere, now stood in direct and scathing opposition to an undeniably large section of the public whose interests it claimed to embody.

It was precisely the "traitorous" nature of this reversal that drew the wrath of Peronist demonstrators to *Crítica,* rather than to the more consistently and predictably anti-Perón newspapers like *La Prensa.* In relating the events of the evening of October 17, an editorialist at *La Época,* the only newspaper to stand by Perón in his fall, commented that, like its building's shutters, the aloof *La Prensa* "had always remained closed to the authentic and legitimate people"; *Crítica,* on the other hand, had proven more insulting: it had seemed to open the door to the popular classes within the media, only to close it at the decisive moment.[102] While the publishers of *La Prensa* and *La Nación* invoked the universality of rights of expression in the abstract, they made absolutely no pretense that their papers served in practice as vehicles for the Argentine popular classes to exercise those rights. *Crítica*'s greatest strength, on the other hand, lay in its successful self-portrayal as the agent of mass, working-class representation in the media. At best, the shattering of this illusion revealed the newspaper's popular character as a mere marketing ploy; at worst, it revealed a conspiracy of the local oligarchy and foreign interests set on silencing popular nationalism and reversing the reforms of the Secretariat of Labor and Social Welfare. Together with the tension built through previous violent confrontations at the newspaper's offices, the abrupt change in the paper's political stance helps to explain not only why *Crítica* came under attack on October 17, but also the ferocity of Peronist reactions against the evening paper: by the nature of its target audience, *Crítica* should have been Peronist, or it simply should not have existed.

The discursive resolution of the contradiction between *Crítica*'s ostensible embodiment of the people's voice and the clearly working-class nature of the October 17 mobilizations centered upon a denial of both the size of the protests and the status of the protesters as members of the public. Furthermore, *Crítica*'s fifth-edition coverage of the early stages of the demonstrations appears to have been consciously calculated to antagonize, even infuriate, those who demanded Perón's release. The paper's bold headline presented the first in a series of dismissals of the demonstrators as both numerically inconsequential and alien to the nation's popular classes: "Isolated groups that do not represent the authentic Argentine proletariat try to intimidate the population." *Crítica*'s editorialized account of the early phase of the march even included a conversation "taken from the street" between "a man" who supported Perón and "a humble worker" who was "detained, pulled from my home under Peronism. Friends of mine who were accused of having proworker ideas were cruelly mistreated."[103] Together with constant allusions to "the people" and "the citizenry" as those who had taken part in the opposition's March of Liberty and the Constitution, the content of *Crítica* journalists' rhetoric both reinforced and explained the absence of any Peronist representation in the pages of the press: the "public" was not, in fact, divided on the issue of Perón, since those

Fig. 9 Public gathering in front of the Casa Rosada, October 17, 1945.

who supported the imprisoned colonel did not constitute "the people." Any dissonance in "public opinion," then, found its elimination in the simple excision from "the public" of what would ultimately prove a majority of the Argentine population.

To assume that this exclusionary message reached the crowds demanding Perón's release, however, is to give exaggerated importance to the reading of newspapers in the heat of what was then Argentina's largest popular mobilization. Yet, since the evening papers constituted the primary source of news, more than a handful of demonstrators surely caught a glimpse of *Crítica's* front page, or heard from those who had, and perhaps even read the incendiary captions to the two photographs on the page. The first photograph shows the crowds gathering in the Plaza de Mayo, "yelling 'vivas' to the ex-Secretary of Labor and Social Welfare, before the indifference of the public," when police allegedly dispersed them with tear gas, "making them cry abundantly." A second, smaller photograph shows a wide avenue from above, empty except for perhaps two dozen people walking separately, casually, without banners of any kind. The photo's particularly derisive and revealing caption has figured in numerous accounts of the events of October 17: "A column of Colonel Perón advances. Here is one of the columns that since this morning stroll through the city in a 'revolutionary' manner. Apart from other small incidents, they have only committed acts against good taste and against the city's aesthetics, made ugly by their presence in our streets. The people saw them pass by, at first a bit surprised and then with glacial indifference."[104] The disjunction between press and public, the contradiction between egalitarian claims of equal representation in the press and the clearly exclusionary nature of access to the media, thus reached its high point in the pages of *Crítica* precisely at the moment in which the supposed "nonpublic"—those incapable or not worthy of citizenship—had suddenly swept the city. The violence at the newspaper's offices would repeat on a greater scale the confrontations of the previous months.

The *Crítica* report on the mobilizations only briefly mentioned "relatively small groups" who stood outside of the newspaper's offices shouting, "Down with rags [*pasquines*]," "Paid by foreigners," and the more ominous "You have little time left."[105] By eight o'clock that evening, just hours before Perón's release, crowds had already overturned one truck carrying the paper's sixth edition in front of the *Crítica* building, scattering and burning its contents.[106] Following Perón's triumphant address from the balcony of the Casa Rosada, over five thousand protesters converged on the *Crítica* offices and attempted to force their way into the building.[107] Sporadic handgun fire gave way to that of automatic weapons, while demonstrators made repeated attempts to set the building ablaze using gasoline, furniture from neighboring businesses, and small explosives. More than two hours later, and with the 3rd Regiment of the Infantry preparing to use artillery against the building, the journalists, printers, and staff members who had not succeeded in escaping through the back door on Rivadavia Street permitted the police to enter and were immediately arrested. Even then, gunmen positioned in the Palacio Barolo across the street continued to fire on *Crítica* for a quarter hour more, and several protesters managed to enter the building, set fire to the machine room, and cause other serious damage. When the siren atop the *Crítica* building finally fell silent nearly three hours after the attack had begun, seventeen-year-old Darwin Pasapompi and twenty-four-year-old Francisco Ramos lay dead, twelve-year-old Roberto Marchi and thirty-five others were injured, and forty-seven were in police custody—most of them minors.[108]

The Defeat of *Crítica;* the Failure of Perón

Crítica, as an institution, also lay moribund. The evening paper appeared again only two weeks later, much more timid, making reference to the events of October 17 only in a short, vague editorial entitled "We have nothing to say."[109] Not until August 1947 did *Crítica* address the attack on the newspaper, in an editorial that answered accusations—true, as would become increasingly clear—that the paper's new director, Natalio Botana's widow, Salvadora Medina Onrubia de Botana, had sold control of *Crítica* to representatives of Perón.[110] In the signed editorial, Salvadora absolved the paper of any culpability for the rhetorical onslaught on the Peronist demonstrators, but did so in a manner that revealed just how damaging the attack had actually proven. The journalists who allegedly produced the editions of October 17, 1945, now formed the backbone of the official press—including César Caminos, who had allegedly first referred to protesters as *descamisados* in the paper's poorly distributed sixth edition.[111] Others abandoned *Crítica* for the recently founded *Clarín*, laying the basis for the daily that would emerge from the Peronist years as Latin America's most widely read newspaper.[112] Deprived of its most talented and experienced journalists, estranged from large sectors of its traditional public, facing significant material losses, and bereft of the symbiotic relations with key state officials that it had maintained for more than a decade, *Crítica* was devastated by the events of October 17.

Yet, if *Crítica*'s turn against Perón left much of the newspaper's installations literally in ruins, it also signaled a defeat for the media strategy of Perón himself. Regular repression and censorship of the daily press by the military regime had done little to generate support for the state authorities and had left the government open not just to ideologically debilitating claims of authoritarianism by the opposition, but to potentially serious international repercussions, especially as a hostile United States began to rebuild international political and economic institutions. Concessions to working journalists, while contingently bringing many newsworkers to the side of the government, neither guaranteed that allegiance at a moment of crisis nor targeted those who had ultimate control over newspaper content.

Even the attempt to resurrect the media strategy forged by General Justo in the 1930s had ended in near-total disaster. Alliances with established newspaper owners like Raúl Damonte Taborda and, to a lesser degree, José Agusti had simply failed; based on political convenience, judicial favors, and official advertising, these arrangements could not fully bring already powerful newspaper owners to depend upon Perón for their papers' continued existence. At the same time, the seeming inevitability of Perón's demise in mid-1945 threatened to make alliance with the colonel more a grave liability than a source of strength. As a result, *Crítica* and other newspapers had lent their power to Perón most readily when he was least threatened, yet found no reason to defend him when he most needed it. With the exception of the activities of the Undersecretariat of Information and the Press, then, Perón's media strategy had failed spectacularly.

Ironically, attempts by Perón and Farrell in 1944 and 1945 to secure the sympathies of the existing commercial press had foundered precisely at the moment of a triumph for Peronism that proved as decisive as it was unexpected. That Perón had emerged strengthened by the crisis of October 1945 cast a pall over the nation's traditional press. For the directors and proprietors of the Buenos Aires newspapers, unbridled opposition not only to the figure of

Perón, but, implicitly or explicitly, to the entire set of reforms brought by the military regime had only served to heighten the urgency of the crisis facing the press. The fact that *Crítica, Noticias Gráficas, La Razón, El Mundo, La Nación,* and *La Prensa* had become crucial weapons of the opposition to the military experiment closely tied the fate of those institutions to a traditional political and social order far less resilient than the proprietors of those papers imagined.

Perhaps more importantly for the long-term stability of the commercial press, however, the questions of *for whom* the press existed and *by whom* its freedoms and power could be exercised had become violently contentious, emerging into the public realm through the now readily apparent chasm between the egalitarian proclamations and exclusionary practice of newspaper proprietors and directors. The profundity of the social changes wrought in the preceding years, together with deep—and structurally related—crises of traditional conceptions of the role of journalism, the rights and expectations of citizenship, and the nature of the state, negated the possibility that the Argentine press could simply return to the status quo ante with the long-anticipated restoration of full constitutional rule. The startling consequences of the first step in that direction—the ouster of Juan Domingo Perón—had made this more than evident.

PART 3

THE DIE IS CAST

> I organized all of this with my spirit and soul centered on the greatness
> of the Patria and on the happiness of her people.
>
> **—Carlos Vicente Aloé, head of Editorial ALEA**

The events of October 1945 revealed a chasm between the "representatives of public opinion" and broad sectors of the Argentine public far deeper than the proprietors of Buenos Aires commercial newspapers cared to admit. Yet the press's unanimity in celebrating Perón's fall from grace and disparaging his supporters was breached by a single newspaper: *La Época*. Owned and run by the Yrigoyenist Radical Eduardo Colóm, the paper had defied what seemed common sense in decrying Perón's ouster, and alone had urged on the popular mobilization that brought Perón's resurgence. With the commercial press assembled in a common front against the colonel and his supporters, the outpouring of popular sentiment in the mobilizations of October 17–18 found its only echo in *La Época*, which alone could now lay claim to representing an undeniably large and suddenly powerful sector of the Argentine population. This incongruity between the profound polarization of the public and the unanimity of the nation's most powerful dailies would prove untenable in the coming months; the small *La Época* alone could not resolve this contradiction.

If only one newspaper backed him in October 1945, however, in five years Perón would succeed not only in building a vast and staunchly loyal media apparatus, but in virtually eliminating the opposition press. The deep inroads into traditional press discourse and the legal status of newspapers made during the military period had laid the basis for a profound transformation of the Argentine press. Beyond bringing many newsworkers to the Peronist cause, the 1944 Journalist's Statute had placed the Argentine newspaper industry on a new juridical footing vis-à-vis the state, lending legal weight to the notion that the press's practical commercial aspects posed a constant threat to the properly cultural and informative mission of journalism. Similarly, the sudden political protagonism of a large sector of Argentine society clearly bereft of representation in the country's traditional media had effectively undermined claims that the existing press reflected the full spectrum of "public opinion." Assertions that only the nation's newspaper entrepreneurs could sustain universal citizen rights to expression and representation in the press simply clashed with the lived experience of much of the newly mobilized Argentine public. As editorialists at one of the new Peronist newspapers would claim, "the big press and public opinion have divorced."[1]

Perón's subsequent assumption of the presidency in the first clean elections in nearly two decades gave his government a degree of legitimacy that both the de facto regime and its opposition had clearly lacked. Rather than signaling a reversal of the previous regime's social project, the return to constitutional rule placed in Peronist hands the means to expand it. That he now ruled in good measure through the constitutional mechanisms that members of the opposition had assumed would halt the Peronist advance lent Perón a tremendous advantage in clashes with the traditional press. Between 1943 and 1946, state-directed attempts to reshape the Buenos Aires press had met with uneven results at best. These experiments did, however, help establish a competing discourse on journalism as a vehicle of collective citizenship—with the state as a barrier against the corrupting influences of commerce—that laid the groundwork for a far more successful media project. Following their electoral victory, Perón and his still amorphous Peronist movement could create a dramatically different media landscape even while portraying their actions as consonant with the constitution, social justice, the public good, and democracy.

The vast para-state media apparatus that Perón would build between 1946 and 1951 clearly also owes much to his control of the patronage capacity of a wealthy, rapidly expanding Argentine state, the particular authoritarian bent of much of his movement, and the lessons he drew from his ill-fated alliance with Raúl Damonte Taborda. Still, to attribute the transformation of the Argentine press in the years of Perón's presidency to nothing more than a mix of coercion and co-optation is to ignore the degree to which traditional, antistatist and market-based understandings of the press were already challenged by a set of circumstances beyond Peronist engineering. The years of constitutional Peronism were, after all, also the years of world recovery from the dual ideological and economic blows of the Great Depression and the Second World War.

In fact, the convergence of a political majority virtually unrepresented in the established press, an increasingly urgent financial crisis in the newspaper industry, and the continued success of the statist economic policies that had emerged by force of necessity during the Depression left little room for a return to the state-press relations that held sway between 1880 and 1930. The outbreak of hostilities in Europe had created a world crisis of newsprint production and distribution that only deepened with the war's end. When this was combined with the inflationary consequences of Peronist redistributive policies and the economic effects of the Journalist's Statute, the import-dependent Argentine newspaper industry faced the possibility of a dramatic market "rationalization" that threatened to undermine both the plurality of a newly vibrant public sphere and the livelihood of organized newsworkers. Economic conditions alone, then, virtually guaranteed that either state or market forces would reshape the landscape of the Buenos Aires commercial press in the wake of World War II. The failure of newspaper owners to organize collectively in response to these crises strengthened the hand of the Peronist government vis-à-vis the press and undermined the possibility that individual proprietors would find any solution to their financial emergency that did not involve some compromise with Peronism.

Largely by invoking claims that only state action could shield the press from ruin, Perón and his allies determined the contours of the media landscape that would emerge. Beyond the press's escalating financial crisis and the clear role played by legal measures, however, the Peronist movement—and Perón himself—also engaged in coercive and co-opting tactics to ensure both the success of allied media and the elimination of opposition newspapers. Yet the targets of these efforts were not simply the traditional commercial dailies, or even the non-Peronist press. Having seen the dangers of alliance with newspaper owners not fully under his control, Perón sought to guarantee the loyalty even of progovernment proprietors by tying them, willingly or not, to a para-state media apparatus. Thus, though at first nearly as eclectic as the Peronist coalition itself, the new press of the Peronist years became progressively more tightly tied to the movement's leading figure. Ironically, this new press would come to serve both as a tool for the consolidation and regimentation of an extremely heterogeneous political movement and as a barrier against the incipient democratization of the Argentine public sphere that the advent of Peronism as an electoral force had fostered.

The Formation and Centralization of the Peronist Press

The presidential campaign, which pitted Perón and former minister of the interior J. Hortensio Quijano against Radicals José Tamborini and Enrique Mosca of the UCR, Socialist, Communist, and Conservative coalition Unión Democrática (UD), also saw the emergence of a new sector of the Argentine press. With the entire traditional press firmly behind the UD, a new set of small, precariously financed newspapers emerged as the propaganda arm of

Perón's backers.[2] This new manifestation of factional journalism included a host of new dailies that, much like the eclectic Peronist coalition itself, initially held little in common beyond support for Perón. As the movement institutionalized, however, this cacophonous early Peronist press became increasingly univocal. If alliance with *Crítica* owner Raúl Damonte Taborda had opened the power of the mass press to Perón and revealed the benefits of a laudatory media, it had also demonstrated the real danger latent in such partnerships with independent newspaper owners. Within five years of Perón's 1946 electoral victory, the array of politically distinct newspapers that had first appeared in the suddenly revitalized Argentine public sphere would become closely tied not just to Perón's allies, but to Perón himself.

A vibrant pro-Perón press appeared almost immediately in the wake of the October 17–18 mobilizations, and continued to function following the electoral victory of Perón four months later. The emergence of commercially significant and politically important newspapers like *La Época, El Laborista, El Líder,* and *Democracia*, beyond providing media support for the Peronist electoral campaign, helped create the impression—not entirely erroneous—that the monopoly on "public opinion" held by the country's traditional press was now broken; the Argentine popular classes now appeared to have gained far greater representation within the national press. Largely within the tradition of factional journalism, these new newspapers served as voices of distinct groups within the pro-Perón public, and the differences in coverage and commentary between the dailies reflected broad debates within the new Peronist political and social coalition. As Perón completed his first six months as head of state, the landscape of the Buenos Aires press had quickly become more variegated, with a set of liberal-conservative, leftist, and popular commercial dailies arrayed against the government, and a new group of more directly partisan newspapers representing disparate social sectors and interests in the now constitutional Peronist regime's corner.

Of the Peronist press, only the afternoon newspaper *La Época* could trace its origins to before October 1945. José Luís Cantilo had founded the paper in the wake of the 1912 Sáenz Peña Law as a means of backing Radical Party leader Hipólito Yrigoyen. *La Época*'s connection to Yrigoyen became so firmly a part of the newspaper's identity, in fact, that crowds attacked the *La Época* offices shortly after the military coup of 1930, burning the paper's installations.[3] In 1937, Eduardo Colóm, of the UCR's Yrigoyenist wing, purchased the paper's name and began publishing weekly editions of what remained an economically insubstantial *La Época*. The military coup of 1943 and the subsequent rise of Perón, however, suggested to many dissident Radicals that Yrigoyen's true political successor had at last appeared. The nationalist sector of the UCR, created in the mid-1930s and whose most prominent figure was writer Raúl Scalabrini Ortiz, broke from the party under the military government and backed Perón in the 1946 elections. Many members of the Fuerza de Orientación Radical de la Juventud Argentina (FORJA) and other dissident Radicals, Colóm included, quickly became part of Peronism's political class in the movement's early years.[4]

More immediately, however, the advent of the military regime in 1943 created new opportunities for Colóm's essentially moribund weekly newspaper that went beyond matters of political sympathy. If initial contacts with Perón in the months following the coup led to little more than vague promises of financial support for *La Época*, Damonte Taborda's and José Agusti's abandonment of Perón in the midst of the 1945 crises made Colóm's adherence to the beleaguered vice president far more important and *La Época* far more crucial to Perón. Faced with the defection of *Crítica* and *Noticias Gráficas*, in late August 1945 Minister of the Interior Quijano placed $50,000 from the government's discretionary funds in the hands of *La Época*'s owner. A subsequent official loan brought the total to $75,000. With the addition of his daughter's personal savings, Colóm managed to bring together $100,000, and on September 17, just as the regime began to crumble, *La Época* began to appear daily.[5] As the only remaining daily sympathetic to the military government and to the figure of Perón specifically, the paper saw its circulation jump from 50,000 to 120,000 copies within three months.[6]

La Época's loyalty to Perón in the crisis of October 1945 owed much to the political convictions of Eduardo Colóm and his faith that the colonel embodied the spirit of Yrigoyenist populism. Yet the nature of the Colóm-Perón alliance also left the *La Época* owner with little choice. Unlike Damonte Taborda, Colóm lacked the advertisers, staff, or capital reserves to continue publishing without government aid. Also, *La Época*'s character as a specifically Peronist newspaper tied its fate to that of the colonel in ways that Raúl Damonte Taborda expected *Crítica* could avoid: since its readership purchased *La Época* precisely for its support of Perón, any change of political orientation would deprive the newspaper of its still tenuous readership base; on the other hand, any post-Perón government surely would not allow a Peronist *La Época* to continue publishing. For Colóm, then, issuing the rallying cry for protesters on October 17—from both the pages of *La Época* and the balcony of the Casa Rosada—was, in fact, more than a move born of political conviction: it was also the most prudent course of action for the newspaper's future.[7] Support for Perón in the elections boosted the political fortunes of the *La Época* owner personally as well: as a candidate of the pro-Perón UCR–Junta Renovadora, Eduardo Colóm won a seat in the national Congress's lower house. The "betrayal" of Damonte Taborda and the loyalty of Colóm in the October crisis helped to demonstrate an important principle that would guide Perón in the coming years: that alliance with important figures with independent potential for political mobilization posed unnecessary risks; weak but dependent allies not only had far more reason to remain loyal, but could themselves be made both more powerful and more dependent as needed.

While *La Época* acted as Colóm's personal mouthpiece and as a media representative of the pro-Perón wing of Yrigoyenist Radicalism, the morning newspaper *El Laborista* served as the voice of the recently founded, pro-Perón Partido Laborista (PL). *El Laborista* began to appear in late 1945 as a formal counterpart to the Socialist Party organ *La Vanguardia* in speaking for the labor movement. The paper's two directors, in fact, came from within the ranks of labor itself: Ángel Borlenghi of the Commercial Employees Union and Leandro Reynés, who, as founding member of the APBA and sitting president of the FAP at the moment of the Journalist's Statute's decree, had experience in both journalism and labor organizing.[8]

Borlenghi and Reynés's hold on the paper, however, proved as ephemeral as the party it represented: following Perón's dissolution of the PL in May 1946, associates of Domingo Mercante, governor of the province of Buenos Aires, assumed control of *El Laborista*.[9] The paper's new directors used it to cultivate Mercante's image until later conflicts over presidential reelection and with President Perón's increasingly powerful wife led to the governor's downfall. Borlenghi, now minister of the interior in the new Peronist government, founded a new newspaper in July 1946, *El Líder*, which acted at once to boost his personal power by portraying the minister as personally close to Perón (the paper's masthead included the president's profile) and to represent on a daily basis the interests of the increasingly disciplined organized labor leadership. Reynés, a candidate together with Colóm on the UCR–Junta Renovadora ticket in 1946, also won a seat in Congress, where he became the staunchest lobbyist for protection and progressive revision of the Journalist's Statute.

The morning newspaper *Democracia* accompanied *La Época* and *El Laborista* in supporting Perón's successful presidential bid. Founded in December 1945 by lawyer Antonio Manuel Molinari and agronomist Mauricio Birabent, the new daily became the voice of support for agrarian reform within the Peronist coalition. Both men had served on the National Agrarian Council (Consejo Agrario Nacional) for the duration of the military regime, where they published the free pro-Perón weekly *Hombres de Campo* and laid the groundwork for what they believed would become a substantial agrarian reform.[10] To this effect, Perón's campaigning in the Argentine interior received wide coverage in *Democracia* and did much to lend credence to Perón's commitment to social justice nationwide and to uprooting the Argentine "oligarchy" precisely at the traditional source of its power: landholding. Perón, of course, had little interest in an extensive agrarian reform that would disrupt agricultural exports—the principal source of funding for his industrialization plans—or drive up food prices for his constituents in the rapidly growing Argentine cities. In May 1946, Miguel Miranda, head of Perón's economic team, convinced

Farrell to relegate the National Agrarian Council to a simple dependency of the National Bank.[11] After Perón assumed the presidency in June 1946, then, not only had Molinari and Birabent's *Democracia* outlived its usefulness to the new president, but the growing disillusionment of the paper's directors with Perón's agrarian policy resulted in fading enthusiasm for the government in the pages of the newspaper.

The surprising plurality of the pro-Perón press in the waning days of the military regime and early months of the first Perón presidency would ultimately fall victim to the centralizing and verticalizing efforts of an increasingly disciplined political organization. In March 1946, just weeks after the national elections, Chief of the Federal Police General Filomeno Velazco approached Eduardo Colóm in an attempt to purchase *La Época*—in Colóm's estimation, on Perón's behalf.[12] Colóm defended himself by making selective aspects of the takeover attempt public through *La Época,* initiating a campaign against Secretary of Industry and Commerce Joaquín Saurí and Undersecretary of Information and the Press Rafael Lascalea for not supporting the paper's increasingly expensive newsprint purchases. This put at risk, Colóm argued, the capacity of the pro-Perón press to respond to the far more solvent traditional commercial press. Underscoring the degree to which Colóm's dependence on Perón grew in the wake of the February electoral victory, the newspaper owner could only protect his hold on *La Época* by accepting as codirector Perón confidante and ex-*Crítica* reporter Emilio Cipolletti, who had recently left his position as interventor of the earthquake-stricken San Juan Province.[13]

Yet the paper's increasingly shaky financial situation meant that Perón's subsequent attempts to reign in Colóm would eventually prove more successful. In 1949, the president's personal secretary, Major Carlos Vicente Aloé, and the president of the Chamber of Deputies, Héctor Cámpora, offered Colóm $500,000 for the newspaper, which he nonetheless rejected. Still, the political marginalization of Colóm would proceed apace with the newspaper's dwindling finances, and by the end of the year Colóm was obliged to surrender ownership of *La Época* to Aloé on the sole condition that he remain the paper's director.[14] However, Colóm's publication of a subsequent series of articles backing the historical legacy of Juan Manuel de Rosas proved unnecessarily divisive for Peronists, and on January 30, 1951, Colóm issued his farewell to *La Época*'s readers, citing not the obvious pressure from fellow Peronists, but his own financial difficulties.[15]

Though *La Época* was the first Peronist newspaper approached by Perón's inner circle, *Democracia* became the first of the progovernment papers to pass fully into what critics would call "the chain."[16] Miguel Miranda, head of the National Economic Council (Consejo Económico Nacional), together with his associates Orlando Maroglio and Alberto Dodero, purchased the financially ailing newspaper from Molinari and Birabent in early 1947 for just $50,000—a mere tenth what would be offered to Colóm only two years later.[17] The real ownership of *Democracia* now stood even closer to Perón himself: Eva Perón, not Miranda, came to own the newspaper and its newly formed parent company, Editorial Democracia. A subsequent infusion of cash from the National Bank, a constant stream of official advertising, and a change away from the paper's narrowly partisan character to appeal more broadly to the urban popular classes quickly made *Democracia* the most successful Peronist paper, much to the chagrin of Eduardo Colóm.[18] Eva Perón quickly acquired her second member of the Peronist press in August 1947 when Editorial Democracia purchased *El Laborista,* just as its patron, Buenos Aires governor Domingo Mercante, began to fall out of favor with the ruling couple.[19]

By mid-1947, then, Peronist newspapers had become an established part of the Buenos Aires press, with *La Época, El Laborista,* and *El Líder* functioning as openly partisan organs within the movement and *Democracia* enjoying a surprising level of success as a more commercially oriented, popular Peronist daily. With the growing institutionalization of Peronism, however, the plurality of newspaper voices that had emerged in the wake of October 1945 had begun to give way to a growing homogenization of the Peronist press. As the Peronist government entered its second full year, the owners of sympathetic newspapers faced the option of coming under direct control of Perón and Eva Perón, or attempting to survive in what would prove extremely trying economic times for the Argentina press. Perón no longer sought allies among newspaper owners; he created dependents incapable of betrayal.

Newsprint Fray or the Financial Crisis of the Commercial Press

Perón and Eva Perón's acquisition of *Democracia* and other papers that had emerged in the wake of the October 1945 demonstrations guaranteed them a newspaper presence that already exceeded that achieved by Justo a decade earlier. Beyond the Peronist press, however, the first eighteen months of Perón's presidency also saw a broad range of previously existing commercial newspapers brought under the control of the Peróns and their closest allies. These would include four of Latin America's five largest dailies at the time of Perón's electoral victory—*El Mundo, Crítica, Noticias Gráficas,* and *La Razón*—signaling the creation of a media apparatus unprecedented in the region.

Scholars have virtually unanimously pointed to the regime's manipulation of the nation's newsprint supply as the primary means by which the Peronist movement managed to appropriate nearly all of the nation's important commercial newspapers.[20] While certainly true, such explanations leave important questions unanswered: How did a Peronist regime jealous of guarding its legal and democratic credentials justify this bureaucratic maneuvering? How did newspaper owners resist government newsprint policies, and why did virtually all fail? What role did other factors, such as steep salary increases for newsworkers, play in the economic crisis of much of the commercial press? What explains the ease and speed with which the regime's media apparatus came to control some of Latin America's most important newspapers? Most basically, what broader set of circumstances opened the possibility for a degree of sustained state intervention in newsprint distribution, as well as more covert forms of state and quasi-state involvement in the press, unthinkable just years earlier?

In fact, a broad set of subjective and objective factors facilitated the legal measures that the Peronist government took with regard to the commercial press. Inroads into the traditional liberal conception of the press as a "fourth estate" had accumulated for over a decade, even if the Journalist's Statute remained the only binding, nonemergency modification of the press's status within Argentine jurisprudence. The statute's legal recognition of the press's character as a commercial industry had powerful implications as the dual blows of Peronist redistributive policies and the worldwide newsprint crisis threatened to devastate the import-dependent Argentine newspaper industry. Most immediately, the Journalist's Statute of 1944 and its 1946 renewal by a democratically elected Argentine Congress added to the financial difficulties of newspaper proprietors even as it benefited in fundamental ways the country's working journalists. Yet the statute also provided a concrete example of broadly legitimate, protective state intervention in the functioning of the

Fig. 10 Perón signs the Estatuto del Periodista Profesional, December 24, 1946. Octavio Palazzolo stands to his immediate right.

newspaper industry even as it lent greater weight to the notion—more explicit in the New Year's decrees that it replaced—that the commercial nature of the modern press posed a constant threat to the proper social role of journalism as a vehicle for the public exercise of citizenship.[21]

If traditional liberalism saw the market as the facilitator of press independence in the face of a necessarily adversarial state, the profound economic crisis facing the newspaper industry reinforced the trend to look to the state as a protector against a now hostile marketplace. At the same time, the severity of the situation added new facets to the possibility of state intervention. With the newsprint crisis threatening to sweep away much of the Buenos Aires commercial press, state intervention of some form seemed the only viable option for maintaining the breadth of the newspaper landscape—in good part due to the failure of newspaper owners to reach an independent corporate solution to the crisis. As much from a growing desperation among proprietors as from the statist appeals of Peronists, then, the Argentine state advanced, both overtly and covertly, to mediate the whole network of relationships that comprised the press: between proprietors and newsworkers; between press and public; between economically weak newspapers and their powerful rivals; and between the newspaper industry as a whole and the world newsprint market.

If doubts remained that Perón might use state action to create a broadly representative press rather than a partisan media apparatus, claims by the owners and editors of the established Buenos Aires commercial press that their papers represented more than a politically suspect fraction of national public opinion had simply become untenable. The Peronist ascendancy placed the directors of *La Nación* in the uneasy position of "guiding" an increasingly marginalized traditional political class while having no sway among the Peronists. The regular implicit affirmations in the pages of *La Prensa* that the paper embodied public opinion itself rang as hollow as claims that the paper "has always been closed to the authentic and legitimate people" proved resonant.[22] This more general crisis of legitimacy for the press was perhaps most severe for *Crítica*, whose owners had revealed themselves as anti-Peronist just as their traditional audience had embraced Perón. That this had become violently apparent on the evening of October 17–18, 1945, marked only the beginning of trouble for the Botana family paper. *Crítica*, economically devastated by the attacks of October 17–18, 1945, and relentlessly ridiculed in the Peronist press for betraying the trust of its core audience, found itself with a dwindling readership precisely as its production costs skyrocketed.[23] Finally, even many newspaper proprietors began to denounce the fundamental liberal claim that the press stood above the mundane world of commercial interests, a notion already weakened by the unionization of journalists and the decree of the Journalist's Statute. In the hostile postwar financial environment, the owners of weaker dailies had good reason to proclaim openly that their newspapers were economic entities in need of aid.

While the roots of the press's crisis of legitimacy are intimately linked to the rise of Peronism, the primary cause of the newspaper industry's financial problems lay beyond the national borders. By disrupting world newsprint production and shipping, the war had placed serious strains on international newsprint markets, with world prices rising over 300 percent between 1936 and mid-1943.[24] At the same time, rapid urbanization throughout the Americas pushed newspaper circulation upward, especially in the United States.[25] Yet, with significant domestic production as well as overland access to Canadian producers, the U.S. newspaper industry could respond to the growing demands of a prosperous public not just with greater circulation, but with more pages per issue as well.

In Argentina, however, the problem was much more acute: not only did the nation's capital have by far the largest newspaper circulation in Latin America—and Argentina among the highest per capita in the world—but the Argentine newspaper industry imported all of the one hundred thirty-six thousand metric tons of newsprint it consumed annually in the 1930s.[26] The Argentine Ministry of Agriculture's occasional attempts to promote domestic production invariably failed, even as the shipping lanes that Argentine importers depended upon grew dangerous with the beginning of the war.[27] Even for the economically powerful *La Prensa*, which had privileged access to producers as well as its own shipping, the situation became increasingly difficult. The paper cut its newsprint imports from twenty-three thousand, eight hundred metric tons in 1939—nearly 20 percent of the nation's total consumption for that year—to about fifteen thousand in 1943, while Gainza Paz imposed limits on the paper's steadily increasing circulation, increased the issue price, and cut the number of pages per issue.[28] The more generalized economic disruptions of the war, furthermore, saw a drop in demand for display advertising as the quantity and variety of previously imported consumer items fell and the shrinking number of newspaper pages reduced advertising space.

Even prior to the military coup of June 1943, then, the rising cost of newsprint and falling advertising revenues had begun to affect the economic fortunes of the national press. Yet, while the world conflict threw the international newsprint market into disarray, the flood of Argentines into the nation's relatively prosperous cities drove circulation steadily upward. In the decade between 1935 and the end of World War II, *La Razón* increased daily sales from 81,000 to 238,000, *La Prensa* from 230,000 to 370,000, *El Mundo* from 207,000 to nearly 306,000, and *Crítica* from 250,000 to 300,000, while *La Nación* and *Noticias Gráficas* showed more modest gains.[29] The strength of Argentina's wartime economy allowed newspaper owners and newsprint distributors like Casa Iturrat to continue importing the newsprint that they required to meet much of this rising demand, though the quality of paper deteriorated after 1939. The capital reserves of newspapers like *La Prensa*, which also had the advantage of its own international shipping, facilitated the advance purchase of relatively large stocks of the commodity, allowing Alberto Gainza Paz to shield his paper against disruptions as well as to resell newsprint in the local market to smaller newspapers and magazines.[30] Revealingly, only Australia imported more high-quality Canadian newsprint than Argentina did in 1944, even though in the final years of the war Argentina received 80 to 90 percent of its newsprint not from Canada, but from Sweden.[31]

The cessation of hostilities, however, presented new problems. European reconstruction saw a dramatic rise in world newsprint consumption not only for newspapers, but also for the official publications of newly reconstituted national states. In Argentina, the rising costs of labor—printers, administrative employees, and truck drivers in addition to journalists had all seen steep wage increases—combined with still rising newsprint prices to steadily erode the solvency of many newspapers. That a solution to this impending crisis of plurality in the Argentine newspaper market might reside in the application of the now well-established economic common sense of state interventionism, Peronists would quickly point out, was hardly threatening; even in Great Britain, the birthplace of individual liberties and traditional notions of the press, the Labour government had begun to investigate newspaper finances with an eye to state regulation.[32] With the idea of the market as an efficient and socially just distributive mechanism increasingly discredited in society and with the labor movement quickly gaining political ground, British economic policy entered the postwar period with a decidedly statist orientation. As a deepening crisis of production of unforeseeable duration threatened to devastate the British newspaper industry and homogenize the public sphere, the Labour government tightened, rather than lifted, the state-managed newsprint rationing begun during the war.[33]

If calls for state action in the newsprint market were hardly unique to Argentina, they came, at first, exclusively from Peronists like Colóm, proprietors of new, pro-Perón newspapers, and government officials. In addition to facing steep initial investments, these new newspaper owners lacked the direct access to newsprint producers and international credit enjoyed by established newspapers. To make matters worse, Eduardo Colóm's allegations of continued "blacklisting" by United States paper companies clearly hold some truth.[34] At the height of Perón's presidential campaign, Colóm and *La Época* stated bluntly what anti-Peronist editors had argued since shortly after the coup of June 1943: "in Argentina there is no freedom of the press."[35] For Colóm, however, censorship was the result not of government action, but of government inaction; he argued that the owners of *La Prensa*, *La Nación*, and *La Razón* had effectively placed a stranglehold on the newsprint supply, pricing the commodity out of reach of newspapers like *La Época*.[36] The business practices of these three dailies, according to Colóm, conspired against the free practice of journalism—and thus against the country itself—as the standard-bearers of the traditional rights of the press hypocritically sought to deny those rights to Perón's supporters. Government officials, Colóm and *La Época* maintained, must actively use state power to rescue the press from the combined forces of avarice, imperialism, and oligarchic antipatriotism that held it hostage.

Still, the first step in alleviating the Peronist press's newsprint difficulties came not before, but immediately following Perón's electoral victory, when the military government claimed the power to expropriate imported newsprint by virtue of a 1939 antispeculation law. That the deepening world crisis in the supply of newsprint threatened to engender a monopoly on the distribution of the commodity in Argentina, the Farrell government argued, made state intervention "even more necessary." Keenly aware of the imminent transition, Farrell justified the measure in terms that reflected the new basis of Perón's political legitimacy: "what is at stake is the assurance in practice of one of the rights consecrated by the National Constitution."[37] On March 7, 1946, another decree called for the expropriation of five hundred tons of newsprint, half from the stocks of *La Prensa* and the remainder from *La Nación*, *El Mundo*, and *La Razón*.[38]

Subsequent government inaction, however, only amplified calls for urgent state intervention. *La Época* escalated its public campaign, while *El Laborista* ominously announced more than once that it lacked sufficient newsprint to publish the following day's edition—surely a convincing claim, given the difficulties faced by the press as a whole.[39] By the time the regime finally did expropriate partial stocks of newsprint in late April, then, the Peronist dailies had already engaged in a concerted effort to portray the measure as protective of the press and the product not of military authoritarianism, but of popular pressure. With the newsprint decrees a new balance between the power of journalism as a vehicle for the exercise of citizenship and the practical aspects of the press's industrial production was struck, with the Argentine state as fulcrum.

The counterattack from *La Prensa* began even before the newsprint decrees became public. In the midst of the presidential campaign, the *La Prensa* editors pointed not to the rapidly expanding and increasingly diverse Argentine newspaper landscape, or even to the actions of the British Parliament, as the origin of Argentine calls for state distribution of newsprint, but to something far more sinister: the German embassy.[40] As usual, the paper made no mention of Perón by name. Yet even the title of the editorial left little room for doubt that Perón, the proposed regulation of the newsprint market, and the defeated Nazis shared a common ideological origin: "Foreign and dictatorial teachings covered with the false banner of sovereignty."

While the equation of Peronism with "Nazi-fascism" had long been common currency among the opposition, the ideological basis of La Prensa's subsequent attacks on the newsprint decree drew upon an exaltation of market economics hardly supported by Communists, Socialists, and left-leaning members of the Radical Party. The paper's editors maintained that "the interference of the state in private activities [has been] brought in our country to extremes known only under totalitarian regimes, [and this] carries with it, with respect to the press, the danger of nullifying the guarantees of freedom established by the constitution."[41] The daily also tied the decree directly to the entire social program of the government, presenting the vast majority of economic reforms as inimical to the country's long-standing political traditions. State intervention in regulating working conditions, commerce, and industry only betrayed protections for individual freedoms and rights. By inhibiting the free exchange of property, the government undercut all other liberties; that it did so in order to supply newsprint to its sympathizers at the expense of the independent press only aggravated an already dangerous situation.[42]

Perón's assumption of the presidency in mid-1946 dealt a serious blow to his detractors in the opposition press. Having won the cleanest elections since 1928, Perón and his followers had captured the ultimate legitimizing mechanism, and the only goal that unified the opposition: full constitutional rule. As the now freely elected but Peronist-dominated Congress proceeded to democratically validate the de facto regime's decrees, arguments that any state intervention in the functioning of the newspaper industry was inherently dictatorial became more difficult to sustain, even as new forms of state power became established.

That measures like the Journalist's Statute might concord with constitutional rule proved particularly disconcerting to Alberto Gainza Paz. As late as August 1946, La Prensa editorialists assured readers that the "totalitarian" Journalist's Statute could not withstand the scrutiny of a democratically elected Congress.[43] However, the Socialist-dominated FAP, now the nation's largest journalist organization, remained firmly behind the measure. Reflecting labor's growing political protagonism, Leandro Reynés, president of the FAP at the moment of the statute's enactment, defended journalists' gains from his seat in Congress. Three months later, disconcerted editorialists at the Paz family paper would remark that they simply could not have imagined that "with a constitutional government established, the imposition of a journalism statute would be approved *unanimously* by the Chamber of Deputies"—especially since non-Peronists still constituted an important voting bloc in the lower house.[44] Before year's end, FAP president Octavio Palazzolo received the new, congressional version of the statute directly from Perón's hands. Military decrees on intervention in the newsprint market similarly received Congress's rapid approval. Increasingly, the measures that the La Prensa directors had denounced as dictatorial restrictions on "freedom of the press" came from an executive and Congress whose electoral legitimacy they could not help but recognize.

Even more menacingly, the tacit alliance that had held since mid-1945 in the opposition press began to crumble as the newspaper industry's deepening economic crisis pitted financially precarious proprietors against their more powerful colleague and competitor. Following the congressional approval of a new Journalist's Statute with even greater wage increases, and with newsprint prices continuing to climb, several newspaper proprietors came to the uncomfortable realization that the crisis they faced was at once more serious and long-lasting than they had imagined. As early as mid-1946, the rising costs of production that threatened Peronist papers like *La Época* and *El Laborista* began to undermine the economic viability even of established newspapers like *Noticias Gráficas*. Thus, while *La Prensa*'s Gainza Paz fought the broad social reforms of the Peronist government on ideological grounds, other proprietors responded to the situation in far more pragmatic terms. Given the likelihood that both the newsprint crisis and Peronist labor reforms would only deepen in the foreseeable future, several newspaper owners approached Gainza Paz for competitive concessions.

In September 1946, *Noticias Gráficas* owner José Agusti and other newspaper proprietors proposed a joint price increase to offset their papers' pressing financial imbalances without altering the media market or turning to the state for aid.[45] More importantly, Agusti also called for the creation of a mechanism that might enable the press to manage this and any future crises with greater coherence: an employers' organization that could bargain collectively with the FAP, the increasingly organized Union of Newspaper and Magazine Vendors, and the printers' Federación Gráfica Bonaerense.[46] The latter proposal was a fundamental and pragmatic recognition that the press was, in fact, a newspaper industry, and that the owners of the nation's newspapers formed a sociologically distinct group from the newsworkers they employed. For the proprietors of *Noticias Gráficas, Crítica,* and other struggling newspapers, the severity of the situation left them with little to gain by continuing to proclaim that the press transcended economics; such arguments had lost much of their power among journalists and even among non-Peronists in Congress, while the ideological purity that such claims bestowed had become dubious at best. Newspaper capital simply could no longer ignore emerging forms of industrial relations.

If these first tenuous moves to create a proprietors' organization marked an important turning point for the nation's newspaper owners, their failure would have devastating consequences for the future of the Argentine press. In December, even as the newsprint crisis worsened, Gainza Paz predictably rejected not just the informal coordination of a newspaper price hike, but Agusti's long-term corporatist proposal. Without the participation of the nation's most economically powerful newspaper, plans for an effective proprietors' organization lay in ruins. In the best of cases, this refusal to cede ground to ideas of the press's economic character demonstrated an ideological intransigence that made Alberto Gainza Paz stand out not just within the Argentine press, but among his international peers.[47] Agusti and others would soon suggest that less pristine motives lay behind Gainza Paz's unwillingness to cooperate. Regardless of his motives, the *La Prensa* owner's veto of the project left the non-Peronist commercial press more vulnerable than he likely imagined. As *Crítica* co-owner Salvadora Medina Onrubia de Botana would later declare, the "no" from *La Prensa* marked the moment when her hopes of avoiding a Peronist takeover of the paper her husband had founded finally evaporated.[48]

Indeed, the failure of proprietors to reach an agreement with the owner of *La Prensa* spurred a public airing of the financial state of the established newspapers and a wave of denunciations against Gainza Paz. With negotiations barely finished, José Agusti announced to readers of *Noticias Gráficas* that since March 1944 the paper had been obliged to concede a 50 percent wage increase to its printers and that the Journalist's Statute had increased the paper's journalist labor costs by 190 percent.[49] The price of scarce newsprint in Buenos Aires, meanwhile, went from $335 per metric ton in March 1945 to $530.40 in July 1946, an increase of nearly 60 percent in just sixteen months—though the American Society of Newspaper Editors placed the price even higher.[50] Agusti even confessed to paying as much as $750 per ton on the black market after Gainza Paz rebuffed his offer to pay cash for just ten tons from *La Prensa*'s enormous fifty-thousand-ton reserves.[51] Rapidly climbing wages for newsworkers and skyrocketing newsprint prices, Agusti explained, had driven production costs up by almost 250 percent; the price of *Noticias Gráficas*, however, remained frozen.[52]

The real fault line in the press, Agusti suggested, lay not between the Peronist papers and the established commercial press, or between the press and the Argentine state, but between "the rich newspapers and the poor newspapers." Yet precisely for this reason, he argued, Gainza Paz's refusal to cooperate made sound business sense. With its monopoly on classified advertising, the morning newspaper *La Prensa* enjoyed monthly advertising revenues of nearly $3 million, dwarfing the $150,000 to $200,000 of the major afternoon papers. Agusti also provocatively suggested that Gainza Paz's rejection of a proprietor alliance had little to do with his principled aversion to corporatist solutions: "With these figures would *La Prensa* need to raise the cost of an issue? And wouldn't its refusal to do so, after having offered its collaboration to the rest of the newspapers, have as justification the creation of a climate such that other newspapers disappear, leaving [*La Prensa*] to constitute itself, practically, as the monopoly of the Argentine press?"[53] A week later, in what retrospectively appears as a direct and final warning to Gainza Paz, the owner of *Noticias Gráficas* declared simply that the national press's "economic freedom," the basis of newspaper independence and the "necessary precondition for freedom of the press," was now extremely precarious.[54]

Crítica quickly seconded the accusations against Gainza Paz. In a front page article, the paper's coproprietors—now Raúl Damonte Taborda's mother-in-law, Salvadora Medina Onrubia de Botana, and her sons—placed the blame for their financial predicament not just on the social reforms of the previous three years, but on the intransigence of the owner of *La Prensa*. Like Agusti, they saw monopolistic intentions in Gainza Paz's rejection of cooperation with other papers, arguing that the owner of the "merciless colossus" realized that any increased circulation revenue *La Prensa* might earn through price increases "would be multiplied in a perfect mathematical progression if, instead of giving alms to its colleagues, it absorbed their lives, coldly condemning them to disappear."[55]

Since its capital reserves and advertising revenue allowed each issue of *La Prensa* to sell at under half the cost of the paper on which it was printed, *Crítica* editorialists assured readers, the free reign of the market would fatally lead to a "concentration of capital predicted, incidentally, by Marxist theoreticians, to whom [*La Prensa*] has reacted with extraordinary horror." Indeed, the arguments that Gainza Paz used to sustain his nineteenth-century liberal view of the press—that the state necessarily inhibited the proper functioning of what was a purely cultural institution—were not only false, but disguised a situation that worked to the *La Prensa* owner's great advantage: "all of the taxes, obligations, and encumbrances [*gabelas*] that threaten to destroy Argentine newspapers," *Crítica* editorialists argued, "only serve to reinforce and give more power to that advertising colossus which *Crítica* permits itself to say is not journalism, not a newspaper, not anything; just a brutal, insolent, and monstrous commercial business."[56]

The following morning, editors at the Irish-Argentine bilingual daily the *Standard*, in whose offices much of the ill-fated proprietor negotiations had taken place, lamented the infighting that had erupted within the Buenos Aires press.[57] Yet even the traditionally measured tone of the paper gave way to categorical recriminations against the owner of *La Prensa*. Pointing to the obvious incompatibility between Gainza Paz's rhetoric of the press as utterly distinct from economic activity and the vast wealth that his paper generated in practice, the editors of the *Standard* dismissed the core of the *La Prensa* owner's stance as simply archaic and contradictory: "[*La Prensa*] is inclined to demand the old freedoms, the pretension of being the fourth estate, reserving for itself, at the same time, the right to be a prosperous commercial business. We maintain that *La Prensa* cannot have it both ways.'"[58] If its commercial nature had so obviously overcome its journalistic mission, how could *La Prensa* continue to seek shelter in outdated notions of the press's unsullied status as a vehicle of citizenship and the noble right of "freedom of the press"?

The denunciations by the owners of *Noticias Gráficas*, *Crítica*, and the *Standard* pointed to the rapidly narrowing range of options that many newspapers proprietors faced with Gainza Paz's refusal to negotiate. While the state remained a potential threat to the independence of their papers, the market posed an immediate threat both to the existence of much of the Buenos Aires press and to the personal wealth of many newspaper owners. Given the gravity of the situation, the *La Prensa* owner's intransigence seemed less a principled stance than a convenient blindness to the undeniable evolution of the press into a commercial enterprise—a transformation illustrated most vividly precisely by *La Prensa*. If Gainza Paz seemed prepared to take advantage of the crisis to establish a stranglehold on journalism in Buenos Aires and, by extension, Argentina as a whole, other powerful interests had also begun to work behind the scenes. In the postwar environment, only two forces were capable of sustaining a press landscape now on the verge of collapse; in rejecting joint action with other newspaper proprietors, Gainza Paz unwittingly paved the way for others to play a far more active role in "rescuing" the Argentine press.

The Peronist Appropriation of the Commercial Press

The Peronist years did see the creation of a newspaper monopoly, but not one controlled by Gainza Paz. In addition to increasing state regulation of newsprint imports, another factor directly mitigated the market conditions that might have facilitated a *La Prensa* monopoly: the machinations of Perón and Eva Perón's associates, both behind closed doors and in the streets. Through a combination of popular violence against newspaper buildings, the denial of paper quotas and official advertising, labor slowdowns, and bureaucratic foot-dragging, Perón and his closest allies managed to assume direct control of nearly all of the important Buenos Aires dailies, including those already within the Peronist orbit. The papers of what the opposition called "the official chain," in addition to receiving state subsidies for production costs, would also share journalists with each other and with the rapidly expanding Undersecretariat of Information and the Press. As a result, the disruptive creation of a publishing monopoly tied to *La Prensa* did not come about; instead, the broad contours of the Buenos Aires editorial landscape remained fairly stable, with the name, target audience, and interpellative tone of each different newspaper relatively unchanged except in political orientation. In the midst of increasing economic difficulties and mounting official and extraofficial harassment, most Buenos Aires newspapers did not disappear; they became Peronist.

This superficial continuity barely masked the sweeping transformation that Perón's success in constructing a loyal media apparatus produced. Yet, despite the scale of the Peronist effort, this was not the first quasi-state venture into the realm of newspaper property. The relationship between General Justo and *Crítica*'s Natalio Botana a decade earlier served as a model for the far more ambitious Peronist media project. Like Justo, Perón avoided unnecessary changes in tone and journalistic style that might alienate an established audience even as a paper's political orientation shifted toward the government; Perón's objective was to create not a "Peronist" journalism, but a Peronist public. He also followed Justo's lead in using a system of hidden private ownership, rather than direct nationalization—even, in some cases, maintaining previous proprietors as figureheads in an attempt to make a newspaper's "independent" status an asset to the regime. Perón's own bitter earlier experience with *Crítica*, however, meant that this Peronist project would exceed Justo's not just in quantity but in quality: through his strict but surreptitious control of newspaper stock titles and state intervention in newsprint distribution, Perón created not allies, but dependents. The tight economic and administrative control that Perón, Eva Perón, and their inner circle maintained over the papers of "the chain" made it unthinkable that newspaper owners or editors might rebel in a moment of crisis.

Justo and Minister of the Economy Federico Pinedo, of course, had also looked beyond *Crítica* for the creation of a sympathetic commercial press. The legacy of their efforts did more than set an example for Perón; in the case of *La Razón*, it also provided the legal and economic grounds for the appropriation of an opposition newspaper. Although the Justo-Pinedo arrangement with Ricardo Peralta Ramos and *La Razón* appears to have been something of an open secret among journalists and government officials as early as 1936, the military government's administrative takeover of the Instituto Movilizador in October 1945 brought the matter to public light.[59] Eduardo Colóm immediately began a campaign against *La Razón* and Peralta Ramos in the pages of *La Época*, and continued to do so well into 1946 as much out of adherence to the general offensive that the Peronist press had launched against the commercial dailies as out of his own hopes of purchasing the paper.[60]

Far more powerful figures than Colóm, however, moved behind the scenes. According to the 1958 judicial resolution returning the paper to Peralta Ramos, in late 1946, apparently reacting to the failed attempt to form a united front with Gainza Paz, *La Razón*'s investors sold the totality of their interests in the paper to Miguel Miranda, head of the Central Bank, for just $3.5 million.[61] Miranda, in turn, passed on the anonymous stock certificates—property of the bearer, to ensure secrecy and ease of transfer—to Eva Perón.[62] The financial crisis facing the Argentine press as a whole had weakened *La Razón* financially with no hope of relief, while the history of the newspaper, its tangled financial dealings with Justo and Pinedo in the 1930s, and Peralta Ramos's willingness to cooperate with Perón made the incorporation of the paper into the government orbit even easier than that of the Peronist *Democracia*. Peralta Ramos continued as *La Razón*'s director, leaving readers with the impression that little had changed at the paper other than an appropriately moderate and measured turn in support of Perón. Yet, with *La Razón*'s stock in the hands of the Peróns, the paper's loyalty to the regime became unconditional: unlike Damonte Taborda one year earlier, Peralta Ramos no longer owned his newspaper, making him completely incapable of using the power of the press to "betray" Perón.

Unlike *La Razón*, *Crítica* came under the full control of the Peróns through a lengthy and complex legal procedure, though the process began in the immediate aftermath of the attacks of October 17, 1945.[63] Beyond soaring newsprint costs, *Crítica* suffered from a series of unique factors. The physical destruction caused by demonstrators on October 17 left the *Crítica* printing plant in dire need of repairs, while the legacy of the fierce opposition to Perón and denigration of his followers precisely in their moment of glory seriously eroded the paper's readership base among an urban popular class more confident in the colonel than ever. Disloyalty to the democratically elected president left Raúl Damonte Taborda little room for political maneuvering; in early 1946, he left for exile, dissolving *Crítica*'s debt-ridden publishing company and passing ownership of the paper to his mother-in-law, Salvadora Medina Onrubia de Botana, and her sons Jaime and Helvio.[64] In an odd reunion based less on familial love than on mutual convenience, the heirs of Natalio Botana once again took possession of *Crítica*.

The paper emerged from the Damonte Taborda period, according to both Helvio Botana and his mother, financially "wrecked."[65] Helvio Botana, by then himself a Peronist of sorts, would later remember, "They took away our newsprint quotas, and we had to buy paper on the black market. They denied us bank credits. For the first time in our history artificial worker problems were created for us. They would stop the editions because a toilet had backed up, even though there were twenty more. The personnel engaged in slowdowns [*trabajaba a reglamento*] in solidarity with all kinds of world events. The delivery trucks were stopped for hours in the middle of the day to check the headlights, knowing that in delivery every second counts."[66] In mid-April 1946, the secretary of labor and social welfare fined *Crítica* $160,000—a full month's worth of wages—for not paying the annual bonus to the paper's employees as demanded by law, a willful oversight the Botanas ascribed directly to Damonte Taborda.[67] Though Salvadora and her son continually placed blame for the paper's recent political equivocations and financial disarray on the head of her exiled son-in-law, this did little to remedy *Crítica*'s dire situation.

The economic damage done to *Crítica* led to the slow dismantling of much of the paper's infrastructure, with the death throes of the paper ironically contributing to the birth of the new Peronist press. In the process of dissolving Buenos Aires Poligráfica, Damonte Taborda sold the centrally located offices and production plant of his and Natalio Botana's ill-fated attempt to create a "serious" newspaper. Molinari and Birabent paid Damonte Taborda $1.3 million for the installations of *El Sol* (Avenida de Mayo 654). Following *Democracia*'s sale to Eva Perón, the plant came to serve as the first headquarters of "the official chain": the Peronist newspaper holding company Editorial ALEA.[68]

Faced with falling circulation but unable to dismiss employees due to the new labor laws, the Botana family signed a contract for the printing of Roberto Noble's *Clarín*, a morning newspaper founded in September 1945. The contract barely covered labor costs, a fact that had brought the similarly desperate José Agusti to reject Noble's offer of the same terms.[69] The arrangement proved awkward from the start, but became even more contentious when *Clarín*'s payments to *Crítica* abruptly dropped by 10 percent even as labor costs rose.[70] Together with the fact that many of the more talented and experienced journalists began to abandon *Crítica* for *Clarín*—and, more generally, for the Peronist press proper—this arrangement subsidized the emergence of what is today the world's most widely read Spanish-language newspaper and the centerpiece of an enormous media conglomerate.

In the wake of the proprietors' failure to reach an agreement with Gainza Paz in late 1946, two newly powerful former *Crítica* journalists initiated the arrangements through which the evening paper began its tortured passage into official hands. Emilio Cipolletti, undersecretary of information and the press since October 1946, blocked the distribution of newsprint to *Crítica* even as he made repeated suggestions to Salvadora that she speak with Eva Perón about the newspaper's financial problems. The Undersecretariat's director of the press, Orestes Confalonieri—expelled from *Crítica* after the events of September 1945—arranged a meeting between Salvadora and President Perón on January 4, 1947. The following morning she had her first meeting with Miguel Miranda at the Central Bank.[71] *Crítica* would find funding, but not without its owners making important concessions.

One month later, on February 5, 1947, Salvadora and her sons signed a contract at the Central Bank by which their Editorial Crítica became associated with a group of investors representing Miranda and Eva Perón.[72] Though the arrangement saved the newspaper from disappearance by binding *Crítica* in the final instance to Perón and his associates, the Botana family continued to encounter bureaucratic problems. A fierce exchange of polemic began between Salvadora and editors at Minister of the Interior Ángel Borlenghi's *El Líder* in August 1947, while Cipolletti's demand that Salvadora personally pen a defense of Eva Perón following her famous European tour produced an editorial that only served to infuriate the first lady.⁷³ The following year the Botana family's Editorial Crítica dissolved itself into the Peronist investors' Compañía Argentina de Ediciones y Publicidad, S.A. (CADEPSA), and in September 1948 Jaime Botana transferred his shares of the company's stock to one of Perón's representatives.⁷⁴ Just over two years later, in the midst of the final Peronist consolidation of the media, the last Botana left the paper—"removed, in fact, by the police"—and all financial interests in *Crítica* passed into the hands of Perón's investors.⁷⁵ Salvadora Medina continued to receive payments from CADEPSA even after her removal from *Crítica,* further weakening her legal claims for the return of the paper following the overthrow of Perón in 1955.⁷⁶

El Mundo and its associated publications fell into the Peronist orbit in a far less complicated fashion. With the distribution of expensive newsprint controlled by the government, negotiations with Gainza Paz failed, and following a timely attack by protestors, the owners of *El Mundo* stood prepared to bargain with Miranda in early 1947.⁷⁷ Although rumor held that Miguel Miranda "found" the stock certificates for *El Mundo* publishers Editorial Haynes in the safe of the recently nationalized British railroad Ferrocarril Oeste, this version of events is far too convenient for all involved.⁷⁸ Carlos Aloé, who headed the Peronist media enterprise, later provided a more convincing explanation: "The English [sic] made a magnificent deal because they sold us half the stock and used the money to invest in other businesses. They continued to receive dividends from their participation [in Editorial Haynes] and two of them received salaries and honoraria as directors."⁷⁹ By mid-1947 the immense Editorial Haynes—owners of Latin America's second-largest newspaper as well as the magazines *Mundo Argentino, P.B.T.,* and *El Hogar,* among others, and owners of a chain of radio stations—was firmly in Peronist hands, while the company's old owners shared in what could now only remain a profitable enterprise only in the shadow of the Argentine state.

Finally, José Agusti saw the futility of continuing to resist the pressure of the Peróns and their associates and negotiated favorable conditions for the inevitable transfer. For *Noticias Gráficas* Agusti received not only a large sum of money, but also an appointment as ambassador to the General Assembly of the United Nations in Paris in 1948 and membership in official delegations to Italy and the United States.⁸⁰ While his acceptance of the posts lead to his expulsion from the Radical Party, he did maintain a nominal connection with his former newspaper.⁸¹

Between 1946 and 1951, virtually all of the Buenos Aires newspaper industry together with the autonomous Peronist press had succumbed to the offensive of Perón, Eva Perón, and their most trusted subordinates. *Democracia, El Laborista, Noticias Gráficas, El Mundo, La Razón, Crítica,* and *La Época,* as well as eleven newspapers beyond the Federal Capital, had all become not just Peronist, but closely tied to the first couple. In addition, they controlled an advertising agency, all twenty-one radio stations and ten magazines associated with Editorial Haynes, *La Razón*'s eighteen radio stations, the Argentine news agency Saporiti, and the Rio de Janeiro-based Agencia Latina de Noticias.[82] Far exceeding anything within Justo's reach a decade earlier, Perón had assembled what was, in effect, Latin America's largest media empire, even before the expropriation of *La Prensa*.

Journalism, Power, and the Peronist State

Despite this enormous transformation, the relationship between press and state had not explicitly changed. Commercial newspapers like *Crítica* and *El Mundo* remained in private hands, with their institutional structures legally distinct from that of the formal state media apparatus, the Undersecretariat of Information and the Press. In practice, however, a virtual monopoly on the power of journalism had accumulated in the hands of those who also held tight control of the reins of the state. At the same time, Peronist management of the press blurred boundaries not just between different newspapers, but between this "private" press and the Undersecretariat. In their transformation of the Argentine newspaper industry, Peronists had created a media apparatus that functioned as a complex hybrid: of the factional-commercial press of the Justo years; of the explicitly factional journalism never fully absent from the Argentine media landscape; and of a dramatically expanded state propaganda machine.

Legal ownership of most of these "private" newspapers rested with the anonymous holding company Editorial ALEA, provocatively named from Caesar's *alea jacta est* (the die is cast).[83] Run by Perón's personal secretary (and later governor of the province of Buenos Aires), Carlos Vicente Aloé, the organization was, strictly speaking, simply a private printing company. In the midst of the press's escalating financial crisis in 1946, Editorial ALEA provided economically troubled newspaper owners with cash advances for future government advertising, effectively opening the door for the subsequent financial machinations of Miranda, Domingo Mercante, Orlando Maroglio, Alberto Dodero, and Alfredo Gorostiza.[84] Aloé's position as head of Editorial ALEA revealed the priorities that drove the project: he apparently became administrator of the rapidly growing official newspaper "chain" simply by virtue of having Perón's and Eva Perón's absolute confidence and knowing marginally more about journalism than the first lady herself.[85]

Administrative divisions between ALEA, individual newspapers, and the host of other companies for which Aloé acted as figurehead quickly became more apparent than real. Although Editorial Democracia, owner of *Democracia*, *El Laborista*, and *Noticias Gráficas*, technically had no legal relationship with

Editorial ALEA, the two organizations shared offices in the former *El Sol* plant at Avenida de Mayo 654. Similarly, Aloé exercised the presidency not just of ALEA, but of Editorial Democracia and Editorial Haynes as well, while Alfredo Gorostiza acted as a major shareholder in both ALEA and *Crítica's* CADEPSA.[86] Blurring the already fuzzy lines between the new press conglomerate and the Argentine state, the Eva Perón Foundation's primary notary, Raúl Gaucherón, handled the legal documentation for both organizations. By 1948, not only had Perón assembled a set of newspapers that exceeded in scale anything imagined by President Justo in the 1930s, but the complex web of ownership of those papers made the financial machinations of Justo, Natalio Botana, Antonio De Tomaso, and Federico Pinedo appear simplistic in comparison.

The Undersecretariat of Information and the Press stood alongside the "private" newspapers managed by Aloé as the second pillar of the regime's media structure. The Undersecretariat acted as the Peronist government's literal ideological state apparatus, forming a line of communication from the upper reaches of the regime to Argentine society as a whole. Former *Crítica* political editor Emilio Cipolletti, appointed head of the Undersecretariat in October 1946, just as the ALEA project began, made clear that his tenure would see an expansion of the Undersecretariat in ways that could not help but confirm the suspicions of opposition newspaper proprietors. Upon taking office, Cipolletti declared that his agency would serve three functions: first, to ensure "easy public access" to information regarding government actions; second, to counter incorrect reporting in the media (that is, to produce formal responses to criticism from the opposition press); and, finally, to engage in "preventive propaganda to inculcate in the working masses the necessity of discerning [the truth] when faced with ill-intentioned propaganda."[87] In the process of fulfilling these functions, the Undersecretariat quickly blended into the "private" Peronist media, financially, administratively, and even journalistically, even as it served to undermine continually the public legitimacy of the financially precarious commercial press.

Born in 1943 as the military regime's coordinator of censorship and government propaganda, the Undersecretariat of Information and the Press formally abandoned the role of official censor with the return to constitutional normality on June 4, 1946. Yet even with the end of censorship—or, more likely, *because of* the end of censorship—the agency's range of duties grew precipitously. Under the new Peronist government, the Undersecretariat acted as both official state news service, distributing official speech transcripts and other information to the daily press, and personal propaganda arm of the president and first lady. The distinction between the two duties was rarely clear: in early 1947, for example, the Undersecretariat issued a communiqué explaining that Perón had arrived seven minutes late to the office one morning due to the crowds of citizens insistent upon greeting him personally.[88] For a brief, chaotic period the Undersecretariat even became the central information clearinghouse for the entire government, with the communications of all government dependencies and ministries passing through the agency.[89]

The Undersecretariat's budget and staff grew accordingly. Now a direct counter to the still formidable power of the Argentine press, especially *La Prensa*, the Undersecretariat received an infusion of cash through the Five Year Plan, which explicitly included $12 million to publicize government aims and achievements. In addition, discretionary funds for the bureau (excluding salaries) totaled nearly $4 million in 1946 and just over $5 million in 1947.[90] Just prior to Perón taking office, the Undersecretariat employed 182 persons with an annual payroll budget of $628,860; by 1947 that sector of the budget surged to $3,678,100, while the staff had swelled to as many as seven thousand—more than quadruple that of *La Prensa*.[91]

In late 1946, the state agency assumed an even more powerful function, one that helped coordinate the Peronist offensive vis-à-vis the financially vulnerable commercial press. By executive decree, the advertising requests of all government agencies were channeled through the Undersecretariat of Information and the Press, giving the agency tremendous power not just over cash-strapped newspapers, but over other sectors of the state as well.[92] The management of lucrative official advertising fell to the Office of Publicity (Dirección de Publicidad), a subsection of the Undersecretariat's General Press Office (Dirección General de Prensa), headed at that time by Cipolletti's former *Crítica* colleague Orestes Confalonieri.[93] With Cipolletti's Undersecretariat controlling official advertising, Aloé's ALEA providing cash advances to financially desperate newspaper owners, and Miguel Miranda coordinating both official loans and groups of Peronist investors, the Peronist media apparatus grew at an astonishing rate.

Yet this sudden expansion of the Peronist and Peronist-controlled commercial press produced a serious challenge for the state agency. After a bureaucratic shake-up of the General Press Office in late 1947, the tasks of journalists working with the Undersecretariat became more strictly regimented as the activities and personnel of the Undersecretariat began to merge with those of the newspapers controlled by Editorial ALEA. In essence, Peronist and quasi-Peronist newspapers "delegated" the writing of substantial portions of their dailies directly to the General Press Office, which in turn warned that each of the Undersecretariat's journalists "should know the deadlines of the newspapers for which he is writing the assigned article"—and even be prepared to write coverage of official speeches before they occurred in order to meet those deadlines.[94] This same resolution also reveals the degree to which the Undersecretariat controlled the editorial decision-making process of the "friendly press": "Recommendations on news items should be sent to the

Casa de Gobierno in a closed enveloped *with the name of the director of each newspaper* and the inscription 'URGENT—INFORMATION,' and should be placed in the mailbox of the Dirección General de Prensa."[95] Journalists with the Undersecretariat were also the pool for the ALEA-controlled newspapers, and the bureaucracy of the state agency assumed important functions of the "private" bureaucracy of a rapidly growing sector of the Buenos Aires press.

The coordination of reporting in the quasi-state press demanded a corresponding bureaucratic oversight, a task that fell to the General Press Office's administrative divisions. In January 1948, Confalonieri's successor, Raúl de Oromí, would call for a better organization of the Office's Archival Division (División Archivo), which collected the nation's publications; the Articles and Commentary Division (División Notas y Comentarios), which coordinated the assignments of the Undersecretariat's journalists; and the Reading and Synthesis Division (División Lectura y Síntesis), in charge of monitoring press content. Oromí instructed the three divisions to prepare folders with newspaper clippings accompanied by the instructions sent to the newspapers as part of a "rigorous control of the form in which the friendly newspapers follow the instructions that we have sent in commenting certain topics of national interest."[96] The success of this control, combined with the concomitant centralization of a Peronist press increasingly dependent on the Undersecretariat's pool of journalists, often led to an uncanny sameness in the coverage by papers as different as *El Mundo* and *Crítica*. The Undersecretariat's coordination of newspaper content quickly led to formulaic, standardized, and stale bureaucratic journalism.

In addition to acting both openly and covertly as the regime's mouthpiece, the Undersecretariat also acted as the government's media eyes and ears. This monitoring of the press was hardly limited to the "friendly newspapers," or even to the national press as a whole; the staff of the Undersecretariat also closely followed foreign newspaper, magazine, and radio coverage deemed of interest. The Undersecretariat's predecessor, the Uriburu-era Oficina de Prensa, had prepared brief synthetic commentary on the day's news for the president and his advisers. This task became significantly simplified by the military government's decree of December 31, 1943, which required that all publications submit several copies of each edition to the new Undersecretariat.[97] Teams at the General Press Office's Archival and Reading and Synthesis Divisions prepared thematically ordered folders of newspaper clippings from these materials, passing the completed booklets to the presidency and then on to the archive. At the height of the Peronist administration's conflict with *La Prensa* in early 1951, for example, the officials at the General Press Office—surely out of Perón's concern about the international repercussions of the dispute—closely monitored not just local coverage of events, but also the editorials and reporting of *Le Monde*, the *New York Times*, the *Christian Science*

Monitor, and Montevideo's *El Día,* as well as radio commentary in Chile, Uruguay, Britain, and the United States.[98]

Perhaps the Undersecretariat's most visible role, however, was that of propaganda arm for Perón, Eva Perón, and the Peronist "New Argentina." As the quantity of publications, state advertising, and cultural events grew quickly under Cipolletti as a result of the need to "publicize" the Five Year Plan, the "preventive propaganda" efforts of the Undersecretariat became even more frenetic. Just as the Peronist state and para-state media apparatus became consolidated in late 1948, Cipolletti unexpectedly died. After a brief interim, Raúl Alejandro Apold, then acting director of *Democracia,* took the reins of the organization; he, not Cipolletti, would become most closely identified with the Peronist propaganda efforts.[99]

Between 1949 and June 1951, the Undersecretariat distributed over 33 million units of propaganda, including nearly 3 million laminated portraits of the Perón and Evita, almost 7 million postcards of the couple, and over two hundred fifty thousand volumes of Peronist doctrine.[100] Similarly, between 1948 and 1955 the Undersecretariat paid $165 million in advertising, more than a third of which formed just one of the many state subsidies to the Editorial ALEA publications.[101] Apold also coordinated a regular radio program of short political commentary by famous entertainers, the most important of whom was tango author Enrique Santos Discépolo, whose undeniable humor drew an audience that included even the opposition that he mercilessly mocked.[102] By 1955, Apold managed a state agency—by then a ministry-level entity named the Secretariat of the Press and Dissemination (Secretaría de Prensa y Difusión)— whose annual budget topped $40 million.[103] The Secretariat's breadth of activities far exceeds the scope of the present study, and historians have only begun to scratch the surface of the ministry's political and cultural significance in Peronist Argentina.[104]

The Limits of the State as Journalist

In the wake of October 1945, the Buenos Aires press faced a profound crisis born less from concerted Peronist attacks than from the convergence of external economic shocks and the consequences of local social transformation. The disarray of the world newsprint market began to hit the import-dependent Argentine press mercilessly in early 1946, draining the finances of otherwise solvent newspaper organizations just as working journalists solidified their gains under the Journalist's Statute. More importantly, the Peronist electoral victory brought to power representatives of a movement whose very existence had shattered the illusion that the commercial press embodied in practice the egalitarian promise that lay at the heart of liberal press discourse. By mid-1946, the Buenos Aires press's entire network of relationships had begun to fray, with signs of strain between press and public, proprietors and journalists, and the ideological claims and actual practices of the commercial press more visible than ever. With audiences in flux, production costs soaring, and press legitimacy challenged as never before, vast sectors of the Buenos Aires newspaper industry teetered on the brink of ruin.

The ensuing public confrontation among newspaper owners—sparked by the refusal to negotiate of the one proprietor upon whom any viable independent solution depended—revealed another fissure within the press. As the owners of *Crítica, Noticias Gráficas,* and other papers feuded with an intransigent Alberto Gainza Paz over the practical implications of the crisis, the Peronist state both overtly and surreptitiously inserted itself into the breach. Coercion, enticement, hidden state subsidy, and official manipulation of the nation's newsprint supply allowed the Peronist government to do precisely what the owner of *La Prensa* had refused: to "rescue" vulnerable newspapers from certain disappearance. In the process, Perón and his allies took control of opposition and sympathetic newspapers alike, fashioning from the Argentine newspaper industry a massive state and para-state media apparatus centered around the dual poles of the Undersecretariat of Information and the Press and Editorial ALEA.

For many convinced first-generation Peronists, the ambiguous nature of the "new" newspaper industry's relationship to the national state did not mark a degeneration of press autonomy, but was a testament to the revolutionary character of a regime set on overcoming vast disparities in the distribution of power and the exercise of citizenship. In mid-1949, Peronist journalist Carlos Dalmiro Viale reminded his readers that with the revolutionary Junta's 1811 founding of *La Gazeta de Buenos-Ayres* "our first free newspaper was of the government" and that this paper "only responded to one interest: the national."[105] In contrast to the "financially powerful" newspapers, he argued, only the Peronist press realized in practice the liberal ideal of the press as a vehicle of public expression open to all. By extending media representation to the nation's previously marginalized, the Peronist press served as the voice of the less powerful in the public sphere; in doing so in collective fashion and in close relationship to the state, it was simply responding to the "practical impossibility" of the universal individual exercise of the right of expression in the press given the capital-intensive character of the modern media and the scale of mass politics.[106]

Viale's claims notwithstanding, the Peronist transformation of the Argentine press did less to extend the power of the press to Argentine workers than it did to expand the power of an increasingly centralized Peronist movement. As early as mid-1946, Perón had already begun to undermine the independence not just of the opposition commercial press, but even that of those newspapers founded specifically to support the movement that brought him to power. For many later, more radical Peronists, this tightening grip on the press marked a missed opportunity, with the bureaucratic wing of the movement derailing the popular, anti-imperialist impulses in order to create a meaningless propaganda apparatus. As Peronist journalist Rodolfo Walsh, the father of Argentine investigative journalism, would later remark, "bureaucratic centralism imposed the path of least resistance. . . . To write the history of the Peronist government, the publications of the Central Bank are more useful than the complete collection of the chain's newspapers and magazines."[107]

In fact, the regimentation of the Argentine press in the hands of Perón's and Eva Perón's most trusted subordinates is inseparable from the broader transformation of Peronism that this same media project helped to engender. By 1950, the spontaneous, chaotic pluralism of early Peronism was clearly succumbing to increasingly ritualized forms of political participation, a process bolstered by the formulaic and bureaucratic acclamation of Perón, Eva Perón, and the Peronist state through the quasi-official media apparatus. Their assertions of having "liberated" the press notwithstanding, Perón and his allies had created a tightly controlled, dependent newspaper industry charged with the task of generating consensus rather than serving as a forum for the expression of citizen opinion. With papers traditionally as divergent as *El Mundo, La Razón,* and *Crítica* praising the regime and deriding the opposition from different perspectives, using what remained distinct journalistic styles directed toward disparate audiences, Peronists could claim that the press "mirrored" society more faithfully than ever. Indeed, the veneer of diversity within the newspaper landscape only seemed to confirm that rising enthusiasm for the Peronist project had begun to encompass ever-broader sectors of the Argentine public; for Peronists, the increasing isolation of the few remaining opposition newspapers, in turn, revealed nothing more than the fading relevance of the Old Argentina.

THE FOURTH ENEMY

> If *La Prensa* was born a forum of ideas, it soon set that characteristic aside and structured itself as a purely commercial enterprise.
>
> **—Congressman Antonio J. Benítez**

> The press itself abolished freedom of the press with its own commercialization, putting itself at the service of oppression and exploitation.
>
> **—*La Época*, April 12, 1951**

The consolidation of the Peronist media project left the Argentine journalism landscape utterly transformed. In October 1945, at Perón's moment of greatest crisis—and greatest political victory—the major Buenos Aires dailies had stood unanimously against him; five years later, most of those same papers had become his unconditional supporters. Reflecting the ongoing accumulation of power in Perón's hands, even the disparate range of pro-Perón newspapers created in the midst of the political opening that followed the 1945 crisis had become subsumed within a disciplined, and increasingly homogenous, media framework set on solidifying that same centralization of power. In addition, the success of Perón's steady drive toward an ever-increasing presence in the organs of "public opinion" expressed both a fundamental claim of his movement and a deeply held aspiration of its leader: Peronism would achieve not mere hegemony, but unanimity.[1]

Yet *La Nación* and *La Prensa*, the two dailies most closely tied to the social order that Peronists claimed to displace, daily belied the notion that full public consensus reigned in the New Argentina. Of the country's major newspapers, only they remained defiantly out of reach, while *Clarín*, the small newcomer in the non-Peronist commercial press, maintained a quasi-oppositional form of "constructive engagement" with the Peronist government.[2] Much to the consternation of Peronists, the circulation of these papers continued to rise, in good measure thanks to their position as opposition media in a press landscape that, despite official claims to the contrary, had grown increasingly univocal by 1950. Even more troubling for the Peronist government, *La Prensa*'s firm monopoly on classified advertising lent Gainza Paz's intransigently anti-Peronist newspaper a substantial readership among the Argentine popular classes—Perón's natural constituency.

The paper's financial power, furthermore, continued to pose a challenge to a Peronist media project heavily dependent on both massive state subsidies and increasingly expensive imported newsprint. The absorption of most of the country's major commercial dailies had done much to resolve a political problem for Peronism, but had failed to answer the basic question that had plagued those papers' previous owners: how could the press weather the postwar financial storm without the cooperation of *La Prensa*? In fact, the financial crisis facing the newspaper industry only deepened, threatening to undermine the viability of *Democracia* and the Editorial ALEA papers just as Perón and his allies stood on the verge of consolidating their control of the commercial press. By mid-1949, *La Prensa*'s status as Latin America's most powerful nongovernmental media corporation, which had protected the paper from Peronist pressures, now made it an increasingly enticing political and economic prize as the regime entered its crucial fifth year. Just as the owners of *Crítica* and *Noticias Gráficas* had needed the cooperation of Alberto Gainza Paz to stabilize the market situation of their newspapers, the new proprietors of those papers set their sights on the only other media organization left in the country that mattered: *La Prensa*.

If the inability of the Peronist press to overcome the acute world newsprint shortage made stronger action against *La Prensa* an economic imperative, by late 1950 there were also a host of political reasons to take the Peronization of the Argentine press further. As the economic boom that had sustained Peronism began to falter, *La Prensa*'s political influence posed a growing threat to a regime that owed its existence to a set of redistributive social policies that were becoming untenable. Growing labor unrest, including an unprecedented wildcat printers' strike and increasing militancy among railway workers, signaled labor's waning enthusiasm for a government that had already begun to step away from its social commitments. That signs of exhaustion had already begun to appear in the Peronist economic project well before the presidential elections of 1952 only made continued working-class patronage of Gainza Paz's newspaper that much more threatening. By early 1951, Peronists were set to take *La Prensa*, and with it to "recapture" those segments of Peronism's natural constituency that had yet to heed the leader's call for a boycott of the paper.

Action against *La Prensa*, however, required a markedly different set of strategies from those that had allowed Perón and his allies to fashion their media project from more vulnerable commercial newspapers. Since the military coup of 1943, newspaper closures had been limited to the strictly political press, with commercial newspapers facing only brief punitive suspensions, such as that of *La Prensa* itself in April 1944. These previous actions were justified by government-declared states of siege, "exceptional" circumstances that at some point had to reach a resolution. The subsequent transformation of the commercial press under constitutional Peronism, in turn, had taken place in a purposefully secretive manner, with newspapers like *La Razón* and *El Mundo* passing into the Peronist camp through hidden machinations and anonymous stock certificate trades. Either approach, however, posed serious problems with regard to *La Prensa*. On the one hand, any clearly arbitrary closure of the paper would at once undermine the relative success with which Peronists had tied the legitimacy of their actions regarding the press to a modified form of the traditional liberal press discourse, place in even greater relief the degree to which the remaining press answered to Perón's directives, and threaten the power lent to the government by its status as a constitutional democracy. On the other hand, Alberto Gainza Paz had shown himself more than capable of refusing the material advantages that any relationship with the government might bring, and *La Prensa* remained solvent in an economic environment that had made other newspapers ripe for the picking. Instead, the takeover of *La Prensa* differed dramatically from these earlier experiences: through the well-publicized actions of a democratically elected Congress in a situation of constitutional normality, the Argentine government directly expropriated all of the news organization's property. Not only did the expropriation of *La Prensa* affect one of the world's more important newspapers—and by far the most powerful of the Latin American dailies—but the action was permanent, legal, and public.

The Press as Culture; *La Prensa* as Commerce

By the time news vendors mounted a strike against *La Prensa* in January 1951, the conflict between the owners of the newspaper and the Peronist movement had dragged on for six years. The tactics that had brought the rest of the commercial press into the Peronist camp—a mix of intimidation, co-optation, and financial enticement—also came into play against *La Prensa*, but to no avail. Even Perón's personal appeals for a sustained boycott of the paper had little practical impact.[3] Unlike the newspapers incorporated into "the chain," *La Prensa* remained economically sound even as newsprint costs soared and newsworker wages climbed. As Perón and his followers steadily built the New Argentina, *La Prensa* stood as a tangible daily reminder that they had not yet truly swept away the Old Argentina. The power of the state rested unequivocally in Peronist hands; without *La Prensa*, the power of the fourth estate did not. Yet, if *La Prensa*'s continued economic strength and his own famed personal fortune allowed Alberto Gainza Paz to resist the overt pressures and surreptitious advances of the Peronist state, they also made the paper vulnerable to other forms of attack.[4] With greater and more prolonged effort than protestors' hurling of paving stones, Peronists sought to undermine the ideological foundations of *La Prensa*'s defiance by consolidating a discourse of "freedom of the press" that centered upon the contradiction between the egalitarian promise embodied in the liberal understanding of the press and the press as it actually operated. By centering their attacks on the breach between the press's ideal role as an open forum of public expression and the reality of the newspaper industry's closed, private, and commercial nature, Peronists challenged the legitimacy of *La Prensa* by turning the language of its owners against the reality of the institution they had created. When the final confrontation with *La Prensa* came, Peronists simply extended their argument to its logical conclusion: the passage of the paper into the hands of the state did not constitute a violation of freedom of the press; instead, it helped to restore freedom of the press by liberating *La Prensa* from the corruption of commerce.

As we have seen, for decades the paper's owners had denounced any attempts to characterize the press—and, in particular, *La Prensa*—as anything but a purely cultural forum for the expression of opinion and the exercise of citizenship, arguing, in essence, that the press *was not* a commercial enterprise simply because it *should not be*. Much of the newspaper rhetoric surrounding the growing financial difficulties of the press in the wake of World War II adopted essential portions of the language regarding both the ideal function and actual character of the press that had formed the heart of 1943–46 military decrees, and even of Sánchez Sorondo's failed 1934 press bill. In December 1945, Eduardo Colóm and *La Época* had called for state action to protect "freedom of the press" from the consequences of commercialism, chiding the opposition press as simple "commercial entities, with boards of directors, managers, balances, and dividends. Journalism has thus become a way of earning money, rather than of defending noble causes."[5] By late 1946, as pressure on the commercial press as a whole grew stronger, the proprietors of *Noticias Gráficas* and *Crítica* had similarly decried the dangers posed to the press by the operation of the market, pointedly accusing Gainza Paz of valuing his hopes for a *La Prensa* monopoly over the preservation of journalistic pluralism.[6] In objecting to the popular Journalist's Statute almost three years earlier, Gainza Paz had rejected "any attempt to take from the newspaper its physiognomy as a tribunal of government to assign it that of a profit-making business or industry."[7] Now the corollary to that understanding of the press became explicit: if, by definition, the press could not be a profit-making industry, then the economically powerful *La Prensa* had long ago forfeited its legitimacy as a newspaper and, thus, its right to protection under articles 14 and 32 of the national constitution. As one *Crítica* editorialist would write, "that advertising colossus . . . is not journalism, not a newspaper, not anything; just a brutal, insolent, and monstrous commercial business."[8]

The rhetorical attacks on *La Prensa* received a significant boost when Emilio Cipolletti's Undersecretariat of Information and the Press began to expand its range of operations. While the Peronist press seemed to occupy as much space in replying to *La Prensa* as it did in praising the government, the expansion of the Undersecretariat extended what was already an active radio campaign aimed at "correcting" the paper. By December 1946, the Undersecretariat began to broadcast daily formal replies to *La Prensa* editorials and articles through Radio del Estado. Through the radio editorials the journalists at the General Press Office bombarded *La Prensa* with accusations of willful inaccuracy and open deception in reporting government policies, pointing to the paper's supposed deformation of the truth as a serious violation of journalistic ethics and a negation of the "social function of freedom of the press."[9] Radio editorialists found the source of this constant distortion of information as much in the Paz family's economic interests as in the imperialist powers the paper ostensibly served. *La Prensa,* editorialists would repeatedly comment, "examines economic questions with an original conception of what is Argentine," repeatedly favoring foreign capital over Argentine capital.[10] More bluntly, the paper maintained "a notoriously anti-Argentine position" on virtually all matters of national interest.[11] Only once did Radio del Estado and the editorialists of the Undersecretariat bring *La Prensa* to a retraction of sorts, with the paper printing in full the Undersecretariat's refutation of an editorial on national monetary policy.[12] Still, the following day one of the paper's editorialists asked, "Who speaks when Radio del Estado speaks?" to which *El Laborista* countered, "The people and their government speak. . . . Who speaks when *La Prensa* speaks? The enemies of our sovereignty speak."[13]

Enemy Number One

The mounting rhetorical assault on *La Prensa* stood in tension with continued physical attacks against the paper. These never reached the scale of the attacks that had ensured the end of *Crítica*, however; the regime's local and international claims to institutional legitimacy depended in part on maintaining legal order and "normality." In combating *La Prensa*, then, the Peronist movement looked to an array of often improvised and contradictory coercive strategies. The inability of Perón and his supporters to fashion a more coordinated confrontation with the newspaper is indicative not only of the time it took to transform Peronism into a coherent movement, but of the reasons that so many Peronists, Perón chief among them, sought to do just that.

By early 1947, the limits of spontaneous action against *La Prensa* became increasingly apparent. In mid-January, editorialists at *Democracia* cautioned readers against attacking the newspaper's offices, declaring that "we know that this would just become propaganda [for *La Prensa*]."[14] Only two weeks after the *Democracia* editorial, however, crowds attacked *La Prensa* following a Perón address supporting the Five Year Plan and denouncing its opponents.[15] Located less than fifty meters from the scene of the gathering, the Plaza de Mayo, *La Prensa* was the obvious reference. Groups of demonstrators began throwing stones toward *La Prensa* immediately after the speech, made several attempts to set fire to the building, and left much of the exterior ornamentation and lighting destroyed.[16] Similar actions took place at the offices of *El Mundo*, which had not yet come under the control of Miranda and Eva Perón, as well as at the Socialist Party newspaper *La Vanguardia*. Gainza Paz, however, had placed employees within the building in anticipation of the assault, who managed to extinguish small fires until the police and fire departments cleared the streets.[17] More importantly, journalists and photographers surveyed the damage to the building, and, given *La Prensa*'s international reach, detailed news and images of the assault spread throughout the Americas. Despite *La Época*'s claim that the action marked "a deserved sanction against a certain press," the incident seems to have confirmed *Democracia*'s warnings: for nearly a month, *La Prensa*, *La Nación*, *El Mundo*, and *La Vanguardia* carried reproductions of foreign and domestic articles on the attacks, as well as notes of solidarity.[18] While the owners of Editorial Haynes (*El Mundo*) soon accepted incorporation into the growing Peronist media apparatus, for *La Prensa* the attack provided more ammunition for denunciations of Peronist "democracy" as superficial and Peronism as little more than fascism.[19]

In the wake of the January attacks, Perón began to position himself strategically as the only barrier containing growing public wrath against *La Prensa*. In his March 1947 address to the labor confederation CGT at the Teatro Colón, Perón emphatically denounced the "blind opposition" of "*la prensa*" as the "fourth enemy" of the deepening of government economic and social reforms. At the same time, however, he rejected calls for a renewed assault on the newspaper's offices, instead echoing *Democracia*'s earlier calls for a reader and advertiser boycott of "those newspapers that knowingly lie and lie" as a means of bringing *La Prensa* into line with the population as a whole.[20] The coordinated refusal of Argentine workers to buy or advertise in these papers, Perón declared, would mean that "within six months those newspapers will write the exact opposite of what they publish today." For workers to do otherwise, Perón declared, "would be to pay them to continue betraying us."[21] By the time the participants in the Teatro Colón event poured into the streets, they found the walls of the downtown area already plastered with the latest radio commentary denouncing *La Prensa* as "anti-Argentine," lending immediate reinforcement to Perón's call for a boycott against the paper.[22] As if by design, *La Prensa*'s reporting of the CGT event at the Teatro Colón seemed to confirm Peronist claims: while the Peronist press covered its pages with photos of Perón addressing workers in the erstwhile sanctum of the Argentine oligarchy, *La Prensa* simply reproduced in small print the text of Perón's speech, reserving space for not one but *two* photographs of the English cruiser *Sheffield* on its arrival in Buenos Aires.[23] The previous issue contained a nearly full-page transcription of an address on commerce by Harry Truman, and the subsequent days' editorials commented not on the Perón speech, but on Truman's and on another by former ambassador Spruille Braden.[24]

Just three days later, the head of the news vendors' union abandoned any ambiguity in the denunciations. Under the title "The Newspaper *La Prensa*: Enemy No. 1 of News Vendors [*canillitas*] and Workers in General," Napoleón Sollazo delivered a communiqué praising Perón and endorsing his call for a boycott against the paper. *La Prensa*, Sollazo maintained, "never opened a space in its columns for the working masses" and had always been "the most genuine representative of the powerful" in their quest to exploit labor—including the very workers that generated the enormous wealth of the paper's owners.[25] By the time the statement appeared in the afternoon dailies, it was already papered across the walls of the city, bearing Sollazo's signature.[26]

The international press saw Perón's call for a *La Prensa* boycott and the subsequent papering of the city as signs not only of a shift in Peronist tactics, but that the Buenos Aires commercial press faced increasingly difficult obstacles.[27] Despite repeated calls over the remainder of the year, however, the boycott did little to affect the political tenor or economic viability of *La Prensa*: the paper's tight control of classified advertising gave it an assured audience among all those looking for housing and employment, and thus, paradoxically, a guaranteed Peronist readership.[28] Even the installation across the street from the *La Prensa* offices of an "oral newspaper" whose deafening loudspeakers blared denunciations of the paper day and night failed to undermine the paper's sales seriously.[29]

The Coming Confrontation

The assault on the *La Prensa* offices in January 1947 nonetheless did not mark the end of vandalism at the newspaper; *La Prensa*, after all, stood just a stone's throw away from the Plaza de Mayo, the privileged stage of Peronist public gatherings. Yet subsequent acts of vandalism remained much more simply symbolic, with demonstrators hurling more insults than paving stones.[30] Actions against the paper instead centered on attempts to convert into coherent policy the twin pillars of the understanding of the social role of the press that had gained ground under the military regime: that an essential function of the press is to represent *all* citizens; and that the press's commercial nature distorts this mirror of society, leaving state intervention as the only means of "protecting" the true function of the press. In the coming years, far more than violence, the Peronist government and Peronist movement would combine claims of La Prensa's "oligarchic" and "anti-Argentine" character with denunciations of commercialism in order to build opposition to the paper and lay the grounds for a series of state actions; the very real newsprint crisis and, after 1949, the growing Argentine financial problems would provide the government with substantive economic grounds for implementing these policies.

The fact that Napoleón Sollazo and the Union of Newspaper and Magazine Vendors (Sindicato de Vendedores de Diarios, Revistas y Afines) escalated their own confrontations with the newspaper added a new element to the mounting conflict between Peronism and La Prensa. Just prior to Teatro Colón meeting, La Prensa had given a prominent place to coverage of the final report on the Argentine labor movement issued by a delegation of the American Federation of Labor.[31] On the evening of March 12, as a result, the leaders of the vendors' union met with the secretariat of the CGT with the express of purpose of studying "the measures that we will adopt with respect to certain newspapers—subsidized [*costeados*] by the oligarchy and foreign imperialism—that are engaged in a campaign against the goals of social justice that motivate the Superior Government of the Nation."[32] In less than a week, the vendors' union issued a statement demanding the end to La Prensa's self-run subscription service as well as a lower price to street vendors for the paper's widely read Sunday edition.[33]

If the *canillitas*' demands remained within the realm of a labor conflict, the Union statement justifying those demands before the Secretariat of Labor and Social Welfare placed the dispute within a much broader political struggle:

> [La Prensa's management] seeks to eliminate vendors in order to keep for itself the benefits gained by the vendor and to eliminate him, because [La Prensa's management] knows that he is fully identified with the principles of social justice that motivate the government of the Most Excellent President of the Nation, Brigadier General Juan D. Perón. This position awakens fear at that newspaper that our union, reacting against the ill-intentioned criticism and systemic opposition that [La Prensa] uses in its daily preaching, might assume an attitude that could one day silence its voice.[34]

Eduardo Colóm's *La Época* similarly accused *La Prensa* of benefiting from the exploitation of news vendors, and rejected Gainza Paz's claims that the *canillitas*' demands threatened freedom of the press by imposing restrictions on *La Prensa*'s management. Instead, editorialists at Colóm's paper argued that "*La Prensa* is a mercantile publicity business. It is interested in the freedom to exploit advertisers, not freedom of the press."[35] Despite the union's withdrawal of the politically inspired—and prophetic—prologue, Gainza Paz and the *La Prensa* administrators rejected the *canillitas*' demands.[36] In 1947, the vendors' union remained relatively weak and insufficiently organized; in the coming years, however, the situation would change dramatically.

The vendors' union's withdrawal of the political charges leveled against *La Prensa*, more than a concession to the owner and administrators of the paper, marked a final recognition that all *official* demands and accusations against the opposition press had to remain couched in economic and legal terms. While editorialists of the Peronist press and the Undersecretariat of Information and the Press continued to attack the opposition press—primarily *La Prensa*—as "anti-Argentine," "oligarchic," and even politically treasonous, moments of government and labor action against the remaining non-Peronist newspapers stayed within the bounds of a discourse of freedom of the press centered on the press's economic character. Thus, even as Eduardo Colóm's *La Época* would blend condemnation of *La Prensa* as a politically regressive "oligarchic" newspaper with denunciations of the "international newsprint trust" to which it maintained close ties, Eduardo Colóm the congressman largely maintained his remarks on the press within the limits of the economic understanding of freedom of the press.[37] In commenting on the ongoing state appropriation at just below market price of 10 percent of all newsprint imports, effective since March 1946, Colóm limited his declarations to saying that "the only thing that the government has done is guarantee in part freedom of the press, which in practice would not exist if all of the newspapers in the country didn't have a bit of paper."[38]

If the Union of Newspaper and Magazine Vendors would act as the primary mechanism by which *La Prensa* passed to Peronist hands in 1951, state measures ostensibly in response to the international newsprint crisis marked the path for both the weakening of *La Prensa* and the strengthening of the "friendly" press. When José Emilio Visca introduced a bill to reduce the number of pages allowed in newspaper editions, in fact, he could summon as precedent not the decrees of the 1943–46 military regime, but *La Prensa*'s own perpetual example of liberal-democratic practice and respect for individual liberties: Visca's bill came on the heels of a nearly identical action by the British government, itself struggling with the impact of the world newsprint shortage.[39] Yet this bill, along with an attempt by the same congressman to resurrect, with only slight modification, the 1934 Law for the Protection of the

Press, was met with little enthusiasm even by Peronist lawmakers, and was firmly rejected by the minority opposition.[40]

Passage of the bills, however, soon became irrelevant: faced with delays in Congress, on July 14 Central Bank head Miguel Miranda simply included newsprint on a list of imported commodities for which the bank would not release foreign currency reserves.[41] Even if newsprint imports constituted only a fraction of total Argentine hard currency expenditures, Miranda cited the rate of change in newsprint prices as justification for their inclusion in the measure: at U.S. $17 million, the exchange permits for the first *half* of 1947 exceeded by U.S. $2.5 million the total spent on the commodity for *all* of the previous year.[42] The response by *La Prensa* editorialists failed to address the underlying economic question, even if it made the gravity of the situation clear: the U.S. $17 million granted by July 1947 corresponded to purchases of little more than a *third* of the quantity imported in 1946. Newsprint inflation thus stood at approximately 320 percent yearly at the time of Miranda's decree, even as the Argentine economy began to feel the first effects of a more global hard currency drain.[43] Still, the move drew loud protests from the opposition press. *La Nación* even began to run a regular column, On the Measures Restricting the Labor of Journalism, which chronicled press-related activity in both Congress and the Central Bank.[44] The title of the column is far from accidental, since it served largely as a space for the reproduction of communiqués denouncing the measure not just from the FAP and the printers' unions, but even from the unquestionably Peronist Union of Newspaper and Magazine Vendors.[45] By early September, however, the measure began to have an effect, as *La Prensa* began to cut its acceptance of larger-print classified advertisements in order to conserve newsprint space.[46]

By the first months of the following year, a potentially more far-reaching blow struck both *La Prensa* and *La Nación,* one that centered even more squarely on the economic elements of "freedom of the press" and the legal implications of Peronist influence for the entire state apparatus. In October of 1946, Argentine Customs had begun an investigation of the two newspapers to determine whether their use of imported newsprint violated the conditions of a 1939 law which had ostensibly freed the commodity from import duties.[47] The 1939 law, the Customs lawyers argued, contained a clear case of exception: it did not cover the newsprint used for commercial purposes, thus leaving the portion of newsprint consumed in the publication of advertising subject to import duties. After a prolonged legal battle, in February of 1948 the courts ruled that while the two newspapers were not necessarily commercial publications, the use of duty-free newsprint for classified and display advertising did violate the provisions of the 1939 legislation. Both *La Prensa* and *La Nación* thus became liable for import duties on that portion of newsprint occupied by advertising *retroactively* to the date of the passage of the original law. With well over 65 percent of each issue space occupied by advertising, combined with high circulation, the directors of *La Prensa* and *La Nación* potentially owed Customs more than the net worth of their newspapers.[48] Yet the Peronist press had grown immensely during the course of the litigation, and any immediate enforcement of the ruling would only too obviously beg the question of Editorial ALEA's use of newsprint as well. Perón, then, simply let the court ruling and as yet unevaluated penalties hang over the heads of the opposition press, only to come down firmly in the wake of *La Prensa*'s expropriation.

The Press and *La Prensa* in the Souring of the Postwar Boom

While one can clearly attribute much of this governmental and extragovernmental harassment of *La Prensa*, and to a lesser extent *La Nación*, to the authoritarian bent of a political movement set on constructing total power, many government economic measures affecting the press remained plausible responses to changing world conditions. Even as early as 1947, as we have seen, state economic initiatives affecting the press could find reasonable justification in what most understood was only the beginning of a serious financial crisis for the newspaper industry. That the origins of this crisis lay in no small part in forces beyond the control of the Peronist government served to fortify government claims that state intervention protected, rather than hindered, the right of freedom of the press. In fact, as Peronists liked to point out, by mid-1950 the deepening newsprint crisis had even led *La Prensa*'s model of liberal democratic practice, the British Parliament, to limit London newspapers to four pages, while the U.S. Congress had begun its own investigation of monopoly practices in the newsprint industry.[49] For Argentina, however, the problem became even more complicated due to local economic conditions: as world newsprint prices continued to rise, the capacity of the Argentine economy to sustain the hard currency drain of importing the commodity fell rapidly. The situation was actually quite serious for the Argentine press, since the combination of a weakening Argentine peso against the dollar and rising world newsprint prices had a combined effect of producing a 200 percent increase in the price of the commodity for Argentine importers between August 1949 and August 1950, or 635 percent in comparison with 1939.[50]

By late 1950, then, the Argentine newspaper industry—totally dependent upon imports at a time of dangerously low national hard currency reserves and impending balance of payments problems—faced a serious dilemma. The continued absorption of economically ailing newspapers into the ALEA chain had kept the newspaper marketplace relatively unchanged from the previous period of prosperity. Similarly, the emergence of a variety of explicitly Peronist dailies that in 1947 had provided each sector of Peronism with a distinctive mouthpiece was quickly becoming superfluous as the movement centralized at the close of the decade. In addition, the social policies of the government vis-à-vis labor benefits and newsprint prices began to take a serious toll even on the Peronist press.[51] The situation could not help but affect the growing number of people in Buenos Aires for whom "freedom of the press" was intimately tied not just to ideological questions, but to workplace and, by implication, economic issues.

In early 1949, a massive wildcat printer's strike, directed as much against the ALEA papers as against the opposition press, presented the "worker's government" with the horrifying specter of its own deepening internal contradictions: Peronist labor combating Peronist capital. Any market "rationalization" that might lead to the elimination of an ALEA newspaper, then, would strike a highly visible simultaneous blow to both labor and the particular sector of the Peronist movement behind the paper. The rise of the Peronist media apparatus and its maintenance through direct and indirect state subsidies, however, could not resolve one of the fundamental problems that had made its creation possible: the newspaper industry's total dependence on increasingly scarce and expensive imported newsprint. By late 1950, the Peronist state found itself subsidizing a steadily growing array of commercial newspapers, most of which had come under state control when faced with economic ruin. The appropriation of most of the Buenos Aires commercial press had now left the quasi-state Editorial ALEA with a host of financially draining newspaper businesses while doing nothing to solve what remained a very real crisis in the economic situation of the national press. To make matters worse, the souring of the Argentine postwar economic boom beginning in 1949 coincided with a still sharper increase in world newsprint prices—even as the Argentine government sought to cut overall imports to protect dwindling currency reserves. By building the Peronist media empire from the debris left by the financial crumbling of the commercial press, Perón and his allies had also inherited the dilemma that had played such a crucial role in the creation of that wreckage: how to weather the postwar economic storm without the aid of *La Prensa*. At the same time, the wholesale elimination of the only other media organization that economically mattered—*La Prensa*—could only occur in such a way as to minimize the impact on the regime's democratic legitimacy in the international sphere. Perón, then, needed to maintain the ability to plausibly deny any equation of the death of *La Prensa* with the death of "freedom of the press" itself.

By late 1950, a host of political reasons to take the Peronization of the Argentine press further presented themselves: growing labor unrest, especially among printers and railway workers, as the regime began to step away from its growing social commitments; the first indications that the Peronist economic trajectory would begin to reverse course to attract foreign capital; and the coming presidential elections of 1951. The continuing economic crisis of the Buenos

Aires commercial press, whose most serious repercussion would be a massive printers' strike against Peronist and non-Peronist newspapers alike, made that extension of control imperative for the viability of the Peronist media. Just as the owners of *Crítica* and *Noticias Gráficas* needed the cooperation of Alberto Gainza Paz to stabilize the market situation of their newspapers, the new proprietors of those papers necessarily fixed as final target the only other media organization left in the country that mattered: *La Prensa*.

The Politics of Confrontation

Just as the absorption of Gainza Paz's newspaper became an enticing way to break the growing bottleneck in the press industry, a variety of political reasons also made the move attractive. In addition to the growing urgency of the press' economic crisis in late 1950, Perón surely sought to avoid the embarrassing scenario of a vocal opponent like *La Prensa* openly contradicting the Argentine nation's unanimous Peronism during the following year's presidential elections. Growing middle-class and labor discontent with the worsening national economic situation also began to boost *La Prensa*'s capacity to discredit the regime's own promises of prosperity through "objective" reporting of local news. Thus, *La Prensa*'s favorable coverage of a newly resuscitated strike by Socialist-led railway workers in January of 1951—an unusual but transparently interested prolabor stance for the paper—determined the timing of government action against the paper.

If the undeniable authoritarian drive of the Peronist movement assured the takeover of the paper, *La Prensa*'s handling of the press's economic crisis helped grant the move greater legitimacy. Like the printers, who had seen their social gains slowly eroded by inflation, news vendors faced worsening conditions. Actual newspaper prices, of which the *canillitas* received a percentage, had generally lagged behind local inflation levels.[52] In addition, the deepening gravity of the newsprint crisis had, by mid-1950, limited the multiple-edition evening papers like *Crítica*, *Noticias Gráficas*, and *La Razón* to a single daily edition, a situation not fully compensated for by increased sales. Later that year, however, circumstances changed dramatically when the Undersecretariat of Information, now in charge of newsprint distribution, abruptly reduced quotas by 20 percent. Whereas previously the state distribution of newsprint had allowed all dailies to either maintain or increase their circulation, since only the permitted number of pages changed, the new measure simply lowered overall newsprint supply, allowing individual newspapers to decrease pages or reduce circulation. Making a move whose consequences they could not foresee, the directors of *La Prensa* decided to lower the paper's street circulation by 90,000 issues weekdays and over 110,000 for the Sunday edition, while maintaining its self-distributed subscription service untouched.⁵³ With fewer newspapers to sell, the *canillitas*' incomes fell accordingly.

When the long-standing dispute between the vendors' union and *La Prensa* suddenly evolved into a strike against the paper on January 26, 1951, the Peronist movement could thus plausibly shift blame for the paper's disappearance, if not onto *La Prensa* itself, at least away from the Peronist government. In fact, *La Prensa*'s years of opposition to the labor movement as well as the constant radio and press campaign against the "excessively commercial" newspaper only muddled the issue of government coercion of the paper's directors. The *canillita* strike had the added benefit of returning the initiative to Peronist labor, now against an institution at least as strategically important to the opposition as were the state-owned railroads to the government.

The *canillitas*' demands also remained within prevailing labor legislation, and the union consciously avoided indications that its actions might infringe upon "freedom of the press." In demanding that 20 percent of the value of the paper's classified advertising pass to the union's social programs, the *canillitas* based themselves again upon the division between the newspaper's journalistic content and its commercial character: "the nature of that advertising is not on the order of general information, but is exclusively in the private interest of the business and of those who publish [the paper]."⁵⁴ Even more threatening to the directors of *La Prensa*, the union asserted its right to review the newspaper's accounting books. The demand cut to the heart of

Fig. 11 Eva Perón meets representatives of the Sindicato de Vendedores de Diarios, Revistas y Afines, December 2, 1949. Napoleón Sollazo stands to her immediate right.

Gainza Paz's continued proclamation of *La Prensa*'s purely cultural/informative character, and thus to the foundation of the paper's claims to inviolability under the terms of the constitution. The paper, then, could not avoid the strike without fatally negating its own conception of "freedom of the press."

Yet the timing of the union's ultimatum seems designed to preclude even the unlikely possibility that the paper might sacrifice its political stance and meet union demands: the forty-eight-hour deadline established by the union had almost expired when news of the ultimatum reached the *La Prensa* offices at noon on January 25.[55] Within an hour, the Argentine Press Union (Sindicato Argentino de Prensa—SAP), a Peronist union which had since displaced the FAP, and the now subdued printer's union, had not only declared a strike in solidarity with the *canillitas*, but had occupied the paper's presses. Delays in mediation of the dispute by officials at the Secretariat of Labor and Social Welfare appeared interminable. Similarly, constant requests by the directors of *La Prensa* that federal police end the occupation of the paper's presses by strikers and their sympathizers met with bureaucratic indifference. When those journalists who had remained "loyal" to the paper attempted to retake the presses after a month of failed negotiations, the strike turned violent: one journalist was killed and fourteen were wounded when shots were fired from the building where the presses were housed. Most of those gathered were immediately arrested, and the Ministry of the Interior formally declared the closure of the paper.[56] Both sides in the dispute claimed the victim as their own, and in protest the CGT declared a symbolic fifteen-minute general strike both in memory of the fallen journalist—a victim of *La Prensa* thugs, it insisted—and in support of direct government intervention.

Seven weeks after the beginning of the conflict, the Chamber of Deputies created a commission empowered to investigate the newspaper. As much as the Peronist press denounced the conflict as the clearest indication of *La Prensa*'s "counterrevolutionary" and "antiworker" character and attacked the paper on nationalist and class grounds, Congress remained largely consistent with the main thrust of the Peronist redefinition of "freedom of the press." The commission, ostensibly acting on the suspicion that the paper had not only evaded taxes and import duties but received unreported hard currency from its foreign contacts, subjected *La Prensa*'s financial records to close scrutiny. Subsequent leaks of commercial documents from *La Prensa*'s offices brought the Peronist press into line with congressional discourse: *La Época* began a series on the paper entitled "The dark history of *La Prensa*," which proposed to detail the repeated attempts of Ezequiel Paz and Alberto Gainza Paz to eliminate all competition and "deny freedom of the press to others." That congressional orders for the arrest of Gainza Paz on charges of tax evasion found the *La Prensa* director already in Montevideo, bound for New York, only seemed to confirm his guilt.

When the parliamentary commission delivered its final report to Congress a month later, the Peronist Deputy Antonio Benítez raised and then dismissed the relevance of *La Prensa*'s close connection to the "imperialist" United Press. Instead, he founded the commission's recommendation for expropriation on the idea that the flagrantly commercial nature of *La Prensa* removed the paper from the ordinary protections afforded to freedom of expression via the press: "If *La Prensa* was born as a forum of ideas, it soon set that characteristic aside and structured itself as a purely commercial enterprise." Given the fact that advertising alone occupied over 70 percent of the paper, bringing *La Prensa* revenue $30 to $32 million per year in revenue, "how, then, can one consider *La Prensa* a high tribune of doctrine?" If at one time *La Prensa* might have served the high cultural and educational mission of journalism, the paper had devolved into nothing more than a business, and a tax-evading and particularly exploitative one at that. The corrupted newspaper, the instrument of a single family, should instead "be transformed into an instrument of the national interests and into the mouthpiece of the free thought of the Argentine people." Backing the commission's case against the paper, Congress moved to use the constitutional provision that empowered it to expropriate private property of public interest. By a vote of 103 to 16, all property of *La Prensa,* including intellectual property rights and control of the name, immediately passed into the hands of the executive power, to be used "in the general interest and social perfection of the Argentine people."[57] In expropriating *La Prensa,* the Argentine Congress acted as the guardian of the public sphere, seeking to "purify" the press of the corruption engendered by its commercialization and returning popular access to the means of social communication.

The degree to which the Peronists had successfully won the ideological as well as the tactical battle over the nature of "freedom of the press" became apparent in the rebuttal of Benítez by the minority member of the commission (and a future president of the republic), Arturo Frondizi. Rather than appeal to broad notions of freedom of expression, Frondizi questioned the accuracy of the commission's findings, denying that *La Prensa* had received funding from outside the country or evaded taxes. The paper, he argued, operated as an exemplary business. In fact, in suggesting that a similar investigation of other newspapers might prove even more revealing, Frondizi reinforced the notion of the press in general as commercial enterprise: "What else are the Peronist newspapers that currently exist in the country? Are they not commercial enterprises, extraordinary commercial enterprises?"[58] The general weakness of Frondizi's argument was not lost on *La Época:* "freedom of the press was abolished by the press itself as it became commercialized. . . . This explains why the [commission's] minority, upon defending the 'independent' press yesterday, forgot to defend freedom of the press."[59]

Even if much of the opposition to Peronism found little to support in the intransigent and even anachronistic liberalism that had ultimately undermined Gainza Paz and *La Prensa*, the expropriation of the newspaper still marked a crucial point of inflection. With the closure of *La Prensa* and its transfer to the CGT, anti-Peronist forces found themselves without a significant presence in the public sphere. Of the major Buenos Aires dailies, only *La Nación* and, to a lesser extent, *Clarín* remained non-Peronist. Yet *La Nación* became much more muted in its opposition to the government after 1951, in part because the Mitre family and its allies feared a fate similar to that of Alberto Gainza Paz.[60] In addition, the nature of *La Nación* made a moderate oppositional stance logical: not only had the paper long remained far more ideologically flexible than *La Prensa*, but given *La Nación*'s political-pedagogical mission, it took only a simple recognition that the dominant section of the political class had become Peronist for the Mitre family to adopt a more constructive and conciliatory position vis-à-vis Peronism.[61]

During the May Day celebrations, within weeks of the expropriation of *La Prensa*, Perón himself announced that the paper that had previously acted as the mouthpiece of a now-defeated oligarchy would pass directly into the hands of the labor confederation CGT. In June, Argentine Customs finally ruled that *La Prensa* owed over $32 million for its use of newsprint to publish advertising; conveniently, the amount approximated the value of the state's compensation for the expropriation, making any payment to Gainza Paz unnecessary.[62] Even those most affected by the ordeal, the journalists, printers, and administrative employees of *La Prensa*, found a kind of solace in the Peronist regime's maternalism: Evita herself demonstrated the intimacy of all workers' relation to the regime by personally compensating the employees' lost wages from the quickly growing funds of the Eva Perón Foundation.[63] The spectacle of Evita literally reaching out to the victims of Gainza Paz's exploitation solidified Peronist assertions that the conflict was purely a labor dispute. Yet not even the resurrection of a "purified" *La Prensa*, now "at the service of the people" instead of the "capitalist instrument of a small group of proprietors," could halt the deepening of the newsprint crisis before the end of the year, nor stay journalists' continued demands for decisive action.[64] Now, however, CGT's *La Prensa* placed blame for the situation upon the "economic aggression" of international capital and the conspicuous consumption of the U.S. newspaper industry, and saw the solution in state-subsidized local production.[65]

If the November 1951 resurrection of *La Prensa* as the paper of the CGT placed decidedly different content within the traditional layout of the paper, a figure familiar to readers also appeared in a dramatically new context: Napoleón Sollazo, head of the Union of Newspaper and Magazine Vendors, had also become vice president of EPASA, the paper's new publishers. In fact, the Peronist transformation of the Argentine commercial press had created a public sphere

Fig. 12 Eva Perón distributes funds from the Fundación Eva Perón to the staff of *La Prensa,* June 11, 1951.

Fig. 13 Eva Perón with the staff of *La Prensa,* May 23, 1951.

whose institutional surface resembled that of the pre-Perón years. Not only did the directors of the newly Peronist *Crítica, Noticias Gráficas, El Mundo,* and *La Razón* attempt to maintain the prior characteristics and audiences of those papers—simply changing the political line—but even the CGT-owned *La Prensa* retained a format and tone that, to the chagrin of many Peronists, maintained the "predominant atmosphere of the Paz [family]."⁶⁶ Even this near-total occupation of the public sphere on the part of the Peronist regime, however, could not bring the final third of the Argentine population into the Peronist fold. Indeed, as Tulio Halperín has argued, the unanimity of the Peronist public sphere only made the continued electoral presence of a minority opposition that much more disconcerting than it had been under the Radical governments of the 1920s, when opposition was visible daily.⁶⁷

This attempt at continuity was hardly accidental. As Carlos Aloé would later explain, "[Perón] always told me that the 'opinion group' was to maintain an organism necessary for . . . propaganda, and to have within reach the necessary means by which he could address public opinion, at whatever moment and in whatever circumstances. To have his own means and not depend on other companies foreign to his will or purposes."⁶⁸ To achieve this, Aloé balanced the finances of those newspapers incorporated into "the chain" that showed losses—at different times *Crítica*, *El Laborista*, *La Época*, and *Noticias Gráficas*—with profitable newspapers like *Democracia* and the publications of Editorial Haynes.⁶⁹ The resulting flow of resources between the different branches of the Peronist media holdings allowed for the maintenance of the largest possible number of different newspapers, magazines, and radio stations without recourse to any potentially fragile alliances. Military investigators would later find themselves mired in financial records that drew only the most tenuous of lines between the operations of ALEA and those of the formally independent Editorial Democracia, CADEPSA (*Crítica*), Editorial Haynes (*El Mundo*), *La Razón*, S.A. Luz (*La Época*), and a host of smaller companies.⁷⁰ Even Aloé's construction company, Atlas, became entangled in the matter: in 1951 ALEA moved into the newly constructed Alas Building—at forty-three stories the tallest in the city—built by Atlas.⁷¹ Far from the product of careless bookkeeping, the sharing of resources between the organizations linked together through Aloé corresponded to Perón's desire to maximize the social reach of the media empire while maintaining independence from all but the most trusted investors.

Journalism, Power, and the Sublimation of Dissent

The 1951 congressional investigation into *La Prensa* marks a turning point not just in the history of the Argentine press, but in that of international news and journalism organizations. By voting nearly unanimously to expropriate the newspaper, the Argentine Congress sparked protests by publishers around the world, and flags flew at half-mast in front of the offices of the major newspapers of the United States, Western Europe, and Latin America.⁷² Though unprecedented, the seizure of the newspaper caught few entirely off guard; U.S.

Fig. 14 Edificio ALAS, location of the offices of Editorial ALEA.

journalists were not alone in having long predicted a final showdown between Gainza Paz and the government.[73] The liberal-conservative daily, after all, had been the Peronist regime's most consistent, powerful, and vociferous critic since the beginning of Perón's political ascent in early 1944. Yet the relative ease with which the Argentine government expropriated what was perhaps the world's most economically powerful newspaper outside of the United States could not help but alarm journalists and governments around the Western world. The expropriation suddenly and radically altered the nation's political landscape: the disappearance of the anti-Peronist *La Prensa* created an Argentine public sphere devoid of the embarrassing indicator that the Peronist movement had yet to achieve the total consensus of all Argentines long proclaimed by its founder; it did so, however, by further diminishing the range of legal channels for dissent. With eroding electoral prospects and even *La Prensa* in the hands of government supporters, the opposition increasingly found itself with little to gain by remaining within the bounds of Peronist legality and little to lose by stepping beyond them.

It is tempting to argue that, within the urban geography of Buenos Aires, *La Prensa* stood as an obstacle too provocative for the architects and supporters of the New Argentina to ignore, and that a final clash between the forces of Peronism and the Paz family newspaper became increasingly likely from the moment that Peronists assumed constitutional power. For Peronists the building's location between the Congress and the executive raised a serious question: if Perón controlled the Casa Rosada, and Peronists controlled the Congress, why did *La Prensa*—the self-proclaimed *cuarto estado*—remain in the hands of the old regime? Shouldn't it also be "liberated"? By explicitly and physically placing itself on par with the nation's governing institutions as a "fourth estate," the owners of *La Prensa* tied the fate of the newspaper to a redistribution of political power and restructuring of the Argentine state that by the late 1940s had already proven more profound than even its advocates had expected. By standing at the geographic heart of state power, the owners of *La Prensa* suddenly found themselves standing at the center of Peronist power. A taunting coincidence only compounded the problem for Alberto Gainza Paz: *La Prensa* celebrated its anniversary on October 18, only a day after the most sacred of Peronist holidays. For the tens of thousands of demonstrators who crowded into the Plaza de Mayo to commemorate the popular mobilization that forced the release of Perón from prison on October 17, 1945, the offices of *La Prensa* stood literally only a stone's throw away.

Even if the geographic manifestation of the director's political pretensions did not condemn *La Prensa*, the paper could hardly have escaped the rapid social and economic transformations of the Peronist period untouched. Struggles for hegemony are, after all, simultaneously ideological and material struggles for control of the instruments of hegemony. The functioning of the press in all capitalist democracies—of which Peronist Argentina is an admittedly peculiar variation—embodies perhaps more visibly and ambiguously than that of any other social institution one of the fundamental contradictions of liberal democracy itself: the impulse toward equal access to the public sphere and the realm of social decision making, and the centrality of private property rights. It was precisely out of this breach between the egalitarian impulse of democracy and the unequal property relations of capitalism that Peronism arose, and within which it could shape a definition of "freedom of the press" at least as viable as that of any other social sector. The Peronists, however, ultimately proved unwilling or politically unable to move beyond a clearly authoritarian and sublimating "resolution" of the tensions within the newspaper industry, or within Argentine society as a whole.

CONCLUSION:
JOURNALISM AND POWER IN THE NEW ARGENTINA

> We have a press like no other in the world. . . .
> We have the purest press in the world.
> **—Américo Barrios, Secretary General of the First National Congress of Journalists, Buenos Aires, September 7, 1951**

> I found myself in danger of agreeing with *La Prensa,* a serious matter.
> **—Rodolfo Walsh, 1968**

With the expropriation of *La Prensa* and its transfer to the CGT, the dramatic transformation of Latin America's most powerful newspaper industry was complete: *Crítica, La Razón, Noticias Gráficas, El Mundo,* and finally the Paz family's paper had all come under the control of the Peronist movement. In addition, at least a dozen local and regional newspapers beyond the Federal Capital, including *El Día* of La Plata, and nearly forty radio stations now revolved tightly in the Peronist orbit.[1] Opposition newspapers like the Socialist *La Vanguardia* and the Salta provincial newspaper *El Intransigente* had succumbed to legal technicalities and Peronist bureaucratic maneuvering.[2] By the time of his fall from power in 1955, Perón and his allies had not only managed to assemble what was undoubtedly the region's largest media empire, but they had sharply curtailed the spaces available for the public voicing of anti-Peronist dissent.

The Argentine press's dramatic transformation in the 1940s is indicative of the authoritarian tendencies of significant sectors of the Peronist movement, but also of the broader set of debilitating economic, political, and ideological crises that had shaken the country since 1930. Peronism itself had arisen from these social conflicts, less as an ideologically coherent political project than as an aggregation of contingent solutions to the multiple crises that permeated Argentine society. As part of this process, Peronists managed to articulate an eclectic vision for the resolution of fundamental conflicts in Argentine society, one that drew as much from assertions that Peronism embodied a revolutionary break with previous political and social practices as it did from claims that the movement marked the true realization of central liberal-democratic promises.[3] Only under Peronism, its proponents argued, could long-excluded sectors of Argentine society—especially workers and women—exercise the liberal political rights of citizenship, including that of "freedom of the press" and the power of journalism. In addition, Peronists claimed an array of new economic, social, and cultural rights as their own innovations. To underestimate the utopian appeal of an Argentina in which long-standing promises of equality, citizenship, and representation in the cultural life of the nation would at last be fulfilled in practice is to overlook fundamental reasons for the genuine support that the movement attained during Perón's tenure in power; it is also to abandon any hope of understanding many Argentines' continued adherence to Peronism in its moments of crisis, and even in the darkest hours of the subsequent waves of military repression.

It is in this light, I have argued, that we must approach the history of Peronism and the Argentine commercial press. As much as any other sector of Argentine society, and perhaps even more visibly, the newspaper industry was fraught with the tensions from which Peronism emerged. Indeed, the entire network of relationships that constituted the press had already showed signs of significant stress for more than a decade prior to the 1943 military coup that gave birth to Peronism, as heated contests for power within the newspaper industry began to alter the landscape of Argentine journalism. Perón and his allies proved particularly adept at inserting themselves into the multiple conflicts within and around the newspaper industry, instrumentalizing these disputes as part of broader political struggles. If those wielding state power managed to "resolve" these tensions in ways that benefited key sectors of the Peronist movement, they did so within the context of a commercial newspaper industry whose own ambiguous ideological foundations, contested juridical status, and teetering economic stability facilitated the process.

The story of the Peronist transformation of the Argentine press, then, is more than one of political authoritarianism: it is inseparable from the multiple contradictions opened up by the commercial development of the newspaper industry, the sudden emergence of newly powerful sectors of the public whose opinion that press ostensibly represented, and the Argentine manifestations of a worldwide economic crisis of the press that threatened its own homogenizing restructuring of the Buenos Aires newspaper industry. The history of Peronism and the press, then, is as much the history of the whole crisis-ridden network of relationships that comprised the Argentine newspaper industry as it is the history of Peronism.

The Immaculate Press of the New Argentina

The characteristics of this history remained sharply contested not just during the period of Peronist ascent and consolidation, but also in the aftermath of Perón's fall in 1955. Members of opposing political tendencies within Argentina as well as many foreign observers viewed the transformation of the commercial press as the epitome of the Peronist experiment, either as a manifestation of Peronism's potential for liberation or as indicative of the movement's inherent authoritarianism. That the majority of the Argentine press had become so intimately linked to the Peronist regime, furthermore, only made the impact of the Peronist government's collapse that much more traumatic for both Peronism and the Argentine newspaper industry. Indeed, the process of undoing the "Peronization" of the press could ignore neither the depth of that transformation nor the continued existence of the decades-old fundamental disputes within and around the commercial press that had shaped it.

For convinced Peronists the first five years of constitutional Peronist government simply, but crucially, brought the newspaper industry into line with values that much of the press itself had pronounced since the turn of the century, but that had remained largely unrealized in practice. At the Sindicato Argentino de Prensa's First National Congress of Journalists in mid-1951, the Congress's nominal founder, José Gabriel, declared that Peronism had managed to end the practical exclusion of broad sectors of the Argentine public from representation in the pages of the daily press. The national press, he argued, now much more closely "reflected ... the general opinion" of the Argentine public than it ever had prior to the emergence of the movement.[4] His colleague Américo Barrios repeated this evaluation in a sycophantic address to the Congress, adding that only Peronism had brought "authentic freedom of the press [and] Juan Perón with Eva Perón have made possible this immaculate press of the New Argentina." The advent of Peronism had not shackled the press to an authoritarian political project, Barrios asserted; it had instead created "the purest press in the world," one in which the power of journalism had opened to the vast majority of Argentines for the first time.[5]

Opponents of Peronism, on the other hand, rejected such notions out of hand. Instead, they saw in the fate of the commercial press the clearest confirmation of the movement's authoritarianism and superficial respect for democratic principles—and, even more, of the demagoguery of the movement's founder. In this environment, Alberto Gainza Paz became something of a living symbol of the embattled traditional conceptions of press freedom, actively lobbying in the United States and elsewhere not just for the return of his newspaper, but for the international ostracism of Perón and his "henchmen."[6] Even after Perón's fall and the restitution of *La Prensa*, Gainza Paz remained an embodiment of resistance to authoritarianism for many in the United States media: in April 1957, NBC's *Armstrong Circle Theater* aired the docudrama "Slow Assassination: Perón vs. La Prensa," with Gainza Paz himself making an appearance to help "expose the evil of Perón to the white light of truth."[7] The case of *La Prensa*, as media scholar Mary Gardner has argued, even served to unite journalists and proprietors of the U.S. press, engaged in their own confrontations, around the Inter American Press Association, which remains the most vital of the pan-American journalism institutions.[8] The conflict between Perón and *La Prensa* was at once so epic and so unambiguous, she maintains, that Gainza Paz's own account of the conflict, first published in Mexico in 1953, "should be required reading for all journalists."[9]

This dismissal of the Peronist media project as the product of little more than a personalist aberration also guided the public reasoning behind the policies of the Revolución Libertadora military regime that displaced Perón. In their sweeping official investigation of Peronist actions, officials characterized the Peronist transformation of the press as responding to the tenacious authoritarianism of the "second tyranny," a twentieth-century version of the Rosas dictatorship.[10] According to the military and its allies, just as the Libertadora would quickly return the country to its "natural" liberal-democratic historical path with the destitution of Perón, so would the Argentine press emerge from Peronist domination to resume its proper role as a purely cultural vehicle for the exercise of the rights of citizenship and the power of journalism.

Yet neither the more conciliatory approach of General Eduardo Lonardi, who initially allowed *La Prensa* to remain in the hands of the CGT, nor his hardline successor General Pedro Aramburu's sweeping policies of de-Peronization could restore the Argentine press to a status that it had once enjoyed only briefly, if at all. In fact, the return of *La Prensa* to Alberto Gainza Paz and the dismantling of Editorial ALEA followed a logic oriented less toward a restoration of the pre-Perón status quo than toward satisfying the demands of the heterogeneous coalition of various Radical Party factions, Socialist currents, and other political groupings that supported the Libertadora. Newspapers slowly became dissociated from "the chain" not as part of a simple privatization of Editorial ALEA, but in ways that resembled a division of spoils. While *El Laborista* went to Cipriano Reyes as a restoration of the Partido Laborista newspaper, government officials distributed *La Época, Crítica, La Razón*, and *Democracia* among various factions of the Socialist Party, the Radical Party, and newer Conservative and Christian Democratic organizations.[11] *Noticias Gráficas*, briefly organized as a cooperative by its journalists, also quickly became absorbed into the latest version of factional journalism, while military intelligence services even resorted to deadly force in order to ensure that the power of the press never drifted too far beyond reach.[12] Other Peronist newspapers and magazines, meanwhile, faced simple closure.

The equivocal nature of Aramburu's "restoration" of the pre-Perón press formed an integral part of the equally complicated project of returning to liberal democracy that formed the core of the Libertadora's basis of legitimacy. If the restoration of *La Prensa*, the distribution of commercial newspapers among the regime's impatient allies, and the silencing of the remaining Peronist media created a public sphere that might have accurately represented the regime's ideal polity, that polity nonetheless bore scant resemblance to the actual Argentine public. Depriving Peronists of the ability to exercise the power of journalism in socially meaningful ways weakened but could not erase what remained the country's most vibrant political movement. Ceding financially troubled newspapers like *Crítica* to rapidly splintering Radical Party factions did little to ensure loyalty to the regime, and even less to consolidate any viable civilian alternative to Peronism.

The press policies of the Revolución Libertadora, then, proved just as contradictory as the broader political strategy of the military regime. If attempts to orchestrate a return to constitutional democracy became an "impossible game" with the electoral proscription of the Peronist majority, so too did efforts to create a "free" press whose doors remained closed to that same section of the public. Given the surprisingly resilient nature of Peronism, especially within the labor movement, continuing to curtail Peronist participation in the public sphere threatened to recreate the kind of chasm between the press and broad sectors of the Argentine public that had helped spark much of the anti-press violence of October 1945.

Similarly, the hope of military officials and their allies that a de-Peronization of the Argentine public sphere, however incomplete in practice, would fatally undermine the legitimacy of Peronism and foster a corresponding shift in the Argentine public proved even more baseless. Each of Argentina's different political currents, it became apparent, had quickly proven itself devastatingly unable to reestablish even the most basic institutional consensus since the crises of the 1930s. The failed democratic gestures between 1955 and 1966 signaled just how untenable the situation had become, while the continued presence of a fragmenting Peronism did little to encourage the cohesion of the broad spectrum of anti-Peronist forces. Even the more pronounced authoritarianism of the 1966 Revolución Argentina military regime could do little but accelerate the process of Peronism becoming at once more heterogeneous, fragmented, and radical. The "aberration" of Peronism became increasingly impossible to ignore as an intrinsic element of national politics as non-Peronist military and civilian regimes alike floundered in the absence of broad public consent.

The continued relevance of Peronism despite the movement's proscription and its founder's exile only made the ongoing evaluation of the Peronist experience that much more contentious. Yet, in the context of alternating military authoritarianism and civilian pseudodemocracy, competing characterizations of the Peronist transformation of the press also became more candid. The characterization of Peronist press policies as an anachronistic resurrection of *rosista* authoritarianism and, alternatively, as a democratizing liberation of the power of journalism from the stranglehold of economically powerful newspaper proprietors both held important elements of truth. The story of the commercial press under Perón proved particularly problematic for those who sought a solution to Argentina's increasingly dangerous political impasse in radical, egalitarian democracy and who considered a reinvigoration of Peronism's revolutionary potential the only viable path to achieve that goal.

In his 1973 revision of an earlier investigation into the assassination of Ricardo Peralta Ramos's lawyer during the Libertadora's "restoration" of the press, journalist Rodolfo Walsh points to the Peronist appropriation of the newspaper industry as the fundamental turning point in the course of Argentine journalism. Prior to the Peronist intervention, the national press remained subservient at once to the "voice of imperialism" embodied in the international news agencies and to the handful of "press lords" who exercised rights promised to all but "denied to millions."[13] For Walsh, a committed member of the Peronist Left until his assassination by security forces in 1977, the formation of the Peronist press also marked a step toward more egalitarian representation of the nation's popular classes in the public sphere, albeit in a qualified manner: "the Peronist press did not express the working class directly, but defended it from the intermediate heights of a new bourgeoisie in ascent." Rather than becoming a vehicle for the Argentine working class's exercise of collective expression and journalistic power, the Peronist media apparatus essentially substituted Peronist and state capital for oligarchic capital, and "the chain [Editorial ALEA] became the preferred terrain of that parasitic sickness of the Peronist Movement: the bureaucracy."[14]

If for Walsh this nonetheless represented a historically significant step toward a more egalitarian distribution of power in Argentine society and thus an indication of Peronism's underlying revolutionary impulse, it did set Peronism's emancipatory potential in a new light. Walsh's narrative of national and working-class liberation derailed by local capital and bureaucracy embodies an important component of Peronist thought after 1955, the importance of which Walsh at times appears only partially cognizant: the tension between, on the one hand, an aspiration for the realization of an egalitarian Argentina and a movement that might create it and, on the other, the actual, concrete history of the Peronist experience. Capital had in fact constituted a far more central element of early Peronism's multiclass alliance than the Peronist rhetoric of workers "combating capital" might suggest. In addition, Perón and Eva Perón themselves not only did not oppose much of the bureaucratic centralization of the press that Walsh criticizes, they directly orchestrated it. The rapid emergence of a vibrant, more pluralistic Peronist press in the aftermath of October 1945 expressed the contradictory impulses and contentious social alliances of early Peronism. Rather than a simple distortion of any original revolutionary impulse, the subsequent centralization and bureaucratization of the Argentine media responded both to the fundamentally precarious nature of the Peronist coalition and to the continued relevance of the authoritarian currents so crucial to the movement's origins. As Raanan Rein has succinctly noted, "the Peronism of 1946–1947 is not the same as that of the years 1953–1955."[15] Yet the Peronism of 1953 to 1955 is in no small measure the product not just of the social forces that emerged in 1946 and 1947, but of the authoritarian social project of the preceding years that had inadvertently helped unleash them. Indeed, for Walsh and his contemporaries to imagine a different trajectory for the formation of the Peronist media apparatus is, in effect, to run the risk of positing not just a different Peronism from that of 1946 to 1955, but a different Perón and Evita.

The Transnational Crisis of the Press

The fate of the press in Latin America's archetypal populist experiment is a particularly striking example of the broader contradictions inherent in the media's shifting role in midcentury capitalist societies. Since the 1930s the proprietors of Buenos Aires newspapers had struggled to reconcile claims for the press's special status vis-à-vis the state with the realities of a capital-intensive newspaper industry and its complex division of labor. Similarly, the suddenly clear chasm between press and public that the events of October 1945 revealed owed as much to the unfulfilled promise of an open, representative media and the entanglement of economic power and journalism as it did to the specific political inclinations of newspaper proprietors. The operation of the market itself, as we have seen, also threatened its own "rationalization" of the Argentine newspaper industry in the immediate postwar years; the continuation of the press's economic problems even after the Peronist expropriation of *La Prensa* and well into the Libertadora only confirms that this crisis embodied much more than a simple Peronist alibi for the manipulation of newsprint stock.[16]

This more general set of crises that permeated the Buenos Aires press also, to varying degrees, affected newspaper industries well beyond Argentina. A 1936 U.S. Supreme Court ruling declaring that the First Amendment did not shield the media from labor laws came just a year after Argentine courts pronounced newspapers subject to the commercial code.[17] Similarly, journalists in the United Sates and Brazil unionized within years of their Argentine counterparts, reflecting not just the growing tensions within the newspaper industry, but a new conception of just what the exercise of journalism signified.[18] In both the United States and Argentina, the post–World War II spike in newsprint prices and newspaper proprietor attempts to cut labor costs in compensation led to an unprecedented level of unrest within the newspaper industry. Printers' strikes rocked Chicago, Miami, and Detroit after 1947, and the American Newspaper Guild began its own investigations into newspaper owners' responses to the newsprint crisis.[19] By early 1949, the situation had become even more serious as wildcat printers' strikes closed the newspapers of Washington, D.C., and left Buenos Aires without newspapers for nearly three weeks.[20] The British press fared better, if only because the strict wartime rationing of newsprint continued well after the war. Even the American Newspaper Guild, operating within the significantly less statist political atmosphere of the United States, advocated that the government invoke the War Powers Act to secure an adequate supply of newsprint to the economically fragile sectors of the industry.[21] The severity of the worldwide newsprint crisis from 1949 to 1952 underscored the menace that an unregulated market could pose not just for newsworkers, but for proprietors of smaller newspapers and the reading public more generally.

It is not surprising, then, that serious attempts to shield the egalitarian promise of liberal-democratic conceptions of journalism practice from the consequences of the press's own industrial expansion emerged nearly simultaneously in Argentina, the United States, and Great Britain. In the United States, the University of Chicago–based Commission on Freedom of the Press (Hutchins Commission) issued a series of studies that located the principal threat to freedom of the press not in the state, but in the profit-driven, capital-intensive nature of the commercial newspaper industry itself.[22] In their 1947 general report, the members of the Commission pointed out a fundamental irony of the modern newspaper industry: as the press became increasingly important as a means of social communication, the corresponding "development of the press as an instrument of mass communication has greatly decreased the proportion of the people who can express their opinions and ideas through the press." This growing tension between the public nature of the press and the private monopoly of the power of journalism, they warned, undermined the broader exercise of citizenship and justifiably threatened the private ownership of the press: "When an instrument of prime importance to all the people is available to a small minority of the people only, and when it is employed by that small minority in such a way as not to supply the people with the service they require, the freedom of the minority in the employment of that instrument is in danger."[23] In Britain, similar fears that unbridled concentration of ownership might homogenize the British public sphere led Parliament to create the Royal Commission on the Press in 1947, with the economics of newspaper proprietorship constituting the primary focus of the Commission's labors through the 1970s.[24]

The story of the Argentine press in the Peronist years, then, forms part of a far more fundamental, transnational phenomenon: the very real threat, according to a growing consensus, that the scale of industrial newspaper and media production was such that the power of journalism might become inextricably and exclusively linked to those holding economic power, much to the detriment of broader democratic practice. In contrast to the United States and Great Britain, however, in Argentina the resulting contests over the reform of media jurisprudence, the ethical norms of journalism practice, and the growing weight of the state in the press's network of relationships resulted in the sweeping alteration of one of the world's larger media landscapes.

The Chasm Between Ideal and Practice

The reasons for the sharp difference between the fate of the Argentine press and that of the press in other countries whose newspaper industries were fraught with similar conflicts do not lie just in the willingness of Peronist leaders to harness the momentum of these disputes to an explicitly partisan and semiauthoritarian political project, or even with Peronism's virtual monopoly on political power. They also lie in the inability of other political forces to consistently articulate a solution to the dilemmas posed by the modern press.

In the case of the owners of *La Prensa*, this took the form of an unyielding refusal even to recognize the very existence of legitimate concerns over the consequences of the press's industrialization. For Alberto Gainza Paz, the matter appeared quite simple: even the slightest concession to the legitimacy of state authority vis-à-vis the press—indeed, any recognition that the press differed from its nineteenth-century ideal—would lead to nothing less than an unequivocally authoritarian subjugation of the press and the power of journalism. Peronist press policies had indeed channeled disputes over the nature of journalism and the internal fissures within the newspaper industry into the construction of a quasi-state and partisan media apparatus devoted less to open citizen access and legitimate popular representation than to the creation and perpetuation of a particular form of state power. Gainza Paz saw this process not just as preordained, but as confirmation of the wisdom of his intransigence.

Yet to deny the legitimacy of newsworker access to the labor protections extended to other workers and to dismiss the exclusion of broad sectors of the public from adequate and accurate representation in the media as inconsequential, is to remain beholden to notions of the press that clash with other fundamental elements of modern liberal democracy. Peronists, non-Peronists, and anti-Peronists alike had long argued that state power could in fact serve to guarantee citizen rights to collective representation in the press, prevent those wielding economic power from establishing a monopoly on the exercise of power through journalism, provide newsworker labor guarantees, and shield the industry from economic crises. Nor were such concerns unique to Argentina. Gainza Paz's intransigent refusal to recognize this openly contradicted what to newsworkers, judges, advertisers, and readers alike seemed obvious: the modern commercial newspaper industry differed in fundamental ways from the less complex and less capital-intensive nineteenth-century press.

Arguably, this position undermined rather than strengthened the *La Prensa* owner in his confrontations with the Peronist government. When the owners of newspapers like *Crítica* and *Noticias Gráficas* virtually begged him for price concessions in late 1946 as a last-ditch effort to maintain the independence of their papers, the intransigence of Gainza Paz appeared less a disinterested defense of the press as a whole than a pragmatic attempt to further strengthen *La Prensa*'s dominant market position. Thus, if Gainza Paz considered his stance a matter of principle, to many anti-Peronists like Arturo Frondizi it appeared at best a misguided embrace of an anachronistic liberal orthodoxy, and at worst a dubious maneuver that only confirmed the tight grip of economic power over the power of journalism. If nothing else, the unyielding position that Gainza Paz adopted sharply limited the range of options available to him in his confrontations with a far more agile and pragmatic opponent.

Peronists, on the other hand, managed to articulate their own solutions to the set of increasingly acute crises that had surrounded and permeated the Argentine newspaper industry's whole network of relationships since the 1930s. In often spontaneous and organic ways, Peronists tapped into an increasingly legitimate current of press criticism that had also begun to emerge in places like the United States and Great Britain. This shift in the discourse on the social role of journalism posited the state not as a threat to the functioning of the press (as proposed in traditional liberalism), but as a defender: of the "true press" from the corrupting influence of commerce; of public opinion from the distorting effects of powerful private interests; of newsworkers from newspaper proprietors; of smaller news organizations from more powerful ones; and of the newspaper industry as a whole from very real external economic shocks and internal production bottlenecks. Peronists employed this discourse in ways that they hoped would reconcile the movement's self-proclaimed status as a "revolutionary" movement with claims that Peronist press policies embodied nothing more—and nothing less—than a resolution of the conspicuous contradiction between the long-standing egalitarian promise contained in liberal conceptions of journalism practice and the concrete functioning of the modern newspaper industry. At the same time, the opposition's failure to fashion a viable alternative to the specifics of government press policies reveals not just the relative absence of agreement regarding anything but their common anti-Peronism, but the degree to which Peronism's own doctrinal eclecticism allowed the movement to occupy a frustratingly broad spectrum of Argentina's ideological terrain.

Conclusion

By their very nature, the media in capitalist democracies fall outside of easy categories: at once public and private, cultural and economic, national and international, and with a power at once mundane and extraordinary, the media occupy multiple levels of contested social terrain. While the ubiquity of the modern media and their power to shape consciousness make conflicts surrounding the press, such as those of Peronist Argentina, important in and of themselves, they also reveal the contours of more fundamental contests. Struggles over the media at once shape and are shaped by much broader disputes regarding the proper boundaries between the public and private realms, the nature of citizenship, democracy, and representation, and the practical relationship between the state, politicians, civil society, and the market. Even contingent resolutions to the perpetual conflicts regarding modern journalism as a practice in the exercise of power, then, remain intimately bound with more basic struggles over the unrealized egalitarian promise of liberal democracy in the midst of the very real social cleavages at the heart of capitalism.

Indeed, any such resolution of conflicts over the media can be nothing but ephemeral, given the perpetually shifting relations of power in capitalist societies and the increasingly rapid pace of change within the productive relations and technology of the media themselves. These ongoing transformations continually undermine consensus on what at other times appear deceptively simple issues. What *is* and what *should be* the relationship between newsworkers, media proprietors, government officials, commercial interests, international organizations, and other institutions of civil society? Is it possible to reconcile the long-standing egalitarian promise of liberal democracy with capital-intensive, modern mass media that effectively place the socially meaningful exercise of "freedom of the press" beyond the grasp of all but a small minority? Can state action close the gap between media ideals and media practices, or does state power represent an inherent threat to the press?

As print media increasingly give way to digital, and as powerful commercial news organizations compete with those born of more flexible and less capital-intensive forms of production and dissemination, these issues have become even more urgent. What qualifies as legitimate journalism? Who or what is "the press"? What exactly are press-related "rights" and "freedoms"? By what means can the exercise of those rights and freedoms in socially meaningful ways approach the universality promised through the juridical framework of democratic republics? Is there a technological "fix" to the unequal distribution of the power of communication, or do these technological advances carry within them the same potential for commercialization and bureaucratic centralization that initially remained hidden in the printing press?

Anything but tentative consensus around these issues will remain inherently illusory. Consideration of the dialectical relationship between these unfolding contests over the media and the broad array of struggles in an increasingly media-saturated society is more than a task for future historians. Nor is it simply a reminder to contemporary students of history that the experience of the past was profoundly uncertain, contentious, and fleeting for those caught in its grasp; it is also a warning that our own certainties and assumptions regarding even the most mundane elements of the past and present are essentially no different, and will also quickly be swept away.

Notes

INTRODUCTION

1. *Crítica*, March 7, 1947; *La Nación*, March 8, 1947.
2. *La Nación*, March 8, 1947.
3. *La Prensa*, March 19, 1947.
4. See *La Nación*, February 28, 1951.
5. For the text of the resolution, see República Argentina, Senado de la Nación, "La Prensa," 363.
6. *La Prensa*, November 19, 1951.
7. Perón, *Perón y "La Prensa,"* 12.
8. Those five papers were, in descending order of circulation, *La Prensa, El Mundo, Crítica, Noticias Gráficas,* and *La Razón*. The region's sixth-largest, *La Nación*, was also published in the Argentine capital but remained free of Peronist control. For regional circulation figures, see *Editor and Publisher, International Year Book Number for 1946,* 294–316. On Peronist newspaper holdings, see Vicepresidencia de la Nación, Comisión Nacional de Investigaciones, *Documentación, autores y cómplices,* 1:537.
9. Much of this work rests on the well-documented reports issued by the military authorities of the post-Perón Revolución Libertadora government as well as polemical studies written by those linked to either the military or *La Prensa*. See Comisión Nacional de Investigaciones, República Argentina, *Documentación, autores y cómplices;* Comisión Nacional de Investigaciones, República Argentina, *Libro negro de la segunda tiranía;* Sánchez Zinny, *El culto de la infamia;* Gainza Paz, *Por defender la libertad;* Pastor, *La otra faz de la segunda dictadura.* For subsequent popular and academic scholarship that draws from this material and largely endorses this interpretation, see Luna, *Perón y su tiempo;* Page, *Perón;* Crassweller, *Perón and the Enigmas of Argentina;* Fraser and Navarro, *Evita;* Barnes, *Evita First Lady;* Dujovne Ortiz, *Eva Perón;* Lynch et al., *Historia de la Argentina;* Rock, *Argentina, 1516–1987*.
10. See, for example, Sirvén, *Perón y los medios de comunicación;* Panella, *La Prensa y el peronismo;* Capelato, *Multidões em cena;* Waisbord, *Watchdog Journalism in South America;* Plotkin, *Mañana es San Perón;* Rein, *Peronismo, populismo y política;* Gambini, *Historia del peronismo;* Sidicaro, *La política mirada desde arriba;* Ciria, *Política y cultura popular;* Gené, *Un mundo felíz;* Ulanovsky, *Paren las rotativas;* Lavieri, "The Media in Argentina." For appraisals even more damning of Perón, see the transnational studies Gardner, *Inter-American Press Association;* Blanchard, *Exporting the First Amendment;* Álvarez and Martínez Riaza, *Historia de la prensa hispanoamericana;* Garrison and Salwen, *Latin American Journalism*.
11. A notable and encouraging exception to this tendency can be found in the recent collection of essays in Da Orden and Melon Pirro, *Prensa y peronismo*.
12. Buchrucker, "Interpretations of Peronism," 8–9.
13. That this is, in fact, a fruitful approach is ably demonstrated by Nállim, "Crisis of Liberalism in Argentina."

14. My own approach to this complex interaction owes its principal debt to Halperín Donghi, "El lugar del peronismo"; Williams, *Marxism and Literature*, 121–27; and Laclau, *Politics and Ideology in Marxist Theory*, 159–61.

15. Nord, "Plea for *Journalism* History," 11.

16. While scholars have frequently placed greater emphasis on the cultural and ideological components of hegemony, Antonio Gramsci's own articulation of the notion of hegemony suggests that he considered contests for institutional power not just as decisive to the success of any hegemonic project, but as crucial in the process of shaping the specific nature and content of the hegemonic project itself. This is especially apparent in Gramsci's use of the trench-warfare metaphor to describe political struggle. Gramsci, *Selections from the Prison Notebooks*, 229–39.

17. Not only was the mid-1940s consumption of newspapers in Buenos Aires triple that in its nearest Latin American peer (Mexico City), Argentina also ranked third worldwide in per capita newspaper purchases in 1882 as well as in the mid-1930s. *Editor and Publisher, International Year Book Number for 1946*, 294–316; Prieto, *El discurso criollista*, 35; and *La Razón*, January 22, 1938, cited in Ruíz Jiménez, "Peronism and Anti-imperialism," 553.

18. Sarlo, *Una modernidad periférica* and "Modern City."

19. On working-class reading cultures in Argentina, see L. Romero, "Buenos Aires en la entreguerra." My own understanding of the influence of newspaper reading and rituals in shaping consciousness is indebted in large part to Martín-Barbero, *De los medios a las mediaciones*; Anderson, *Imagined Communities*; Debray, *Media Manifestos*; Henkin, *City Reading*; Lefebvre, *Critique of Everyday Life*; and Hardt, *In the Company of Media*.

20. Carey, "Problem of Journalism History," 92. On the notion of "structure of feeling," see Williams, *Marxism and Literature*, 128–38.

21. Waisbord, *Watchdog Journalism in South America*, 17; see also his "Media in South America."

22. On the relationship between the market-driven press and the diffusion and incorporation of dissidence with an emphasis on the British experience, see Curran, "Press as an Agency of Social Control"; and Curran, "Rethinking the Media."

23. Jürgen Habermas has long argued for that autonomy from state power plays a central role in the broader processes of political and social legitimation that take place through the institutions of social communication. Habermas, *Legitimation Crisis*.

24. Hallin, *We Keep America*, 11. For varying approaches to the media as an element in the reproduction of power relations in modern societies, see Althusser, "Ideology and Ideological State Apparatuses"; Martín-Barbero, *De los medios a las mediaciones*; Horkheimer and Adorno, "Culture Industry"; Williams, *Marxism and Literature*; and Antonio Gramsci's conceptions of hegemony and the state in *Selections from the Prison Notebooks*.

25. Historians' continued reliance upon the press as a window into social processes and political discourse is due in no small measure to the important insights that this approach continues to yield. See, for example, Sidicaro, *La política mirada desde arriba*; Ruíz Jiménez, "Peronism and Anti-imperialism"; Mazzei, *Los medios de comunicación y el golpismo*; Alonso, "Ideological Tensions"; the essays in Jaksić, *Political Power of the Word*; and the now classic study by Beatríz Sarlo, *El imperio de los sentimientos*. Two classic studies that move beyond this approach to engage the impact of changes in the form of journalism practice are Halperín Donghi, *José Hernández y sus mundos*; and Ramos, *Desencuentros de la modernidad*.

26. The embracing of this tendency, however, does not fully undermine the contributions of media scholars. See, for example, Lawson, *Building the Fourth Estate*; Hill and Hurley, "Freedom of the Press in Latin America"; Fromson, "Mexico's Struggle for a Free Press"; and Buckman, "Birth, Death, and Resurrection."

27. Nerone, *Violence Against the Press,: Policing the Public Sphere in U.S. History* (New York: Oxford University Press, 1994), 14–15.

28. Media historians Hanno Hardt and Bonnie Brennen are at the forefront in addressing this issue for the historiography of the United States. See in particular the essays collected in Hardt and Brennen, *Newsworkers*.

29. Much of this work has focused on Perón's relationship with organized labor and serves as a revision of the interpretation of Germani, *Política y sociedad*. See, for example, Murmis and Portantiero, *Estudios sobre los orígenes del peronismo*; Matsushita, *El movimiento obrero argentino*; Horowitz, *Argentine Unions*; Tamarin, *Argentine Labor Movement*; and Torre, *La vieja guardia sindical y Perón*. On the influence of the broader political environment of 1930–43 on the origins of Peronism, see Halperín Donghi, *Argentina en el callejón*; Buchrucker, *Nacionalismo y peronismo*; and Zanata, *Del estado liberal a la nación católica*.

30. Among those few works that consider the press policies of the Justo government, the most insightful remains Saítta, *Regueros de tinta*. As its title suggests, however, Saítta's study focuses on the previous decade, straying little beyond 1932 and the newspaper *Crítica*.

31. Peronism encapsulates in a single, heterogeneous movement not just the broad democratic opening common throughout much of Latin America in the immediate post–World War II years, but also the subsequent containment of that same process by the end of the 1940s. On the broader Latin American process, see Bethell and Roxborough, "Latin America"; and Grandin, *Last Colonial Massacre*. In her study of the institutionalization of the forces that brought Perón's electoral victory in 1946, Moira Mackinnon traces a parallel evolution toward a containment of the political opening of the immediate postwar years. Mackinnon, *Los años formativos*.

32. Here I follow Fredric Jameson's emphasis on the centrality of utopian impulses within political ideology. For Jameson, like Louis Althusser before him, the power of any ideology rests primarily in its relative capacity both to explain and provide an imagined resolution to lived social contradictions. See especially Jameson, *Political Unconscious*; and Althusser, "Ideology and Ideological State Apparatuses." For other studies that address this utopian aspect of Peronist appeal, see James, *Resistance and Integration*; Plotkin, *Mañana es San Perón*; Healey, *Ruins of the New Argentina*; Aboy, *Viviendas para el pueblo*; Gené, *Un mundo felíz*; and Elena, "Justice and Comfort."

33. See, in particular, Halperín Donghi, "El lugar del peronismo en la tradición política argentina"; Plotkin, "La 'ideología' de Perón: Continuidades y rupturas," in Amaral and Plotkin, *Perón*, 45–67; Plotkin, *Mañana es San Perón*; Laclau, *Politics and Ideology*; Sigal and Verón, *Perón o muerte*; and De Ipola, *Ideología y discurso populista*.

34. While I follow Laclau in asserting that the shattering of what remained of Argentina's liberal consensus in the ideological crises of the 1930s allowed early Peronism to reassemble the fragments of liberalism in new combinations, with regard to the commercial press—and the case of *La Prensa* in particular—Perón did not progressively seek to discredit liberalism itself as a mere pretext for the oligachy's excercise of class power in the manner that Laclau implies. Instead, Perón continued to point to the gap between liberal theory and liberal practice, deploying notions of Peronism as the practical realization of the egalitarian ideals that undergirded liberal discourse as instruments in specific struggles. Laclau, *Politics and Ideology*, 189. On Perón's navigation between Argentine liberalism and nationalism, see Winston, "Between Rosas and Sarmiento."

35. The circulation of *La Vanguardia* stood at 70,000 copies in 1945, equal to that of *El Mercurio* of Santiago de Chile and *El Tiempo* of Bogotá, Colombia. *Editor and Publisher, International Year Book Number for 1946*, 296, 303–4. On *La Vanguardia* and its place within the early socialist press, see Walter, "Socialist Press."

36. Throughout this work I follow the Argentine usage: "Buenos Aires" and "city of Buenos Aires" refer to the zone of the Federal Capital; "Greater Buenos Aires" refers to the urban conglomeration outside of but surrounding the Federal Capital (e.g., Avellaneda, Quilmes, San Isidro); "province of Buenos Aires" includes all territory of that province, but does not include the federal district of the city of Buenos Aires. Residents of the Federal Capital are typically called *porteños*.

37. Substantive analyses of the commercial press of the province of Buenos Aires in the Peronist period can be found in Quiroga, "Prensa comercial y organización"; and Llull, *Prensa y política en Bahía Blanca*. For a view of disputes surrounding quasi-partisan provincial journalism, see Neiburg, "Intimacy and the Public Sphere."

38. The consequences of this distinction form the basis for the arguments of Pellet Lastra, *La libertad de expression*.

39. For some discussion of the fate of Argentine radio under Perón, see Sirvén, *Perón y los medios de comunicación*; Matallana, *Locos por la radio*; Claxton, *From Parsifal to Perón*; Haussen, *Rádio e política*; and Merkin et al., *Días de radio*, 153–63. More general surveys of Argentine radio history are Sarlo, *La imaginación técnica*; Ford and Rivera, "Los medios masivos de comunicación"; Gallo, *La radio*.

40. These criticisms of the distorting influence of commercial interests on the press as fora of public expression not only came from across the ideological spectrum, but many foreshadowed in important ways elements of the argument presented Habermas, *Structural Transformation of the Public Sphere*.

41. For recent studies of Argentine political philosophy in the 1930s, see Halperín Donghi, *La Argentina y la tormenta del mundo*; Halperín Donghi, *La República imposible*; Loris Zanata, *Del estado liberal a la nación católica*; Nállim, "Crisis of Liberalism"; Tato, *Viento de Fronda*; De Privitellio, *Vecinos y ciudadanos*; the corresponding sections of Sebreli, *Crítica de las ideas políticas argentinas*.

42. James, *Resistance and Integration*, 16, and see generally 14–21. The literature devoted to the question of changing forms of citizenship in Latin America is small but growing. See, for example, Whitehead, "Note on Citizenship," as well as the essays in Sabato, *Ciudadanía política y formación*, and Guerra and Lempèriére, *Los espacios públicos en Iberoamérica*. On Argentina specifically, see Sábato, *La política en las calles*; Karush, *Workers or Citizens*; and Elena, "What the People Want."

43. Much of the work in media studies surrounding the relationship between the media and citizenship focuses less on representation and expression in the media than on political manipulation through the media, or, alternatively, on questions of information access. For notable but partial exceptions, see the essays in Dahlgren and Sparks, *Communication and Citizenship*, especially Dahlgren's introduction, 1–26, and Curran, "Rethinking the Media as a Public Sphere."

44. Perelman, *Como hicimos el 17 de Octubre*, 55.

45. Halperín Donghi, *Argentina en el callejón*, 90.

CHAPTER I

1. Sindicato de Prensa Argentina, *Anuario de prensa argentina*.

2. Greenup and Greenup, *Revolution Before Breakfast*, 223.

3. Clemenceau, *South America Today*, 196; Blasco Ibáñez, *Argentina y sus grandezas*, 411–12.

4. The rise of the ideal of objectivity in United States journalism takes a slightly more linear course than in Argentina, and many of the "serious" Argentine newspapers contain elements modeled on U.S. newspapers. See Schudson, *Discovering the News*; Leonard, *Power of the Press*; and Kaplan, *Politics and the American Press*.

5. On the financial problems of newspaper production in the years of partisan journalism, see in particular Halperín Donghi, *José Hernández y sus mundos*; Galván Moreno, *El periodismo argentino*; Ulanovsky, *Paren las rotativas*; Marco, *Bartolomé Mitre*; and Marco, *Historia del periodismo argentino*.

6. There is an essential continuity in the general liberal "heroic" narrative found in Fernández, *Historia del periodismo argentino*; Galván Moreno, *El periodismo argentino*; Barreiro, *La libertad de prensa*; Gainza Paz, *Por defender la libertad*; as well as in the more recent work by Trotti, *La dolorosa libertad de prensa*; and Ulanovsky, *Paren las rotativas*.

7. Myers, "Las paradojas de la opinion," 75.

8. On the press of the colonial period and the first years of the republic, see Medina, *Historia y bibliografía;* Santa Coloma, *La prensa argentina,* 33–58; and Galván Moreno, *El periodismo argentino,* 19–51.

9. The "Day of the Journalist," established at the initial meeting of the Federación Argentina de Periodistas in 1938 and later declared a press holiday in 1946, is still celebrated on June 7, the day that the *Gazeta de Buenos-Ayres* first appeared. "Primer Congreso Nacional de Periodistas: Primera Sesión Plenaria. Córdoba, 26 de Mayo de 1938: Versión taquigráfica," in Palazzolo, *Diez años de organización sindical,* 61.

10. Cited in Mayer, *El derecho público de prensa,* 73.

11. Ibid., 73–74.

12. Ibid., 71. Funes' influence within the revolutionary process in Argentina is discussed by Halperín Donghi, "Colonial *Letrado.*"

13. The political instability of the independence years only adds more uncertainty to the definitions—both descriptive and normative—of the "public sphere" in the rebellious colonies. For convincing arguments for the emergence of a public sphere in the Río de la Plata and beyond, see Chiaramonte, "Ciudadanía, soberanía y representación"; Myers, *Orden y virtud,* especially 26–34; Guerra and Lempèriére, *Los espacios públicos en Iberoamérica;* and Uribe-Urán, "Birth of the Public Sphere."

14. Recent studies of conflict-ridden nature of the rearticulation of Church/state relations in the course of independence include Di Stefano, Calvo, and Gallo, *Los curas de la revolución;* Stefano, *El púlpito y la plaza,* 93–133; and Bianchi, *Historia de las religions,* 17–39.

15. Mayer, *El derecho público de prensa,* 91–94; Myers, *Orden y virtud,* 26.

16. On the ideological origins of the April 1811 decree, see Mayer, *El derecho público de prensa,* 76. On revisions by the junta affecting libel and disruption of public peace, see Pellet Lastra, *La libertad de expresión,* 38–39.

17. Mayer, *El derecho público de prensa,* 95–97.

18. Myers, *Orden y virtud,* remains the best study of the republican discourse within the pro-Rosas press. See also Beltrán, *Historia del periodismo argentino,* 187–210.

19. A brief survey of journalism practice by Argentine exiles like Sarmiento, Mitre, Florencio Varela, Valentín Alsina, Miguel Cané, Esteban Echeverría, and Juan Bautista Alberdi in Uruguay and Chile is found in Beltrán, *Historia del periodismo argentino,* 211–24. Forサrmiento and Mitre's journalism in exile, see, respectively, Jaksić, "Sarmiento and the Chilean Press"; and Marco, *Bartolomé Mitre,* 72–73 and 81–102.

20. In *El Mercurio,* 1841, cited in Jaksić, "Sarmiento and the Chilean Press," 31.

21. Cited in Mayer, *El derecho público de prensa,* 137–38.

22. Ibid., 138.

23. Alberdi's antecedent appeared as art. 16 of chap. 2 of his draft constitution. It did not contain the phrase "in conformity with the laws that regulate its exercise," and also more explicitly extended the *libertad de imprenta* and other constitutional rights to foreign residents. See Pellet Lastra, *La libertad de expresión,* 48.

24. The offense of *calumnia* consisted in false and public accusation of punishable criminal activity. To qualify as *calumnia,* the accusation had to be false and the author of the accusation had to be aware of its falsity. *Injuria,* on the other hand, consisted of the far more amorphous offense of dishonoring or diminishing the reputation of a person through language that exceeded the limits of "good culture." In contrast to *calumnia,* accusations that were *injuriosas* could be so regardless of their truth, since the crime was one of purposeful offense, or *animus injuriandi. Desacato,* finally, consisted of offending a public official's dignity in the exercise of his or her office. The crime of *desacato* largely amounted to *injuria* directed at a public official, with the added consequence that it affected not only the individual named, but the dignity of the office with which he or she was invested. Accusations of an official's incompetence, however, did not qualify as *desacato,* unless made with *animus injuriandi.* These offenses became arts. 109, 110, and 224 of the revised Penal Code of 1921, respectively. See Mayer, *El derecho público de prensa,* 295–311.

25. See ibid., 152–64.
26. Pellet Lastra, *La libertad de expresión*, 50.
27. Ibid., 47–66.
28. The 1910 Ley de Defensa Social is a case in point. This federal law specifically criminalized "incitement to commit a crime" through the press, as well as other equally serious violations. It was designed as a repressive measure against the surge in anarchist activities, but the Argentine Supreme Court did eventually establish the law as constitutional. Yet even this did not end debate, and these measures were incorporated in a more general way into the 1921 revision of the Penal Code, thereby restoring the precedent of considering these as not as crimes particularly *of* the press, but as common crimes committed *through* the press. See Pellet Lastra, *La libertad de expresión*, 94–95; Santa Coloma, *La prensa argentina*, 153–58.
29. See the classic studies by Botana, *El orden conservador*; and Halperín Donghi, "1880"; as well as the more recent work by Needell, "Optimism and Melancholy"; Salvatore, "Normalization of Economic Life"; Rock, *State Building and Political Movements*; and the preliminary studies in Botana and Gallo, *De la República posible*; and Halperín Donghi, *Vida y muerte*.
30. Here I use the term "factional journalism" as a translation of *periodismo faccioso* rather than the more common English "partisan press" or "political press." The latter expressions do not quite capture the complexity of political fragmentation in the nineteenth-century press, in which specific factions and informal political currents formed the terms of political reference to a greater degree than did more organized political associations. See Halperín Donghi, *José Hernández y sus mundos*; Duncan, "La prensa política." On a regional level, see Alonso, *Construcciones impresas*; and Jaksić, *Political Power of the Word*.
31. On the functioning of the press and its relationship to the broader public sphere in Buenos Aires at this time, see Lettieri, *La república de la opinión*; Halperín Donghi, *José Hernández y sus mundos*; Sabato, *La política en las calles*.
32. Halperín Donghi, *José Hernández y sus mundos*, 26–28, 145.
33. See Marco, *Bartolomé Mitre*, 371–74.
34. For a brief but clear discussion of models of journalism practice in South America, see Waisbord, *Watchdog Journalism in South America*, 8–14.
35. In this, the establishment of liberal hegemony in Argentina after 1880 created a situation analogous to the establishment of the bourgeois constitutional state in Britain, France, and the United States in the 1830s. Habermas, *Structural Transformation of the Public Sphere*, 184.
36. *La Prensa*, October 18, 1869.
37. The significance of layout changes in the transition to commercial journalism is discussed in Barnhurst and Nerone, *Form of News*.
38. *La Prensa*, September 24, 1874.
39. In his 1920 report for the U.S. Department of Commerce, J. W. Sanger points to the following incident as an indicator of the class difference between readers of *La Prensa* and *La Nación*: "A well-known encyclopedia used, among other media, both *La Prensa* and *La Nación*. From the start, the latter led, nearly all its sales being cash sales. *La Prensa* ran a very poor second until 'pay day' for Argentina came, whereupon *La Prensa* coupons began to pour in, nearly all, however, being for the purchase of the set of books on the installment plan. In the final accounting *La Prensa* was found to have led all other media." Sanger, *Advertising Methods*, 22.
40. Rojas Paz, "La prensa argentina," 264; *Editor and Publisher, International Year Book Number for 1947*, 310–12. Because circulation figures for newspapers in this period are sometimes inconsistent, I have chosen to use the generally more conservative figures presented before the American Society of Newspaper Editors, since these numbers were verified by independent observers for the calculation of advertising rates.
41. Rojas Paz, "La prensa argentina," 264.

42. Morris, *Deadline Every Minute*, 107.
43. Ibid., 108. See also Fenby, *International News Services*, 46.
44. Garrison and Salwen, *Latin American Journalism*, 87. Joe Morris also argues that United Press's initial dependence on *La Prensa* played a key role in shaping the kind of reporting that the agency produced: "The Buenos Aires paper required a comprehensive type of news coverage which was not yet popular among UP clients in the USA. Thus *La Prensa* gave the service its first major outlet for dispatches treating vital international problems in a thorough and detailed manner, which had not always been typical of the UP coverage. The acquisition of a large and important client always had an impact on the reporting and writing of the men who produced the UP news report. Now the service had to adjust its approach by putting more emphasis on solid 'think stuff' in order to hold its contract with Don Ezequiel Paz. *La Prensa* was a hard, if well-paying task-master. It never relaxed. The UP had to earn its big fees from Buenos Aires, and in doing so it became a far more substantial and comprehensive press association in North America and, eventually, throughout the world." Morris, *Deadline Every Minute*, 109.
45. Morris, *Deadline Every Minute*, 146.
46. The statue, placed on the building in 1900, is still visible today, and the building itself houses the municipal Casa de la Cultura.
47. Blasco Ibáñez, *Argentina y sus grandezas*, 411–12.
48. Clemenceau, *South America Today*, 196.
49. *La Nación*, January 4, 1870.
50. Ibid. Also cited in a special forty-five-page pamphlet in commemoration of the paper's seventy-fifth anniversary, "Como fue fundada *La Nación*," *La Nación*, January 4, 1945.
51. On the role of *La Nación* as a means of support for the Partido Repúblicano, see Zimmermann, "La prensa."
52. Cited in Sidicaro, *La política mirada desde arriba*, 17.
53. The 1890 revolt marked the last significant national insurrection from within the Argentine elite until 1930, though the sustained electoral abstentionism of the Unión Cívica Radical (UCR) had left further uprisings a possibility. See Rock, *Politics in Argentina*; Halperín Donghi, "Estudio preliminar"; Persello, *El Partido Radical*.
54. Sidicaro, *La política mirada desde arriba*, 19.
55. Sidicaro convincingly argues that, despite the heterogeneity of the *La Nación* editorial board over time, the editorial column does unify those writers into an institutionally based "collective intellectual," thereby depersonalizing the texts of the paper's forums of opinion. Sidicaro, *La política mirada desde arriba*, 520.
56. *Editor and Publisher, International Year Book Number for 1936*, 244–46; *International Year Book Number for 1946*, 294–96.
57. With 210,000 copies daily, Rio de Janeiro's *A Noite* maintained the highest circulation of any Latin American newspaper outside of Argentina in 1946, followed by Mexico City's *La Prensa* at 135,000 copies daily. *Editor and Publisher, International Year Book Number for 1946*, 294–96.
58. *La Nación* was housed on San Martín 344–50 from 1885 to 1929, when it moved to a larger building at Florida 337–47.
59. See Mitre, *"La Nación" y the Associated Press;* Garrison and Salwen, *Latin American Journalism*, 86–87; Morris, *Deadline Every Minute*, 106–7; and Fenby, *International News Services*, 46.
60. On the life of Natalio Botana, perhaps the most fascinating and influential figure in all of mid-twentieth-century Latin American journalism, see Abós, *El tábano*. Botana's equally fascinating wife is the subject of Barrandeguy, *Salvadora;* and Abós, "La Venus Roja."
61. *Crítica* in its golden years forms the subject of the most innovative and detailed of the recent studies of the Argentine press, Saítta, *Regueros de tinta*. See also Senén González and Welp, "Crítica."

62. The extension of suffrage realized through Sáenz Peña Law profoundly altered working class politics and introduced new dilemmas for the more radicalized sectors of labor. See Karush, *Workers or Citizens;* Adelman, "Socialism and Democracy."

63. Reproduced in *Crítica,* September 15, 1927.

64. Saítta, *Regueros de tinta,* 50.

65. Botana and the *Crítica* journalists proclaimed these factors, rather than any failings in journalistic model or practice, as the cause for the paper's precarious finances prior to the 1920s. *Crítica,* September 15, 1927.

66. Raúl González Tuñón, in Salas, *Conversaciones con Raúl González Tuñón,* 53; and González Tuñón, "Crítica y los Años 20."

67. For a revealing analysis of *Crítica* crime reporting in the 1920s, see Caimari, *Apenas un delincuente,* 199–218.

68. See Saítta, *Regueros de tinta,* especially 55–90.

69. Ibid., 73.

70. On the move to the building at Avenida de Mayo 1333, see the multiple issues dedicated to the event in *Crítica,* September 1–15, 1927. *Editor and Publisher, International Year Book Number for 1928,* 290.

71. Among the journalist memoirs and other writings in which Natalio Botana figures prominently are Tálice, *100.000 ejemplares por hora;* Tálice, *El Malevo Muñoz;* Godoy Froy, *Perfiles de Roberto A. Tálice;* Tiempo, *Mi tío Scholem Aleijem;* Huberman, *Hasta el alba con Ulyses Petit de Murat;* Martínez Cuitiño, *El café de Los Inmortales;* Moncalvillo, *Conversaciones con Edmundo Guibourg;* Petorruti, *Un pintor ante el espejo;* Saldías, *La inolvidable bohemia porteña;* Salas, *Conversaciones con Raúl González Tuñón;* González Tuñón, "Crítica y los Años 20"; Nalé Roxlo, *Borrador de memorias;* Llano, *La aventura del periodismo.* Helvio Botana, who periodically assumed joint direction of *Crítica* after his father's death, has also published *Memorias.* See also the images of Botana as master in the "hell for journalists" in Leopoldo Marechal's novel *Adán Buenosayres,* 491–96. Roberto Arlt's intended novel based on Botana's life was written more than sixty years later by Pedro Orgambide, *El escriba.*

72. Raimundo "Calki" Calcagno, film critic with *El Mundo,* recounts his confrontation with his paper's director after writing a negative review of the Baires studio's first release. Carlos Muzio Sáenz Peña informed him that yes, journalists should not distort their own opinions, "but sometimes there are special circumstances, like this one. And you, before writing this review, should have come to consult with me.... This is not a common case: this is the first production by Botana, who has *Crítica* behind him. They employ other methods to impose things. They are like gunmen." All of the other newspapers carried laudatory reviews of the film, and Calcagno saw himself faced with the option of writing a second, positive review or losing his job. Calki, *"El Mundo" era una fiesta,* 51.

73. On the controversies surrounding the mural—which continue today—see Abós, *Cautivo.*

74. Neruda, *Confieso que he vivido,* 161–62.

75. *Editor and Publisher, International Year Book Number for 1936,* 244–46.

76. Haynes had arrived in Argentina in 1877 as an employee of the British-owned Ferrocarril Gran Oeste Argentino. Ulanovsky, *Paren las rotativas,* 27. That much of the stock of Editorial Haynes remained in the hands of the British railway companies ultimately facilitated Perón's eventual takeover of *El Mundo* and Editorial Haynes's radio and magazines: the transfer of ownership took place with the Argentine government's nationalization of the country's rail system. "Powers Reports on Advertising in Argentina," *Editor and Publisher,* February 14, 1948. See chapter 6 below.

77. Fernández, López Barros, and Petris, "*El Mundo* condensado/r e ilustrado/r," 2.

78. *Editor and Publisher, International Year Book Number for 1936,* 244–46; *International Year Book Number for 1946,* 294–96.

79. On the conflicts in the *Jornada/Crítica* newsroom, and the subsequent conflicts between *Noticias Gráficas* and *Crítica*, see Saítta, *Regueros de tinta*, 21, 253–54; and Saítta, "*Crítica* en los años '30."

80. Secretaría de la Presidencia, "Diario 'Noticias Gráficas,'" Archivo General de la Nación, Archivo Augustín P. Justo (cited hereafter as AGN, Justo), box 37, doc. 19.

81. *Editor and Publisher, International Year Book Number for 1936*, 244–46; *International Yearbook Number for 1946*, 294–96.

82. Prieto, *El discurso criollista*; *Editor and Publisher, International Year Book Number for 1928*, 290–300.

83. *Editor and Publisher, International Year Book Number for 1928*, 290–92.

84. *Editor and Publisher, International Year Book Number for 1936*, 17, 19, 244–46, 265.

85. *Editor and Publisher, International Year Book Number for 1946*, 295–316.

86. Even before the 1928 appearance of the tabloid-size *El Mundo*, the newspaper *Crítica* published instructions and diagrams detailing how to fold *Crítica* in order to facilitate reading on buses, trains, and streetcars and in theaters. *Crítica*, September 5, 1927.

87. Sanger, *Advertising Methods*, 13–15. Argentina maintained a per capita GDP roughly three times greater than that of Brazil between 1900 and 1929, and on par with Italy, Austria, and Norway. Solomon, *Transformation of the World Economy*, 178. Wealth in Argentina also remained geographically concentrated in the Federal Capital.

88. Martín-Barbero, *De los medios a las mediaciones*, 135, 155. See also the pathbreaking discussion of the historical evolution of United States' newspaper advertising in Ewen, *Captains of Consciousness*.

89. Lefebvre, *Everyday Life in the Modern World*, 107.

90. Galván Moreno, *El periodismo argentino*, 218.

91. *Crítica*, September 12, 1927.

92. *Crítica*, September 2, 1927. The poem is reproduced in Tálice, *100.000 ejemplares por hora*, 130–32; and Saítta, *Regueros de tinta*, 80–81.

93. Di Tella, *Perón y los sindicatos*, 154.

94. Journalist and playwright Florencio Sánchez christened news vendors with this name in his 1904 play *Canillita*, in reference to the thin legs exposed by the vendors' short pants. On the conditions of vendors in Montevideo, see Baletti Bianchi, *Mirando vivir a los canillitas*; and on Chicago news vendors, see Bekken, "Crumbs from the Publishers' Golden Tables."

95. H. Botana, *Memorias*, 99.

96. For a summary of the strike, see ibid., *Memorias*, 96–100; Saítta, *Regueros de tinta*, 57–60; and Abós, *El tábano*, 119–21.

97. Rama, *La ciudad letrada*, 122–23.

98. Halperín Donghi, *José Hernández y sus mundos*, 145. On the influence journalism on the course of Argentine literature, in addition to Halperín's work on José Hernández see Prieto, *El discurso criollista*; Sarlo, *El imperio de los sentimientos*; and Saítta, *El escritor en el bosque de ladrillos*.

99. See Rivera, "Los juegos de un tímido." Borges' contributions to the *Revista Multicolor* are compiled in Borges, *Obras, reseñas y traducciones inédita*.

100. On Martí the journalist, see Julio Ramos, "Límites de la Autonomía: Periodismo y Literatura," in *Desencuentros de la modernidad*, 82–111.

101. Sidicaro, *La política mirada desde arriba*, 521.

102. Roberto Tálice, *100.000 ejemplares por hora*, 144.

103. Martínez Estrada, *Radiografía de la pampa*, 245.

104. Marechal, *Adán Buenosayres*, 492. Marechal began the novel in 1927 while a journalist at *Crítica*, though the work was not published until 1948.

105. Ibid., 493.

106. Círculo de la Prensa, *Anuario 1996*, 3.

107. Ibid., 3–4; Fernández, *Historia del periodismo argentino*, 201.

108. For example, during the second Yrigoyen presidency (1928–30), the Círculo de la Prensa dedicated significant energy to defending the prerogatives of publishers in the provinces of San Juan (then under federal intervention) and Santiago del Estero. Círculo de la Prensa, *Memoria y Balance, 1928–1929*, 8–9.

109. By 1942 the school boasted ninety-eight students, more than a third of them women. Fernández, *Historia del periodismo argentino*, 203.

110. *La Prensa*, October 19, 1925.

111. Ibid.

112. *La Prensa*, October 19, 1920.

113. Ibid.

114. Angel Bohigas, "El Discurso de D. Ángel Bohigas," in Diario 'La Nación,' *La Nación*, 15–16.

115. *La Prensa*, October 19, 1920; Bohigas, "El Discurso de D. Ángel Bohigas," 16.

116. Siebert, Peterson, and Schramm, *Four Theories of the Press*, 4. This convergence of the so-called libertarian theory of the press between sectors of the Argentine press and that of the United States and Great Britain, however, was neither coincidental nor one-sided. In fact, the Inter American Press Association adopted Ezequiel Paz's 1925 articulation of the idealized role of the journalist as an impersonal conduit of objective information, enshrining it as the journalist's code of ethics at the height of the Perón–*La Prensa* dispute in 1950. Napp, *Para la historia del periodismo*, 292; Gainza Paz, *Por defender la libertad*, 41.

117. Among the abundant examples is the particularly macabre and self-promotional celebration of *Crítica*'s high circulation after the revelation that that one of its journalists had died while investigating a kidnapping case. The following day the paper dedicated nearly a full page to describing its own coverage of the case, proclaiming that "all of the city yesterday was a showcase for CRITICA. It was in all hands, in all parts, at all times." *Crítica*, October 9, 1932.

118. *Crítica*, September 1, 1927.

119. *Crítica*, April 18, 1923. Cited in Saítta, *Regueros de tinta*, 61.

120. *Crítica*, September 1, 1927 (emphasis added).

CHAPTER 2

1. On the Unión Cívica Radical, see Rock, *Politics in Argentina*; Persello, *El Partido Radical*. On the Argentine Right, see Rock, *Authoritarian Argentina*; Deutsch, *Las Derechas*; Tato, *Viento de Fronda*; Deutsch and Dolkart, *Argentine Right*; and Buchrucker, *Nacionalismo y peronismo*.

2. Ibarguren, *La historia que he vivido*, 384, 386, 404.

3. On attempts to build a nationalist project centered on the figure of Uriburu, see Finchelstein, *Fascismo, liturgia e imaginario*.

4. Plotkin, *Mañana es San Perón*, 19–41. On the broader implications of this crisis, see Halperín Donghi, *La República imposible* and *La Argentina en la tormenta del mundo*; J. Romero, *Las ideas en la Argentina del siglo XX*; Zanata, *Del estado liberal*; Jorge Nállim, "Crisis of Liberalism in Argentina"; and Buchrucker, *Nacionalismo y peronismo*.

5. On the tangled web of partisan political intrigue surrounding "patriotic fraud," see Sanguinetti, *La democracia ficta*; Ciria, *Partidos y poder*; Walter, *Province of Buenos Aires*, 114–96; Béjar, *El régimen fraudulento*; and Persello, *El Partido Radical*.

6. Halperín Donghi, *La República imposible* and *La Argentina en la tormenta del mundo*, 14.

7. State-of-siege provisions were invoked four times after the coups of September 1930 and June 1943, the final time beginning in December 1941 and lasting through the final days of World War II. Pellet Lastra, *La libertad de expresión*, 107–8.

8. Saítta, *Regueros de tinta*, 225–27.

9. *Crítica*, August 7, 1927. On the Partido Socialista Independiente, see Sanguinetti, *Los socialistas independientes*.

10. Botana had originally placed *Crítica* in a stridently oppositional position during the first government of the incredibly popular Yrigoyen (1916–22), a fact that likely did little to aid the paper's struggling finances. In 1928, however, it appeared that only Yrigoyen could halt the victory of a broad Conservative coalition that promoted the candidacy of Leopoldo Melo. Abós, *El tábano*, 152.

11. See, for example, the political cartoon "¿No oye o no quiere oir?," in which a frail Yrigoyen is literally incapable of understanding the shouts of "Down with Yrigoyen" and "Revolution" coming from his radio. *Crítica*, September 3, 1930.

12. See accounts in *Crítica*, September 8, 1930; H. Botana, *Memorias*, 58; Tálice, *100.000 ejemplares por hora*, 504–17.

13. Tálice, *100.000 ejemplares por hora*, 511.

14. *Crítica*, September 7–21, 1930; *Crítica*, November 2, 1930.

15. Tálice, *100.000 ejemplares por hora*, 524.

16. *Crítica*, October 25, 1930.

17. *Crítica*, October 28, 1930.

18. "Edmundo Guibourg a Natalio Botana. París, 15 de noviembre de 1930," AGN, Archivo General Uriburu, box 17, doc. 51, reproduced in García Molina and Mayo, *Archivo del general Uriburu*, 2:209–10. Leopoldo Lugones Jr. was the son of the famed Argentine poet.

19. H. Botana, *Memorias*, 63.

20. In keeping with state-of-siege restrictions, the paper printed no commentary to the text of a key Uriburu speech in December 1930. Instead, the headline of the text reads simply, "Disquieting Declarations Made in Speech Today by General José F. Uriburu." *Crítica*, December 18, 1930.

21. Secretaría de la Presidencia, "Memoria Sintética Sobre Funcionamiento de la 'Sección Prensa,'" AGN, Justo, box 37, doc. 18.

22. *Crítica*, April 15, 1931.

23. Círculo de la Prensa, *Memoria y Balance, 1930–1931*, 12.

24. See *Crítica*, April 23–25, 1931.

25. Círculo de la Prensa, *Memoria y Balance, 1930–1931*, 13; *La Nación*, May 7, 1931.

26. Saítta, *Regueros de tinta*, 249; Abós, *El tábano*, 220.

27. H. Botana, *Memorias*, 63–64, 69.

28. Ibid., 69; Abós, *El tábano*, 234.

29. *Jornada*, September 11, 1931.

30. *Jornada*, October 31, 1931; *Jornada*, October 21, 1931.

31. Fraga, *El General Justo*, 286–87.

32. H. Botana, *Memorias*, 150.

33. Ibid., 169–70; Fraga, *El General Justo*, 337–38.

34. See, for example, *Crítica*, November 16, 1933.

35. In his memoirs, exile Francisco Ayala remarks that Botana paid extravagantly for minimal work, both as a way of supporting the exiled intellectuals as well as generating an identification of *Crítica* with the Republican cause. Ayala, *Recuerdos y olvidos*, 272–73. For Córdova Iturburu's coverage of Spain, see the compilation Córdova Iturburu, *España bajo el comando del pueblo*. On the paper's overall portrayal of the conflict, see Montenegro, "La Guerra Civil Española y la política argentina," 211–36.

36. Journalist Francisco Luís Llano, for example, would later recall that Botana made the struggle of Spanish Republicans "his struggle," and casually—and privately—donated the full sum for the purchase of an airplane for the Republicans. Llano, *La aventura del periodismo*, 95. Journalist Ulyses Petit de Murat, similarly, claims that Botana's adherence to the cause of the Spanish Republic and anti-Fascism more generally revealed the *Crítica* owner's "absolute romanticism and great respect for the dignity of man." Huberman, *Hasta el alba con Ulyses Petit de Murat*, 58.

37. See Walter, *Province of Buenos Aire*, 127–41.
38. On the conflict between Lugones Jr. and Botana, see Saítta, *Regueros de tinta*, 258–62; and Abós, *El tábano*, 220–33.
39. Dolkart, "Right in the Década Infame," 83–84.
40. H. Botana, *Memorias*, 112–13.
41. *Crítica*, October 11, 1932; *Crítica*, October 14, 1932.
42. *Crítica*, October 14, 1932.
43. *Crítica*, August 19, 26, 28, and 31, 1932; *Crítica*, September 20, 1932.
44. *Crítica*, September 23, 24, 26 and 28, 1932; *Crítica*, October 4 and 12, 1932.
45. "Nota del Ministro de Agricultura Antonio de Tomaso al Presidente Augustín P. Justo," AGN, Justo, box 37, doc. 26.
46. Ibid.
47. *Crítica*, May 12 and June 14, 1934.
48. Antonio de Tomaso died unexpectedly in August 1933. "Nota de Ulyses Petit de Murat al General Justo," in AGN, Justo, box 37, doc. 24; "Asunto ARSA c/ Botana," in AGN, Justo, box 37, doc. 25.
49. "Proyecto de Organización de un Diario. Entregado por Pérez Ircoreca/Ercoreca [sic] y Garay Díaz," in AGN, Justo, box 37, doc. 23.
50. Ibid.
51. "Proyecto de Organización de un Diario," in AGN, Justo, box 37, doc. 22. This document is the confidential evaluation of the project (document 23) submitted by the *El Mundo* journalists.
52. Ibid.
53. Ibid.
54. *La Época*, December 14, 1945. While the articles in *La Época* are clearly intended to discredit *La Razón*'s 1940s "proprietor," Ricardo Peralta Ramos, they do largely concord with documentation in the Archivo Augustín P. Justo, and are likely based upon documents found in the Central Bank in mid-1945.
55. Newton, *Nazi Menace*, 123.
56. "Memorandum. La Razón," in AGN, Justo, box 37, doc. 15. Félix Laíño, who would become *La Razón*'s editor-in-chief in 1937, remarks that upon his arrival at the paper in 1935, Peralta Ramos began a study of newsroom operations. "Félix Laíño: 45% de publicidad y 55% de texto," in Rivera and Romano, *Claves del periodismo argentino actual*, 192–230.
57. *Editor and Publisher, International Year Book Number for 1936*, 244–46; "Memorandum. La Razón," in AGN, Justo, box 37, doc. 15.
58. "Memorandum. La Razón," in AGN, Justo, box 37, doc. 15. The evaluator advised that the primary owner of the newspaper withdrew substantial sums of money from the *La Razón* operating budget, and that instead "Mrs. H. de Cortejarena should receive what is set for her ... and she should stay peacefully at home, until such time as the situation of the newspaper has improved."
59. *La Razón*'s cost of production had peaked at $4,050,069 in 1931–32, even though net income had peaked at $832,486 three years earlier. For March 1935–March 1936, total cost of production stood at $2,620,306, while net income had fallen to $194,652. Together with the mounting debt, the precipitous fall in income after 1933 surely triggered the paper's financial crisis. Ibid.
60. Ibid.; *La Época*, October 24, 1945; *La Época*, December 14, 1945; *Democracia*, March 2, 1946; Walsh, *Caso Satanowsky*, 22.
61. "Memorandum. La Razón," in Archivo Justo, box 37, document 15.
62. *El Laborista*, October 4, 1946.
63. *La Época*, October 24, 1945; Newton, *Nazi Menace*, 123.
64. Comisión Nacional de Investigaciones, *Documentación, autores y cómplices*, 1:536–38; *Editor and Publisher, International Year Book Number for 1946*, 294–96.
65. Although several right-wing newspapers like *La Fronda, Crisol*, and *Bandera Argentina* did report links between Botana, Justo, and Pinedo, these newspapers maintained

limited circulation that did not overlap with the readership of *Crítica*. I have seen no evidence of reporting of the issue in any of the major commercial newspapers.

66. On the generation of consensus around an expanding role for the state in Argentine economic and social life across much of the political spectrum in the 1930s and early 1940s, see Halperín Donghi, *La república imposible*, 133–51; Béjar, *Uriburu y Justo*; Plotkin, *Mañana es San Perón*, 27–30; Sidicaro, *Los tres peronismos*, 25–54; Díaz Alejandro, *Ensayos sobre la historia económica argentina*; Cramer, "Argentine Riddle"; Horowitz, *Argentine Unions*; Belini, "El Grupo Bunge"; and Zanatta, *Del estado liberal*.

67. Secretaría de la Presidencia, "Memoria Sintética Sobre Funcionamiento de la 'Sección Prensa,'" AGN, Justo, box 37, doc. 18. This document is an early Justo-era evaluation of the Sección Prensa.

68. Ibid. This definition appears as a direct quote from an earlier document establishing the Sección Prensa.

69. Ibid.

70. Ibid.

71. Ibid.

72. Secretaría de la Presidencia, "Diario 'Noticias Gráficas,'" AGN, Justo, box 37, doc. 19.

73. Among the memoranda prepared through the Sección Prensa, see the two documents from mid-1932: "Memorandum de Prensa. Crítica. Buenos Aires," AGN, Justo, box 36, doc. 7; and "Memorandum de Prensa. Noticias Gráficas. Buenos Aires," AGN, Justo, box 36, doc. 6.

74. More ambitiously, the authors of the project also hoped to create an "Anti-Marxist Institute" that would bring together intellectuals closely associated with Argentine Nationalists like Monseñor de Andrea, Monseñor Franceschi, and Gustavo Martínez Zuviría. "Proyecto de Campaña Anti-Marxista," AGN, Justo, box 49, doc. 66.

75. Secretaría de la Presidencia, "Memoria Sintética Sobre Funcionamiento de la 'Sección Prensa,'" AGN, Justo, box 37, doc. 18.

76. República Argentina, Ministerio del Interior, *Memoria del Ministerio del Interior, 1936–1937*, 96. The centralization of government advertising had been enacted by decree on December 2, 1930, and had figured as a key element in the project for the Sección Prensa's formalization under Justo.

77. Kinkelín emerged as the primary military figure associated with the Nationalist movement, and became head of the brownshirted Legión Cívica in the early 1930s.

78. Comisión Pro Ley de Prensa, *Proyecto de ley del Senador Sánchez Sorondo, de Amparo de la Prensa* (Buenos Aires: Imprenta del Congreso, 1934), 9.

79. Ibid., 8.

80. Ibid., 7–8.

81. Ibid., 6–7; 12; Mayer, *El derecho público de prensa*, 71.

82. These offenses would remain largely confined to those of *calumnia* (libel), *injuria* (insult), *desacato* (contempt of a public official), and sedition.

83. Articles 3, 12, and 13 in Comisión Pro Ley de Prensa, *Proyecto de ley del Senador Sánchez Sorondo, de Amparo de la Prensa*, 3–4.

84. Articles 11, 16–18, and 21 in ibid., 4.

85. Ibid., 8.

86. Ibid., 6, 14.

87. On the multiple cases, see *Crisol*, September 8–10 and 23, 1933; *Crisol*, October 1, 5, 10, 11, and 31, 1933; *Crisol*, November 15 and 25, 1933; *Crisol*, February 7 and 9, 1934; *Crítica*, October 9, 1933; *Crítica*, November 23, 1933; *Crítica*, May 12, 1934; *Crítica*, June 14, 1934.

88. Botana wrote the letter in response to learning that Kinkelín had appealed to a federal judge to have the Uruguayan-born Botana stripped of his Argentine citizenship. *Crítica*, May 23, 1934.

89. Just a year later Kinkelín would announce that he had uncovered a Jewish conspiracy to seize control of the Tucumán sugar industry. Rock, *Authoritarian Argentina*, 98.

90. "Asunto ARSA c/ Botana," in AGN, Justo, box 37, doc. 25; "Nota de Ulyses Petit de Murat al General Justo," in AGN, Justo, box 37, doc. 24.

91. Comisión Pro Ley de Prensa, *Proyecto de ley del Senador Sánchez Sorondo, de Amparo de la Prensa*, 3.

92. República Argentina, Cámara de Senadores, *Diario de sesiones 1934*, vol. 2, September 15, 1934, 286, 325–26.

93. Ibid., September 4, 1934, 75; Comisión Pro Ley de Prensa, *Proyecto de ley del Senador Sánchez Sorondo*, 3.

94. República Argentina, Cámara de Senadores, *Diario de sesiones 1934*, vol. 2, September 11, 1934, 138–56. Palacios published a book-length compilations of his speeches in the Senate during the course of the debate. Palacios, *Libertad de prensa*.

95. "Resoluciones de la Comisión Directiva: La Proyectada Ley de 'Amparo a la Prensa'" and "Carta de la Comisión Directiva del Círculo de la Prensa al Honorable Presidente de la Cámara de Diputados, Manuel Fresco, September 25, 1934," in Círculo de la Prensa, *Boletín Oficial* (October 1934), 7–8.

96. *La Nación*, October 7, 1933; August 9, 1934; September 6, 1934; and November 6, 1934.

97. On August 27, 1947, José Emilio Visca, Peronist deputy for the province of Buenos Aires, introduced Sánchez Sorondo's failed bill into the congressional record in its entirety, hoping that it would serve as the basis for a new law regulating the press. This attempt also failed, but this time in large part because Perón himself had other means of addressing the press. See República Argentina, Cámara de Diputados, *Diario de sesiones 1947*, August 27, 1947, vol. 3, 653–66.

98. *El Mercurio*, October 11–15, 1934; and "Resoluciones de la Comisión Directiva: La Publicación en el Extranjero de Crónicas Inexactas Sobre el Congreso Eucarístico," in Círculo de la Prensa, *Boletín Oficial* (December 1934), 7. I am grateful to Pablo Carrasco for locating coverage of both the Eucharistic Congress and the subsequent dispute in *El Mercurio*.

99. *El Mercurio*, October 28–31, 1934; "Ordenando una investigación de los telegramas remitidos al extranjero por el corresponsal de la United Press," in República Argentina, Ministerio del Interior, *Memoria del Ministerio del Interior, 1934–1935*, 32–33.

100. "Resoluciones de la Comisión Directiva: La Publicación en el Extranjero de Crónicas Inexactas Sobre el Congreso Eucarístico," in Círculo de la Prensa, *Boletín Oficial* (December 1934), 7.

101. "Ordenando una investigación de los telegramas remitidos al extranjero por el corresponsal de la United Press," in República Argentina, Ministerio del Interior, *Memoria del Ministerio del Interior, 1934–1935*, 32–33.

102. Decree 63.731 of July 13, 1935. See "Reglamentación del Funcionamiento de Agencias Noticiosas," in República Argentina, Ministerio del Interior, *Memoria del Ministerio del Interior, 1935–1936*, 265–68.

103. *La Nación*, July 20–23, 1935; *La Nación*, August 16, 1935; *La Nación*, September 1, 1935.

104. *La Nación*, August 16, 1935.

105. "Funcionamiento de Agencias Noticiosas," in República Argentina, Ministerio del Interior, *Memoria del Ministerio del Interior, 1935–1936*, 280–84; *La Nación*, September 12, 1935; and "Derogación del decreto que reglamentara la función de agencias informatvias y corresponsales noticiosos," in Círculo de la Prensa, *Boletín Oficial* (Ocober 1935), 8.

106. "Reglamentación del Funcionamiento de Agencias Noticiosas," in República Argentina, Ministerio del Interior, *Memoria del Ministerio del Interior, 1935–1936*, 265–68.

107. "Discurso del presidente de la F.A.P. Octavio Palazzolo. Séptimo Congreso de la Federación Argentina de Periodistas. Sesión Inaugural (Santa Fe, Junio 27 de 1946)," in Palazzolo, *Díez años de organización sindical*, 496.

108. Cincuenta y Tres Periodistas Argentinos, *El libro azul y blanco*, 216–19; Senén González, "Con olor a imprenta."

109. Angel Rama has remarked that the physical closeness between journalists and other workers that emerged as a consequence of the urbanization of the 1920s and 1930s, which brought class conflict more starkly into the consciousness of journalists. Rama, *La ciudad letrada*, 155–57. We might go further: journalists and printers by necessity interacted in the daily process of newspaper production in ways that at least opened the possibility for mutual solidarity.

110. Even when celebrating circulation peaks, *Crítica* journalists denied the paper's commercial nature, instead declaring, "we will not say commercial, because we find repugnant a concept which to others is benevolent and saving." *Crítica*, October 9, 1932. Sylvia Saítta also points to a rejection of the commodity nature of its journalism in the pages of *Crítica*, arguing that this anticommercial discourse reinforced the paper's illusion of "direct contact" with its reading public. Saítta, *Regueros de tinta*, 125.

111. "Resoluciones de la Comisión Directiva: El Régimen de Control de Cambios," in Círculo de la Prensa, *Boletín Oficial* (December 1933), 6; "El Control de Cambios para las Empresas Periodísticas," in Círculo de la Prensa, *Boletín Oficial* (October 1935), 9. This appeal was unsuccessful.

112. Círculo de la Prensa, *Publicaciones del Círculo de la Prensa. Ley de Jubilación de Periodistas* (Buenos Aires: Círculo de la Prensa, 1941), 26; "Resoluciones de la Comisión Directiva," in Círculo de la Prensa, *Boletín Oficial* (October 1932), 6.

113. Círculo de la Prensa, *Proyecto de ley de jubilaciones;* "Resoluciones de la Comisión Directiva. Jubilación de Periodistas," in Círculo de la Prensa, *Boletín Oficial* (October 1934), 10–11.

114. "Resoluciones de la Comisión Directiva. Ley de Jubilación para Periodistas y Gráficos," in Círculo de la Prensa, *Boletín Oficial* (February 1935), 7.

115. "Resoluciones de la Comisión Directiva. Ley de Jubilaciones y Pensiones de Periodistas y Gráficos. Texto Sancionado por la H. Cámara de Diputados de la Nación," in Círculo de la Prensa, *Boletín Oficial* (June 1935), 10–15.

116. "Resoluciones de la Comisión Directiva. Declaración del Círculo de la Prensa sobre el trámite de la Ley de Jubilaciones y Pensiones para Periodistas y Gráficos," in Círculo de la Prensa, *Boletín Oficial* (February 1935), 8.

117. Luís Ramiconi, "Nota de la Federación Gráfica Bonaerense al Presidente de la Nación," Círculo de la Prensa, *Ley de jubilación de periodistas*, 49–50.

118. "Resoluciones de la Comisión Directiva. Las renuncias de los señores Navarro Lahitte, Calisto y Vaccaro," in Círculo de la Prensa, *Boletín Oficial* (October 1935), 2. Though not appearing in the organization's *Boletín Oficial* until October, open letters from the organization about the pension law in June 1935 bore the signature of interim president Augusto de Muro of *La Nación*.

119. *La Prensa*, June 28, 1935; Cincuenta y Tres Periodistas Argentinos, *El libro azul y blanco*, 221. The text of the declaration is also reprinted as "Declaración del Círculo de la Prensa a propósito de la Ley de Jubilaciones y Pensiones, para Periodistas y Gráficos," in Círculo de la Prensa, *Boletín Oficial* (June 1935), 15–17.

120. "Mensaje del P.E. Vetando la Ley de Jubilaciones," in Círculo de la Prensa, *Boletín Oficial* (June 1935), 10–19.

121. Luís R. Praprotnik, "Los periodistas considerados empleados de comercio a los fines de la ley No. 11.729; La indemnización por cesantía y por despido sin previo aviso; Algunas apuntaciones a las sentencias recientes de la magistratura de paz letrado de la Capital Federal," in Círculo de la Prensa, *Boletín Oficial* (April 1936), 6–18.

122. On the expansion of labor law through court decisions on the revised Commercial Code, see Schjolden, "Suing for Justice," 202–26.

123. Praprotnik, "Los periodistas considerados empleados," 18.

124. Ibid., 8.

125. On the court rulings involving the Córdoba paper *La Voz del Interior*, see Luís R. Praprotnik, "Estatutos de Periodistas Profesionales," in Círculo de la Prensa, *Boletín Oficial* (June 1937), 10–59; and "Los periodistas y la ley 11.729," in Círculo de la Prensa, *Boletín Oficial* (December 1937), 11.

126. The letter is reproduced in "Hacia el Congreso de Córdoba," in Círculo de la Prensa, *Boletín Oficial* (February 1938), 11.

127. The Círculo de la Prensa's response is reprinted in ibid., 11–12.

128. The message is reprinted in "Congreso Nacional de Periodistas," in Palazzolo, *Diez años de organización sindical*, 11–12.

129. "Primer Congreso Nacional de Periodistas. Segunda Sesión Plenaria (Córdoba, 27 de Mayo de 1938)," in Palazzolo, *Diez años de organización sindical*, 88.

130. Ibid., 86.

131. "Labor de la Comisión Directiva. Sesión del 24 de Septiembre de 1938," in Círculo de la Prensa, *Boletín Oficial* (October 1938), 38.

132. See, for example, "El Congreso de Córdoba: Su obra," in Círculo de la Prensa, *Boletín Oficial* (June 1938), 15–22.

133. "Labor de la Comisión Directiva. Sesión del 12 de Noviembre de 1938," in Círculo de la Prensa, *Boletín Oficial* (December 1938), 15. Palazzolo repeated the accusation in public on at least one other occasion. "Primer Congreso de la Federación Argentina de Periodistas (Segundo del Gremio). Primera Sesión Plenaria. Mendoza, 10 de Julio de 1939. Versión taquigráfica," in Palazzolo, *Díez años de organización sindical*, 123.

134. Though membership numbers for the new organization are unclear, over sixty Buenos Aires journalists signed a letter of dissent from the Círculo de la Prensa, pledging adherence to the FAP, on the occasion of the first annual meeting of the FAP, held in Mendoza in 1939. Among the signatories were Oscar Lanata, Gregorio Verbitzky, Nicolás Olivari, Alberto Desimone, Dardo Cúneo, Leandro Reynés, Roberto Martínez Cuitiño, Bernardo Verbitzky, Eduardo Pacheco, Juan León Dubini, Ismael Viñas, and Juan Antonio Solari. "Primer Congreso de la Federación Argentina de Periodistas (Segundo del Gremio). Sesión Preparatoria. Mendoza, 9 de Julio de 1939. Versión del Acta," in Palazzolo, *Diez años de organización sindical*, 111.

135. "Segundo Congreso de la Federación Argentina de Periodistas. Primera Sesión Plenaria. Rosario, 23 de Mayo de 1941. Versión taquigráfica," in Palazzolo, *Diez años de organización sindical*, 195.

136. Círculo de la Prensa, *Ley de Jubilación de Periodistas*, 153–60.

137. "Nota No. 3.037 al Señor Jefe de Policía de la Capital, December 19, 1941," in República Argentina, Ministerio del Interior, *Memoria del Ministerio del Interior, 1941–1942* 61.

138. "Acerca del estado de sitio," in Círculo de la Prensa, *Boletín Oficial* (February 1942), 1–6.

139. See "Tercer Congreso. Realizado en Buenos Aires el 9, 10 y 11 de Julio con sesión de clausura en La Plata, el 12 de Julio de 1942," in Palazzolo, *Díez años de organización sindical*, 291–370.

140. Letter from Leandro R. Reynés, President of the Federación Argentina de Periodistas, to Adolfo Lanús, President of the Círculo de la Prensa (Buenos Aires, November 20, 1942); letter from Adolfo Lanús to Leandro Reynés (Buenos Aires, November 21, 1942), in Círculo de la Prensa, *Boletín Oficial* (December 1942), 12–13.

141. Pellet Lastra, *La libertad de expresión*, 99–101.

CHAPTER 3

1. *La Nación*, June 5, 1943. While still a small faction within the military at the moment of the June coup, the secret nationalist military lodge, the GOU (Grupo Obra de

Unificación), would subsequently provide an increasingly important and ideologically powerful parallel command structure within the armed forces. The GOU counted the unknown Juan Domingo Perón among its founding members. For some of the clearer explanations of the complex web of intrigue surrounding the constantly shifting balance of power within the armed forces from 1943 to the election of Perón in 1946, see Rouquié, *Poder militar y sociedad política*; Díaz Araujo, *La conspiración del '43*; Potash, *Army and Politics in Argentina*; Potash, *Perón y el G.O.U.*; and Rodríguez Lamas, *Rawson, Ramírez, Farrell*.

2. Among the numerous studies of the Argentine Right in the 1930s and early 1940s, see Buchrucker, *Nacionalismo y peronismo*; Zanatta, *Del estado liberal*; Deutsch and Dolkart, *Argentine Right*; and Rock, *Authoritarian Argentina*.

3. Sirvén, *Perón y los medios de comunicación*, 25.
4. *La Nación*, June 5, 1943.
5. *La Prensa*, June 5, 1943.
6. *La Nación*, June 5, 1943.
7. *La Prensa*, June 8, 1943.
8. *La Prensa*, June 6, 1943.
9. *La Prensa*, June 7, 1943; Rouquié, *Poder militar y sociedad política*, 28.
10. Sirvén, *Perón y los medios de comunicación*, 19; Larra, *Etcétera . . .*, 28.
11. *La Nación*, June 8, 1943.
12. *La Nación*, June 9, 1943.
13. Ibid.
14. Ibid.
15. Ibid.
16. *La Nación*, June 28, 1943 (emphasis added).
17. Rodríguez Lamas, *Rawson, Ramírez, Farrell*, 20.
18. "The idea of government as reward and pleasure, as conquest and prize, is what has stripped the authority of the political parties that until just yesterday could not even reach agreements to unite under the same banner of principles. The idea of government as public duty immediately establishes that the obligation can only fall upon the best citizens of the republic, upon the most apt and most pure, upon those who have never stained themselves in indecorous business." *La Prensa*, July 17, 1943. See also the editorial of June 17, 1943.
19. *La Nación*, June 18, 1943.
20. Thus, rather than attacking increasing government intervention in the functioning of the economy, the notoriously laissez-faire editors at *La Prensa* instead consistently praised private industrial initiative. See, for example, *La Prensa*, July 26, 1943.
21. *Crítica*, June 7, 1943. This editorial, "Tenga fe el pueblo," apparently pleased General Ramírez enough that the paper reprinted it verbatim five days later. See *Crítica*, June 12, 1943.
22. See, for example, "¿Deben depurarse los partidos políticos?" *Crítica*, June 24, 1943. The tactic was hardly new to the paper, but not since the days of Justo had the newspaper's content so consistently blessed government policies. See Sylvia Saítta, *Regueros de tinta*, especially 298–302.
23. See *Crítica*, June 14 and 16, 1943. Damonte Taborda's attacks on Barceló and Moreno had their immediate roots in the *Crítica* ownership dispute discussed below.
24. *Crítica*, June 24, 1943.
25. See *Crítica*, July 4–6, 1943. On *Crítica* and Mussolini, see *Crítica*, July 25–27, 1943. The strong *Crítica* support for the United States also has another explanation, not at all inconsistent with the paper's role as booster for the regime: Damonte Taborda had long been a recipient of State Department funds, much of which went to directly finance pro-U.S. articles in *Crítica*. See Newton, *Nazi Menace*, 436n61.
26. See, for example, references to litigation against Botana for the paper's "defamation" of German ambassador Heinrich Ritter von Kaufmann-Asser in 1933 and the Italian ambassador in 1938 in *Crítica*, July 26, 1943.

27. *Crítica*, July 7, 1943.
28. *Crítica*, April 26, 1943.
29. Fraga, *El General Justo*, 480.
30. See H. Botana, *Memorias*, 192–93 and 204; "Destino de un diario y de mil familias," *Qué sucedió en 7 días*, May 16, 1946 (test run), 32.
31. *Crítica*, May 22, 1945.
32. *Crítica*, November 17, 1943. See also Newton, *Nazi Menace*, 437n62. While Newton mentions only that the funds had a mysterious official origin, it seems apparent that the funding came through the Instituto Movilizador, which also carried official loans for *La Razón*.
33. See *Crítica*, August 4, 1943 (emphasis added).
34. Ibid.
35. *Crítica*, August 4, 1943.
36. *La Nación*, August 6, 1943.
37. *La Prensa*, August 6, 1943.
38. *La Prensa*, August 6–7, 1943.
39. *Crítica*, August 6–7, 1943.
40. See Rock, *Authoritarian Argentina*, 250–51; and Rodríguez Lamas, *Rawson, Ramírez, Farrell*, 30.
41. *La Prensa*, August 8, 1943.
42. Ibid.
43. *La Prensa*, August 30, 1943.
44. Ibid.
45. Ibid.
46. The titles of the majority of the clandestine papers either denounced the repression of the regime or equated the Ramírez government with foreign—German and Italian—domination of what was a fundamentally liberal Argentina: *El Garrote, El Himno Nacional, ¡Urquiza, Despierta!, La Voz de Mayo, Maipú, Libertad, Resistencia, Mayo, Libertad y Reforma*, and perhaps the most imaginative, *En la pendiente de la humillación*. See Comisión Nacional de Investigaciones, *Documentación*, 2:404.
47. The paper, *Búho*, was distributed free to newspaper vendors, who sold it at $0.05—half the cost of the major dailies. Ibid, 402.
48. See letter from Adolfo Lanús, president of the Círculo de la Prensa, to President Pedro Pablo Ramírez (Buenos Aires, August 24, 1943), and telegram from Adolfo Lanús, president of the Círculo de la Prensa, to the minister of the interior (Buenos Aires, September 28, 1943), in Círculo de la Prensa, *Memoria y Balance*, 105–14; *La Prensa*, September 24, 1943.
49. Letter from Adolfo Lanús, President of the Círculo de la Prensa, to President Pedro Pablo Ramírez (Buenos Aires, October 11, 1943), Círculo de la Prensa, *Memoria y Balance*, 115–16; *New York Times*, October 12, 1943; *La Prensa*, October 12, 1943; *La Nación*, October 16, 1943. The editorialists of *La Nación*, while lamenting the closure of the Jewish press in Argentina, stated bluntly that "there have never existed racial or religious persecutions on our soil, nor could they ever exist without harming the sentiments and going against the will of the people." *La Nación*, October 24, 1943.
50. *Crítica*, September 12, 1943. *La Capital* was (and still is) the country's oldest continuously published periodical.
51. Air defense drills for Buenos Aires began with rotating neighborhood blackouts on October 11, 1943, and culminated with a mock air raid and practice bombing of the city—sirens and antiaircraft guns included—on November 23, 1943. *Crítica* published photos of crowds that had gathered along the Avenida General Paz, which rings the Argentine capital, to enjoy the brief and ultimately harmless spectacle of the European war brought home. See *Crítica*, October 11–November 24, 1943; *La Nación*, October 10–13, 1943; and *La Prensa*, October 14–16, 1943.
52. *La Prensa*, September 9, 1943.

53. *Crítica*, September 30, 1943.
54. Letter from Adolfo Lanús, President of the Círculo de la Prensa, to Minister of the Interior General Alberto Gilbert (Buenos Aires, September 8, 1943), in Círculo de la Prensa, *Memoria y Balance 1943–1944*, 113–12.
55. "Sesión del 16 de Octubre de 1943," in Círculo de la Prensa, *Boletín Oficial* (December 1943), 8–10.
56. "La Federación de Periodistas presentó un memorial al ministro del Interior," *La Nación*, September 16, 1943.
57. Comisión Nacional de Investigaciones, *Documentación*, 2:400. The restrictions on reporting newspaper closures, nonetheless, did not end editorial commentary or reporting on the question of the role of the press. Instead, discussions of the issue became alternatively increasingly abstract, or commentary involved only international events and pronouncements by foreign officials. For example, see Sumner Welles article on the European press and the subsequent editorial in *La Nación*, December 22–23, 1943.
58. Letter from Adolfo Lanús, President of the Círculo de la Prensa, to President Pedro Pablo Ramírez (Buenos Aires, December 29, 1943), and letter from Jefe de la Mesa de Entradas to Director of the Círculo de la Prensa, Adolfo Lanús (Buenos Aires, January 12, 1944), in Círculo de la Prensa, *Memoria y Balance 1943–1944*, 122–23.
59. Decreto No 12.937/43 (October 21, 1943), reproduced in Comisión Nacional de Investigaciones, *Documentación*, 2:384.
60. The significant leverage that the Undersecretariat gave national authorities in the realm of ideology production has ensured its survival—in various forms and under various names—to the present day.
61. Ibid.
62. Decreto No 11.644/43 (November 9, 1943), reproduced in Comisión Nacional de Investigaciones, *Documentación*, 2:385. The Undersecretariat's power to intervene in the distribution of newsprint would remain unused until the final months of the de facto government.
63. Comisión Nacional de Investigaciones, *Documentación* 2:385.
64. In its "Blue Book" on Argentina, the United States Department of State would later claim that the creation and pattern of internal organization of the Undersecretariat of Information and Prensa came at the suggestion of German Nazi advisers hidden in the upper reaches of the government. The charge is unlikely, since the Undersecretariat clearly marked a broadening of the already existing Oficina de Información, albeit with greatly expanded powers and an ideological mission that corresponded to the increasing dominance of the GOU in the regime. Even the commission assigned to investigate the Undersecretariat after the fall of Perón in 1955 hesitated in considering direct Nazi influence in the organization of the repartition. See Comisión Nacional de Investigaciones, *Documentación*, 2:388.
65. *Crítica*, November 12, 1943.
66. *La Nación*, November 18, 1943.
67. *La Prensa*, November 15, 1943. Like the *La Nación* editorial, this editorial ostensibly addressed statements made by journalists in the United States, in this case by the American Society of Newspaper Editors. *La Prensa*'s owner, Alberto Gainza Paz, maintained close professional ties to the organization and personal ties to members of its direction. While the editorial does not mention the Undersecretariat of Information and the Press by name, the timing, content, and direct commentary on the local situation leave no doubt as to the subject of the commentary.
68. Ibid.
69. Ibid.
70. *La Prensa*, June 8, 1943.
71. The justification for the dissolution lay in that "the party organizations do not respond to the reality of the political life of the nation, nor are they representative of the authentic national opinion, for having denatured their specific function [by] going against

elemental norms of political ethics; using fraud, bribery, and venality as weapons and making personal benefit their end, totally forgetting the legitimate interests of the fatherland." Decree 18.409 (December 31, 1943), *Anales de la legislación argentina,* 1944, 72.

72. On the arguments against the applicability of the Commercial Code to the Argentine press, see Luís Praprotnik, "Los periodistas considerados empleados de comercio a los fines de la ley No. 11.729; La indemnización por cesantía y por despido sin previo aviso; Algunas apuntaciones a las sentencias recientes de la magistratura de paz letrado de la Capital Federal," in Círculo de la Prensa, *Boletín Oficial* (April 1936), 6–18.

73. Decree 18.407 (December 31, 1943), *Anales de la legislación argentina,* 1944, 70 (emphasis added).

74. Ibid. For a brief, generally approving contemporary commentary on the broad bases of the decree, see the work by University of Buenos Aires professor of law Jorge Mayer, *El derecho público de prensa,* 449–58.

75. Decree 18.407 (December 31, 1943), *Anales de la legislación argentina,* 1944, 70.

76. Decree 18.406/43 rearranged and expanded the Undersecretariat bureaucracy, while Decree 18.408/43 required publishers to submit fifteen copies of each edition of each newspaper published in the country, ten copies of each national magazine, five of each foreign publication, and three of each book.

77. The newly created section of the Undersecretariat, the Archivo de Prensa, sorted newspaper articles by topic, producing daily reports of important stories for government officials as well as thematic binders for consultation on a particular topic. This latter collection, in fact, has aided significantly in the elaboration of the present work.

78. Decree 18.407/43 prohibited any publication "a) Contrary to the general interest of the Nation or that disturbs public opinion; b) That offends Christian morality or good customs; c) That disturbs the good relations that the Nation maintains with friendly countries; d) That contains derogatory [*injuriosas*] assertions against public functionaries, private institutions and individuals in general; e) That lowers the moral or cultural level or the people; f) Of any news that is totally or partially false, or [that is presented in such a form] that might deceive the population, harming general or private interests." Decree 18.407 (December 31, 1943), *Anales de la legislación argentina,* 1944, 70.

79. *La Nación,* January 6, 1944.

80. *La Prensa,* January 6, 1944.

81. For example, the editors justified the measure dissolving the political parties and swore continued faith in the ultimate intentions of the regime: "The man on the street walks disoriented, looking for his ranks. He feels with honor, he loves his country, what occurs hurts and wounds him, but he is like a current that goes jumping between stones without finding its channel. He even tells himself, before the obstinate repetition of fraud: govern alone, and be done with it. . . . Don't continue with the farce of elections. . . . It is the worst moment. . . . But the faith of the people has not died." *Crítica,* January 5, 1944.

82. See, in particular, "Reconocimiento de una libertad esencial," *Crítica,* February 26, 1944.

83. Letter from Adolfo Lanús, President of the Círculo de la Prensa, to President Pedro Pablo Ramírez (Buenos Aires, January 29, 1944), in Círculo de la Prensa, *Memoria y Balance 1943–1944,* 137–44.

84. Ibid., 141–48. Lanús was acquitted in late April.

85. On the broad political and social ramifications of the San Juan quake, see Healey, *Ruins of the New Argentina.*

86. For details of the mission and the rupture in relations with the Axis, see Newton, *Nazi Menace,* 283–314.

87. The removal of Ramírez coincided with the dissolution of the GOU itself, apparently in order to free its members from an oath of loyalty to the deposed president. See Potash, *Perón y el G.O.U.,* 182–83.

CHAPTER 4

1. An important exception is Contreras, "Los trabajadores gráficos." On newsworkers in the United States, see especially the essays collected in Hardt and Brennen, *Newsworkers*; Brennen, "Newsworkers During the Interwar Era"; and *American Journalism* 15 (Summer 1998), special issue devoted to labor and newsworkers. Two important earlier studies that focus on the idea of "objectivity," an important element of the professional ideology of journalists in the United States, are Schudson, *Discovering the News*; and Schiller, *Objectivity and the News*. Hallin, *We Keep America*, 18–39, also provides a suggestive analysis of the relationship between ideology and technical and social change within the journalism profession. Leab, *Union of Individuals*, provides an account of the founding of the U.S. counterpart to the Argentine Federation of Journalists.

2. In the case of the Argentine press, Sylvia Saítta's examination of the internal workings of *Crítica* in *Regueros de tinta* is a welcome exception to this tendency.

3. Joel Horowitz notes that reforms favoring labor initially came slowly, with only twenty-seven labor contracts enacted in the Federal Capital between November 27, 1943, and June 30, 1944. Horowitz, *Argentine Unions*, 183.

4. Sirvén, *Perón y los medios de comunicación*, 24. Omar Lavieri similarly overlooks the role of journalists in shaping the regulations that affected them, arguing simply that under Perón "journalists had to register with the government or be barred from practicing their craft." Lavieri, "Media in Argentina," 190–91.

5. Luís Praprotnik, "Los periodistas considerados empleados de comercio a los fines de la ley No. 11.729; La indemnización por cesantía y por despido sin previo aviso; Algunas apuntaciones a las sentencias recientes de la magistratura de paz letrado de la Capital Federal," in Círculo de la Prensa, *Boletín Oficial* (April 1936), 10.

6. "Primer Congreso Nacional de Periodistas. Segunda sesión plenaria (Córdoba, 27 de Mayo de 1938). Versión taquigráfica," in Palazzolo, *Díez años de organización sindical*, 84–93.

7. The view of Peronism as largely co-optative of labor in its initial phase has long been contested by historians, and the experience of Argentine journalists in the early moments of the Peronist experiment confirms the protagonistic role that labor played in initiating social reform. See especially Murmis and Portantiero, *Estudios sobre los orígenes del peronismo*; Matsushita, *Movimiento obrero argentino*; Torre, *La vieja guardia sindical*; Horowitz, *Argentine Unions*; and James, *Resistance and Integration*.

8. This account of the drafting of the Estatuto del Periodista is taken primarily from the comments of the journalists Octavio Palazzolo, Santiago Senén González, Leandro Reynés, and Domingo Varea during the FAP's 1944 national congress. See "Quinto Congreso de la Federación Argentina de Periodistas. Primera sesión plenaria (Buenos Aires, Octubre 21 de 1944). Versión taquigráfica," in Palazzolo, *Díez años de organización sindical*, 406–12.

9. The statement was published in full in *La Nación*, December 2, 1943.

10. Comments by Octavio Palazzolo in "Quinto Congreso de la Federación Argentina de Periodistas. Primera sesión plenaria (Buenos Aires, Octubre 21 de 1944). Versión taquigráfica," in Palazzolo, *Díez años de organización sindical*, 407.

11. Ibid. (emphasis added).

12. Ibid.

13. The commission consisted of two representatives from the Círculo de la Prensa (Capital Federal), two from the FAP, one from the APBA, and five proprietors. For the Círculo de la Prensa, Alberto Gerchunoff of *La Nación* and Mauricio Bornand of *La Prensa* participated. Leandro Reynés, president of the FAP, likely occupied the second FAP seat alongside Palazzolo. "Sesiones de la Comisión Directiva. Sesión del 14 de febrero de 1944," in Círculo de la Prensa, *Boletín Oficial* (April 1944), 19–20; "Quinto Congreso de la Federación Argentina de Periodistas. Primera sesión plenaria (Buenos Aires, Octubre 21 de 1944). Versión taquigráfica," in Palazzolo, *Díez años de organización sindical*, 409–10;

"Quinto Congreso de la Federación Argentina de Periodistas. Sesión de Clausura (Buenos Aires, Octubre 22 de 1944), Versión taquigráfica," in Palazzolo, *Díez años de organización sindical*, 441; *Quien es quien en la Argentina*, 4th ed., s.v. "Agusti, José Wenceslao" and "Palazzolo, Octavio."

14. *Crítica*, March 28, 1944.
15. Ibid.
16. Ibid.
17. Ibid.
18. Estatuto del Periodista, decree 7.618/44 (March 25, 1944), *Anales de la legislación argentina*, 1944.
19. Art. 49. The statute divided employers into three categories of descending financial stature, and this classification was specified by decree 14.200 on June 3, 1944. *La Nación*, *La Prensa*, and *Crítica* each fell into "category one" and consequently paid the highest wages to journalists. Others in this category included *La Razón*, the *Standard*, the *Buenos Aires Herald*, United Press / Prensa Unida, Associated Press / Prensa Asociada, and Editorial Haynes (*El Mundo*). The evening paper *Noticias Gráficas* was conditionally classified as category two. "Clasificación de Empresas Periodísticas," in Círculo de la Prensa, *Boletín Oficial* (July 1944), 25.
20. Estatuto del Periodista, art. 52.
21. I have calculated the figures from statistics given in *Noticias Gráficas*, December 6, 1946. On March 1, 1944, the paper's proprietor, José W. Agusti, was prepared to spend $18,937.60 for total journalists' salaries that month. The decree of the Journalist's Statute signified an immediate increase of $6,175.50 over that figure, while the reclassification of *Noticias Gráficas* as a category one paper on April 10, 1945, meant a further increase of $5,900 monthly. Employees of other newspapers saw similar or even greater gains.
22. See, for example, the discussion of expenses in *Crítica*, December 7, 1946.
23. Estatuto del Periodista, arts. 27, 35.
24. Estatuto del Periodista, art.37b.
25. Estatuto del Periodista, art. 67.
26. The strategy, of course, extends to other corporate interests as well: "Libertarians argue that the corporation is a legal person and must have the same rights as a biological person, though the former has greater resources and more social, economic and political power." Nerone, *Last Rights*, 140.
27. *La Nación*, January 6, 1944.
28. *Estatuto del Periodista*, preamble.
29. Estatuto del Periodista, arts. 62–64.
30. Estatuto del Periodista, arts. 50.
31. Only three legitimate reasons could determine a rejection of any petition for inclusion in the registry or later cancellation of registration: the use of false statements in applying for inclusion; subsequent conviction of a serious crime; and if the journalist has stopped practicing the profession for two consecutive years. Estatuto del Periodista, arts. 8–10.
32. Estatuto del Periodista, preamble (emphasis added).
33. "Quinto Congreso de la Federación Argentina de Periodistas. Primera sesión plenaria (Buenos Aires, Octubre 21 de 1944). Versión taquigráfica," in Palazzolo, *Diez años de organización sindical*, 408.
34. *La Nación*, February 29, 1944.
35. "Sesiones de la Comisión Directiva. Sesión del 14 de febrero de 1944," in Círculo de la Prensa, *Boletín Oficial* (April 1944), 19.
36. *La Nación*, March 30, 1944. Significantly, no specific criticism of the conduct of Luís Mitre or other proprietors of *La Nación* emerged at the FAP's October 1944 congress.
37. *La Prensa*, February 22, 1944.
38. Ibid.
39. Ibid. (emphasis added).

40. Ibid.

41. References to the Italian and French laws began as early as Luís Proprotnik's 1937 studies for the Círculo de la Prensa, in which he did point to the "collective contracts" for journalists in those countries as providing both precedents for Argentine proposals, as well as raw material for the elaboration of a local proposal. See Luís R. Proprotnik, "Estatutos de Periodistas Profesionales. Contribución al estudio de las condiciones de vida y de trabajo de los periodistas y de las cuestiones que atañen al ejercicio y organización de la profesión," *Boletín del Círculo de la Prensa* (June 1937), 10–59.

42. *La Prensa,* February 22, 1944.

43. See "Courage in Argentina," *Editor and Publisher,* February 26, 1944.

44. As a young journalist from Mendoza, the future anti-Peronist Eduardo García was shocked upon learning of the compensation arrangements at *La Prensa,* where he worked as a member of the editorial staff and as a contributor to the "Actualidad" section starting in the late 1920s. Newswriters faced even more demanding working conditions at some the other dailies in the same period, especially those at the emerging popular newspapers. See García, *Yo fuí testigo,* 129.

45. "Quinto Congreso de la Federación Argentina de Periodistas. Primera sesión plenaria (Buenos Aires, Octubre 21 de 1944). Versión taquigráfica," in Palazzolo, *Diez años de organización sindical,* 408; Estatuto del Periodista, art. 67.

46. *Editor and Publisher, International Year Book Number for 1946,* 294–316; "Quinto Congreso de la Federación Argentina de Periodistas. Primera sesión plenaria (Buenos Aires, Octubre 21 de 1944). Versión taquigráfica," in Palazzolo, *Diez años de organización sindical,* 410. The circulation levels of *Noticias Gráficas* far exceeded those of category one papers like the *Buenos Aires Herald,* the *Standard,* and *El Avisador Mercantil.* The classification most likely came in compensation to Agusti for sympathetic coverage of the work of the Secretariat of Labor and Social Welfare, which would also explain why, after breaking with Perón, Agusti's paper suddenly became category one in October 1945.

47. "Quinto Congreso de la Federación Argentina de Periodistas. Primera sesión plenaria (Buenos Aires, Octubre 21 de 1944). Versión taquigráfica," in Palazzolo, *Diez años de organización sindical,* 409.

48. Ibid.

49. Morris, *Deadline Every Minute,* 316.

50. Pablo Sirvén asserts that the Farrell government also closed AP at this time, although I have found no evidence to support this claim. Sirvén, *Perón y los medios de comunicación* 30.

51. Morris, *Deadline Every Minute,* 316.

52. Ibid. A survey of *La Prensa* during the closure reveals that UP cables appeared in *La Prensa* as "Especial. Vía Montevideo" or "Especial. Vía Nueva York."

53. Kelly, *Ruling Few,* 313.

54. *La Nación,* April 28, 1944.

55. See *La Prensa,* August 7, 1946; Gainza Paz, *Por defender la libertad,* 82–83.

56. Pablo Sirvén remarks that "on April 26, 1944, the newspapers complained more than usual" in response to *La Prensa*'s closure. The terms of the state of siege, however, prohibited this, and my own survey of the Buenos Aires press that day does not reveal any violation of government restrictions in reporting the incident. See Sirvén, *Perón y los medios de comunicación,* 31.

57. *La Nación,* May 22, 1944; *La Nación,* May 23, 1944.

58. Rumor at the time held that Mitre's public disavowal of Forn de Oteiza Quirno led not only to Victoria Ocampo, founder of the legendary literary magazine *Sur,* ending her contributions to *La Nación*'s literary supplement, but also to her falling out with the supplement's director, Eduardo Mallea. Ocampo's work does not, in fact, appear in *La Nación* after the incident. I am grateful to Dr. Tulio Halperín-Donghi for pointing this out.

59. The move did not succeed in ending the country's diplomatic isolation. See *Crítica,* August 9, 1944; *La Razón,* August 9, 1944; and *La Nación,* August 10, 1944.

60. The employees of the United Press in Buenos Aires had appealed to Perón in his capacity as secretary of labor and social welfare to end the closure, arguing not that the measure violated freedom of the press, but that it had left over a hundred journalists without work. "Sesiones de la Comisión Directiva. Sesión del 20 de Marzo de 1944," in Círculo de la Prensa, *Boletín Oficial* (April 1944), 20.

61. "Historia del Peronismo. Clausura de *La Vanguardia*," *Primera Plana*, March 7, 1967.

62. Police detained Santander on the evening of August 18, 1944, following a raid on the offices of *Crítica*. He was later released to exile in Montevideo. *Crítica*, August 7, 1945. "Quinto Congreso de la Federación Argentina de Periodistas. Sesión preparatoria (Buenos Aires, Octubre 20 de 1944). Versión taquigráfica," in Palazzolo, *Diez años de organización sindical*, 396.

63. Upon its creation, the Secretariat of Labor and Social Welfare occupied the massive, ornate offices of the Buenos Aires City Council. The building, just a block from the Plaza de Mayo, had remained for the most part unoccupied since President Castillo's dissolution of the Council (Consejo Deliberante) in October 1941, following a series of corruption scandals. See *Politics and Urban Growth*, 211–34.

64. "Quinto Congreso de la Federación Argentina de Periodistas. Sesión inaugural (Buenos Aires, Octubre 20 de 1944). Versión taquigráfica," in Palazzolo, *Diez años de organización sindical*, 399–404.

65. Ibid., 402.
66. Ibid.
67. Ibid., 401.
68. Ibid., 402.
69. Ibid. (emphasis added).
70. Ibid. (emphasis added).
71. Ibid., 402.

72. The outspoken APBA delegates were Octavio Palazzolo, Leandro Reynés, Oscar Ares, and Santiago Senén González. Those from the Círculo de la Prensa de Rosario included Domingo Varea and Dino Cinelli. Mariano Forcat of the Asociación de Periodistas de Santa Fe also consistently sided with his Rosario colleagues.

73. "Quinto Congreso de la Federación Argentina de Periodistas. Segunda sesión plenaria (Buenos Aires, Octubre 21 de 1944). Versión taquigráfica," in Palazzolo, *Diez años de organización sindical*, 421–22.

74. Ibid., 422.

75. "Quinto Congreso de la Federación Argentina de Periodistas. Primera sesión plenaria (Buenos Aires, Octubre 21 de 1944). Versión taquigráfica," in Palazzolo, *Diez años de organización sindical*, 410.

76. Ibid.

77. "Quinto Congreso de la Federación Argentina de Periodistas. Segunda sesión plenaria (Buenos Aires, Octubre 21 de 1944). Versión taquigráfica," in Palazzolo, *Diez años de organización sindical*, 422; "Sexto Congreso de la Federación Argentina de Periodistas. Sesión preparatoria (Buenos Aires, June 28, 1945)," in *Diez años de organización sindical*, 460. Upon leaving the FAP, the Círculo de la Prensa de Rosario divided, with dissident journalists forming the local FAP affiliate Asociación de Periodistas del Sur de Santa Fe, Rosario.

CHAPTER 5

1. Some of the more important examinations of the events of October 17, 1945, are included in Torre, *El 17 de Octubre de 1945*, published on the fiftieth anniversary of the mobilization. See also Luna, *El '45*. Three contradictory participatory accounts are Perel-

man, *Como hicimos el 17 de Octubre;* Reyes, *Yo hice el 17 de Octubre;* and Colóm, *17 de Octubre.* On the institutionalization of October 17 as Peronist Loyalty Day, see Plotkin, "Rituales políticos"; Plotkin, *Mañana es San Perón,* 75–140.

2. In his study of the press under Perón, for example, Pablo Sirvén gives only a half-page description of the attacks on *Crítica,* despite the event's pivotal importance for what was then Buenos Aires' premier popular newspaper. Sirvén, *Perón y los medios de comunicación,* 40.

3. *El Mundo,* October 18, 1945.

4. James, "October 17th and 18th, 1945."

5. Ibid., 454.

6. *El Mundo,* October 18, 1945; *La Nación,* October 18, 1945.

7. "Quinto Congreso de la Federación Argentina de Periodistas. Primera sesión plenaria (Buenos Aires, Octubre 21 de 1944). Versión taquigráfica," in Palazzolo, ed., 410.

8. Only one Buenos Aires newspaper, in fact, consistently backed Perón, even after his detention: *La Época.* While the paper would later emerge as an important voice within the Peronist movement, in 1945 *La Época'*s circulation could not compare with that of *La Prensa, La Nación, Crítica, Noticias Gráficas, La Razón,* and *El Mundo.* In fact, *La Época* had become a daily newspaper only four weeks prior to the demonstrations of October 17. On the relationship between *La Época* and Perón, see chapter 6 below.

9. See, for example, "El trabajo y sus antecedentes legislativos," *La Nación,* December 4, 1943; as well as the positive evaluations of the military government on its anniversary, "Un año de gobierno," *La Nación,* June 3, 1944 and "La labor de un año de gobierno," *La Nación,* June 4, 1944. On the initial support of *La Nación* editorialists for the economic policies of the military regime, see Sidicaro, *La política mirada desde arriba,* 177–86.

10. *La Nación,* July 1, 1944. On the speech and U.S. State Department reactions, see Page, *Perón,* 72–75.

11. *La Nación,* July 4, 1944.

12. By mid-1944, the activities of the Undersecretariat of Information and the Press had grown both in quantity and quality. In March 1944, Oscar Lomuto (*La Razón*) became the first professional journalist to assume the head of the Undersecretariat, and, together with Marcial Rocha de María (*Crítica*) and Eduardo J. Pacheco (*Noticias Gráficas*), made the institution much more capable of producing positive propaganda for the regime rather than simply coordinating censorship. Luna, *El '45,* 159. On the development of the Undersecretariat of Information and the Press, see chapter 6 below. Not coincidentally, both Lomuto and Rocha de María played small but crucial roles in the initial stages of the Journalist's Statute's elaboration.

13. Both phrases were the traditional usage at the respective papers. In editorials on the second election of Yrigoyen as president in 1928, *La Prensa* editorialists reasserted the paper as the *órgano de opinión pública,* while *Crítica'*s writers similarly reminded their readers that the paper was an *expresión del sentimiento popular. La Prensa,* October 12, 1928; *Crítica,* October 12, 1928, cited in Fernández, López Barros, and Petris, "*El Mundo.*"

14. This characteristic, as noted in chapter 1, forms the basis of the newspaper's legendary status within Latin American journalism history. For an excellent examination of specific interpellative strategies of the *Crítica* staff at the paper's height in the 1920s, see Saítta, *Regueros de tinta,* especially 55–90.

15. *Noticias Gráficas,* established by Jorge Mitre to take advantage of the closure of *Crítica* in the wake of the 1930 coup, maintained a short-lived rivalry first with the *Crítica* substitute *Jornada* and then with *Crítica* itself. By the middle of the decade, however, *Noticias Gráficas* teetered on the verge of bankruptcy. Llano, *La aventura del periodismo,* 113.

16. Luna, *El '45,* 248, 200–201, 215–19.

17. H. Botana, *Memoria,* 205.

18. Ibid.

19. Newton, *Nazi Menace in Argentina,* 437n62. On March 8, 1945, the United Press carried an item from Río de Janeiro stating the Raúl Damonte Taborda was visiting the

Brazilian capital on a "special confidential mission," presumably at the behest of the military authorities. Although *La Prensa* printed the story together with a UP retraction of the news in the same issue, the denial of any official motive for the visit does not make the scenario any less likely. *La Prensa*, March 8, 1945; *Crítica*, March 11, 1945. Damonte Taborda also later claimed that Perón had repeatedly offered him the position of minister of foreign relations, which he apparently refused. Damonte Taborda, *Ayer fué San Perón*, 239.

20. Although Salvadora Medina Onrubia de Botana would later find it convenient to claim that Cipolletti had only worked as her personal employee, and not in *Crítica* "since he was not a journalist," he does appear in the paper as the "Government House reporter." See Medina Onrubia de Botana, *Crítica y su verdad;* and *Crítica*, October 12, 1945. On Cipolletti's tenure as interventor of the province of San Juan, see Healey, *Ruins of the New Argentina*.

21. *Crítica* extensively reproduced photographs of the event, including the quasi-Nazi official stage and Argentine-made "DL-DL" tanks and artillery. The modern nature of the armament in particular seems to have fascinated the paper's journalists and editors. *Crítica*, July 9, 1944 (6th ed.).

22. Eight years later, the core of Bemberg's economic holdings in the beer industry came under state control after a long series of investigations for tax evasion and antitrust violations. Buchrucker, *Nacionalismo y Peronismo*, 370.

23. *Crítica*, July 4, 1944, June 30, 1944.

24. *Crítica*, November 22, 1944.

25. For example, following a March 1944 speech in which Farrell called on the audience to "look in the past for those examples that can strengthen our spirit," a group of Nationalists began to chant, "¡Rosas, Rosas!" The following day, a *Crítica* editorialist not only cast suspicion on the "nationalism" of a political sector that drew its cues from international fascism, but even rhetorically removed Rosas from the flow of Argentine history, since he did not contribute to the nation's freedom. President Farrell, the editorialist insisted, was referring to figures from "the true Argentine past": that is, those who established the liberal institutions of the country and who were "the sincere defenders of liberty." *Crítica*, March 12, 1944.

26. *Crítica*, December 29, 1944.

27. Ibid.

28. See, for example, "El lenguaje de Caseros," *Crítica*, January 2, 1945.

29. *Crítica*, March 22, 1945.

30. Ibid.

31. In October 1944, eight months after breaking relations with the Axis, the military government prohibited "all forms of direct or indirect propaganda that favors the cause or political regimes with which the Argentine Republic has broken diplomatic relations." The government also decreed the immediate closure of the newspapers *Il Matiino d'Italia* and *Deutsche La Plata Zeitung*, pro-Fascist and pro-Nazi, respectively. *Crítica*, October 18, 1944.

32. See *Crítica*, March 10, 1945; April 23 1945; April 24, 1945.

33. Senén González and Welp, *"Crítica,"* 52. Rudnitzky would later form part of the group of journalists that penned the most damning polemic against the non-Peronist press. See Cincuenta y Tres Periodistas Argentinos, *El libro azul y blanco de la prensa argentina*, 36–37.

34. *Noticias Gráficas*, June 29, 1945.

35. See, for example, "Hitler recurrió a la justicia argentina para silenciar la voz de CRITICA," *Crítica*, May 3, 1945.

36. On Perón's relationship with the Nationalist Right in this period, see Walter, "Right and the Peronists," 105–8; Rock, *Authoritarian Argentina*, 138–83.

37. See, for example, "Procesos y clausuras jalonan nuestra lucha," *Crítica*, March 27, 1945.

38. H. Botana, *Memorias*, 205.

39. Sidicaro, *La política mirada desde arriba*, 209. Sidicaro's phrase is *editoriales por interpóstitos editoriales*. While Sidicaro limits this to the reprinting of foreign editorials in 1949, the practice was in fact used more broadly to favor certain news coverage, and had become common by 1945 as a way of circumventing official censorship.

40. See, for example, articles by Paris correspondents Ricardo Sáenz Hayes and Alberto Cellario, "Cuando la Libertad Cae Encadenada, lo Primero que Enmudece es el Editorial" and "Posee un Alto Concepto del Periodismo el Comando Aliado," *La Prensa*, June 16, 1945; "Conceptos de Truman y Stettinus Acerca de la Libertad de Prensa," *La Prensa*, June 23, 1945; the editorial centered around praise for comments by the acting U.S. secretary of state, Joseph Grew, and members of the American Society of Newspaper Editors, "Libre Información y Libre Opinión Periodística," *La Prensa*, June 26, 1945. See also "Prensa Libre," an editorial on the proposed press arrangements in a postwar Germany, *La Nación*, February 20, 1945; and "La Libertad de Prensa en el Mundo," opinion essay by Mario Mariani, *Crítica*, June 28, 1945.

41. In the years of constitutional Peronism (1946–55), the practice of "editorial by proxy" would serve to maintain media focus on the question of freedom of the press and government policy by allowing for constant space devoted to the issue, regardless of any lull in events in Argentina. As a product of his attempt to create a portrait of "the Argentine," James Bruce, U.S. ambassador to Argentina in the late 1940s, attributes this tactic to less circumstantial, more exotic factors: "Instead of attacking the government's antipress campaign outright, for instance, *La Prensa* might editorially praise Dean Carl W. Ackerman of Columbia University's School of Journalism for a speech on freedom of the press. In this it reflected Argentine temperament—and the Spanish habit of circumlocution to make a point." Bruce, *Those Perplexing Argentines*, 205–6.

42. Cited in *Crítica*, March 7, 1945.

43. *La Prensa*, June 18, 1945.

44. *La Nación*, June 8, 1945.

45. *The New York Times*, June 9, 1945, cited in *La Vanguardia*, June 19, 1945.

46. Braden, *Diplomats and Demagogues*, 328.

47. In a later interview with Félix Luna, Oscar Lomuto claimed that both he and Braden "understood that the assurances that I transmitted to him were of a private character, and should remain between us [*no habrían de trascender*]." According to Lomuto, upon reading the newspapers the following morning an infuriated Perón demanded that Lomuto sue the ambassador "for breaking his word of honor." Luna, *El '45*, 160. Relating the discussion to the press that afternoon, however, Braden remarked that he was doing so to fulfill his agreement with Lomuto. Upon questioning, he stated that local papers could now carry the transmitted cables of U.S. correspondents in Argentina, and that the discussion with Lomuto could be taken as a formal promise on the part of the Argentine authorities. *La Razón*, June 13, 1945. On the incident Lomuto seems the more reliable source; not only is his characterization more in keeping with the normal functioning of government, but Braden's memoirs, rife with other errors and spectacular exaggerations, place the meeting two days later and misspell Lomuto's name. Braden, *Diplomats and Demagogues*, 327.

48. *La Vanguardia*, June 19, 1945.

49. Luna, *El '45*, 103.

50. By decree, on June 6 the regime lifted all existing suspensions of newspapers, declared that any new suspensions could only come about through direct decree of the national Executive Power, and rescinded all orders for arrest affecting journalists. The decree also declared that the government had long sought to guarantee full freedom of the press but found it necessary to condition that freedom due to "exceptional circumstances that culminated with the total uncovering of a vast conspiracy designed to derail the country in its rapid march toward the full recuperation of its values and international conduct." "Acerca de las suspensiones de diarios o periódicos," in Círculo de la Prensa, *Boletín Oficial* (June 1945), 9.

51. The FAP had asked its member organizations throughout the country to cancel all celebration of the Day of the Journalist and to engage in a coordinated ten-minute suspension of activity at 6:00 p.m. that day to protest the newspaper suspensions. *La Vanguardia*, June 5, 1945.

52. Ghioldi, who upon release had headed for exile in Chile, returned after reaching the border city of Mendoza. In Buenos Aires he was greeted by sizable demonstrations, and his remarks to the crowd regarding the necessity of elections were carried in the commercial press. *La Razón*, June 11, 1945; *La Nación*, June 11, 1945. *Crítica*'s coverage, not surprisingly, walked a fine line between support for Ghioldi and loyalty to Perón: unlike the other papers, it omitted the Socialist leader's remarks that he would continue to "struggle for freedom," printing only that he would "collaborate so that constitutional order could be restored." In their respective portrayals in Damonte Taborda's paper, then, Ghioldi would appear to have much in common with Perón. *Crítica*, June 11, 1945.

53. Kelly, *Ruling Few*, 313.

54. Braden claims in his memoirs that his public association with Gainza Paz and others led Perón to imply that "fanatics" might plan an assassination attempt against the ambassador, due to his clear friendly relations with leading figures of the opposition. Braden, *Diplomats and Demagogues*, 329–30.

55. See the articles by and about Arnold Cortesi of the *New York Times* and Joseph Newman of the *New York Herald Tribune* in *Crítica*, June 28, 1945 and July 3, 1945; *La Nación*, July 4, 1945; and *La Prensa*, July 6, 1945. For the impact of the incident on the U.S. State Department's approach to Argentina, see Blanchard, *Exporting the First Amendment*, 34–36.

56. "The Secretary of State to the Ambassador in Argentina (Braden)," July 3, 1945, *FRUS: 1945*, vol. 9, 513.

57. "El Círculo de la Prensa firma un Manifiesto en que se Solicita el Restablecimiento de la Normalidad Institucional," and "Visita del Embajador de los Estados Unidos," in Círculo de la Prensa, *Boletín Oficial* (July 1945), 8–11; *La Nación*, July 15, 1945.

58. Braden sits at the center of nearly all accounts of the mobilizations against the Farrell/Perón government, and the discussion of his Argentine tenure forms the most lively part of his memoirs. In addition, see Scenna, *Braden y Perón*; and Frank, *Juan Perón vs. Spruille Braden*.

59. *La Nación*, June 16, 1945.

60. *La Nación*, June 17, 1945.

61. "Sexto Congreso de la FAP. Quinta Sesión Plenaria y de Clausura (Buenos Aires, June 30, 1945)" and "Sexto Congreso de la FAP. Resoluciones del Sexto Congreso de la Federación Argentina de Periodistas (Buenos Aires June 28–30, 1945)," in Palazzolo, *Diez años de organización sindical*, 474–75 and 485, respectively.

62. See declarations in *Noticias Gráficas*, September 1, 1945; and *El Litoral*, October 14, 1945.

63. Reports on meetings to annul the Journalist's Statute appeared in *La Época*, October 4, 1945.

64. On union positions in mid-1945, see Baily, *Movimiento obrero*; and Torre, "La CGT en el 17 de Octubre."

65. Cited in *Crítica*, September 15, 1945; *La Nación*, September 16, 1945.

66. Cited in *Crítica*, September 15, 1945.

67. Perelman, *Como hicimos el 17 de Octubre*, 55.

68. Cited in Sirvén, 36.

69. Cited in "The Ambassador in Argentina (Braden) to the Secretary of State," July 20, 1945, *FRUS: 1945*, vol. 9, 397.

70. "En el Local del Círculo Estalló un Petardo," in Círculo de la Prensa, *Boletín Oficial*, July 1945, 1.

71. *La Prensa*, July 26, 1945.

72. Damonte Taborda, during his subsequent Brazilian exile, disingenuously claimed that he had always been in opposition to Perón, explaining that *Crítica* began a systematic campaign against the colonel after Damonte Taborda became the paper's director in May 1945. Not only does this fail to account for why *Crítica* continued to support Perón during June—when other papers stepped up their antigovernment rhetoric—but Raúl Damonte Taborda clearly had control over the paper since early 1943. Damonte Taborda, *Ayer fué San Perón*, 239.

73. For Perón's full-page response to the *fuerzas vivas*, see *Crítica*, June 16, 1945; the long rebuttal to the Manifesto by several unions appears in *Crítica*, June 23, 1945.

74. *Crítica*, June 29–30, 1945.

75. On August 2, 1945, second-tier Radical politician Hortensio Quijano assumed the post of minister of the interior (vacant since General Perlinger's resignation in July 1944), while Juan I. Cooke became minister of foreign relations.

76. *Crítica*, August 28, 1945.

77. *Crítica*, September 4, 1945.

78. *Crítica*, September 5, 1945.

79. Luna, *El '45*, 408n46.

80. *Crítica*, September 15, 1945. The editorial "Prensa Venal" challenged Perón to back his claims of press corruption by providing the names and information of those papers supposedly sustained by foreign sources or by the Argentine state. Damonte Taborda, who would clearly have found such revelations prejudicial to his own interests, could remain confident such information would not be forthcoming: Perón had only just begun a massive subsidy to transform the pro-Perón *La Época* into a daily paper. See chapter 6.

81. Ibid.

82. *Crítica*, September 17, 1945.

83. *Crítica*, October 13, 1945.

84. *Crítica*, August 7, 1945; Llano, *La aventura del periodismo*, 128.

85. See, for example, photos of demonstrators celebrating the end of World War II in *Crítica*, August 14–16, 1945.

86. *Crítica*, May 8–12, 1945. The precise nature of the confrontation is unclear, since the state of siege prohibited the full reporting of the event.

87. "Sesión del 18 de Mayo de 1945," in Círculo de la Prensa, *Boletín Oficial* (April/May 1945), 18.

88. *Crítica*, August 14–17, 1945; *La Nación*, August 16, 1945.

89. *La Nación*, August 16, 1945; *Crítica*, August 16, 1945.

90. "Círculo de la Prensa Repudia los Atentados Contra Diarios," in Círculo de la Prensa, *Boletín Oficial* (August/September 1945), 3.

91. Cited in *Crítica*, August 16, 1945 (emphasis added). While the attacks appear the work primarily of members of the ALN together with several soldiers, Damonte Taborda would later claim that it was a concerted assault carried out under Perón's direct orders. This seems unlikely, given that the attack failed. Damonte Taborda, *Ayer fué San Perón*, 240.

92. Cowles, *Bloody Precedent*, 219.

93. "Sesiones de la Comisión Directiva. Sesión del 27 de Septiembre de 1945," in Círculo de la Prensa, *Boletín Oficial* (October/November, 1945), 29.

94. "Reimplantación del Estado de Sitio," in Círculo de la Prensa, *Boletín Oficial* (August/September, 1945), 4.

95. This "blackout" occurred on October 11 for evening papers and October 12 for the morning papers. For explanations of the proprietors' motives, see "Libertad de Prensa" in *La Razón*, October 14, 1945; "El Editorial que no Ha Sido Escrito" in *Crítica*, October 12, 1945; "Libertad de Prensa," *La Vanguardia*, October 16, 1945; and "Era una Cuestión de Dignidad, y la Resolvimos Dicidiendo no Salir," *Noticias Gráficas*, October 14, 1945.

96. *Córdoba*, September 27, 1945.

97. *Crítica*, October 12, 1945. "Diarios Clausurados y Periodistas Detenidos," in Círculo de la Prensa, *Boletín Oficial* (October/November, 1945), 3.
98. *Crítica*, October 12, 1945.
99. Ibid.
100. Ibid.
101. Damonte Taborda, like other newspaper owners, refused to publish on the evening of October 11, in accordance with the newspaper "blackout." The journalists who supposedly stood with Quijano in his plans to make *Crítica* once again a Peronist paper were fired immediately: Orestes Confalonieri, Juan Valencia, Alfredo Tissera, Amadeo Dante Brunetti, and Helvio Casal Cabrera. Emilio Cipolletti, acting governor of the earthquake-stricken province of San Juan at the behest of Perón, was also finally removed from *Crítica* payrolls that day. His continued presence as an employee of the paper until then suggests one of two things: that Damonte Taborda had remained much more cautious in his opposition to Perón than the pages of *Crítica* would indicate; or that it simply proved more economical to maintain Cipolletti on the payroll than to abide by the Journalist's Statute's strict compensation regulations. Ibid.
102. *La Época*, October 18, 1945.
103. *Crítica*, October 17, 1945.
104. Ibid.
105. Ibid.
106. *La Nación*, October 18, 1945.
107. The following account draws largely from *Noticias Gráficas*, October 18, 1945; *El Mundo*, October 18–19, 1945; and *La Época*, October 18, 1945.
108. *El Mundo* would later report that the judicial investigation found no proof that any shots had been fired from *Crítica*, and that all had been fired from the street below or from the Pasaje Barolo into the *Crítica* building, and that police found only two .32 caliber revolvers in their subsequent search of the building. While those inside the newspaper offices surely did not match the firepower of those outside, *Crítica* staff no doubt expected another attack on the building, given the events of the previous several months, and it is highly unlikely that they left the building without a fairly coordinated system of defense. In this sense, the Peronist *La Época*'s assertion—supported by photographs—that police found a large cache of arms and Molotov cocktails at the newspaper's offices seems just as credible. *El Mundo*, October 21, 1945; *La Época*, October 18, 1945. *Crítica*, August 8, 1947, also makes references to Damonte Taborda maintaining a private, armed security force at the building—a precaution started in the Botana era.
109. *Crítica*, November 1, 1945.
110. "La Verdad Sobre el 17 de Octubre y el Balcón de CRITICA," *Crítica*, August 8, 1947.
111. Ibid. The list includes Caminos, head of the newsroom in *Democracia;* former *Crítica* business managers Ernesto Contreras and Mario Aubone and journalists Luís Rivero, Roberto Caminos, and Máximo Miguez, also with *Democracia;* Armando Di Tella, head of the *La Época* newsroom; Manrique Washington, Jorge Barberis, Eduardo Barberis, and José Rebollo also of *La Época;* and Raúl López, a former armed guard at the *Crítica* offices, a supposed "elevator operator" at the Undersecretariat of Information and the Press.
112. *Clarín*, founded by Roberto Noble, first appeared on August 28, 1945. Present and former *Crítica* journalists and staff who passed to *Clarín* included Horacio Maldonado, Andrés Guevara, Armando Lena, Juan Carlos Petrone, Raúl González Tuñón, José Portogalo, Ignacio Covarrubias, Moisés Schebor Jacoby, Horacio Estol, Carlos Martínez Cuitiño, Héctor Agosti, Cayetano Córdova Iturburu, and Conrado Nalé Roxlo. Following the events of October 17, 1945, a financially troubled *Crítica* also received the printing contracts for the new newspaper. Llano, *La aventura del periodismo*, 119–28; Ramos, *Los cerrojos a la prensa*, 63–64.

CHAPTER 6

1. *El Laborista*, November 14, 1946.
2. For the support given by *La Prensa, La Nación, Crítica*, and *Noticias Gráficas* to the candidates of the UD, see Ruíz Jiménez, "Peronism and Anti-imperialism."
3. See Plotkin, *Mañana es San Perón*, 325.
4. Among other works, see Jauretche, *FORJA*; Scenna, *FORJA;* and Rock, *Authoritarian Argentina*, 122–24, 220.
5. *La Época*, November 8, 1946; "Historia del Peronismo, La Primera Presidencia, XXXII: La Cadena de Diarios," *Primera Plana*, February 21, 1967, 35. Sirvén places the initial meeting between Perón and Colóm on September 8, 1943, and states that Perón sent the *La Época* owner to the Undersecretariat of Information and the Press to see Oscar Lomuto. This timing seems highly unlikely since not only did the $100,000 that Colóm insisted he needed to convert *La Época* into a daily newspaper not appear until almost two years later, but Lomuto himself did not assume the head of the Undersecretariat until March 1944. Sirvén, *Perón y los medios de comunicación*, 27–28.
6. "Historia del Peronismo, XXXII," 35.
7. For Colóm's version of the events of October 17, 1945, see Colóm, *17 de Octubre*.
8. *La Época*, March 11, 1946.
9. Plotkin, *Mañana es San Perón*, 326. On the dissolution of the Partido Laborista and the formation of the Partido Peronista, see Moira Mackinnon, *Los años formativos*.
10. Plotkin, *Mañana es San Perón*, 326.
11. "Historia del Peronismo, La Primera Presidencia, XIV, Política Agraria," in *Primera Plana*, August 16, 1966, 35.
12. "Historia del Peronismo, XXXII," 35; Sirvén, *Perón y los medios de comunicación*, 65.
13. See *La Época*, March 28–April 1, 1946; June 10, 1946; and November 8, 1946; *Quien es quien en la Argentina*, 4th ed., s.v. "Cipolletti, Emilio."
14. "Historia del Peronismo, XXXII," 35.
15. *La Época*, January 30, 1951.
16. Luna, Sirvén, and Hugo Gambini have all placed *Democracia* as the "first link in the chain," but, as explained below, it appears that *La Razón* and *Crítica*—and possibly *El Mundo*—came under Perón's direct control even before *Democracia*. Luna, *Perón y su tiempo*, 1:85; Sirvén, *Perón y los medios de comunicación*, 66; and "Historia del Peronismo, XXXII," 34.
17. "Historia del Peronismo, XXXII," 34; "Historia del Peronismo, XIV, 36. Both articles, based on interviews with Molinari, place the transfer of *Democracia* at "mid-1947," but news of the sale—delayed by at least one week—appears in *Editor and Publisher*, March 15, 1947.
18. Colóm openly complained about the government's unequal treatment of the different Peronist papers and decried *Democracia*'s larger subsidies. *Editor and Publisher*, March 15, 1947.
19. *Editor and Publisher*, August 23, 1947.
20. Mariano Plotkin, for example, correctly states that "at the beginning of Perón's regime the pressure upon the opposition press was applied above all through the quotas of imported paper granted to each newspaper, and by means of the denial of official advertising." A similar argument forms the basis for Sirvén's discussion of the fates of *Crítica, Noticias Gráficas, La Razón*, and *El Mundo* in 1946–47, as well as Félix Luna's look at the appropriation of those papers by the Peronists. Plotkin, *Mañana es San Perón*, 329; Sirvén, *Perón y los medios de comunicación;* and Luna, *Perón y su tiempo*, 1:81–94.
21. This same argument and the same newsprint crisis lay at the heart of the creation of the British Royal Commission on the Press in 1947. On the long-running Commission, see Curran, "Press Freedom as a Property Right."
22. *La Época*, October 18, 1945.

23. See, for example, the extensive diatribe against *Crítica*—complete with six photographs of rifles and ammunition confiscated in the paper's building—in the pages of *La Época*, October 18, 1945; and the polemic against *Crítica* in *El Líder*, August 8–21, 1947, which emphasized Botana's connections with the long-discredited Argentine Conservatives.

24. *Editor and Publisher*, June 5, 1943.

25. Los Angeles and San Francisco, California, showed the most dramatic gains in newspaper circulation, with both cities doubling the number of newspapers sold in the decade between the outbreak of the Spanish Civil War and the end of World War II. See *Editor and Publisher, International Yearbook Number for 1936; International Year Book Number for 1946*.

26. This figure represents average Argentine annual consumption for the years 1930–41. República Argentina, Ministerio de Agricultura, *La industria de papel*, 3.

27. Ibid.

28. *Editor and Publisher*, June 5, 1943.

29. *Editor and Publisher, International Year Book Number for 1936; International Year Book Number for 1946*.

30. The Paz family owned 50 percent of the steam freighter *Río Grande*, which it used to assure constant shipping of the imported industrial inputs needed to maintain *La Prensa*. República Argentina, Cámara de Senadores, *La Prensa*, 77.

31. *Editor and Publisher*, July 28, 1945; *Editor and Publisher*, June 1, 1946.

32. Debates in the British House of Commons on the establishment of a committee to investigate the finances of British newspapers—what would become the Royal Commission on the Press—received wide coverage in the Argentine press. See *La Época*, April 20, 1946; *La Prensa*, July 17, 1946; and *La Prensa*, September 29–30, 1946.

33. Gerald, *British Press*, 26–35. For an overview of state media policies in the immediate postwar, see Curran, "Press Freedom as a Property Right," 59–82; and the contemporaneous studies by Martin, *Press the Public Wants*; and Gerald, *British Press*.

34. See, for example, *La Época*, December 20, 1945. On wartime boycotts imposed by the United States Department of State, see Friedman, *Nazis and Good Neighbors*.

35. *La Época*, December 19, 1945.

36. See, for example, *La Época*, November 5, 1945; December 19, 1945; and December 20, 1945.

37. Decreto 6219/46 (February 28, 1946), cited in *La Prensa*, March 5, 1946. The irony of the measure was lost on few of the regime's opponents; the constitutional guarantees were still, after all, suspended under the terms of the state of siege.

38. Decreto 6629/46 (March 7, 1946), cited in *La Nación*, April 28, 1946.

39. See *La Época*, March 1, 1946, through April 11, 1946; *El Laborista*, March 30, 1946, and April 1, 1946.

40. *La Prensa*, January 20, 1946.

41. *La Prensa*, March 5, 1946.

42. Ibid.; *La Prensa*, March 9, 1946.

43. *La Prensa*, August 27, 1946.

44. *La Prensa*, November 24, 1946 (emphasis added).

45. "El aumento, como posible solución," *Qué sucedió en 7 días*, September 12, 1946, 33.

46. Medina Onrubia de Botana, *Crítica y su verdad*, 232.

47. Newspaper owners in the United States had founded the American Society of Newspaper Editors in 1922. British proprietors abandoned their own ideological objections in 1953 to form the Press Council as a buffer against further government regulation. See Gerald, *British Press*, 163–67.

48. Medina Onrubia de Botana, *Crítica y su verdad*, 233.

49. *Noticias Gráficas*, December 6, 1946. The increase of 190 percent corresponds to the increase in the total amount paid by the newspaper to journalists, not to the rate of

increase for individual journalists. Journalists' wages increased by 78 percent in this period, while working hours decreased; as a result, *Noticias Gráficas* and other papers paid their existing journalists more and, in addition, hired more journalists to compensate for the shortened work schedule imposed by the Journalist's Statute.

50. *Editor and Publisher,* June 1, 1946.
51. In February 1946, *La Prensa*'s annual newsprint consumption—reduced because of the crisis—stood at twenty-six thousand tons, making the fifty-thousand-ton reserve nearly a two-year supply. Rojas Paz, "La prensa argentina," 264. While Agusti attributes the *La Prensa* owner's refusal to selfish greed, the legality of such a sale after the Farrell newsprint decrees is questionable. Both Gainza Paz and the Mitre family argued that newsprint imports could not fall under the 1939 antispeculation law since both *La Prensa* and *La Nación* imported not for sale or speculation, but for their own use.
52. *Noticias Gráficas,* December 6, 1946.
53. Ibid.
54. *Noticias Gráficas,* December 12, 1946.
55. *Crítica,* December 7, 1946.
56. Ibid.
57. *Standard,* December 8, 1946; Medina Onrubia de Botana, *Crítica y su verdad,* 233.
58. *Standard,* December 8, 1946.
59. Setaro, *La vida privada del periodismo,* 60–61.
60. See, for example, *La Época,* October 24, 1945; October 30, 1945; December 14, 1945; June 11, 1946; October 3–5, 1946. Colóm stated his interest in the paper to journalist Pablo Sirvén in Sirvén, *Perón y los medios de comunicación,* 70.
61. Cited in Walsh, *El caso Satanowsky,* 20. In her memoirs, Salvadora Medina Onrubia de Botana states that she believed that Peralta Ramos still maintained control of *La Razón* at the time of the proprietors' meeting at the *Standard.* Salvadora Medina Onrubia de Botana, *Crítica y su verdad,* 233. Peralta Ramos himself declared in a subsequent investigation that explicit pressure from Miguel Miranda began in October of 1946, and that after some resistance, the paper's investors gave in to the head of the Central Bank. *La Nación,* February 3, 1956.
62. Rodolfo Walsh, *El caso Satanowsky,* 20 and 47.
63. The case of *Crítica* is at least as complex as that of *La Razón.* Like the affairs of Peralta Ramos, those surrounding the newspaper founded by Natalio Botana are veiled in the secrecy of backroom deals and shady financial transactions. To make matters more complicated, the memoirs of Helvio Botana are filled with such basic inaccuracies as the date of Perón's assumption of the presidency, which Helvio Botana inexplicably places on May 1, 1946. H. Botana, *Memorias,* 211. Similarly, his mother's self-published memoirs were written with the explicit purpose of pleading her case before the authorities of the Revolución Libertadora for the return of *Crítica,* and contain similar inaccuracies and suspect interpretations. Medina Onrubia de Botana, *Crítica y su verdad.* While I have used both sources here, I have done so only where they coincide with each other and either the investigations conducted by the post-1955 military authorities or other sources, or are in accord with known circumstances.
64. By dissolving the paper's publishing company, Damonte Taborda halted any legal action that might have followed Salvadora's denunciations of financial mismanagement against her son-in-law. H. Botana, *Memorias,* 206.
65. Ibid.; Medina Onrubia de Botana, *Crítica y su verdad,* 224, 305. Salvadora places the length of *Crítica*'s closure after October 17, 1945 at three months; in fact, *Crítica* returned to the streets in two weeks.
66. H. Botana, *Memorias,* 209–10.
67. "Destino de un diario y de mil familias," *Qué sucedió en 7 días,* May 16, 1946 (test run), 32.
68. "Historia del Peronismo, XIV," 36, 37n3. Salvadora claims that "la señora"—Eva Perón—purchased the offices of *El Sol* for her paper, but *Democracia* moved to Avenida de

Mayo 654 nearly a year before the first lady's purchase of the paper. Salvadora Medina Onrubia de Botana, *Crítica y su verdad*, 326; *Democracia*, April 4, 1946.

69. *Clarín* had used the plant of *Noticias Gráficas* for its printing until José Agusti broke his contract with Noble over the price of the service. According to Salvadora, out of desperation the Botanas accepted the same contract that Agusti rejected. Salvadora Medina Onrubia de Botana, *Crítica y su verdad*, 306.

70. Ibid., 225.

71. Ibid., 309–11.

72. Ibid., 307–8; Comisión Nacional de Investigaciones, *Documentación*, 2:629.

73. See *Crítica*, Jul 21–August 11, 1947; *El Líder*, August 7–21, 1947. On the letter in defense of Eva Perón, see *Crítica*, June 17, 1947; Medina Onrubia de Botana, *Crítica y su verdad*, 313; and Barrandeguy, *Salvadora*, 165–69. The spur for this defense allegedly came from *Crítica*'s printing of an Associated Press bulletin which stated that Eva Perón "began her career at fifteen when she left home," a clear reference to Evita's supposed work as a prostitute. *Editor and Publisher*, August 9, 1947.

74. Comisión Nacional de Investigaciones, *Documentación*, 2:629.

75. H. Botana, *Memorias*, 210.

76. Comisión Nacional de Investigaciones, *Documentación*, 2:628, 633.

77. The attack against *El Mundo*, as well as *La Prensa* and the Socialist *La Vanguardia*, occurred as the CGT gathered in the Plaza de Mayo to celebrate Perón's announcement of the Five Year Plan. See *La Prensa*, January 25–26, 1947; *La Nación*, January 25–26, 1947; *El Mundo*, January 25–27, 1947.

78. *Editor and Publisher*, February 14, 1948; Ramos, *Cerrojos a la prensa*, 84.

79. Cited in "Historia del Peronismo, XXXII," 35. By 1947 the proprietors of Editorial Haynes, though of English descent, were Argentine nationals.

80. Ibid.; *Quien es quien en la Argentina*, 6th ed., s.v. Agusti, José. Perón also named Agusti ambassador to the U.S.S.R. upon Argentina's renewal of diplomatic relations with that country, though Agusti never assumed the post. "Su historia ya tiene un cuarto de siglo: Biografía y encrucijada de NOTICIAS GRAFICAS," *Qué sucedió en 7 días*, May 22, 1956, 32.

81. See José W. Agusti, "Carta Abierta al Presidente del Comité Metropolitano del Radicalismo, Dr. J. W. Perkins. Cómo Sirviendo al País se Llega a una 'Manifiesta Inconducta Partidaria,'" *Noticias Gráficas*, September 4, 1948.

82. Comisión Nacional de Investigaciones, *Documentación*, 1:536–38. Ángel Borlenghi maintained sole control of *El Líder*.

83. "Historia del Peronismo, XXXII," 36.

84. *La Vanguardia*, May 5, 1947; Comisión Nacional de Investigaciones, *Documentación*, 1:536.

85. In a 1967 interview Aloé claimed that, impressed with his explanation of the purpose of *Democracia*'s special year-end edition, the first lady tapped him for the post upon the Peronist acquisition of Editorial Haynes. "Historia del Peronismo, XXXII," 34–35. Though this story certainly resonates with Eva Perón's political style, it appears to contain at least some factual error. Testifying before military authorities a decade earlier, Aloé stated that he assumed control of ALEA in 1946—while Editorial Haynes did not come under Peronist control until early 1947. *La Nación*, February 3, 1956.

86. *Quien es quien en la Argentina*, 6th ed., s.v. Aloé, Carlos; Comisión Nacional de Investigaciones, *Documentación*, 2:543.

87. *La Nación*, October 22, 1946; *La Prensa*, October 22, 1946.

88. See *Tribuna Democrática*, January 1, 1947. It is noteworthy that such sycophantic expressions preceded Raúl Alejandro Apold's assumption as head of the office.

89. The centralization of official news stayed in effect for the first half of 1947, after which each ministry returned to addressing the media directly. See *La Nación*, November 22, 1946; *La Época*, January 15, 1947; July 1, 1947.

90. Comisión Nacional de Investigaciones, *Documentación*, 2:411.

91. Ibid., 410–11; *Editor and Publisher*, August 23, 1947; Rojas Paz, "La prensa argentina," 264. If the budget for salaries only quintupled in face of the much steeper increase in the number of employees, the figure still seems reasonable, given that many of these new employees surely worked part-time for the government bureau, a common practice among journalists.

92. Comisión Nacional de Investigaciones, *Documentación*, 2:409.

93. *La Acción* (Rosario), February 3, 1947.

94. "Resolución No. 35 [del Director General de Prensa], Octubre 21 de 1947," in Archivo de Prensa, folder "Archivo de Prensa: Antecedentes, 1943–1948. Vol. I."

95. Ibid. (emphasis added).

96. "Raúl Oromí, Director General de Prensa a Antonio Carregal, Jefe de la División Archivo. Enero 26 de 1948," in Archivo de Prensa, folder "Archivo de Prensa: Antecedentes, 1943–1948. Vol. I."

97. Decree 18.408/43 required publishers to submit fifteen copies of each edition of each newspaper published in the country, ten copies of each national magazine, five of each foreign publication, and three copies of each book.

98. See, for example, Archivo de Prensa, folder "Conflicto del diario *La Prensa*, 16/3/51," and folder "Conflicto del diario *La Prensa*, 17/3/51 al 18/3/51." Monitoring of foreign radio coverage predates this conflict but, not surprisingly, becomes increasingly common at moments of heightened tensions with foreign governments.

99. Cipolletti's successor, Carlos Pereyra Rozas, also died shortly after assuming the post. Apold became undersecretary of information and the press in early March 1949. See *La Nación*, March 9, 1949.

100. Comisión Nacional de Investigaciones, *Documentación*, 2:435.

101. Ibid., 586–87. The remainder of the official advertising took the form of street posters and other forms of nonnewspaper advertising.

102. Pujol, *Discépolo*, 328–29. Some of Discépolo's monologues from the program *Pienso . . . y digo lo que pienso* are collected in Discepolín, *¿A mí me la vas a contar?*

103. "Historia del Peronismo, La Primera Presidencia, LV: El Zar de la Propaganda," *Primera Plana*, August 8, 1967, 34.

104. Two groundbreaking studies of the Secretariat's propaganda activities are Plotkin, *Mañana es San Perón*, and the more recent Gené, *Un mundo felíz*.

105. Carlos Dalmiro Viale, "La Libertad Argentina de Prensa," *Argentina*, August 1949, 11.

106. Carlos Dalmiro Viale, "Prensa Libre y Responsible," *Argentina*, July 1949, 5–6.

107. Walsh, *El caso Satanowsky*, 210.

CHAPTER 7

1. This drive toward "deep unanimity" profoundly shaped Peronist politics, but was by no means unique to Peronism. See Halperín Donghi, "El lugar del peronismo," 36–42.

2. On Roberto Noble's small but growing *Clarín* in the Peronist period, see Ramos, *Cerrojos a la prensa;* and Walsh, *El caso Satanowsky*. Noble's behavior vis-à-vis the Peronist state and the traditional commercial press forms almost as much a part of Salvadora Medina Onrubia de Botana's memoirs as her complaints against the Peronist government itself. See Medina Onrubia de Botana, *Crítica y su verdad*.

3. *Democracia*, January 11, 1947; *Crítica*, March 7, 1947; *La Nación*, March 8, 1947.

4. Beyond the wealth held in the newspaper itself, Gainza Paz allegedly had a personal fortune in excess of $100 million (about U.S. $25 million), which provided a financial cushion for the operations of *La Prensa*. *Editor and Publisher*, April 5, 1947.

5. *La Época*, December 12, 1945.

6. See chapter 6.

7. *La Prensa*, February 22, 1944.
8. *Crítica*, December 7, 1946.
9. See Subsecretaría de Informaciones. Dirección General de Prensa, "Función Social de la Libertad de Prensa," radio editorial transmitted by the Radio del Estado network, December 23, 1946, 8:30 p.m. in Archivo de Prensa; Subsecretaría de Informaciones. Dirección General de Prensa, "'La Prensa' y la Verdad," radio editorial transmitted by the Radio del Estado network, January 3, 1947, 8:30 p.m., in Archivo de Prensa.
10. Subsecretaría de Informaciones. Dirección General de Prensa, "El Diario 'La Prensa' y el Interés Nacional," radio editorial transmitted by the Radio del Estado network, March 4, 1947, 1:30 p.m., in Archivo de Prensa.
11. Subsecretaría de Informaciones. Dirección General de Prensa, "Acción y Espíritu del Diario 'La Prensa,'" radio editorial transmitted by the Radio del Estado network, March 6, 1947, 8:30 p.m., in Archivo de Prensa; and Subsecretaría de Informaciones. Dirección General de Prensa, "Doctrina del Diario 'La Prensa,'" radio editorial transmitted by the Radio del Estado network, March 10, 1947, 8:30 p.m., in Archivo de Prensa.
12. *La Prensa*, September 20 and 21, 1947.
13. *La Prensa*, September 22, 1947; *El Laborista*, September 23, 1947.
14. *Democracia*, January 11, 1947.
15. *La Nación*, January 25, 1947.
16. Ibid.; *La Prensa*, January 25, 1947; *El Mundo*, January 25, 1947.
17. One journalist would later report that Gainza Paz had received warning about the impending assault and took these precautions. Given the political climate in Buenos Aires, however, such warnings were most likely superfluous. *Editor and Publisher*, March 15, 1947.
18. *La Época*, January 31, 1947. On the attacks against *La Prensa*, *El Mundo*, and *La Vanguardia* see *La Prensa*, January 25, 1947; *El Mundo*, January 25, 1947; and *La Nación*, January 25, 1947. International condemnation can be found in *La Prensa*, January 27, 1947; Círculo de la Prensa, *Boletín Oficial* (December 1946–January 1947), 1; and Círculo de la Prensa, *Boletín Oficial* (February–March 1947), 1–2; 7. On earlier calls for a boycott of *La Prensa*, see *Democracia*, January 11, 1947.
19. The *La Prensa* editorial on the attack, "Against Democracy and Liberty," included thinly veiled accusations of Peronism's Nazi sympathies, while the title itself spoke to the regime's alleged failings in adhering to the rules of political liberalism. *La Prensa*, January 26, 1947.
20. *Editor and Publisher*, April 5, 1947. This article reflects the continued characterization of the Peronist movement as essentially fascist that would remain the staple of U.S. reporting on Argentina well in the late twentieth century: "He came onto the stage and theatrically took off his coat. Immediately, he was joined in the ritual by the hundreds in the house. This taking off one's coat at a Peronist meeting is something like the 'Roman Salute' of Mussolini's Venice Palace balcony days." Perón's removal of the coat, in fact, corresponded not to dreams of imperial greatness, but to identification with the poor *descamisados* that formed not only the basis of much of Peronist political mythology, but also the electoral base of the movement.
21. *La Nación*, March 8, 1947.
22. *La Prensa*, March 19, 1947.
23. *La Prensa*, March 8, 1947.
24. *La Prensa*, March 7, 1947; *La Prensa*, March 9, 1947; *La Prensa*, March 15, 1947.
25. *El Laborista*, March 10, 1947.
26. *New York Times*, March 20, 1947.
27. See, for example, "El gobierno de Perón contra los diarios democráticos," in *El Plata* (Montevideo), March 17, 1947; "El periodismo bajo el gobierno de Perón," in *El Plata* (Montevideo), March 20, 1947; and "Perón posters ask boycott of Prensa," in *The New York Times*, March 20, 1947.
28. In late September the Food Workers Union [Sindicato de Empleados y Obreros de la Industria de la Alimentación] and the Confederation of State Personnel [Confederación

del Personal del Estado] again called for a boycott of *La Prensa*, and again met with little success. *La Época*, September 21, 1947; *El Laborista*, September 30, 1947.

29. Gainza Paz, *Por defender la libertad*, 98.

30. See for example, the attacks on October 17, 1947, in *La Prensa*, October 18, 1947. Events at newspaper offices during various October 17 celebrations are examined in Plotkin, "Rituales políticos."

31. *La Prensa*, March 10, 1947. On March 12 and 13, *La Prensa* published the formal responses by the CGT and other unions to the AFL report, and on March 16 reproduced various declarations of support for the AFL report from dissident Argentine unions.

32. *La Prensa*, March 12, 1947.

33. *La Nación*, March 19, 1947. By January 1947 *La Prensa*'s average daily circulation had grown to 397,384 copies, of which 38,000 corresponded to subscribers in the city of Buenos Aires and the rest of the country. *La Prensa*, March 19, 1947.

34. *La Nación*, March 19, 1947.

35. *La Época*, March 22, 1947.

36. *La Prensa*, March 29, 1947; *La Nación*, April 2, 1947; and *La Prensa*, April 2, 1947.

37. See, for example, *La Época*, June 14, 1947.

38. República Argentina, Cámara de Diputados, *Diario de sesiones 1947*, July 31, 1947, 894.

39. Ibid., July 4, 1947, 356–58. In reporting the British restrictions, *La Prensa* editorialists chose to emphasize not the extreme crisis which lead to the limitations, but rather the protests of the more powerful British commercial newspapers. See, for example, *La Prensa*, January 16–19, 1947.

40. Visca introduced the 1934 Matías Sánchez Sorondo into the congressional record in its totality, along with the latter's speech supporting the bill. See República Argentina, Cámara de Diputados, *Diarios de sesiones 1947*, August 27, 1947, 653–66.

41. See *La Nación*, July 15, 1947; *La Prensa*, July 16, 1947.

42. *Editor and Publisher*, August 16, 1947.

43. The paper reported that between January 20 and July 5, 1947, the Central Bank had approved $74 million for newsprint purchases, with 51,064 metric tons arriving in the port. In 1946 142,576 tons arrived at a total expense of $65 million. Not only was Argentine spending significantly more on newsprint, then, but nearly a third less was coming into the Buenos Aires port. *La Prensa*, July 16, 1947.

44. The section "Ante las medidas restrictivas de la labor periodística" ran from mid-August through the end of September.

45. The *canillitas* in particular complained that the Central Bank decree would force the typically multiedition evening papers like *La Razón*, *Crítica*, and *Noticias Gráficas* to reduce runs to a single evening edition. See *La Nación*, July 20, 1947; *La Prensa*, July 20, 1947.

46. *La Prensa*, September 8, 1947; *Editor and Publisher*, September 20, 1947.

47. The argument depended in part on a slight alteration of the text of the 1939 law. The law had originally left exempt from import duties paper "destined for the printing of newspapers, periodicals, books, pamphlets, and magazines, except *those* of commercial character [*los de carácter comercial*]." In presenting their arguments against *La Prensa* and *La Nación*, however, Customs lawyers claimed that the newsprint exempt from import duties was paper "destined for the printing of newspapers, periodicals, books, pamphlets, and magazines, except *that* of commercial character [*lo de carácter comercial*]." This shifted the commercial exception from the entire publication to images printed on the newsprint. *La Prensa*, August 22, 1947.

48. By comparison, *La Prensa* editorialists would point out, advertising space in the *New York Times* typically stood at just over 65 percent of each edition, similar to *La Prensa*. *La Prensa*, December 3, 1947.

49. For commentaries on the restriction of paper use for the British press, see *La Época*, June 9, 1950; on the United States, see *La Prensa*, June 21, 1950.

50. *La Nación*, August 30, 1950; *La Prensa*, December 17, 1950.

51. In late January of 1951, even the first Peronist paper, *La Época*, faced an economic crisis, leading to the resignation of its long-time director, the Peronist congressman Eduardo Colóm, and a restructuring of the paper's finances. *La Época*, January 30, 1951.

52. On newspaper prices and the rising costs of production, see chapter 6.

53. *La Prensa*, January 10, 1951.

54. *Los Andes* (Mendoza), January 27, 1951.

55. Ibid.

56. See *La Nación*, February 28, 1951.

57. See *La Nación*, April 12, 1951.

58. Ibid. A much more compelling argument seems to have escaped the future president of the republic: if *La Prensa* was primarily a commercial institution, did not Gainza Paz have much more to gain in subordinating the paper to Perón than it did in opposing him—especially when such opposition meant the dissolution of the enterprise itself?

59. *La Época*, April 12, 1951.

60. On pressures for *La Nación*'s adoption of a more staid editorial policy, see Seoane, *El burgués maldito*, 71–72.

61. Ricardo Sidicaro also convincingly argues that the economic reorientation adopted in Perón's second term coincided with the policies advocated by the *La Nación* editors for some time. See Sidicaro, *La política mirada desde arriba*, 219–39.

62. *La Nación*, June 28, 1951. The convenience of the ruling was twofold: Perón could simultaneously offer compensation without having to actually pay it; and, since essentially nothing was offered, Gainza Paz could not boost his own case against the regime by refusing the compensation.

63. The Foundation's compensation to the *La Prensa* employees totaled over $3 million. *La Nación*, June 12, 1951.

64. *La Prensa*, November 19, 1951.

65. The entire Peronist press drove home the inequity of world newsprint distribution, pointing to the 384-page editions of *The New York Times* and the 110-page edition of *The New York Herald* in early December of 1951—in the midst of the Argentine press's most severe shortage. See *La Prensa*, December 11, 1951; *La Prensa*, December 14, 1951; and *La Prensa*, December 17, 1951.

66. "Elogiado y repudiado, vuelve," *Qué sucedió en 7 días*, January 18, 1956, 23.

67. Halperín Donghi, "El lugar del peronismo," 40–41.

68. Comisión Nacional de Investigaciones, *Documentación*, 1:539.

69. Ibid., 540; Aloé, *Gobierno, proceso, conducta*, 249.

70. Comisión Nacional de Investigaciones, *Documentación*, 2:543.

71. The building, at Bouchard 722, also housed apartments for navy and air force officers. "Historia del Peronismo, La Primera Presidencia, XXXII: La Cadena de Diarios," in *Primera Plana*, February 21, 1967, 36; Comisión Nacional de Investigaciones, *Documentación*, 2:411.

72. In her history of the Inter American Press Association (IAPA), Mary Gardner remarks that "it was really the cause of *La Prensa* (Argentina) which united the United States press in its support of the Inter American Press Association." Gardner, *Inter American Press Association*, 96.

73. See, for example Ernie Hill, "Threat to Wreck *La Prensa* Caps Climax of Perón's Fight," *Editor and Publisher*, July 21, 1945.

CONCLUSION

1. Comisión Nacional de Investigaciones, *Documentación*, 1:536–38.

2. On the case of *El Intransigente*, see Torino, *Desde mi celda*; and Neiburg, "Intimacy and the Public Sphere."

3. On Perón's use of elements of liberalism, see also Plotkin, "La 'ideología' de Perón."
4. Gabriel, *La libertad de prensa*, 7.
5. Barrios, *La verdad periodística y la prensa amarilla*, 46.
6. See, for example, "Gainza Paz Sees La Prensa Gaining in Popular Esteem," *Editor and Publisher*, April 7, 1951, 7–8; and "Gainza Paz Tells La Prensa's Fate," *Editor and Publisher*, October 6, 1951, 56.
7. Armstrong Circle Theater, "Slow Assassination: Perón vs. La Prensa," NBC Television Network Master Broadcast Report in T.V. Network Master Books (Sunday, April 14, 1955–Tuesday, April 16, 1957).
8. Gardner, *Inter American Press Association*, 96–99.
9. Ibid., 99; Gainza Paz, *Por defender la libertad*.
10. See Comisión Nacional de Investigaciones, *Documentación*; Comisión Nacional de Investigaciones, *Libro negro de la segunda tiranía*; Sánchez Zinny, *El culto de la infamia*.
11. On the struggles over the distribution of the ALEA newspapers and *Democracia*, see "Embrollo en los eslabones," *Qué sucedió en 7 días*, January 25, 1956, 39; "Alza y papel: S.O.S. de ocho diarios," *Qué sucedió en 7 días*, February 15, 1956, 37; "Diarios en capilla," *Qué sucedió en 7 días*, April 25, 1956, 4–5; "La revolución y la libertad de prensa," *Qué sucedió en 7 días*, September 18, 1956, 6–7; Medina Onrubia de Botana, *Crítica y su verdad*; Walsh, *El caso Satanowsky*; and Melon Pirro, "La prensa de oposición."
12. See "Su historia ya tiene un cuarto de siglo," *Qué sucedió en 7 días*, May 22, 1956, 32–33. On the interest of military intelligence in the commercial press of the Libertadora period, see Walsh, *El caso Satanowsky*.
13. Walsh, *El caso Satanowsky*, 199.
14. Ibid., 200.
15. Rein, *Peronismo, populismo y política*, 16.
16. On the continued newsprint problem under Aramburu, see "'La Prensa': 80 Toneladas y 160 Gramos," *Qué sucedió en 7 días*, February 8, 1956, 36; and "Alza y Papel: S.O.S. de Ocho Diarios," *Qué sucedió en 7 días*, February 15, 1956, 37.
17. Brasch, "AP v. NLRB."
18. See Owensby, *Intimate Ironies*, 55, 168; and Salcetti, "Competing for Control."
19. On the strikes, see "Slowdown Reported in Chicago, Detroit," *Editor and Publisher*, November 22, 1947; "Miami Strike," *Editor and Publisher*, January 1, 1949; "Chicago Strikers Lose $9,000,000 in Wages," *Editor and Publisher*, February 12, 1949; "Chicago Printers Ask New Negotiation," *Editor and Publisher*, April 9, 1949; "Chicago Printers Told Offer Won't Be Raised," *Editor and Publisher*, April 16, 1949. On the American Newspaper Guild's investigations, see American Newspaper Guild, *Newsprint Problem*; American Newspaper Guild and Friedman, *Newsprint*; "Guild Urges Action on Newsprint Supply," *Editor and Publisher*, January 29, 1949; and "ANPA Says Guild Report on Newsprint Is Slanted," *Editor and Publisher*, February 26, 1949.
20. "1-Day Wildcat Strike Havocs Capital Routine," *Editor and Publisher*, April 9, 1949; "Pay, Hour Compromise Ends Strike in D.C.," *Editor and Publisher*, April 16, 1949; and *La Nación*, February 2–7, 1949; March 4, 1949.
21. "Guild Urges Action on Newsprint Supply," *Editor and Publisher*, January 29, 1949.
22. On the Hutchins Commission, see Bates, *Realigning Journalism*; Blanchard, *Hutchins Commission*; McIntyre, "Repositioning a Landmark"; and Nerone, *Last Rights*.
23. Hocking, *Freedom of the Press*, 1–3.
24. Curran, "Press Freedom as a Property Right"; and the contemporaneous studies by Martin, *Press the Public Wants*; and Gerald, *British Press*.

Bibliography

ARCHIVES

Archivo General de la Nación
Archivo del Círculo de la Prensa (Capital Federal)
Archivo de la Subsecretaría de Prensa, Secretaría de la Presidencia de la Nación
Archivo del diario *La Nación*
Archivo del diario *La Prensa*
Biblioteca del Congreso
Biblioteca Nacional
Biblioteca del diario *La Prensa*
Biblioteca del Comité Central del Partido Comunista Argentino
Biblioteca del Instituto Ravignagni, Universidad de Buenos Aires
Biblioteca de la Sociedad Argentina de Escritores
Biblioteca de la Unión de Trabajadores de Prensa de Buenos Aires
Library of Congress (U.S.A.)

NEWSPAPERS AND PERIODICALS

La Acción (Rosario, Argentina)
Anales de la legislación argentina
Los Andes (Mendoza, Argentina)
Argentina
C.G.T.
El Canillita
La Capital (Rosario, Argentina)
Córdoba (Córdoba, Argentina)
Crítica
Democracia
El Día (Montevideo, Uruguay)
Editor and Publisher (New York, U.S.A.)
La Época
La Hora
El Laborista
El Líder
El Mundo
La Nación
New York Times (New York, U.S.A.)
Noticias Gráficas
Octubre
Orientación

Página/12
El Plata (Montevideo, Uruguay)
La Prensa
Primera Plana
Qué sucedió en 7 días
La Razón
La Vanguardia

PUBLISHED PRIMARY AND SECONDARY LITERATURE

Abós, Alvaro. *Cautivo: El mural argentino de Siqueiros.* Buenos Aires: Libros del Zorzal, 2004.
———. *El tábano: Vida, pasión y muerte de Natalio Botana, el creador de "Crítica."* Buenos Aires: Sudamericana, 2001.
———. "La Venus Roja: Salvadora Medina Onrubia de Botana: Anarquista, poeta, periodista." *Todo es Historia,* no. 480 (2001): 6–29.
Aboy, Rosa. *Viviendas para el pueblo: Espacio urbano y sociabilidad en el barrio Los Perales, 1946–1955.* Buenos Aires: Fondo de Cultura Económica, 2005.
Acha, Omar. "Sociedad civil y sociedad política durante el primer peronismo." *Desarrollo Económico* 44, no. 174 (2004): 199–230.
Adelman, Jeremy. "Socialism and Democracy in Argentina in the Age of the Second International." *Hispanic American Historical Review* 72, no. 2 (1992): 211–38.
Agbaje, Adigun A. B. *The Nigerian Press, Hegemony, and the Social Construction of Legitimacy (1960–1983).* Lewiston, U.K.: Edwin Mellen Press, 1992.
Aguinaga, Carlos, and Roberto Azaretto. *Ni década ni infame: Del '30 al '43.* Buenos Aires: Jorge Baudino, 1991.
Alexander, Robert J. *Juan Domingo Perón: A History.* Boulder, Col.: Westview Press, 1979.
Allison, Victoria Caudery. "The Bitch Goddess and the Nazi Elvis: Peronist Argentina in the U.S. Popular Imagination." Ph.D. diss., State University of New York at Stony Brook, 2001.
Aloé, Carlos Vicente. *Gobierno, proceso, conducta.* Buenos Aires: Sudestada, 1969.
Alonso, Paula, ed. *Construcciones impresas: Panfletos, diarios y revistas en la formación de los estados nacionales en América Latina, 1820–1920.* Buenos Aires: Fondo de Cultura Económica, 2004.
———. "Ideological Tensions in the Foundational Decade of 'Modern Argentina': The Political Debates of the 1880s." *Hispanic American Historical Review* 87, no. 1 (2007): 31–41.
Althusser, Louis. "Ideology and Ideological State Apparatuses (Notes Towards an Investigation)." In *Lenin and Philosophy and Other Essays,* edited by Ben Brewster, 127–86. New York: Monthly Review Press, 1971.
Alvarez, Jesús Timoteo, and Ascensión Martínez Riaza. *Historia de la prensa hispanoamericana.* Madrid: Editorial MAPFRE, S.A., 1992.
Amaral, Samuel, and Mariano Ben Plotkin, eds. *Perón: Del exilio al poder.* Buenos Aires: Cántaro, 1993.
American Newspaper Guild. *The Newsprint Problem: Ten Questions and Answers.* New York: Guild, 1948.
American Newspaper Guild and Clara H. Friedman. *Newsprint: Summary of a Report on Newsprint Supply and Distribution.* New York: Guild, 1949.
Anderson, Benedict. *Imagined Communities: Reflections on the Origin and Spread of Nationalism.* Rev. ed. London: Verso, 1991.
Armus, Diego, ed. *Mundo urbano y cultura popular: Estudios de historia social argentina.* Buenos Aires: Sudamericana, 1990.

Arrighi de Garibotti, Francisca. *La odisea de la prensa libre (1945–1955)*. Gualeguay (Entre Ríos): n.p., 1964.
Asociación de Periodistas de Buenos Aires. *Estatutos*. Buenos Aires: Asociación de Periodistas de Buenos Aires, 1939.
Ayala, Francisco. *Recuerdos y olvidos*. Madrid: Alianza Editorial, 1988.
Baily, Samuel L. *Movimiento obrero, nacionalismo y política en la Argentina*. Buenos Aires: Paidós, 1984.
———. "The Role of Two Newspapers in the Assimilation of Italians in Buenos Aires and São Paulo, 1893–1913." *International Migration Review* 12, no. 3 (1978): 321–40.
Baletti Bianchi, Julieta. *Mirando vivir a los canillitas*. Montevideo: Casa A. Barreiro y Ramos, 1938.
Barbrook, Richard. *Media Freedom: The Contradictions of Communication in the Age of Modernity*. London: Pluto Press, 1995.
Barnes, John. *Evita, First Lady: A Biography of Eva Perón*. New York: Grove Press, 1978.
Barnhurst, Kevin G., and John Nerone. *The Form of News: A History*. New York: Guilford Press, 2001.
Barrandeguy, Emma. *Salvadora, una mujer de "Crítica."* Buenos Aires: Ediciones Vinciguerra, 1997.
Barreiro, José P. *La libertad de prensa y de pensamiento en la Argentina durante el siglo xix*. Buenos Aires: Colegio Libre de Estudios Superiores, 1949.
Barrios, Américo. *La verdad periodística y la prensa amarilla: Discurso pronunciado en la última sesión plenaria del Primer Congreso Nacional de Periodistas por el señor Américo Barrios, Secretario General del organismo*. Buenos Aires: Primer Congreso Nacional de Periodistas, 1951.
Bates, Stephen. *Realigning Journalism with Democracy: The Hutchins Commission, Its Times, and Ours*. Washington, D.C.: Annenberg Washington Program in Communications Policy Studies of Northwestern University, 1995.
Beasley-Murray, Jon. "Peronism and the Secret History of Cultural Studies: Populism and the Substitution of Culture for State." *Cultural Critique* 39 (1998): 189–217.
Béjar, María Dolores. *El régimen fraudulento: La política en la Provincia de Buenos Aires, 1930–1943*. Buenos Aires: Siglo Veintiuno, 2005.
———. *Uriburu y Justo: El auge conservador (1930–1935)*. Buenos Aires: Centro Editor de América Latina, 1983.
Bekken, Jon. "The Chicago Newspaper Scene: An Ecological Perspective." *Journalism and Mass Communication Quarterly* 74, no. 3 (1997): 490–500.
———. "Crumbs from the Publishers' Golden Tables: The Plight of the Chicago Newsboy." *Media History* 6, no. 1 (2000): 45–57.
Belini, Claudio. "El Grupo Bunge y la política económica del primer peronismo, 1943–1952." *Latin American Research Review* 41, no. 1 (2006): 27–50.
Beltrán, Oscar. *Historia del periodismo argentino*. Buenos Aires: Sopena, 1943.
Benjamin, Walter. "The Author as Producer." In *Reflections: Essays, Aphorisms, Autobiographical Writings*, edited by Peter Demetz, translated by Edmund Jephcott, 220–38. New York: Schocken Books, 1978.
———. "The Work of Art in the Age of Mechanical Reproduction." In *Illuminations*, edited by Hannah Arendt, translated by Harry Zohn, 217–51. New York: Schocken Books, 1968.
Beresford Crawkes, J. *533 días de historia argentina: 6 de setiembre de 1930–20 de febrero de 1932*. Buenos Aires: Mercatali, 1932.
Bethell, Leslie, and Ian Roxborough. "Latin America Between the Second World War and the Cold War: Some Reflections on the 1945–8 Conjuncture." *Journal of Latin American Studies* 20 (May 1988): 167–89.
Bianchi, Susana. *Historia de las religiones en la Argentina: Las minorías religiosas*. Historia Argentina. Buenos Aires: Sudamericana, 2004.
Blanchard, Margaret A. *Exporting the First Amendment: The Press-Government Crusade of 1945–1952*. New York: Longman, 1986.

———. *The Hutchins Commission: The Press and the Responsibility Concept.* Lexington, Ky.: Association for Education in Journalism, 1977.
Blasco Ibáñez, Vicente. *Argentina y sus grandezas.* Madrid: La Editorial Española Americana, 1910.
Bohigas, Angel. "El Discurso de D. Ángel Bohigas." In Diario 'La Nación,' *La Nación*, 15–16.
Bonasso, Miguel. *Don Alfredo.* Buenos Aires: Planeta, 2000.
Borges, Jorge Luís. *Obras, reseñas y traducciones inéditas: Colaboraciones de Jorge Luís Borges en la "Revista Multicolor de los Sábados" del diario Crítica, 1933–1934.* Buenos Aires: Editorial Atlántida, 1999.
Botana, Helvio I. *Memorias: Tras los dientes del perro.* Buenos Aires: Peña Lillo, 1977.
Botana, Natalio. *El orden conservador: La política argentina entre 1880 y 1916.* Buenos Aires: Sudamericana, 1977.
Botana, Natalio, and Ezequiel Gallo. *De la República posible a la República verdadera (1880–1910).* Vol. 3 of *Biblioteca del Pensamiento Argentino.* Buenos Aires: Espasa Calpe, 1997.
Boyle, Maryellen. "Capturing Journalism: Press and Politics in East Germany, 1945–1991." Ph.D. diss., University of California–San Diego, 1992.
Braden, Spruille. *Diplomats and Demagogues: The Memoirs of Spruille Braden.* New Rochelle, N.Y.: Arlington House, 1971.
Brasch, Walter M. "AP v. NLRB: The Right to Union Membership." In Brasch, *With Just Cause*, 89–95.
———, ed. *With Just Cause: Unionization of the American Journalist.* Lanham, Md.: University Press of America, 1991.
Brennan, James P., ed. *Peronism and Argentina.* Wilmington, Del.: Scholarly Resources, 1998.
Brennen, Bonnie. *For the Record: An Oral History of Rochester, New York, Newsworkers.* New York: Fordham University Press, 2001.
———. "Newsworkers During the Interwar Era: A Critique of Traditional Media History." *Communication Quarterly* 43 (1995): 197–209.
Bruce, James. *Those Perplexing Argentines.* New York: Longmans, Green, 1953.
Buchrucker, Cristián. "Interpretations of Peronism: Old Frameworks and New Perspectives." In Brennan, *Peronism and Argentina*, 3–28.
———. *Nacionalismo y peronismo: La Argentina en la crisis ideológica mundial (1927–1955).* Buenos Aires: Sudamericana, 1987.
Buckman, Robert T. "Birth, Death, and Resurrection of Press Freedom in Chile." In Cole, *Communication in Latin America*, 155–81.
Bueno, Javier. *Mi viaje a América.* Paris: Garnier, 1913.
Caimari, Lila. *Apenas un delincuente: Crímen, castigo y cultura en la Argentina, 1880–1955.* Colección Historia y Cultura. Buenos Aires: Siglo Veintiuno, 2004.
Calki (Raimundo Calcagno). *"El Mundo" era una fiesta.* Buenos Aires: Corregidor, 1977.
Camaño, Juan C., and Osvaldo Bayer. *Los periodistas desaparecidos.* Buenos Aires: Norma, 1998.
Capelato, Maria Helena Rolim. *Multidões em cena: Propaganda política no varguismo e no peronismo.* Campinas, SP: Papirus, 1998.
Carey, James. "The Problem of Journalism History." In *James Carey: A Critical Reader*, edited by Eve Stryker Munson and Catherine A. Warren, 86–94. Minneapolis: University of Minnesota Press, 1997.
Carulla, Juan E. *Al filo del medio siglo.* Entre Ríos: Llanura, 1951.
Casullo, Nicolás. *Pensar entre épocas: Memoria, sujetos y crítica intelectual.* Buenos Aires: Grupo Editorial Norma, 2004.
Cattaruzza, Alejandro. *Historia y política en los años treinta: Comentarios en torno al caso radical.* Buenos Aires: Biblos, 1991.
Chafee, Zechariah. *Free Speech in the United States.* Cambridge, Mass.: Harvard University Press, 1941.

———. *Government and Mass Communications*. 2 vols. Chicago: University of Chicago Press, 1947.
Chiaramonte, José Carlos. "Ciudadanía, soberanía y representación en la génesis del Estado argentino (c. 1810–1852)." In *Ciudadanía política y formación de las naciones: Perspectivas históricas de América Latina*, edited by Hilda Sábato, 94–116. Mexico City: Fondo de Cultura Económica, 1999.
Cincuenta y Tres Periodistas Argentinos. *El libro azul y blanco de la prensa argentina*. Buenos Aires: Organización Nacional del Periodismo Argentino, 1951.
Cipolletti, Emilio. *Ante los ojos de América*. Buenos Aires: Ediciones Justicia Social, 1947.
Círculo de la Prensa (Capital Federal). *Anuario*, 1896–1997.
———. *Boletín Oficial*, 1928–56.
———. *Ley de jubilación de periodistas*. Buenos Aires: Círculo de la Prensa, 1941.
———. *Memoria y Balance, 1928–1929*. Buenos Aires: Círculo de la Prensa, 1929.
———. *Memoria y Balance, 1930–1931*. Buenos Aires: Círculo de la Prensa, 1931.
———. *Proyecto de ley de jubilaciones para periodistas y gráficos de la República: Enviado al H. Congreso de la Nación por el P.E., con fecha Agosto 26 de 1932*. Buenos Aires: Círculo de la Prensa, 1932.
Ciria, Alberto. *Partidos y poder en la Argentina moderna (1930–1946)*. 3rd ed. Buenos Aires: Ediciones de la Flor, 1975.
———. *Política y cultura popular: La Argentina peronista, 1946–1955*. Buenos Aires: Ediciones de la Flor, 1983.
Claxton, Robert H. *From Parsifal to Perón: Early Radio in Argentina, 1920–1940*. Gainesville: University Press of Florida, 2007.
Clemenceau, Georges. *South America Today: A Study of the Conditions, Social, Political, and Commercial in Argentina, Uruguay, and Brazil*. New York: Knickerbocker Press, 1911.
Coca, Joaquín. *El contubernio*. Buenos Aires: Claridad, 1932.
Cole, Richard, ed. *Communication in Latin America: Journalism, Mass Media, and Society*. Wilmington, Del.: Scholarly Resources, 1996.
Colóm, Eduardo. *17 de Octubre: La revolución de los descamisados*. Buenos Aires: La Época, 1946.
Colominas, Norberto, and Enrique Sdrech. *Cabezas: Crímen, mafia y poder*. Buenos Aires: Atuel, 1997.
Comisión Nacional de Investigaciones, República Argentina. *Documentación, autores y cómplices de las irregularidades cometidas durante la segunda tiranía*. 3 vols. Buenos Aires: Gobierno de la Nación, 1958.
———. *Libro negro de la segunda tiranía*. Buenos Aires: Gobierno de la Nación, 1958.
Comisión Pro Ley de Prensa. *Proyecto de ley del Senador Sánchez Sorondo, de Amparo a la Prensa*. Buenos Aires: Congreso de la Nación, 1934.
Commission on Freedom of the Press (Hutchins Commission). *A Free and Responsible Press*. Chicago: University of Chicago Press, 1947.
Confalonieri, Orestes. *Perón contra Perón*. Buenos Aires: Editorial Antygua, 1956.
Conniff, Michael L., ed. *Populism in Latin America*. Tuscaloosa: University of Alabama Press, 1999.
Contreras, Gustavo Nicolás. "Los trabajadores gráficos, la prensa y la política durante el peronismo." In *Prensa y peronismo: Discursos, prácticas, empresas (1943–1958)*, edited by María Liliana Da Orden and Julio César Melon Pirro. Rosario, Argentina: Prohistoria, 2007.
Córdova Iturburu, Cayetano. *España bajo el comando del pueblo*. Buenos Aires: Ediciones FOARE, 1938.
Cossio, Carlos. *La opinión pública*. 4th ed. Buenos Aires: Paidós, 1973.
Cowles, Fleur. *Bloody Precedent*. New York: Random House, 1952.
Cox, David. "The Rise and Decline of *La Prensa*." M.A. thesis, University of South Carolina, 1995.

Cramer, Gisela. "Argentine Riddle: The Pinedo Plan of 1940 and the Political Economy of the Early War Years." *Journal of Latin American Studies* 30, no. 3 (1998): 519–50.
Crassweller, Robert D. *Perón and the Enigmas of Argentina*. New York: W. W. Norton, 1987.
Crawley, Eduardo. *A House Divided: Argentina, 1880–1980*. London: C. Hurst, 1984.
Curran, James. "The Press as an Agency of Social Control: An Historical Perspective." In *Newspaper History from the Seventeenth Century to the Present Day*, edited by George Boyce, James Curran, and Pauline Wingate, 51–75. London: Constable, 1978.
———. "Press Freedom as a Property Right: The Crisis of Press Legitimacy." *Media, Culture and Society* 1 (1979): 59–82.
———. "Rethinking the Media as a Public Sphere." In *Communication and Citizenship: Journalism and the Public Sphere in the New Media Age*, edited by Peter Dahlgren and Colin Sparks, 27–57. Communication and Society. London: Routledge, 1991.
Curran, James, and Jean Seaton. *Power Without Responsibility*. London: Routledge, 1993.
Da Orden, María Liliana, and Julio César Melon Pirro, eds. *Prensa y peronismo: Discursos, prácticas, empresas (1943–1958)*. Rosario, Argentina: Prohistoria, 2007.
Dahlgren, Peter, and Colin Sparks, eds. *Communication and Citizenship: Journalism and the Public Sphere in the New Media Age*. London: Routledge, 1991.
———. *Journalism and Popular Culture*. London: Sage, 1992.
Damonte Taborda, Raúl. *¿A dónde va Perón? De Berlín a Wall Street*. Montevideo: Ediciones de la Resistencia Revolucionaria Argentina, 1955.
———. *Ayer fué San Perón: 12 años de humillación argentina*. Buenos Aires: Gure, 1955.
Debray, Régis. *Media Manifestos: On the Technological Transmission of Cultural Forms*. Translated by Eric Rauth. London: Verso, 1996.
De Ipola, Emilio. *Ideología y discurso populista*. 2nd ed. Buenos Aires: Folios Ediciones, 1983.
Del Campo, Hugo. *Sindicalismo y peronismo: Los comienzos de un vínvculo perdurable*. Biblioteca de Ciencias Sociales. Buenos Aires: CLACSO, 1983.
Delgado, Ariel. *Agresiones a la prensa*. Buenos Aires: Asociación Madres de la Plaza de Mayo, 1995.
De Privitellio, Luciano. *Augustín Justo: Las armas en la política*. Buenos Aires: Fondo de Cultura Económica, 1997.
———. *Vecinos y ciudadanos: Política y sociedad en la Buenos Aires de entreguerras*. Buenos Aires: Siglo Veintiuno, 2003.
Deutsch, Sandra McGee. *Las Derechas: The Extreme Right in Argentina, Brazil, and Chile, 1890–1939*. Palo Alto: Stanford University Press, 2002.
Deutsch, Sandra McGee, and Ronald Dolkart, eds. *The Argentine Right: Its History and Intellectual Origins, 1910 to the Present*. Wilmington, Del.: Scholarly Resources, 1993.
Dewey, John. *Freedom and Culture*. Buffalo: Prometheus Books, 1939.
Díaz Alejandro, Carlos. *Ensayos sobre la historia económica argentina*. Buenos Aires: Amorrortu, 1975.
Díaz Araujo, Enrique. *La conspiración del '43: El GOU: Una experiencia militarista en la Argentina*. Buenos Aires: Ediciones La Bastilla, 1971.
Di Stefano, Roberto. *El púlpito y la plaza: Clero, sociedad y política de la monarquía católica a la república rosista*. Historia y cultura. Buenos Aires: Siglo Veintiuno, 2004.
Di Stefano, Roberto, Nancy Calvo, and Klaus Gallo, eds. *Los curas de la revolución: Vidas de eclesiásticos en los orígenes de la Nación*. Buenos Aires: Emecé, 2002.
Di Tella, Torcuato S. *Perón y los sindicatos: El inicio de una relación conflictiva*. Buenos Aires: Ariel, 2003.
Diario La Nación. *"La Nación" y los premios María Moors Cabot de 1942*. Buenos Aires: La Nación, 1942.
Díaz Alejandro, Carlos F. *Essays on the Economic History of the Argentine Republic*. New Haven: Yale University Press, 1970.
Diez Periodistas Porteños. *Al margen de la conspiración*. Buenos Aires: Biblos, 1930.
Discepolín (Enrique S. Discépolo). *¿A mi me la vas a contar? Mordisquito*. Buenos Aires: Freeland, 1973.

Dolkart, Ronald H. "The Right in the década infame, 1930–1943." In Deutsch and Dolkart, *Argentine Right*, 65–98.
Dujovne Ortiz, Alicia. *Eva Perón: La biografía*. Buenos Aires: Aguilar, 1995.
Duncan, Tim. "La prensa política: 'Sud-América,' 1884–1892." In *La Argentina del Ochenta al Centenario*, edited by Gustavo Ferrari and Ezequiel Gallo, 761–83. Buenos Aires: Sudamericana, 1980.
Editor and Publisher: International Year Book Number for 1946. New York: Editor and Publisher, 1946.
Elena, Eduardo. "Justice and Comfort: Peronist Political Culture and the Search for a New Argentina, 1930–1955." Ph.D. diss., Princeton University, 2002.
———. "What the People Want: State Planning and Political Participation in Peronist Argentina, 1946–1955." *Journal of Latin American Studies* 37 (February 2005): 81–108.
Ellner, Steve. "The 'Radical' Thesis on Globalization and the Case of Venezuela's Hugo Chávez." *Latin American Perspectives* 29, no. 6 (2002): 88–93.
Ellner, Steve, and Daniel Hellinger, eds. *Venezuelan Politics in the Chávez Era: Class, Polarization, and Conflict*. Boulder, Col.: Lynne Rienner, 2003.
Ellner, Steve, and Miguel Tinker Salas, eds. *Venezuela: Hugo Chávez and the Decline of an "Exceptional Democracy."* Lanham, Md.: Rowman and Littlefield, 2007.
Esti Rein, Mónica. *Politics and Education in Argentina, 1946–1962*. Latin American Realities. Armonk, N.Y.: M. E. Sharpe, 1998.
Ewen, Stuart. *Captains of Consciousness: Advertising and the Social Roots of the Consumer Culture*. New York: McGraw-Hill, 1976.
Federación Argentina de Periodistas. *VIII Congreso de la Federación Argentina de Periodistas*. Buenos Aires: Federación Argentina de Periodistas, 1947.
———. *IX Congreso de la Federación Argentina de Periodistas*. Buenos Aires: Federación Argentina de Periodistas, 1948.
———. *Resoluciones del IX Congreso*. Buenos Aires: Federación Argentina de Periodistas, 1948.
———. *X Congreso de la Federación Argentina de Periodistas*. Buenos Aires: Federación Argentina de Periodistas, 1949.
———. *XI Congreso de la Federación Argentina de Periodistas*. Buenos Aires: Federación Argentina de Periodistas, 1951.
———. *Resoluciones aprobadas por el XI Congreso*. Buenos Aires: Federación Argentina de Periodistas, 1951.
Fenby, Jonathan. *The International News Services: A Twentieth Century Fund Report*. New York: Schocken Books, 1986.
Fernández, José Luís, Claudia López Barros, and José Luís Petris. "*El Mundo* condensado/ r e ilustrado/r." In *Noveno Congreso Nacional y Regional de Historia Argentina*. Rosario, Argentina: Academia Nacional de Historia, 1996.
Fernández, Juan Rómulo. *Historia del periodismo argentino*. Buenos Aires: Librería Perlado Editores, 1943.
Fernández Llorente, Antonio, and Oscar Balmaceda. *El caso Cabezas: El crimen del reportero gráfico y la investigación del asesinato que conmovió al país*. Buenos Aires: Planeta, 1997.
Finchelstein, Federico. *Fascismo, liturgia e imaginario: El mito del general Uriburu y la Argentina nacionalista*. Buenos Aires: Fondo de Cultura Económica, 2002.
Floria, Carlos A., and César A. García Belsunce. *Historia política de la Argentina contemporánea, 1880–1983*. Buenos Aires: Alianza Editorial, 1988.
Ford, Aníbal, and Jorge B. Rivera. "Los medios masivos de comunicación en la Argentina." In Ford, Rivera, and Romano, *Medios de comunicación*, 24–45.
Ford, Aníbal, Jorge B. Rivera, and Eduardo Romano, eds. *Medios de comunicación y cultura popular*. Buenos Aires: Legasa, 1990.
Fowler, Roger. *Language in the News: Discourse and Ideology in the Press*. London: Routledge, 1991.

Fraga, Rosendo, ed. *Autopercepción del periodismo en la Argentina*. Buenos Aires: Belgrano, 1997.
———. *El General Justo*. Buenos Aires: Emecé, 1993.
Frank, Gary. *Juan Perón vs. Spruille Braden: The Story Behind the Blue Book*. Lanham, Md.: University Press of America, 1980.
Fraser, Howard M. *Magazines and Masks: "Caras y Caretas" as a Reflection of Buenos Aires, 1898–1908*. Tempe: Center for Latin American Studies, 1987.
Fraser, Nicholas, and Maryssa Navarro. *Evita: The Real Life of Eva Perón*. New York: W. W. Norton, 1996.
Friedman, Max Paul. *Nazis and Good Neighbors: The United States Campaign Against the Germans of Latin America in World War II*. New York: Cambridge University Press, 2003.
Fromson, Murray. "Mexico's Struggle for a Free Press." In Cole, *Communication in Latin America*, 115–37.
Gabetta, Carlos, ed. *Periodismo y ética: Jornadas sobre periodismo y ética del diario "La Nación."* Buenos Aires: Espasa, 1997.
Gabriel, José. *La libertad de prensa: Declaración aprobada por el Primer Congreso Nacional de Periodistas celebrado en Buenos Aires del 1 al 8 de septiembre de 1951, y fundada por José Gabriel, delegado al congreso y presidente y relator de la Comisión de Libertad de Prensa, que formuló el despacho correspondiente*. Buenos Aires: Primer Congreso Nacional de Periodistas, 1951.
Gainza Paz, Alberto. "Eyes and Tongues of Our People." *Vital Speeches of the Day* 18 (1953): 73.
———. *Por defender la libertad*. 2nd ed. Buenos Aires: Diario "La Prensa," 1957.
Gallo, Ricardo. *La radio: Ese mundo tan sonoro*. Buenos Aires: Corregidor, 1991.
Galván Moreno, C. *El periodismo argentino: Amplia y documentada historia desde sus orígenes hasta el presente*. Buenos Aires: Editorial Claridad, 1944.
Gambini, Hugo. *El 17 de octubre de 1945*. Buenos Aires: Brújula, 1969.
———. *Historia del peronismo: El poder total (1943–1951)*. Buenos Aires: Planeta, 1999.
García, Eduardo Augusto. *Yo fui testigo: Antes, durante y después de la segunda tiranía (Memorias)*. Buenos Aires: Luís Lasserre y Cia., 1971.
García Canclini, Néstor. *Culturas híbridas: Estrategias para entrar y salir de la modernidad*. Mexico City: Grijalbo, 1989.
García Molina, Fernando, and Carlos A. Mayo, eds. *Archivo del general Uriburu: Autoritarismo y ejército*. 2 vols. Biblioteca Política Argentina 261–62. Buenos Aires: Centro Editor de América Latina, 1986.
García Sebastiani, Marcela. "The Other Side of Peronist Argentina: Radicals and Socialists in the Political Opposition to Perón (1946–1955)." *Journal of Latin American Studies* 35 (2003): 311–39.
Gardner, Mary A. *The Inter American Press Association: Its Fight for Freedom of the Press, 1926–1960*. Austin: University of Texas Press, 1967.
Garrison, Bruce, and Michael B. Salwen. *Latin American Journalism*. Hillsdale, N.J.: Lawrence Erlbaum Associates, 1991.
Garvie, Alejandro. *La economía peronista, 1946–1955: Los límites de la voluntad*. Buenos Aires: Longseller, 2002.
Gay, Luís. *El Partido Laborista en la Argentina: La historia del partido que llevó a Perón al poder*. Buenos Aires: Editorial Biblos, 1999.
Gené, Marcela. *Un mundo feliz: Imágenes de los trabajadores en el primer peronismo, 1946–1955*. Buenos Aires: Fondo de Cultura Económica, 2005.
Gerald, J. Edward. *The British Press Under Government Economic Controls*. Minneapolis: University of Minnesota Press, 1956.
Germani, Gino. *Política y sociedad en una época de transición*. Buenos Aires: Paidós, 1962.
Giusti, Roberto. *Visto y vivido. Anécdotas, semblanzas, confesiones y batallas*. Buenos Aires: Losada, 1965.

Godoy Froy, Martha Lía. *Perfiles de Roberto A. Tálice*. Buenos Aires: Corregidor, 1990.
Goldman, Aaron L. "Press Freedom in Britain During World War II." *Journalism History* 22, no. 4 (1997): 146–55.
González Tuñón, Raúl. "*Crítica* y los años 20." *Todo es Historia* 32 (1969): 53–67.
Gramsci, Antonio. *The Antonio Gramsci Reader: Selected Writings, 1916–1935*. Edited by David Forgacs. New York: New York University Press, 2000.
———. *Selections from the Prison Notebooks*. Edited and translated by Quintin Hoare and Geoffrey Nowell Smith. New York: International, 1971.
Grandin, Greg. *The Last Colonial Massacre: Latin America in the Cold War*. Chicago: University of Chicago Press, 2004.
Greenup, Ruth, and Leonard Greenup. *Revolution Before Breakfast: Argentina, 1941–1946*. Chapel Hill: University of North Carolina Press, 1947.
Guerra, François-Xavier, and Annick Lempèriére. *Los espacios públicos en Iberoamérica: Ambigüedades y problemas, siglos XVIII–XIX*. Mexico City: Fondo de Cultura Económica, 1998.
Guibourg, Edmundo. *El último bohemio: Conversaciones con Edmundo Guibourg (Entrevistas de Mona Moncalvillo)*. Buenos Aires: Editorial Celtia, 1981.
Gurevitch, Michael, Tony Bennett, James Curran, and Janet Woollacott, eds. *Culture, Society and the Media*. London: Routledge, 1982.
Gutiérrez, Leandro, and Luís Alberto Romero. *Sectores populares: Cultura y política. Buenos Aires en la entreguerra*. Buenos Aires: Sudamericana, 1995.
Guyot, Joëlle. *La presse moderniste en Argentine de 1896 à 1905*. Paris: Presses de la Sorbonne Nouvelle, 1999.
Habermas, Jürgen. *Legitimation Crisis*. Translated by Thomas McCarthy. Boston: Beacon Press, 1975.
———. *The Structural Transformation of the Public Sphere: An Inquiry into a Category of Bourgeois Society*. Translated by Thomas Burger with the assistance of Frederick Lawrence. Cambridge, Mass.: MIT Press, 1989.
Hall, Stuart. "The Rediscovery of 'Ideology': Return of the Repressed in Media Studies." In *Culture, Society and the Media*, edited by Michael Gurevitch, Tony Bennett, James Curran, and Janet Woollacott, 52–86. London: Routledge, 1982.
Hallin, Daniel C. *We Keep America on Top of the World: Television Journalism and the Public Sphere*. London: Routledge, 1994.
Halperín Donghi, Tulio. *Argentina en el callejón*. Buenos Aires: Espasa Calpe Argentina/Ariel, 1994.
———. *La Argentina y la tormenta del mundo: Ideas e ideologías entre 1930 y 1945*. Buenos Aires: Siglo Veintiuno, 2003.
———. "The Colonial *Letrado* as a Revolutionary Intellectual: Deán Funes as Seen Through His *Apuntamientos para una Biografía*." In *Revolution and Restoration: The Rearrangement of Power in Argentina, 1776–1860*, edited by Mark D. Szuchman and Jonathan C. Brown, 54–73. Lincoln: University of Nebraska Press, 1995.
———. "Estudio preliminar." In Halperín Donghi, *Vida y muerte*, 21–272.
———. *José Hernández y sus mundos*. Buenos Aires: Sudamericana, 1985.
———. "1880: Un nuevo clima de ideas." In *El espejo de la historia: Problemas argentinos y perspectivas latinoamericanas*, 239–51. Buenos Aires: Sudamericana, 1987.
———. "El lugar del peronismo en la tradición política argentina." In *Perón: Del exilio al poder*, edited by Samuel Amaral and Mariano Ben Plotkin, 15–44. Buenos Aires: Cántara, 1993.
———. *La República imposible (1930–1945)*. Vol. 5 of *Biblioteca del Pensamiento Argentino*. Buenos Aires: Ariel, 2004.
———. *Vida y muerte de la República verdadera (1910–1930)*. Vol. 4 of *Biblioteca del Pensamiento Argentino*. Buenos Aires: Ariel, 1999.
Hardt, Hanno. *Critical Communication Studies: Essays on Communication, History and Theory*. London: Routledge, 1992.

———. *In the Company of Media: Cultural Constructions of Communication, 1920s–1930s.* Boulder, Col.: Westview Press, 2000.
Hardt, Hanno, and Bonnie Brennen, eds. *Newsworkers: Toward a History of the Rank and File.* Minneapolis: University of Minnesota Press, 1995.
Harrison, Stanley. *Poor Men's Guardians: A Record of the Struggles for a Democratic Newspaper Press, 1763–1973.* London: Lawrence and Wishart, 1974.
Haussen, Doris Fagundes. *Rádio e política: Tempos de Vargas e Perón.* Porto Alegre: EDIPUCRS, 2001.
Healey, Mark Alan. *The Ruins of the New Argentina: Peronism and the Remaking of San Juan After the 1944 Earthquake.* Durham: Duke University Press, 2011.
Henkin, David. *City Reading: Written Words and Public Spaces in Antebellum New York.* New York: Columbia University Press, 1998.
Hill, Kim Quaile, and Patricia A. Hurley. "Freedom of the Press in Latin America: A Thirty-Year Survey." *Latin American Research Review* 15 (Spring 1980): 212–18.
Hocking, William E. *Freedom of the Press: A Framework of Principle.* Chicago: University of Chicago Press, 1947.
Horkheimer, Max, and Theodor W. Adorno. "The Culture Industry: Enlightenment as Mass Deception." In *Dialectic of Enlightenment,* translated by John Cumming, 120–67. New York: Herder and Herder, 1972.
Horowitz, Joel. *Argentine Unions, the State and the Rise of Perón, 1930–1945.* Berkeley: Institute of International Studies, University of California–Berkeley, 1990.
Horvath, Ricardo. *Revolución y periodismo (Guevara-Masetti-Walsh).* Ediciones del Instituto Movilizador de Fondos Cooperativos. Buenos Aires: Centro Cultural de la Cooperación, 2003.
Huberman, Silvio. *Hasta el alba con Ulyses Petit de Murat.* Buenos Aires: Corregidor, 1979.
Humphreys, Peter J. *Mass Media and Media Policy in Western Europe.* European Policy Research Unit Series. Manchester: Manchester University Press, 1996.
———. *Media and Media Policy in West Germany: The Press and Broadcasting Since 1945.* German Studies Series. New York, Oxford, Munich: Berg, 1990.
Ibarguren, Carlos. *La historia que he vivido.* Buenos Aires: Eudeba, 1969.
Ickes, Harold L. *America's House of Lords: An Inquiry into Freedom of the Press.* New York: Harcourt-Brace, 1939.
———, ed. *Freedom of the Press Today: A Clinical Examination by Twenty-Eight Specialists.* New York: Vanguard, 1941.
Jaksić, Iván. "The Machine and the Spirit: Anti-technological Humanism in Twentieth-Century Latin America." *Revista de Estudios Hispánicos* 30 (1996): 179–201.
———, ed. *The Political Power of the Word: Press and Oratory in Nineteenth-Century Latin America.* London: Institute of Latin American Studies, University of London, 2002.
———. "Sarmiento and the Chilean Press, 1841–1851." In *Sarmiento: Author of a Nation,* edited by Tulio Halperín Donghi, Iván Jaksić, Gwen Kirkpatrick, and Francine Masiello, 31–60. Berkeley: University of California Press, 1994.
James, Daniel. "October 17th and 18th, 1945: Mass Protest, Peronism and the Argentine Working Class." *Journal of Social History* 21 (Spring 1988): 441–61.
———. *Resistance and Integration: Peronism and the Argentine Working Class, 1946–1976.* New York: Cambridge University Press, 1988.
Jameson, Fredric. *The Political Unconscious: Narrative as a Socially Symbolic Act.* Ithaca: Cornell University Press, 1981.
Jauretche, Arturo. *FORJA y la década infame: Con un apéndice de manifiestos, declaraciones y textos de volantes.* Buenos Aires: Coyoacán, 1962.
Jones, Aled. *Powers of the Press: Newspapers, Power and the Public in Nineteenth-Century England.* Hants: Scolar Press, 1996.
Kaplan, Richard L. *Politics and the American Press: The Rise of Objectivity, 1865–1920.* New York: Cambridge University Press, 2002.

Karush, Matthew B. *Workers or Citizens: Democracy and Identity in Rosario, Argentina (1912–1930)*. Albuquerque: University of New Mexico Press, 2002.
Kelly, David. *The Ruling Few; Or the Human Background to Diplomacy*. London: Hollis and Carter, 1952.
Knudson, Jerry W. *Bolivia: Press and Revolution, 1932–1964*. Lanham, Md.: University Press of America, 1986.
———. "Veil of Silence: The Argentine Press and the Dirty War, 1976–1983." *Latin American Perspectives* 24, no. 6 (1997): 93–112.
Laclau, Ernesto. *On Populist Reason*. New York: Verso, 2005.
———. *Politics and Ideology in Marxist Theory: Capitalism, Fascism, Populism*. London: New Left Books, 1977.
Larra, Raúl. *Etcétera . . .* Buenos Aires: Anfora, 1982.
———. *Mundo de escritores*. Buenos Aires: Ediciones Sílaba, 1973.
Lavieri, Omar. "The Media in Argentina: Struggling with the Absence of a Democratic Tradition." In Cole, *Communication in Latin America*, 183–98.
Lawson, Chappell H. *Building the Fourth Estate: Democratization and the Rise of a Free Press in Mexico*. Berkeley: University of California Press, 2002.
Leab, Daniel. *A Union of Individuals: The Formation of the American Newspaper Guild, 1933–1936*. New York: Columbia University Press, 1970.
Lefebvre, Henri. *Critique of Everyday Life*. Vol. 2, *Foundations for a Sociology of the Everyday*. Translated by John Moore. London: Verso, 2002.
———. *Everyday Life in the Modern World*. Translated by Sacha Rabinovitz. London: Transaction, 1994.
Leigh, Robert D., and Llewellyn White. *Peoples Speaking to Peoples: A Report on International Mass Communication from the Commission on Freedom of the Press*. Chicago: University of Chicago Press, 1946.
Lence, José R. *Memorias de un periodista*. Buenos Aires: Centro Difusor del Libro, 1945.
León-Dermota, Ken. *. . . And Well Tied Down: Chile's Press Under Democracy*. Westport, Conn.: Praeger, 2003.
Leonard, Thomas C. *The Power of the Press: The Birth of American Political Reporting*. New York: Oxford University Press, 1986.
Lettieri, Alberto. *La república de la opinión: Política y opinión pública en Buenos Aires entre 1852 y 1862*. Buenos Aires: Biblos, 1998.
Llano, Francisco Luís. *La aventura del periodismo*. Buenos Aires: Peña Lillo, 1978.
Llull, Laura. *Prensa y política en Bahía Blanca: "La Nueva Provincia" en las presidencias radicales, 1916–1930*. Bahía Blanca: EdiUNS, 2005.
Luna, Félix. *El 45: Crónica de un año decisivo*. Buenos Aires: Jorge Álvarez, 1969.
———. *Perón y su tiempo*. 3 vols. Buenos Aires: Sudamericana, 1984–86.
Lynch, John, Roberto Cortés Conde, Ezequiel Gallo, Juan Carlos Torre, and Liliana de Riz. *Historia de la Argentina*. Buenos Aires: Planeta, 2002.
Mackinnon, Moira. *Los años formativos del Partido Peronista (1946–1950)*. Buenos Aires: Siglo Veintiuno, 2002.
Manzoni, Celina. "La Revista de Avance (La Habana, 1927–1930) y su articulación con otras publicaciones modernizadoras en América Latina a comienzos del siglo XX." In *51o Congreso Internacional de Americanistas*. Santiago de Chile: Secretaría General de 51o Congreso Internacional de Americanistas, 2003.
Marco, Miguel Ángel de. *Bartolomé Mitre*. Buenos Aires: Planeta, 1998.
———. *Historia del periodismo argentino: Desdo los orígenes hasta el centenario de mayo*. Buenos Aires: Editorial de la Universidad Católica Argentina, 2006.
Marechal, Leopoldo. *Adán Buenosayres*. Critical ed. Edited by Jorge Lafforegue and Fernando Colla. Santiago de Chile: Editorial Universitaria, 1997.
Marshall, T. H. *Citizenship and Social Class, and Other Essays*. Cambridge: Cambridge University Press, 1950.
Martin, Kingsley. *The Press the Public Wants*. London: Hogarth Press, 1947.

Martín-Barbero, Jesús. *De los medios a las mediaciones: Comunicación, cultura y hegemonía.* Barcelona: Gustavo Gili, 1987.
Martínez Cuitiño, Vicente. *El café de Los Inmortales.* Buenos Aires: Kraft, 1954.
Martínez Estrada, Ezequiel. *Radiografía de la pampa.* 13th ed. Buenos Aires: Losada, 1991.
Martuccelli, Danilo, and Maristella Svampa. *La plaza vacía: Las transformaciones del peronismo.* Buenos Aires: Editorial Losada, 1997.
Marx, Karl. *On Freedom of the Press and Censorship.* New York: McGraw-Hill, 1974.
Matallana, Andrea. *Locos por la radio: Una historia social de la radiofonía en la Argentina, 1923–1947.* Buenos Aires: Prometeo Libros, 2006.
Matsushita, Hiroshi. *El movimiento obrero argentino, 1930–1945: Sus proyecciones en los orígenes del peronismo.* Buenos Aires: Ediciones Siglo Veinte, 1983.
Mayer, Jorge. *El derecho público de prensa.* Buenos Aires: Imprenta de la Universidad, 1944.
Mayobre, José Antonio. "Venezuela and the Media." In *Latin Politics, Global Media,* edited by Elizabeth Fox and Silvio Waisbord, 176–86. Austin: University of Texas Press, 2002.
Mazzei, Daniel H. *Los medios de comunicación y el golpismo: La caída de Illia, 1966.* Avellaneda, Argentina: Grupo Editor Universitario, 1997.
McCann, Bryan. *Hello, Hello Brazil: Popular Music in the Making of Modern Brazil.* Durham: Duke University Press, 2004.
McIntyre, Jerilyn S. "Repositioning a Landmark: The Hutchins Commission and Freedom of the Press." *Critical Studies in Mass Communications* 4 (1987): 136–60.
McKee, Alan. *The Public Sphere: An Introduction.* New York: Cambridge University Press, 2005.
McKercher, Catherine. *Newsworkers Unite: Labor, Convergence, and North American Newspapers.* Critical Media Studies, Institutions, Politics, and Culture. New York: Rowman and Littlefield, 2002.
Medina, José Toribio. *Historia y bibliografía de la imprenta en el antigüo virreinato del Río de la Plata.* La Plata: Taller de Publicaciones del Museo, 1961.
Medina Onrubia de Botana, Salvadora. *Crítica y su verdad.* Buenos Aires: privately printed, 1958.
Melon Pirro, Julio César. "La prensa de oposición en la Argentina post-peronista." *Estudios Interdiciplinarios de América Latina y el Caribe* 13, no. 2 (2002): 115–37.
Merkin, Marta, Juan José Panno, Gabriela Tijman, and Carlos Ulanovsky. *Días de radio: Historia de la radio argentina.* Buenos Aires: Espasa Calpe, 1995.
Miri, Héctor F. *Yrigoyen, Perón, Frondizi y el cuarto poder.* Buenos Aires: Corto y Claro, 1959.
Mitre, Jorge. *"La Nación" y the Associated Press.* Buenos Aires: La Nación, 1941.
Mochkofsky, Graciela. *Timerman: El periodista que quiso ser parte del poder (1923–1999).* Buenos Aires: Sudamericana, 2003.
Moncalvillo, Mona. *Conversaciones con Edmundo Guibourg: El último bohemio.* Buenos Aires: Celtia, 1983.
Montenegro, Silvina. "La Guerra Civil Española y la política argentina." Ph.D. thesis, Universidad Complutense de Madrid, 2002.
Morris, Joe Alex. *Deadline Every Minute: The Story of the United Press.* Garden City, N.Y.: Doubleday, 1957.
Munck, Ronaldo. "Mutual Benefit Societies in Argentina: Workers, Nationality, Social Security and Trade Unionism." *Journal of Latin American Studies* 30 (1998): 573–90.
Murmis, Miguel, and Juan Carlos Portantiero. *Estudios sobre los orígenes del peronismo.* Sociología y Política. Buenos Aires: Siglo Veintiuno, 2004.
Myers, Jorge. *Orden y virtud: El discurso repúblicano en el régimen rosista.* Buenos Aires: Universidad Nacional de Quilmes, 1995.
———. "Las paradojas de la opinion: El discurso político *rivadaviano* y sus dos polos: El 'gobierno de las luces' y 'la opinión pública, reina del mundo.'" In *La vida política*

en la Argentina del siglo XIX: Armas, votos y voces, edited by Hilda Sabato and Alberto Lettieri, 75–95. Buenos Aires: Fondo de Cultura Económica, 2003.
Nalé Roxlo, Conrado. *Borrador de memorias*. Buenos Aires: Plus Ultra, 1978.
Nállim, Jorge A. "The Crisis of Liberalism in Argentina, 1930–1946." Ph.D. diss., University of Pittsburgh, 2002.
Napp, Guillermo. *Para la historia del periodismo: El Primer Congreso Panamericano de Periodistas*. Buenos Aires: Sociedad Anónima de Ediciones e Impresiones, 1987.
Needell, Jeffrey. "Optimism and Melancholy: Elite Response to the *fin de siècle bonaerense*." *Journal of Latin American Studies* 31 (1999): 551–88.
Negretto, Gabriel L., and José Antonio Aguilar-Rivera. "Rethinking the Legacy of the Liberal State in Latin America: The Cases of Argentina (1853–1916) and Mexico (1857–1910)." *Journal of Latin American Studies* 32 (2000): 361–97.
Neiburg, Federico. *Los intelectuales y la invención del peronismo*. Buenos Aires: Alianza Editorial, 1998.
———. "Intimacy and the Public Sphere: Politics and Culture in the Argentinian National Space, 1946–1955." *Social Anthropology* 11 (February 2003): 63–78.
Nerone, John C., ed. *Last Rights: Revisiting "Four Theories of the Press."* History of Communication. Urbana: University of Illinois Press, 1995.
———. *Violence Against the Press: Policing the Public Sphere in U.S. History*. New York: Oxford University Press, 1994.
Neruda, Pablo. *Confieso que he vivido*. Buenos Aires: Planeta, 1992.
Neustadt, Bernardo. *No me dejen solo*. Buenos Aires: Planeta, 1995.
Newton, Ronald C. *The Nazi Menace in Argentina, 1931–1947*. Palo Alto: Stanford University Press, 1992.
Nord, David Paul. "A Plea for *Journalism* History." *Journalism History* 15 (Spring 1988): 8–15.
Novick, Susana. *IAPI: Auge y decadencia*. Buenos Aires: Centro Editor de América Latina, 1986.
Nudelman, Santiago. *El régimen autoritario: Torturas, presos políticos, negociados*. Buenos Aires: privately printed, 1960.
Oficina Argentino—Chileno de Intercambio Intelectual. *Homenaje a "La Prensa" y "La Nación"*. Buenos Aires: Oficina Argentino—Chileno de Intercambio Intelectual, 1944.
O'Malley, Tom, and Clive Soley. *Regulating the Press*. London: Pluto Press, 2000.
Orgambide, Pedro. *El escriba*. Buenos Aires: Norma, 1996.
Owensby, Brian P. *Intimate Ironies: Modernity and the Making of Middle-Class Lives in Brazil*. Stanford: Stanford University Press, 1999.
Page, Joseph A. *Perón: A Biography*. New York: Random House, 1983.
Palacios, Alfredo L. *Libertad de prensa*. Buenos Aires: Claridad, 1935.
Palazzolo, Octavio, ed. *Diez años de organización sindical*. Buenos Aires: Federación Argentina de Periodistas, 1949.
Panella, Claudio, ed. *La Prensa y el peronismo: Crítica, conflicto, expropiación*. La Plata: Universidad Nacional de La Plata, 1999.
Pastor, Reynaldo. *La otra faz de la segunda dictadura*. Buenos Aires: Bases, 1960.
Pellet Lastra, Arturo. *La libertad de expresión*. 2nd ed. Buenos Aires: Abeledo-Perrot, 1993.
Perelman, Ángel. *Como hicimos el 17 de octubre*. Buenos Aires: Coyoac, 1961.
Pérez-Linan, Aníbal. "Television News and Political Partisanship in Latin America." *Political Research Quarterly* 55, no. 3 (2002): 571–88.
PERIODISTAS para la Defensa del Periodismo Independiente. *Ataques a la prensa: Informe 1999*. Buenos Aires: Planeta Espejo de la Argentina, 1999.
Perón, Juan Domingo. *Libro azul y blanco (respuesta al Libro azul y blanco del Departamento de Estado de los Estados Unidos)*. Buenos Aires: Freeland, 1973.
———. *Perón y "La Prensa" de la era justicialista*. Buenos Aires: Presidencia de la Nación, Subsecretaría de Informaciones, 1953.

———. *Política y estrategia (No ataco, critico)*. Buenos Aires: Editorial Democracia, 1952.
Persello, Ana Virginia. *El Partido Radical: Gobierno y oposición, 1916–1943*. Buenos Aires: Siglo Veintiuno, 2004.
Petorruti, Emilio. *Un pintor ante el espejo*. Buenos Aires: Hachette, 1968.
Pinedo, Federico. *En tiempos de la república*. Buenos Aires: Mundo Forense, 1946.
Pineta, Alberto. *Verde memoria: Tres décadas de literatura y periodismo en una autobiografía: Los grupos de Boedo y Florida*. Buenos Aires: Ediciones Antonio Zamora, 1962.
Plotkin, Mariano Ben. "The Changing Perceptions of Peronism." In Brennan, *Peronism and Argentina*, 29–54.
———. "La 'ideología' de Perón: Continuidades y rupturas." In *Perón: Del exilio al poder*, edited by Samuel Amaral and Mariano Ben Plotkin, 45–67. Buenos Aires: Cántaro, 1993.
———. *Mañana es San Perón: Propaganda, rituales políticos y educación en el régimen peronista (1946–1955)*. Buenos Aires: Ariel Historia Argentina, 1994.
———. "Rituales políticos, imágenes y carisma: La celebración del 17 de Octubre y el imaginario peronista 1945–1951." In Torre, *El 17 de Octubre de 1945*, 171–217.
Portogalo, José. "Balada con nudos de bronce sobre mis años." In *Tumulto*, 54. Buenos Aires: Ediciones Imán, 1935.
Potash, Robert A. *The Army and Politics in Argentina, 1928–1945: Yrigoyen to Perón*. Palo Alto: Stanford University Press, 1969.
———, ed. *Perón y el G.O.U.: Los documentos de una logia secreta*. Buenos Aires: Sudamericana, 1984.
Prieto, Adolfo. *El discurso criollista en la formación de la Argentina moderna*. Buenos Aires: Sudamericana, 1988.
Pujol, Sergio. *Discépolo: Una biografía argentina*. Buenos Aires: Emecé, 1996.
Quiroga, Nicolás. "Prensa comercial y organización del Partido Peronista en la provincia de Buenos Aires: Una mirada desde el espacio local, 1945–1955." In *El gobierno de Domingo A. Mercante en Buenos Aires (1946–1952): Un caso de peronismo provincial*, edited by Claudio Panella, 321–44. La Plata: Asociación Amigos del Archivo Histórico de la Provincia de Buenos Aires, 2005.
Rama, Ángel. *La ciudad letrada*. Hanover, N.H.: Ediciones del Norte, 1984.
Ramos, Julio A. *Los cerrojos a la prensa*. Buenos Aires: Editorial Amfin, 1993.
———. *Desencuentros de la modernidad: Literatura y política en el siglo xix*. Mexico City: Fondo de Cultura Económica, 1989.
Rein, Raanan. *Peronismo, populismo y política*. Buenos Aires: Editorial de Belgrano, 1998.
República Argentina, Cámara de Diputados. *Diario de sesiones 1947*. Buenos Aires: Imprenta del Congreso Nacional, 1947.
República Argentina, Cámara de Senadores. *Diario de sesiones 1934*. Buenos Aires: Imprenta del Congreso Nacional, 1934.
———. *La Prensa: Antecedentes relacionados con la ley 14.021*. Buenos Aires: Imprenta del Congreso Nacional, 1951.
República Argentina, Comisión Nacional de Investigaciones. *Documentación, autores y cómplices de las irregularidades cometidas durante la segunda tiranía*. 3 vols. Buenos Aires: Gobierno de la Nación, 1958.
———. *Libro negro de la segunda tiranía*. Buenos Aires: Gobierno de la Nación, 1958.
República Argentina, Ministerio de Agricultura de la Nación. *La industria del papel y las posibilidades de expansión a base de materias primas nacionales*. Buenos Aires: Ministerio de Agricultura de la Nación, Dirección de Propaganda y Publicaciones, 1943.
República Argentina, Ministerio del Interior. *Memoria del Ministerio del Interior presentada al honorable Congreso de la Nación, 1934–1935*. Buenos Aires: Imprenta del Congreso Nacional, 1935.
———. *Memoria del Ministerio del Interior presentada al honorable Congreso de la Nación, 1935–1936*. Buenos Aires: Imprenta del Congreso Nacional, 1936.

———. *Memoria del Ministerio del Interior presentada al honorable Congreso de la Nación, 1936–1937*. Buenos Aires: Imprenta del Congreso Nacional, 1937.

———. *Memoria del Ministerio del Interior presentada al honorable Congreso de la Nación, 1941–1942*. Buenos Aires: Imprenta del Congreso Nacional, 1942.

República Argentina, Ministerio de Relaciones Exteriores y Culto. *La República Argentina ante el "Libro Azul."* Buenos Aires: Dirección de Información al Exterior, 1946.

República Argentina, Senado de la Nación. *"La Prensa": Antecedentes relacionados con la ley 14.021*. Buenos Aires: Imprenta del Congreso Nacional, 1951.

República Argentina, Subsecretaría de Información y Prensa, Dirección General de Prensa. *Estatuto del periodista*. Buenos Aires: Imprenta del Congreso Nacional, 1944.

Reyes, Cipriano. *Yo hice el 17 de Octubre*. Buenos Aires: CEAL, 1984.

Rivas Rojas, Raquel. "Tales of Identity in the Shadow of the Mass Media: Populist Narrative in 1930s Venezuela." *Journal of Latin American Cultural Studies* 10, no. 2 (2001): 193–204.

Rivera, Jorge B. "Los juegos de un tímido: Borges en el suplemento de *Crítica*." In Ford, Rivera, and Romano, *Medios de comunicación*, 181–96.

Rivera, Jorge B., and Eduardo Romano. *Claves del periodismo argentino actual*. Buenos Aires: Ediciones Tarso, 1987.

Roberts, Kenneth. "Social Correlates of Party System Demise and Populist Resurgence in Venezuela." *Latin American Politics and Society* 45, no. 3 (2003): 35–57.

———. "Social Polarization and the Populist Resurgence in Venezuela." In *Venezuelan Politics in the Chávez Era: Class, Polarization, and Conflict*, edited by Steve Ellner, and Daniel Hellinger, 55–72. Boulder, Col.: Lynne Rienner, 2003.

Rock, David. *Argentina, 1516–1987: From Spanish Colonization to the Falklands War*. Berkeley: University of California Press, 1987.

———. *Authoritarian Argentina: The Nationalist Movement, Its History and Its Impact*. Berkeley: University of California Press, 1995.

———. *Politics in Argentina, 1890–1930: The Rise and Fall of Radicalism*. Cambridge: Cambridge University Press, 1975.

———. *State Building and Political Movements in Argentina, 1860–1916*. Stanford: Stanford University Press, 2002.

Rodríguez Lamas, Daniel. *Rawson, Ramírez, Farrell, 1943–1946*. Biblioteca Política Argentina 41. Buenos Aires: Centro Editor de América Latina, 1983.

Rojas Paz, Pablo. "La prensa argentina." In *Historia del periodismo*, edited by Clemente Cimorra, 219–70. Buenos Aires: Editorial Atlántida, 1946.

Romero, José Luís. *Las ideas en la Argentina del siglo XX*. Buenos Aires: Biblioteca Actual, 1983.

Romero, Luís Alberto. "Buenos Aires en la entreguerra: Libros baratos y cultura de los sectores populares." In *Mundo urbano y cultura popular: Estudios de Historia Social Argentina*, edited by Diego Armus, 39–67. Buenos Aires: Sudamericana, 1990.

Rotenberg, Abrasha. *Historia confidencial: La Opinión y otros olvidos*. Buenos Aires: Sudamericana, 1999.

Rouquié, Alain. *Poder militar y sociedad política en la Argentina*. Vol. 2. Buenos Aires: Hyspamérica, 1986.

Ruíz Jiménez, Laura. "Peronism and Anti-imperialism in the Argentine Press: 'Braden or Perón' Was Also 'Perón Is Roosevelt.'" *Journal of Latin American Studies* 30 (October 1998): 551–71.

Sabato, Hilda. "Citizenship, Political Participation and the Formation of the Public Sphere in Buenos Aires, 1850s–1880s." *Past and Present* 136 (1992): 139–63.

———, ed. *Ciudadanía política y formación de las naciones: Perspectivas históricas de América Latina*. Mexico City: Fondo de Cultura Económica, 1999.

———. *La política en las calles: Entre el voto y la movilización, Buenos Aires, 1862–1880*. Buenos Aires: Sudamericana, 1998.

Saítta, Sylvia. "*Crítica* en los años '30: Entre la conspiración y el exilio." *Entrepasados* 2 (1992): 25–41.

———. *El escritor en el bosque de ladrillos: Una biografía de Roberto Arlt.* Buenos Aires: Sudamericana, 2000.

———. *Regueros de tinta: El diario "Crítica" en la década de 1920.* Colección Historia y Cultura. Buenos Aires: Sudamericana, 1998.

Salas, Horacio. *Conversaciones con Raúl González Tuñón.* Buenos Aires: Ediciones La Bastilla, 1975.

Salcetti, Marianne. "Competing for Control of Newsworkers: Definitional Battles Between the Newspaper Guild and the American Newspaper Publishers Association, 1937–1938." Ph.D. diss., University of Iowa, 1992.

Saldías, José Antonio. *La inolvidable bohemia porteña.* Buenos Aires: Freeland, 1968.

Salvatore, Ricardo D. "The Normalization of Economic Life: Representations of the Economy in Golden-Age Buenos Aires, 1890–1913." *Hispanic American Historical Review* 81, no. 1 (2001): 1–44.

Sánchez, Florencio. *Canillita.* In *Teatro completo de Florencio Sánchez: Veinte obras compiladas y anotadas, con los juicios que merecieron sus estrenos*, ed. Dardo Cúneo, 232–51. Buenos Aires: Claridad, 1941.

Sánchez Zinny, E. F. *El culto de la infamia: Historia documentada de la segunda tiran argentina.* 2nd ed. Buenos Aires: Ediciones Gure, 1958.

Sanger, J. W. *Advertising Methods in Argentina, Uruguay and Brazil.* Washington, D.C.: Government Printing Office, 1920.

Sanguinetti, Horacio. *La democracia ficta, 1930–1938.* Buenos Aires: Editorial Astrea, 1975.

———. *Los socialistas independientes.* Buenos Aires: Editorial de Belgrano, 1981.

Santa Coloma, Francisco. *La prensa argentina: Antecedentes, legislación y jurisprudencia.* Buenos Aires: Casa Editora F. Álvarez y Cia, 1912.

Sarlo, Beatriz. *El imperio de los sentimientos: Narraciones de circulaciónon periódica en la Argentina (1917–1927).* 2nd ed. Buenos Aires: Norma, 2004.

———. *La imaginación técnica: Sueños modernos de la cultura argentina.* Buenos Aires: Nueva Visión, 1992.

———. "The Modern City: Buenos Aires, the Peripheral Metropolis." In *Through the Kaleidoscope: The Experience of Modernity in Latin America*, edited by Vivian Schelling, 108–23. London: Verso, 2000.

———. *Una modernidad periférica: Buenos Aires, 1920 y 1930.* Buenos Aires: Nueva Visión, 1988.

Sarobe, José María. *Memorias sobre la revolución del 6 de setiembre de 1930.* Buenos Aires: Gure, 1957.

Scenna, Miguel Ángel. *Braden y Perón.* Buenos Aires: Editorial Korrigan, 1974.

———. *FORJA: Una aventura argentina (de Yrigoyen a Perón).* Buenos Aires: La Bastilla, 1972.

Schement, Jorge Reina, and Everett M. Rogers. "Media Flows in Latin America." *Communication Research* 11, no. 2 (1984): 305–20.

Schiller, Daniel. *Objectivity and the News: The Public and the Rise of Commercial Journalism.* Philadelphia: University of Pennsylvania Press, 1981.

Schjolden, Line. "Suing for Justice: Labor and the Courts in Argentina, 1900–1943." Ph.D. diss., University of California–Berkeley, 2002.

Schramm, Wilbur, ed. *Communications in Modern Society.* Urbana: University of Illinois Press, 1948.

———. *Mass Communications.* Urbana: University of Illinois Press, 1949.

———. *The Process and Effects of Mass Communications.* Urbana: University of Illinois Press, 1954.

Schudson, Michael. *Discovering the News: A Social History of American Newspapers.* New York: Basic Books, 1978.

———. "Toward a Troubleshooting Manual for Journalism History." *Journalism and Mass Communications Quarterly* 74, no. 3 (1997): 463–76.
Sebreli, Juan José. *Crítica de las ideas politicas argentinas.* 3rd ed. Buenos Aires: Sudamericana, 2003.
———. *Los deseos imaginarios del peronismo.* Buenos Aires: Sudamericana, 1992.
Senén González, Santiago. "Con olor a imprenta." *Todo es Historia*, no. 358 (1997): 50–53.
Senén González, Santiago, and Yanina Welp. "*Crítica*: Un hito en el periodismo argentino." *Todo es Historia*, no. 375 (1998): 36–54.
Seoane, María. *El burgués maldito.* Buenos Aires: Planeta, 1998.
Setaro, Ricardo M. *La vida privada del periodismo.* Buenos Aires: Fegrabo, 1936.
Sidicaro, Ricardo. *La política mirada desde arriba: Las ideas del diario "La Nación," 1909–1989.* Buenos Aires: Sudamericana, 1993.
———. *Los tres peronismos: Estado y poder económico, 1946–1955/1973–1976/1989–1999.* Buenos Aires: Siglo Veintiuno, 2002.
Siebert, Fredrick Seaton. *Freedom of the Press in England, 1476–1776.* Urbana: University of Illinois Press, 1952.
Siebert, Fredrick Seaton, Theodore Peterson, and Wilbur Schramm. *Four Theories of the Press: The Authoritarian, Libertarian, Social Responsibility, and Soviet Communist Concepts of What the Press Should Be and Do.* Urbana: University of Illinois Press, 1956.
Sigal, Silvia, and Eliseo Verón. *Perón o muerte: Los fundamentos discursivos del fenómeno peronista.* Buenos Aires: Legasa, 1986.
Sindicato Argentino de Prensa. *Declaración de propósitos.* Buenos Aires: Sindicato Argentino de Prensa, 1948.
Sindicato Luz y Fuerza (Capital Federal) and Arturo Jauretche. *Cien años contra el país.* Buenos Aires: 2 de Octubre, 1970.
Sindicato de Prensa Argentina. *Anuario de prensa argentina.* Buenos Aires: Argent-Press Guía Solana de Publicaciones, 1939.
Sirvén, Pablo. *Perón y los medios de comunicación (1943–1955).* Biblioteca Política Argentina. Buenos Aires: Centro Editor América Latina, 1984.
Smith, Anne-Marie. *A Forced Agreement: Press Acquiescence to Censorship in Brazil.* Pittsburgh: University of Pittsburgh Press, 1997.
Smith, Peter H. "La base social del Peronismo." *Hispanic American Historical Review* 52, no. 1 (1972): 55–73.
Sodre, Nelson Werneck. *História da imprensa no Brasil.* Rio de Janeiro: Edições do Brasil, 1977.
Solomon, Robert. *The Transformation of the World Economy, 1980–1993.* 2nd ed. New York: St. Martin's Press, 1999.
Stryker Munson, Eve, and Catherine A. Warren, eds. *James Carey: A Critical Reader.* Minneapolis: University of Minnesota Press, 1997.
Sunkel, Guillermo. *Razón y pasión en la prensa popular: Un estudio sobre cultura popular, cultura de masas y cultura política.* Santiago de Chile: Instituto Latinoamericano de Estudios Transnacionales, 1985.
Tálice, Roberto A. *100.000 ejemplares por hora: Memorias de un redactor de "Crítica," el diario de Botana.* Buenos Aires: Corregidor, 1989.
———. *El Malevo Muñoz (Carlos de la Púa): Mi amistad con el autor de "La crencha engrasada."* Buenos Aires: Freeland, 1969.
Tamarin, David. *The Argentine Labor Movement, 1930–1945.* Albuquerque: University of New Mexico Press, 1985.
Tato, María Inés. *Viento de Fronda: Liberalismo, conservadurismo y democracia en la Argentina, 1911–1932.* Buenos Aires: Siglo Veintiuno, 2004.
Terán, Oscar. "Ideas e intelectuales en la Argentina, 1880–1980." In *Ideas en el siglo: Intelectuales y cultura en el siglo XX latinoamericano*, edited by Oscar Terán, 13–95. Buenos Aires: Siglo Veintiuno, 2004.

———. *Vida intelectual en el Buenos Aires fin-de-siglo (1880–1910): Derivas de la "cultura científica."* Buenos Aires: Fondo de Cultura Económica, 2000.
Ternavasio, Marcela. "Hacia un régimen de unanimidad. Política y elecciones en Buenos Aires, 1828–1850." In *Ciudadanía política y formación de las naciones: Perspectivas históricas de América Latina,* edited by Hilda Sabato, 119–41. Mexico City: Fondo de Cultura Económica, 1999.
Tiempo, César. *Mi tío Scholem Aleijem y otros parientes.* Buenos Aires: Corregidor, 1978.
Torino, David Michel. *Desde mi celda: Historia de una infamia.* Buenos Aires: Impresora Rumbos, 1953.
Torre, Juan Carlos, ed. "La CGT en el 17 de Octubre." In Torre, *El 17 de octubre de 1945,* 23–81.
———. *El 17 de octubre de 1945.* Buenos Aires: Ariel, 1995.
———. *La vieja guardia sindical y Perón: Sobre los orígenes del peronismo.* Buenos Aires: Sudamericana, 1990.
Trotti, Ricardo. *La dolorosa libertad de prensa: En busca de la ética perdida.* Buenos Aires: Editorial Atlántida, 1993.
Ulanovsky, Carlos. *Paren las rotativas: Historia de los grandes diarios, revistas y periodistas argentinos.* Buenos Aires: Espasa, 1997.
Uribe-Urán, Víctor. "The Birth of a Public Sphere in Latin America During the Age of Revolution." *Comparative Studies in Society and History* 42 (April 2000): 425–57.
Verbitsky, Bernardo. *En esos años.* Buenos Aires: Editorial Futuro, 1947.
Verbitsky, Horacio. *Un mundo sin periodistas: Las torturosas relaciones de Menem con la prensa, la ley y la verdad.* Espejo de la Argentina. Buenos Aires: Planeta, 1998.
———. *Rodolfo Walsh y la prensa clandestina, 1976–1978.* Colección El Periodista de Buenos Aires. Buenos Aires: Ediciones de la Urraca, 1985.
Verga, Alberto, Nelson Domínguez, León Zafran, and Horacio Martorelli. *El periodismo por dentro.* Buenos Aires: Ediciones Líbera, 1965.
Vicepresidencia de la Nación, Comisión Nacional de Investigaciones. *Documentación, autores y cómplices de las irregularidades cometidas durante la segunda tiranía.* Vol. 1. Buenos Aires: Gobierno de la Nación, 1958.
Waisbord, Silvio. "Media in South America: Between the Rock of the State and the Hard Place of the Market." In *De-Westernizing Media Studies,* edited by James Curran and Myung-Jin Park, 50–62. New York: Routledge, 2000.
———. "Media Populism: Neo-Populism in Latin America." In *The Media and Neo-Populism: A Contemporary Comparative Analysis,* edited by Gianpietro Mazzoleni, Julianne Stewart, and Bruce Horsfield, 197–216. Westport, Conn.: Praeger, 2003.
———. *Watchdog Journalism in South America: News, Accountability, and Democracy.* New York: Columbia University Press, 2000.
Walsh, Rodolfo J. *Caso Satanowsky.* Buenos Aires: Ediciones de la Flor, 1973.
Walter, Richard J. *Politics and Urban Growth in Buenos Aires, 1910–1942.* Cambridge: Cambridge University Press, 1993.
———. *The Province of Buenos Aires and Argentine Politics, 1912–1943.* Cambridge: Cambridge University Press, 1985.
———. "The Right and the Peronists, 1943–1955." In Deutsch and Dolkart, *Argentine Right,* 99–118.
———. *The Socialist Party of Argentina, 1890–1930.* Austin: University of Texas Press, 1977.
———. "The Socialist Press in Turn-of-the-Century Argentina." *Americas* 37, no. 1 (1980): 1–24.
Whitehead, Laurence. "A Note on Citizenship in Latin America Since 1930." In *Latin America: Politics and Society Since 1930,* edited by Leslie Bethell, 67–73. New York: Cambridge University Press, 1998.
Williams, Daryle. *Culture Wars in Brazil: The First Vargas Regime, 1930–1945.* Durham: Duke University Press, 2001.
Williams, Raymond. *Communications.* New York: Barnes and Noble, 1967.

———. *Marxism and Literature*. Oxford: Oxford University Press, 1977.
———. *The Sociology of Culture*. Chicago: University of Chicago Press, 1995.
Winston, Colin M. "Between Rosas and Sarmiento: Notes on Nationalism in Peronist Thought." *Americas* 39, no. 3 (1983): 305–32.
Zanatta, Loris. *Del estado liberal a la nación católica: Iglesia y ejército en los orígenes del peronismo, 1930–1943*. Buenos Aires: Universidad Nacional de Quilmes, 1996.
Zimmermann, Eduardo. "La prensa y la oposición política en la Argentina de comienzos del siglo: El caso de *La Nación* y el Partido Repúblicano." *Estudios Sociales* 8, no. 15 (1998): 45–70.

Index

NOTE: Cities, provinces, and regions are located in Argentina unless otherwise specified.

Act of Chapultepec, 157
Adán Buenosayres (novel), 43
Agencia Latina de Noticias, 199
Agencia Noticiosa Argentina, S.A. (ANDI), 132
Agosti, Héctor P., 165, 270 n. 112
Agote, Carlos, 36
Agusti, José W., 46, 197. See also *Noticias Gráficas*
  alliance with Perón, 153, 181, 198, 263 n. 46
  arrest, 106
  criticism of *La Prensa*, 191–93, 273 n. 51
  and Journalists Statute, 122, 131, 262 n. 21
Alas Building, 224–25
Alberdi, Juan Bautista, 31, 103, 130, 245 n. 23
Alfaro Siqueiros, David, 44
Alianza Civil, 64
Alianza Libertadora Nacionalista (ALN), 154
Almacenes Reunidos Sociedad Anónima (ARSA), 67–68, 76. See also Sánchez Sorondo, Matías
Aloé, Carlos V., 177, 183, 198–201, 224, 290 n. 85. See also Editorial ALEA
Alvarez, Eduardo, 98
American Federation of Labor, 213
American Newspaper Guild, 235
American Society of Newspaper Editors (ASNE, United States), 130, 192, 259 n. 67, 272 n. 47
Los Andes (newspaper), 95
Antille, Armando, 149
Antonini de Cortejarena, Helvicia, 45, 69, 252 n. 58
APBA (Asociación de Periodistas de Buenos Aires)
  founding of, 86–87
  influence of, 134, 182
  Journalist's Statute and, 120–22, 127, 264 n. 72
  stance on nature of journalism, 137–38
Apold, Raúl A., 203, 274 n. 88, 275 n. 99
Aramburu, Pedro, 231–32
Ares, Oscar, 122, 138–41, 264 n. 72
Argentina Libre (newspaper), 95
Argentine Federation of Journalists. See FAP (Federación Argentina de Periodistas)
Argentine Press Union (SAP), 220, 230
Arica-Tacna dispute (Chile–Peru), 36
Arlt, Roberto, 52
Armstrong Circle Theater (television program, United States), 231
Associated Press (AP), 41, 109, 156, 159, 262 n. 19, 263 n. 50, 274 n. 73
Asociación de Periodistas de Buenos Aires. See APBA
Avellaneda, Nicolás, 35, 40

Baires Film, 44
Banco Central. See Central Bank
Banco Hipotecario, 69
Bandera Argentina (newspaper), 252 n. 65
Barabraham, Ernesto, 84
Barceló, Alberto, 98–99
Barrios, Américo, 228, 230
Bedoya, Eduardo, 99
Beltrán, Alberto, 166
Bemberg, Otto, 151, 266 n. 22
Benítez, Antonio J., 206, 221
Birabent, Mauricio, 182–84, 197
Blasco Ibáñez, Vicente, 25
Bohigas, Ángel, 54
Bordabehere, Enzo, 64
Borges, Jorge Luís, 52
Borlenghi, Ángel, 182, 197
Bornand, Mauricio, 106, 128, 261 n. 13

302 / INDEX

Botana, Helvio, 65, 99, 150, 196, 273 n. 63
Botana, Jaime, 99, 196, 198
Botana, Georgina, 99
Botana, Natalio. See also *Crítica* (newspaper)
  conflicts with Matías Sánchez Sorondo, 67–68
  coup of September 1930, participation in, 58, 62
  as cultural figure, 43–44, 51
  death of, 99
  exile of, 41, 46, 63
  extortion by, 43–44, 65
  founding of *Crítica*, 41–42
  litigation against, 76
  police persecution of, 63
  relation with politicians, 58, 62–65, 98
Braden, Spruille, 158–59, 161–65, 212, 268 n. 54
Bramuglia, Juan, 121–23, 134
Broquen, Eduardo, 82–83
Buchrucker, Cristián, 4
Buenos Aires (city)
  federal status of, 16, 32–34
  newspaper readership in, 3, 7, 16, 25, 28, 46–48
Buenos Aires Herald (newspaper), 25, 262 n. 19, 263 n. 46
Buenos Aires Poligráfica, 76, 99–100, 165, 197. See also *Crítica*

Cabezas, José Luís, ix–x
Calisto, Alfredo, 82
Canada, 188
Cantilo, José Luís, 180
Caminos, César, 172, 270 n. 101
Cámpora, Héctor, 183
canillita. See news vendors
Capone, Al, 44, 162
Carey, James, 8
Carreras, Ernesto C., 166–67
Casa Iturrat, 187
Casal Cabrera, Helvio, 120, 270 n. 101
Casarino, Armando, 73
Castillo, Ramón, 87–88, 91–92, 94, 99
censorship
  coordination of, 108–9, 265 n. 12
  criticism of, 102–4, 109–10
  effects of, 62, 106, 128, 132–33, 156
  imposition of, 60, 72, 86, 92, 106
  legal basis for, 29, 31–32, 114, 117
  lifting of, 28, 157, 159, 164, 200
  penalties for violating terms of, 106, 132–33, 167

  Perón and, 136, 148–49
  protest against, 107
Central Bank (Banco Central)
  newspaper deposits in, 78
  newspapers purchased by, 195, 197, 273 n. 61
  newsprint and, 215, 277 n. 43, 277 n. 45
  reporting on, 205, 215
  subsidies to newspapers, 69–72, 99, 184
CGT (Confederación General de Trabajo)
  confrontation with *La Prensa*, 213, 220
  meetings of, 1–3, 211
  ownership of *La Prensa*, 2, 222–24, 231
Chávez, Hugo, x–xi
Chile, 15, 30, 32, 36, 77–78, 205, 243 n. 35
Cipolletti, Emilio
  Crítica and, 149–50, 197, 266 n. 20, 270 n. 101
  death of, 203
  government posts, 150, 183, 197, 200–201
Círculo de Periodistas (province of Buenos Aires), 53
Círculo de la Prensa (city of Buenos Aires)
  appeals to government officials, 78, 81, 106
  conflict within, 61, 80, 85
  criticism of, 162
  founding of, 53
  ideology of, 56, 87
  journalist pension law and, 81–83, 86, 120
  Journalist's Statue and, 122, 127–28
  newspaper proprietors and, 53–54, 137
  protests by, 77, 106–7, 114, 167
  relation with FAP, 85–87
  violence against, 163
Círculo de la Prensa (province of Córdoba), 83–4
Círculo de la Prensa (city of Rosario), 137–40, 264 nn. 72, 77
Círculo de la Prensa (province of Tucumán), 128
citizenship. See also Constitution of 1853; freedom of the press; journalism; liberalism; press
  class and, 19, 148, 171, 204
  Peronism and, 4, 14, 17, 19, 134–37, 204–5, 229–31
  press and, 4, 22, 27–31, 54–56, 81, 94–96, 134–42, 213, 235–39
  social aspects of, 19–21, 204
Clarín (newspaper), 167, 172, 197, 206, 222, 270 n. 112

Clemenceau, Georges, 25, 39
Colóm, Eduardo, 149, 177, 184, 195. See also *La Época* (newspaper)
 alliance with Perón, 181–82, 195
 criticism of *La Prensa*, 214
 newsprint distribution, views on, 188–89, 209
 ownership of *La Época*, 180, 183
Colombia, 15, 65, 243 n. 35
Commercial Code, 27, 82–3, 111–12, 119, 234
Commission on Anti-Argentine Activities, 98
Commission on Freedom of the Press (Hutchins Commission, United States), 235
Communists, 65, 95, 104, 165–68, 179, 190
Compañía Argentina de Ediciones y Publicidad, Sociedad Anónima (CADEPSA), 198, 200, 224. See also *Crítica*
Concordancia, 64–8, 71, 73, 91. See also Justo, Augustín P.
Confalonieri, Orestes, 168, 197, 201–2, 270 n. 101
Confederación General de Trabajo. See CGT
Constitution of 1853, 16, 28, 33, 54, 110, 139, 189. See also freedom of the press
 article 14, 30–32, 114, 152, 210, 245 n. 23
 article 32, 30, 32, 77, 114, 210
 calls for return to, 62, 92–4, 101–2, 105, 159–60, 190
 suspension of, 56, 60, 86, 139, 190
Cooke, Juan I., 149, 269 n. 75
Cordone, Alberto, 46, 73
Córdoba (newspaper), 122
Córdova Iturburu, Cayetano, 65, 165, 270 n. 112
Cortejarena, José A., 45
Correa, Francisco, 77
coups
 of 1930, 5, 33, 46, 58–59, 61–63, 72, 87, 180
 of 1943, 88, 91–94, 99, 139, 151, 180
 of 1955, 198, 228, 230, 259 n. 64
 of 1966, 232
 of 2002 (Venezuela), x
Crisol (newspaper), 71, 76, 252 n. 65
Crítica (newspaper). See also Buenos Aires Poligráfica
 attacks on, 4, 21, 143–46, 166–67, 170–72, 270 n. 108
 circulation, 43, 47, 187
 closures of, 46, 63, 168
 commercialism, 41–43
 competition, 45
 finances of, 186, 192, 196–97, 218, 224
 founding of, 41–42
 journalism style of, 42–43, 53, 55–56, 146–48, 169
 journalists, 52–53
 Journalist's Statute and, 131
 oppposition to Perón, 164–6, 168
 opposition to *La Prensa*, 193–94, 204
 ownership of, 72, 76, 99–100, 196, 198, 200, 273 n. 63
 as partisan press, 65–69, 71, 97–100, 109, 147, 151–55
 production of, 49–50
 readership, 55–56, 148–49
Crocco, Eduardo, 166
Culaciati, Miguel, 98

Damonte Taborda, Raúl. See also *Crítica*
 exile, 95, 144, 269 n. 72
 opposition to Journalist's Statute, 122, 131
 ownership of *Crítica*, 99–100, 114, 150, 197
 relation with Perón, 98, 149–55, 164–65, 168, 172, 181
Darío, Rubén, 52
De la Torre, Lisandro, 64
De Tomaso, Antonio, 62–67, 200
decree 18.407. See New Year's decrees
Democracia (newspaper), 180, 196, 198, 203, 231, 270 n. 111
 finances of, 207, 224, 271 n. 18
 founding of, 182–83
 opposition to *La Prensa*, 211
 Peronist purchase of, 183–84, 271 nn. 16–17
Departamento Nacional de Trabajo, 117, 119–20
El Día (newspaper, La Plata), 167, 228
El Día (newspaper, Uruguay), 203
Di Leo, Oscar, 82
Dirección General de Correos y Telégrafos, 78
Dirección General de Prensa, 201–2, 210
Discépolo, Enrique Santos, 203
Dodero, Alberto, 183, 199
Dorrego, Manuel, 30
Dughera, Eduardo, 50

Editorial ALEA. See also Aloé, Carlos V.
 administration of, 177, 200–202, 224, 233
 dismantling of, 231

Editorial ALEA *(continued)*
  finances of, 199, 201, 203, 207, 216, 217
  founding of, 4, 197, 274 n. 85
  offices of, 200, 224–25
  strikes against, 217
Editorial Crítica, 198. See also *Crítica*
Editorial Democracia, 199–200, 224. See also *Democracia* (newspaper)
Editorial Haynes, 45, 198–200, 211, 224, 248 n. 76, 274 n. 85. See also *El Mundo*
La Época (newspaper)
  attacks against, 180
  criticism of opposition press, 143, 195, 206, 211, 214, 220–21, 252 n. 54, 270 n. 108
  circulation, 181
  finances of, 181, 183, 191, 224, 269 n. 80, 271 n. 5
  newsprint distribution and, 183, 188–89, 209
  ownership of, 177, 180, 183, 198, 231
  support for Perón, 169, 177, 181, 265 n. 8
  support for Yrigoyen, 180
Estatuto del Periodista Profesional. See Journalist's Statute
Eucharistic Congress, 77–78
Eva Perón Foundation, 200, 222–23

FAP (Federación Argentina de Periodistas). See also Journalist's Statute
  congresses, 83–87, 134–40, 160
  founding of, 84, 256 n. 134
  goals of, 84, 88, 120, 190
  relation with other journalist organizations, 85–87, 128, 137–39, 158–59, 220, 264 n. 77
  relation with government, 102, 106, 120, 134–35, 140, 145–56, 160, 215
  relation with proprietors, 122–23, 126, 131, 138–39, 191, 261 n. 13
Farrell, Edelmiro J.
  government posts, 105, 115
  Journalist's Statute and, 117, 123, 126, 128
  media strategy of, 146–49, 172, 189
  political strategy, 117–18, 134, 139, 143
  relations with United States, 132
  views on press, 95–97, 107, 109
Farrell, T. P., 78
fascism. See also Sánchez Sorondo, Matías
  Argentine military and, 95, 98, 105, 151, 155–56, 165

  Argentine nationalism and, 67, 84, 99, 152, 154, 266 n. 25
  media policies, inspiration for, 75–76, 108, 130
  Peronism and, 4, 13, 147, 168, 190, 211, 276 n. 20
  La Razón and, 70
Federación Argentina de Periodistas. See FAP
Federación Gráfica Bonaerense (FGB), 50, 62, 80, 82, 191
Federación de Vendedores de Diarios, 50
Forn de Oteiza Quirno, Mila, 133, 147, 279 n. 58
For the Protection of the Press (legislation), 74–79, 81, 101, 214–15
France, 36, 130, 246 n. 35, 263 n. 41
La Fraternidad (union), 105
freedom of expression. See freedom of the press
freedom of the press. See also censorship; Constitution of 1853; press, ideas of; journalism, social role
  constitutional ambiguity on, 16, 32
  foreign pressure for, 157–58
  individual rights and, 103, 138, 160, 162, 190
  legal protection of, 16, 28–29
  limits on, 29, 31
  military views on, 101, 136, 152
  newsprint and, 188–90, 215, 217
  newsworker unions and, 214, 219–20
  Peronist views on, 19, 226–27, 229–30
  positive and negative conceptions of, 31, 33, 52
  press ownership and, 20, 162, 173, 193, 238
  profit motive and, 20, 193–94, 206, 209, 219, 221
  Sarmiento and, 30
  scholarship on, 10, 15
  state action and, 31, 54, 75, 127, 191, 209, 216
  threats to, 128, 188, 190, 210
La Fronda (newspaper), 71, 252 n. 65
Frondizi, Arturo, 221, 237
Fuerza de Orientación Radical de la Juventud Argentina (FORJA), 181
fuerzas vivas, 160–64
Fulle, Miguel, 166
Funes, Gregorio, 29, 74, 76

Gabriel, José, 80, 230
Gainza, Alberto, 36

Gainza Paz, Alberto. See also *La Prensa*
  arrest of, 167, 220
  criticism of, 138, 191–94, 209, 222, 237
  exile of, 220, 230–31
  Journalist's Statute and, 116, 122, 129–31, 190
  liberalism and, 113–14, 141, 160, 191, 193, 222
  news vendors and, 214
  opposition to military regime, 139
  opposition to Peronism, 207–8, 211, 225, 278 n. 62
  personal wealth of, 209, 275 n. 4
  relation with foreign ambassadors, 159, 268 n. 54
  relation with foreign newspaper proprietors, 259 n. 67
  relation with newspaper proprietors, 191–94, 198, 204
  television appearance by, 231
  views on nature of journalism, 129–30, 220, 236–37
García Lorca, Federico, 44
Gardel, Carlos, 64–65
Gazeta de Buenos-Ayres (newspaper), 28, 30, 204, 245 n. 9
General Confederation of Labor. See CGT (Confederación General de Trabajo)
General Press Office (Dirección General de Prensa), 201–2, 210. See also Undersecretariat of Information and the Press
Gerchunoff, Alberto, 52, 106–7, 128, 261 n. 13
Ghioldi, Américo, 159, 268 n. 52
Gilbert, Alberto, 100–102, 105, 115
Giudice, Ernesto, 65, 165
González, Enrique P., 107, 114–15
González Alberti, Paulino, 165
González Tuñón, Enrique, 52
González Tuñón, Raúl, 49, 52, 65, 165, 270 n. 112
Gorostiza, Alfredo, 199–200
GOU (Grupo de Oficiales Unidos)
  dissolution of, 260 n. 87
  influence of, 97, 107–8, 111, 256–57 n. 1, 259 n. 64
  members of, 95, 105
  role in 1943 coup, 91–92, 97, 256–57 n. 1
Granier, Marcel, x
Great Britain
  Argentine press and, 132, 156, 159, 250 n. 116
  foreign relations with Argentina, 64, 115, 150
  newsprint distribution in, 188–89, 214, 216, 235
  press in, 54, 188, 235–67, 272 nn. 32, 47
Guibourg, Edmundo, 52, 63

Halperín Donghi, Tulio, 19, 59, 224
Havas, 41. See also wire services
Haynes, Alberto, 45, 248 n. 76. See also Editorial Haynes
Hearst, William Randolph, 44, 64
Hernández, José, 34, 51
El Hogar Argentino (periodical), 45
Hombres de Campo (periodical), 182
La Hora (newspaper), 95
Hoy (newspaper), 167
Hull, Cordell, 105

Independent Socialist Party (PSI), 61–63, 66
Inter American Press Association (IAPA), 231, 250 n. 116, 278 n. 72
El Intransigente (newspaper), 228
Instituto Movilizador de Inversiones Bancarias. See Central Bank
Italy, 36, 130, 249 n. 87

James, Daniel, 19, 144
Jantus, Luís María, 62
Jornada (newspaper), 64. See also *Crítica*
journalism. See also censorship; citizenship; journalists; press; *individual newspapers*
  commodification of, 51–54
  debates on nature of, x–xi, 75, 80–87, 116, 129–37, 238–39
  democracy and, x, 226–27, 229, 236, 238
  factional, 15, 30, 33–35, 40
  objectivity and, 26, 53–54
  Peronism and, 13–14, 121–23
  scholarship on, 3, 6, 10–12, 117–18
  social role of, 7, 12, 16–17, 19, 237; military view of, 93–97, 101–2, 111–12, 126–27; Peronist view of, 135–37, 141, 234
journalists. See also Círculo de la Prensa; FAP; journalism; Journalist's Statute; newsworkers
  arrest of, 63, 92, 95, 99, 106, 114, 144, 166–67, 171, 264 n. 62, 267 n. 50
  class status of, 8–9, 20, 26–27, 51–54, 80–87, 116–22

journalists *(continued)*
    disputes among, 84–87, 137–40
    dismissal of, 124–25, 131, 133
    employment of, by state 124, 147, 153, 194, 200–203, 265 n. 12
    labor legislation affecting, 81–87, 119–27, 185–86
    Perón and, 134–37, 140, 146, 149, 160–61, 168, 204, 222
    persecution of, 2–4, 62–63, 95, 157, 159, 220
    popular image of, 43–44, 52–55, 148
    professionalization of, 52–54
    registry of, 83, 112, 126, 262 n. 31
    relations with other newsworkers, 9, 80, 220
    relations with proprietors, 8, 12, 51–52, 82–85, 117–18, 122–29, 231
    responsibility for content, 74–78, 101–2, 112–13
    scholarship on, 9–12, 117–18
    strikes by, 80, 159
    unionization of, 80, 84–87, 234–35
    violence against, ix–xi, 168–71, 220, 250 n. 117
    working conditions of, 51–52, 80, 84, 124, 191–92
Journalist's Day, 84, 159
Journalist's Statute. *See also* Círculo de la Prensa; FAP; journalism; journalists
    disputes among journalists over, 137–40
    consequences of: financial, 124–25, 192, 262 n. 21; ideological, 117–21, 125–31, 140–42, 185–86; legal, 118, 121–27, 140–41
    origins of, 83–84, 119–21
    Perón and, 119–23
    proprietor opposition to, 122–23, 128–31, 150, 190–91, 209
    provisions of, 123–25, 131, 262 n. 19
    revision of, 182, 185, 190–91
    wages and, 124, 131, 192, 262 n. 21, 272–73 n. 49
Justo, Augustín P. *See also* Botana, Natalio; *Crítica*; Perón, Juan Domingo; wire services
    coup of 1930, participation in, 59, 62
    death of, 99
    election of, 61, 64, 73
    media strategy of, 61, 64–72, 76–79, 99, 146, 195–96
    ownership of *Crítica*, 64, 72, 76–77, 99, 165
    political approach of, 62–66
    relationship with Botana, Natalio, 62–65, 146, 195, 252 n. 65
    relationship with newsworkers, 83
    regulation of press by, 78–79
    scholarship on, 13
Justo, Juan B., 40

Kelly, David, 159
Kinkelín, Emilio, 72–74, 76, 108, 253 n. 77

El Laborista (newspaper), 180, 182, 184, 189, 191, 210, 224, 231. *See also* Editorial Democracia
Ladvocat, Héctor, 107–9, 120
Laíño, Félix, 70, 252 n. 56
Lanús, Adolfo, 87, 106–7, 114, 133
Larra, Raúl, 165
Lascalea, Rafael, 183
Lefebvre, Henri, 48
Legión Cívica Argentina, 66–67, 253 n. 77
liberalism. *See also* citizenship; Constitution of 1853; journalism; Journalist's Statute; freedom of the press; press
    anti-liberalism and, 74–75, 96
    crisis of, 58–59, 77, 79, 108
    economic, 101–3
    egalitarianism and, 14–15, 17, 110, 140, 144–45, 203–4, 209, 226, 231, 238
    hegemony of, 33–34
    Peronism and, 14, 19, 136–38, 151–54, 208–9, 226, 237–38
    political, 30, 92, 94–95, 139, 155–56, 231
    role of press in, 9, 12, 14, 27, 54–57, 101–2, 118, 125, 141, 237, 250 n. 116
    state and press in, 18, 31, 72, 93–96, 110–12, 186
Libertad (newspaper), 63
El Líder (newspaper), 180, 182, 184, 197, 272 n. 23
Liga Patriótica, 50
Lomuto, Oscar, 120, 158, 265 n. 12, 267 n. 47
Lonardi, Eduardo, 231
Los Angeles (California), 47, 272 n. 25
Lugones, Leopoldo, 52
Lugones, Leopoldo Jr., 63, 66
Luna, Félix, 158

Mallea, Eduardo, 52, 263 n. 58
"Manifesto of Commerce and Industry," 160–64
March of the Constitution and Liberty, 165, 169
Marchi, Roberto, 171

Marechal, Leopoldo, 43, 52, 53, 249 n. 104
Mariño, Cosme, 49
Maroglio, Orlando, 183, 199
Marotta, Sebastián, 80
Martí, José, 52
Martínez de Hoz, Federico, 66
Martínez Estrada, Ezequiel, 52
Martínez Zuviría, Gustavo A. (Hugo Wast), 105
media. *See* journalism; press
Medina Onrubia de Botana, Salvadora, 63, 150, 171, 192–93, 196–98
Melo, Leopoldo, 66, 82, 251 n. 10
Menem, Carlos, ix, xi
Mercante, Domingo, 135, 153, 182, 184, 199
El Mercurio (newspaper, Chile), 77–78, 243 n. 35
Mexico City (Mexico), 47, 242 n. 17, 247 n. 57
Miranda, Miguel, 182–84, 195, 197, 198–99, 201, 211, 215, 273 n. 61
Mitre, Bartolomé, 30, 34, 39–40, 51, 53. See also *La Nación*
Mitre, Emilio, 40, 64. See also *La Nación*
Mitre, Jorge, 41–42, 46, 148, 265 n. 15. See also *La Nación*; *Noticias Gráficas*
Mitre, Luís, 41–42, 113, 133, 147, 263 n. 58. See also *La Nación*
Molinari, Antonio M., 182–84, 197
Le Monde (newspaper, France), 202
Morales, Emilio B., 45
Moreno, Mariano, 28, 84, 151
Moreno, Rodolfo, 98–99
Mosca, Enrique, 165, 179
Muello, Ernesto, 122
El Mundo (newspaper). *See also* Editorial Haynes; radio
  attacks on, 4, 211, 274 n. 77
  circulation, 46–47, 184, 187, 241 n. 8
  finances of, 198–99, 224, 262 n. 19
  founding, 45
  journalism style of, 45–46, 48, 202, 205, 223
  journalists of, 53, 66, 69, 120
  newsprint and, 189, 271 n. 20
  ownership of, 45, 198–99, 208, 248 n. 76, 271 n. 16
  Peronism and, 167, 173, 211, 265 n. 8
Mundo Argentino (periodical), 198
Myers, Jorge, 27

La Nación (newspaper). *See also* Mitre, Bartolomé; Mitre, Emilio; Mitre, Jorge; Mitre, Luís
  attacks on, 168
  censorship and, 109, 133, 157
  circulation, 15, 41, 46–47, 187
  Círculo de la Prensa (city of Buenos Aires) and, 53–54, 85
  denunciations of, 138, 153, 163, 188
  finances of, 26, 215–16, 262 n. 19
  founding of, 34, 39
  journalism style of, 34, 39–42, 44, 53–54, 74, 222
  journalists of, 52
  litigation against, 215–16
  military rule and, 94–97, 100–102, 113, 148, 160
  newsprint and, 188–89, 215–16
  ownership of, 34, 39, 46
  Peronism and, 105, 147, 186, 211, 215, 222
  press regulations and, 77–78, 111, 113–14, 128, 173
  readership of, 40–41, 246 n. 39
  wires services and, 36, 41, 156
La Nación Argentina (newspaper), 34, 39
El Nacional Argentino (newspaper), 34
National Agrarian Council (Consejo Agrario Nacional), 182–83
National Bank. *See* Central Bank
National Congress of Journalists, 83–85. *See also* Círculo de la Prensa; FAP
National Economic Council (Consejo Económico Nacional), 183
National Labor Department, 117, 119–20
Navarro Lahitte, Juan José, 82, 85
Nerone, John, 11
Neruda, Pablo, 44
New Year's decrees, 111, 202
  decree 18.407, 91, 111–14, 117
  repeal of, 123, 128
New York Times (newspaper, United States), 157, 202
news vendors
  dispute with *La Prensa*, 2, 4, 208, 212–14, 218–20
  newsprint crisis and, 214–15, 218, 277 n. 45
  Peronism and, 4, 218, 222
  strikes by, 2, 50, 219–20
  unionization of, 50–51, 191
newsprint
  consumption of, 35, 43, 187–88, 273 n. 51
  distribution of, 4, 15, 108, 127, 185, 188–98, 218
  expropriation of, 189–92, 214
  importation of, 81, 187–88, 207, 215, 277 n. 43

newsprint *(continued)*
  litigation involving, 215–16, 222, 277 n. 47
  newsworkers and, 215, 218, 234–35
  price of, 18, 183, 185–86, 191–92, 203, 215–17
  production of, 179, 187–88, 222
newsworkers. *See also* journalists; news vendors; printers
  labor disputes and, 268 n. 51
  legislation affecting, 61, 82–83, 117, 236–37
  newsprint crisis and, 179, 235
  Peronism and, 5, 17, 117–18, 122, 172
  relations with proprietors, 10, 18, 106, 127–28, 186, 191, 236–38
  relationship among, 9–12
  scholarship on, 12, 117–18
  wages of, 124, 179, 192, 208
  violence against, 2
Newton, Ronald, 69
Noble, Roberto, 197, 270 n. 112
A Noite (Río de Janeiro, newspaper), 46, 47, 247 n. 57
Nord, David Paul, 6–7, 9
Noriega, Enrique, 69
Noticias Gráficas (newspaper). *See also* Agusti, José W.; Mitre, Jorge
  circulation, 46–47, 187, 241
  closure of, 105–6
  criticism of *La Prensa*, 191–94, 204
  finances of, 46, 124, 191–94, 207, 218, 224, 262 n. 21
  founding of, 46
  journalism style of, 46, 223
  Journalist's Statute and, 124, 131, 262 n. 19
  litigation against, 82
  military rule and, 73, 105–6, 153
  newsprint and, 218, 187, 192
  ownership of, 46, 106, 198, 231
  Peronism and, 173, 181, 184, 263 n. 46, 265 n. 8
Nueva Gaceta (newspaper), 95

Ocampo, Victoria, 263 n. 58
October 17–18, 1945 mobilizations
  Crítica and, 21, 143–46, 165–73, 186, 196, 270 n. 108
  newspaper coverage of, 169–73, 177, 180–81
  Peronism and, 143–46, 165–73, 177
  press and, 19, 21, 144–46, 169, 177, 180–86, 232

La Prensa and, 145, 226
  scholarship on, 144
Office of Publicity (Dirección de Publicidad), 201
Oficina de Información, 108, 259 n. 64
Oficina de Prensa, 73, 202
Onetti, Juan Carlos, 52
Orientación (newspaper), 95
Ortiz, Roberto, 87

P.B.T. (periodical), 198
Palacio Barolo, 171
Palacios, Alfredo, 77
Palazzolo, Octavio, 80, 85–86, 116, 120–23, 138–40, 145, 185, 190
Partido Comunista. *See* Communists
Partido Demócrata Nacional (PDN), 66–67
Partido Laborista (PL), 182, 231. *See also El Laborista* (newspaper)
Partido Socialista. *See* Socialists
Partido Socialista Independiente (PSI), 61–63, 66
partisan press. *See also* journalism, models of
Pasapompi, Darwin, 171
Paz, Ezequiel, 36, 53–55, 82, 250 n. 116. *See also La Prensa* (newspaper)
Paz, José C., 34–35, 49. *See also La Prensa* (newspaper)
Penal Code, 31–2, 74–6, 245 n. 24, 246 n. 28
Peralta Ramos, Ricardo, 69–71, 122, 195–96, 233, 252 n. 54, 273 n. 61. *See also La Razón* (newspaper)
Perelman, Ángel, 19, 161–62
Perlinger, Luís, 105, 123
Perón, Juan Domingo. *See also* October 17–18 mobilizations; Perón, Eva; Peronism; Peronist press; *individual newspapers*
  arrest of, 143, 165, 167–68
  coups against, 3, 198, 228, 259 n. 64
  denunciation of press, 1–3, 161, 208, 211–12
  diplomacy of, 147, 158, 202
  election of, 47, 153, 178, 188, 190
  Journalist's Statute and, 119–23
  journalists and, 134–37, 140, 146, 149, 160–61, 168, 204, 222
  Justo administration, as precedent for, 21, 135, 146, 172, 195
  media strategy of, 4–5, 17–21, 172–73, 179–80, 211, 224

political strategy of, 115–18, 140, 146–47, 149, 189
relation with Damonte Taborda, Raúl, 98, 149–55, 164–65, 168, 172, 181
Secretariat of Labor and Social Welfare and, 120–23, 127, 133–35, 149, 170, 264 n. 60
social reforms of, 149, 155, 160, 162
Perón, Eva. See also *Democracia* (newspaper); Peronism
authoritarianism of, 4, 14, 233
newspapers, ownership of, 184, 194–99, 230, 273 n. 68
newsworkers and, 219, 222–23
Peronism. See also October 17–18 mobilizations; journalism; Peronism; Peronist press; press; *individual newspapers*
appeal of, 14, 19, 156, 226, 229, 236–38
authoritarianism of, 3–4, 178, 183, 227, 233–34
fascism and, 4, 13, 147, 154–56, 168, 189–90, 211, 276 n. 20
freedom of the press, conception of, 19, 209, 226–27, 229–30
liberalism and, 6, 14–15, 17, 19, 136–38, 151–54, 208–9, 226, 237–38
ideology of, 4, 14–15, 17, 19, 136–37, 230, 237
news vendors and, 4, 218–23
newsworkers and, 5, 17, 117–18, 122, 172
scholarship on, 3–4, 13–15, 19
view of journalism in, 13–17, 121–23, 126, 135–37, 141, 234, 237
Peronist press. See also Editorial ALEA; Perón, Juan Domingo; Perón, Eva; Peronism; Undersecretariat of Information and the Press; *individual newspapers*
commercial press and, 194–99, 222–24, 230
dissolution of, 231–32
financial problems of, 203–4, 217–18
founding of, 179–84
management of, 199–203
Petit de Murat, Ulyses, 52, 251 n. 36
Pinedo, Federico
newspaper finances and, 69–71, 81, 195–96, 252 n. 65
political allies of, 62, 64–68
Plotkin, Mariano, 14, 59
populism, 3–4, 70, 97, 148–49, 181, 234
Portogalo, José, 25, 65
Praprotnik, Luís, 83, 119, 123

La Prensa (newspaper). See also Círculo de la Prensa; Gainza Paz, Alberto; journalism; liberalism; Paz, Ezequiel; Paz, José C.; press; United Press
attacks against, 4, 145, 163, 166, 168, 210–12
boycott against, 1–2, 211–12
censorship and, 103–5
CGT and, 2, 220, 222–23, 231
circulation of, 35, 46–47, 187, 218, 241 n. 8
closure of, 132–33, 208, 220
commercialism of, 83, 138, 193, 206, 208–10, 214, 221–22
denunciations of, 1–2, 138–39, 189, 192, 211–14
expropriation of, 2–3, 17, 22, 221
finances of, 35, 187–88, 192–93, 207–8, 212, 221–24
foreign press and, 156–57, 224, 231
founding of, 34, 226
journalism style of, 34–36, 53–56, 110–11, 169
Journalist's Statute and, 116, 129–31, 190
labor conflicts and, 2, 80–82
liberalism and, 22, 54, 139, 206, 209, 226
litigation against, 82–83, 215–16, 221–22
military rule and, 94–97, 102–7, 110–14, 160
news vendors and, 212–15, 218–22
newsprint and, 35, 187–89, 215, 218, 222
offices of, 36–39
production of, 49–50
readership of, 35, 207, 246 n. 39
scholarship on, 3
strikes against, 80–81, 220–23
United Press and, 36, 41, 156, 221, 247 n. 44
press. See also censorship; freedom of the press; journalism; Journalist's Statute; Justo, Augustín P.; liberalism; newsprint; newsworkers; Perón, Juan Domingo; Peronist press; *individual newspapers*
circulation, 3, 7, 25, 35, 41, 45–47, 187, 218, 246 n. 40
class nature of, 161–62, 230, 233
class tensions within, 20, 80–84, 87, 118–19, 128–31
commercialism and, 9, 15, 17, 44 48, 209–10, 213–14, 219–21
democracy and, x, 226–27, 229, 236, 238

press *(continued)*
  ethnic, 25
  financial problems of, 188–89, 191–94, 203–4, 207, 216–17, 224
  as fourth estate, 9, 27, 36, 42, 54, 75, 185, 193, 226
  ideological influence of, 5, 7–9, 39–40, 155
  industrialization of, 9, 17–18, 26–27, 34, 47–56, 118, 229
  Justo administration and, 62–72
  legal status of, 27–33, 77–79, 82–87, 121, 127, 141, 185–86
  libertarian conception of, 54–55, 103, 114, 250 n. 115
  readers and, 54–55
  scholarship on, 10–11
  state and, 18, 58, 75, 107–13, 126–27, 216, 237–38
  strikes against, 80, 159, 217, 219–20, 235
  violence against, 4, 144–45, 163, 166–71, 194, 211, 220
printers. *See also* Federación Gráfica Bonaerense (FGB); newsworkers
  employment of, 27, 35, 47–50
  labor actions by, 62, 80–81, 207, 217–18, 235
  labor legislation and, 81–83, 191–92
  union of, 50, 62, 220
Puiggrós, Rodolfo, 165

Quijano, J. Hortensio, 149, 167–68, 179, 181, 269 n. 75, 270 n. 101

Radical Party. *See also* Yrigoyen, Hipólito
  corruption and, 65, 68
  crisis of, 58–59
  elections, participation in, 42, 59, 64–65, 94, 179
  factions of, 58, 61, 66, 181, 231–32
  political alliances of, 94, 149–51, 164–65
  press and, 104, 134, 152, 177, 180, 198, 231–32
radio
  government monitoring of, 202–3
  legal status of, 16, 32
  newspapers and, 16, 70, 198–99, 224, 228
  propaganda, 73, 203, 210, 212, 219
Radio Caracas Televisión (RCTV), x
Radio del Estado, 210.
railway workers, 105, 207, 217–18
Rama, Ángel, 51
Ramiconi, Luís, 82

Ramírez, Pedro
  authoritarianism of, 95, 102, 105–7
  diplomacy of, 115
  journalist appeals to, 106–7, 114, 133
  policies of, 103
  political offices held by, 94
  press reaction to, 97–99, 105
  resignation of, 117, 122
Ramos, Francisco, 171
Rawson, Arturo, 93–95, 167
La Razón (newspaper)
  attacks on, 163, 166, 168
  circulation, 45–47, 184, 187, 241 n. 8
  denunciations of, 163
  finances of, 45, 69–71, 195–96, 218, 224
  founding of, 45
  journalism style of, 42–43, 70, 205, 223
  Journalist's Statute and, 122, 262 n. 19
  Justo administration and, 69–71
  modernization of, 69–71
  newsprint and, 188–89
  ownership of, 45, 69–71, 195–99, 231, 271 n. 16, 273 n. 63
  readership of, 69
  strikes against, 50
Registry of Intellectual Property, 74, 77
Rein, Raanan, 234
Repetto, Nicolás, 64
Republican Party (Mitrista), 40
Reuters, 132. *See also* wire services
Revolución Libertadora, 231–34, 241 n. 9, 273 n. 63
Reyes, Cipriano, 231
Reynés, Leandro, 87, 182, 190, 256 n. 134, 264 n. 72
Río de Janeiro (Brazil), 46–47, 199, 247 n. 57
Rivadavia, Bernardino, 151
Rocha de María, Marcial, 120, 265 n. 12
Rojas Paz, Pablo, 52
Roosevelt, Franklin D., 64, 105
Roosevelt, Eleanor, 157
Rosas, Juan Manuel de, 30, 33, 77, 151, 183, 266 n. 25
Royal Commission on the Press (Great Britain), 235
Rudnitzky, Alberto, 153, 266 n. 33

Sabattini, Amadeo, 149–50, 152
Sáenz Peña Law, 40, 42, 58, 180, 248 n. 62
Saítta, Silvia, 42, 43, 255 n. 110
San Francisco (California), 47, 272 n. 25
San Juan (province), 114–15, 150, 183, 250 n. 108

San Martín, José de, 147, 151
Sánchez Sorondo, Matías. *See also* For the Protection of the Press (legislation)
Crítica and, 63, 67–68, 76–77, 98–99
fascism and, 66–67, 75, 108
litigation by, 68, 76
views on press, 58, 74–79, 84, 95
Santander, Silvano, 134, 264 n. 62
Santiago de Chile (Chile), 47, 243 n. 35
São Paulo (Brazil), 47
Saporiti, 199
Sarmiento, Domingo F., 30, 151
Saurí, Joaquín, 183
Scalabrini Ortiz, Raúl, 180
Sección Prensa, 72–73, 79, 108
Secretariat of the Press and Dissemination (Secretaría de Prensa y Difusión), 203. *See also* Undersecretariat of Information and the Press
Secretaría de Trabajo y Previsión (STP). *See* Secretariat of Labor and Social Welfare
Secretariat of Labor and Social Welfare
  FAP and, 134–35
  founding of, 119–20
  Journalist's Statute and, 120–23, 126–27, 130–31, 196
  news vendors and, 213
  opposition to, 160–61, 169
  Perón, Juan Domingo, and, 120–23, 127, 133–35, 149, 170, 264 n. 60
  press coverage of, 151, 153–54
  social reforms by, 143
Senén González, Santiago, 138–39, 264 n. 72
Shaw, George Bernard, 52
Sidicaro, Ricardo, 40, 157
Sindicato Argentino de Prensa (SAP), 220, 230
Sindicato de Periodistas y Afines, 80
Sindicato de Vendedores de Diarios, Revistas y Afines (SVDRA). *See* Union of Newspaper and Magazine Vendors
Socialists. *See also* Independent Socialist Party; *La Vanguardia* (newspaper)
  divisions among, 58, 98, 231
  elections and, 64, 73, 179
  labor and, 62, 82, 190, 218
  military rule and, 104, 231
  press regulations and, 77, 190
Sociedad Interamericana de Prensa (SIP). *See* Inter American Press Association
Sociedad Poligráfica Argentina, 64. *See also Crítica*

Sofovich, Manuel, 82
El Sol (newspaper), 197, 200, 273 n. 68
Solari, Juan Antonio, 98, 256 n. 134
Sollazo, Napoleón, 212–13, 219, 222
Sottosegretario per la Stampa e Propaganda, 108
Soviet Union, 70, 73, 98, 165–66
Spain, 36, 63, 65–66, 70, 98
Special Section (police), 63, 164, 167
Standard (newspaper), 193, 262 n. 19, 263 n. 46
Storni, Saturnino, 105
Subsecretaría de Información y Prensa. *See* Undersecretariat of Information and the Press
Sweden, 188

Tálice, Roberto, 52
Tamborini, José, 179
El Telégrafo Mercantil, Rural, Político, Económico e Historiográfico del Río de la Plata (newspaper), 28
Teisaire, Alberto, 134, 158
Undersecretariat of Information and the Press. *See also* Oficina de Prensa
  activities, 108–9, 112–13, 194
  censorship by, 108–9, 127
  formation of, 107–9
  journalists employed by, 150, 153, 158, 197, 201, 265 n. 12
  newsprint and, 218
  opposition to, 109–10
  Peronist press and, 199–204
  precedents for, 108
  propaganda and, 108, 115, 156, 203, 210, 214
  structure of, 201–2, 260 n. 77
La Unión (newspaper), 134
Unión Cívica Radical (UCR). *See* Radical Party
Unión Democrática (UD), 179
Unión Ferroviaria, 105
Union of Newspaper and Magazine Vendors, 191, 213–15, 219, 222. *See also* news vendors
United Press (UP). *See also* wire services
  La Nación and, 41
  La Prensa and, 36, 41, 156, 221, 247 n. 44
  reporting by, 78, 131–32, 134, 159
  suspension of, 132
United States
  foreign relations with Argentina, 98, 105, 109, 132, 150, 172, 259 n. 64
  labor legislation, 234

United States *(continued)*
  newsworker strikes, 235
  newsprint distribution, 235, 188, 235–36
  press of, 41, 54, 156, 224, 230–31, 250 n. 116
  scholarship on, 11, 117
Uriburu, Alberto, 67
Uriburu, José F.
  authoritarianism of, 58–60, 66–67, 72–73
  coup of 1930, participation in, 58–59
  dictatorship of, 59–62
  political rivalries, 59, 62–64
  press policies of, 60, 72–73, 88, 108, 202
Urquiza, Justo José de, 31, 151

Valmaggia, Juan, 85
La Vanguardia (newspaper)
  attacks on, 211
  circulation, 15, 243 n. 35
  closure of, 105, 134, 228
  journalism style of, 71
  labor and, 182
  Peronism and, 158–59
Varea, Domingo, 138–39, 264 n. 72
Velazco, Filomeno, 183
Venezuela, ix–xi
Verbitsky, Bernardo, 167, 256 n. 134
Verbitsky, Gregorio, 256 n. 134
Viale, Carlos Dalmiro, 204
Villafañe, Benjamín, 77
Visca, José Emilio, 214, 254 n. 97

Waisbord, Silvio, 8
Walsh, Rodolfo, 205, 228, 233–34
Wells, H. G., 52
wire services, 41, 78–79, 81–82, 112–13, 156. *See also* Associated Press; United Press

Yrigoyen, Hipólito
  comparison with Perón, 165, 181–82
  election of, 42, 62
  press and, 73, 177, 180, 251 n. 10
  overthrow of, 58–59

www.ingramcontent.com/pod-product-compliance
Lightning Source LLC
Chambersburg PA
CBHW021354290426
44108CB00010B/234